97851

1975

ELEMENTARY PROBABILITY MODELS
AND STATISTICAL INFERENCE

Elementary
Probability
Models
and
Statistical
Inference

Douglas G. Chapman
University of Washington

Ronald A. Schaufele
York University, Toronto

Xerox College Publishing Company

Waltham, Massachusetts | Toronto

To Isobel and Mary

Preface

The aim of this text is to introduce the concepts of statistical inference, the foundations of which lie in probability theory. Statistical methods are of widespread and increasing importance in many areas of science and business. An understanding of statistical concepts is basic to a wise use of statistical methods in such areas; such statistical methods in turn are basic to many decision-making procedures as well as to investigations designed to help our understanding of the universe.

The creator of statistical methods must have a strong foundation in mathematics as well as in statistics. The user of statistical methods does not need such a foundation, and it is the opinion of the authors that many elementary statistics texts and courses become courses in algebra rather than statistics if what is supposed to be mathematical rigor is emphasized. Mathematical derivations do not always clarify *statistical concepts* even for the mathematically able, and more usually they only confuse and confound the typical applied statistics student. Thus, mathematical proofs and derivations are almost entirely omitted in this text.

Although we have tried to be as mathematically careful in our definitions and theorems as is possible at the level at which this book is aimed, we acknowledge that some of the definitions represent compromises with absolute mathematical rigor, and we warn students who continue to study mathematical statistics or probability that they will encounter slightly more complete definitions later, particularly in dealing with jointly continuous random variables. Yet we believe that no one who studies and understands our book will be misled by the definitions or material given here. Mathematical notation is used because it is a useful and labor-saving language and because the student will need this language in attempting to extend his knowledge, read statistically oriented articles, and so on. For the same reason we have chosen to emphasize probability models but have excluded most material on combinatorial probabilities.

While the text is specifically designed for nonmathematics majors in any of the natural or social sciences, we believe that it can be equally well used as a text for a lower-division statistics course for mathematics students. Many mathematics students learn the formal mathematics associated with statistical methods but do not learn the basic concepts or how to apply them in real problems. Yet most mathematically trained students who use their mathematical training in a technical vocation are more likely to be problem solvers than creators of new methods. The text has been used in a one-quarter five-hour course at the University of Washington, though to cover all of the material under this arrangement is rather difficult. The substance can easily be fitted into a one-quarter five-hour course or a three-hour one-semester course either by the omission of the material on operating characteristic curves or the section of Chapter 10 on tests and confidence intervals, or by the omission of one of Chapters 11 or 12. It will fit nicely into a two-quarter three-hour sequence.

Statistical concepts come most easily when the student has been motivated by real data. This is, however, seldom possible in an undergraduate statistics course. As a substitute for this, the authors believe that sampling experiments have an important place in any introductory course. In this text there is a wide variety of experiments highly recommended both for student individual work and for class projects.

The introduction of real data and real situations is also desirable in the problems of an elementary statistics textbook. Most real-world problems are beyond the level of an introductory course; there is the additional difficulty that often a great deal of background information is necessary, so that much time and space is used up in the introduction to the problem. For these reasons most problems are abstractions of varying degrees of reality of real-life situations. The instructor will need to emphasize this and the reason for it to students who are concerned for the involvement of their studies in the real world. Nevertheless we have attempted to include some problems that are as close to realism as possible, which do require long explanations. Some of these are carried over to different chapters to emphasize the continuity of the methods and to utilize the extra effort initially applied. These problems should help the student to gain some appreciation for model building, which is such an important part of modern scientific method but which is difficult to illustrate at an elementary level.

Nonmathematical textbooks in statistical methods are traditionally referred to as "cookbooks," for obvious reasons. It is true that many such books are collections of methods. Such an approach can be avoided by eliminating a treatment of most methods now being used widely in statistics, but if this is done, the student who learns only statistical concepts may have difficulty bridging the gap between his formal statistics course and what he is going to see, read about, and use in other courses where standard methods are used. This text attempts to bring in some of these standard methods and ground them solidly on basic concepts.

The writer of an elementary textbook in this field must not only resolve the question of degree of mathematical emphasis and the question of concepts versus methods; he must face the fact that there are several schools of statistical analysis with variations within schools. The present textbook is built upon the Neyman–Pearson "classical" theory, which the authors believe to be the most solid foundation for statistical inference in science at present. In business, where decisions may be personal, a statistical analysis based on personal or subjective probability may be rational. In science, an objective method which serves to provide information as well as make decisions seems to us to be more appropriate. The introduction of prior probabilities means additional arbitrary choices that may confuse the beginning student. Once basic concepts of the classical theory are well understood, it should be easy to develop Bayesian theory in a second course.

Starred Sections. Some topics are more difficult than others. These have been starred. Some users may wish to omit these from their study. In our experience, both the operating characteristic curves and Chebyshev's inequality cause difficulty for students. We believe that operating characteristic curves are quite important in obtaining a thorough understanding of concepts of hypothesis testing but also agree that the topic can be omitted. Problems and exercises dealing with material in starred sections as well as some others of perhaps more than usual difficulty have been starred.

Comments on Usage. It is possible to emphasize hypothesis testing as a decision procedure or as information acquisition. The latter is the approach due to Fisher; the former is particularly associated with Wald, though also implicit in the Neyman–Pearson theory. We believe that both points of view are useful, the emphasis varying according to the type of problem and the use to which the analysis is to be put. Therefore, we have included sections on hypothesis testing as a decision rule procedure as well as sections giving the significance probability approach. The user may wish to emphasize one of these points of view more than the other and there should be no trouble in doing so.

Some users may wish to place less emphasis on multivariate probability models (Chapter 9). These have often received scant treatment in elementary texts. However, the authors believe that, with the advent of the computer, multivariate statistical analysis is becoming much more important, and therefore statistical users should receive as thorough a grounding in this area as has been traditionally the case for univariate models.

It is quite feasible to omit the nonparametric section (Chapter 12) but retain the two-sample t test that is included there. We have included the two-sample t test with nonparametric tests to emphasize the existence of alternatives to the two-sample t test—alternatives which some statisticians believe should be preferred to the two-sample t test. Some readers will also regret the omission of treatment of the paired-sample t test. While no treatment of this topic is included in the textual material, numerous problems use the pairing technique, so that the teacher who wishes to can use these as a basis for elaborating on this topic and its relationship to the two-sample t test.

Users of the book are invited to write to either of the authors about their experiences with the book. Naturally, we are interested in hearing about sections and problems which were thought to be particularly helpful to students, but we are more interested in finding out which sections or problems cause undue difficulty or are confusing. We also welcome any suggestions for improvement.

The authors wish to express their thanks to Professors William Harkness, James Holstein, and Donald Truax, who read the manuscript and made a large number of valuable comments. A number of the authors' colleagues and students have also contributed useful suggestions for which we are grateful. We express thanks to Sharyn Lindsey, who typed some versions of the manuscript and did many of the figures. We are indebted to the literary executor of the late Sir Ronald A. Fisher, F.R.S., to Dr. Frank Yates, F.R.S., and to Oliver & Boyd Ltd., Edinburgh, for permission to reprint Tables 4 and 6 from their book *Statistical Tables for Biological, Agricultural and Medical Research*. Acknowledgment of support of the Canadian National Research Council is also gratefully noted.

D. G. CHAPMAN

Seattle, Washington   R. A. SCHAUFELE

Contents

CHAPTER SIX

Continuous Distributions, the Normal Probability Model, and Approximations

CHAPTER SEVEN

Point Estimation and Hypothesis Testing for the Mean of a Normal Population

CHAPTER EIGHT

Confidence Intervals

CHAPTER NINE

Joint Probability Models

CHAPTER TEN

Regression and Correlation

CHAPTER ELEVEN

Chi-Square Tests

CHAPTER TWELVE

Nonparametric Tests

APPENDIX ONE

Summarization of Data

APPENDIX TWO

Tables, 322–338

List of Examples

ELEMENTARY PROBABILITY MODELS
AND STATISTICAL INFERENCE

CHAPTER ONE

Introduction

What Is Statistics?

"Statistics" is a singular noun and a collective one. In the latter sense it refers to a body of numerical data, often collected by governmental agencies, that is, the state; hence the name. But in recent usage it is applied more commonly to the methods of analysis of such numerical data or the analysis of any data resulting from physical or biological observations. In this text we are concerned with *statistics as a method of treatment of numerical data.*

There are several aspects to statistical problems:

1. Collection of the data.
2. Summarization and graphical representation of the data.
3. Analysis proper.

Our primary interest in this book concerns the methods of analysis proper. In the body of the text, we touch slightly on some phases of summarization of the data necessary to analysis. Summarization and graphical presentation of data are useful tools and are not to be regarded as unimportant. With the rapid advance in the use of computers, however, their importance has been diminished and their study here has been relegated to Appendix 1.

Finally, collection of the data may be the most important part of the statistical study. Data improperly collected may be of no use whatsoever, or worse still, may suggest false conclusions. Proper methods of data collection can best be studied after a course in statistical analysis; there are courses in this area which go under the names of Theory of Sampling and Design of Experiments.

Experiments

We will use the term "experiment" generally for any study involving data, numerical or otherwise; i.e., it may include any or all of the following: the collection of the data, the summarization and graphical representation of the data, the analysis of the data, including the drawing of a conclusion. Numerical data, i.e., statistics in its collective usage, are a feature of modern life. We encounter, in newspapers and magazines, reports on numbers of accidents, population changes, electoral votes, cost of living indices, etc. In scientific experiments this concern with numbers is even greater inasmuch as most experiments are designed to produce results that can be measured and reported quantitatively.

If asked to characterize such data, it is improbable that the uninitiated would agree on any particular single characterization. However, if we think of some familiar examples of "statistics," e.g., grade point averages, heights, times to travel from residence to university, number of colds in a year, we note that the prime characteristic is the variability of such data. This variability makes statistical analysis necessary. *Statistical experiments* refer to experiments where the numerical results may vary from one trial to another and are not completely predictable.

Example 1.1   Coin tossing

Anyone can perform a statistical experiment (a very trivial one) by obtaining an ordinary coin and tossing it ten times. After each toss the result is recorded: heads or tails. This is the collection of data.

The data may be summarized by counting, say, the number of heads. Suppose ten tosses result in eight heads. Do you think that the coin is "fair," i.e., properly made and balanced so that heads and tails are equally likely to appear? Statistical analysis is necessary here, and the aim of this course is to answer just such questions.

Example 1.2   Body temperatures

A more useful sampling experiment that each individual can perform is to take his or her temperature each morning for a week. Thus a typical set of seven temperature readings might be 98.4, 98.0, 98.3, 98.7, 98.9, 98.2, 98.5. Note that none of these is 98.6 degrees, the supposed "normal" human temperature. It might well be asked if this person's average temperature is indeed 98.6. By "average" temperature is meant the average over a long period of time, which is of course to be distinguished from the average of the seven observations actually made. The average of these seven is 98.43.

Example 1.3 Travel times

In the previous experiments, data were collected and then some questions posed. More properly, the question is posed before the collection of the data. A student may ask, "How long does it take me to travel from my home to the university?" He may carefully time himself each day for two weeks. He then has collected ten observations of travel time. He can summarize these simply by taking the average. He may then ask further, "How reliable is the result I have obtained?" To make precise this question and to answer it is, again, the function of statistical analysis.

Example 1.4 Who was Einstein?

A famous university president stated in a commencement address, "The present education in the universities is completely out of balance. Students do not even know who the great thinkers of our time are, let alone their philosophy and the reason for their importance." The *Daily* editor decided to write a story around this, and so a reporter was sent out to make a campus survey. He interviewed 20 students and asked each: "Who was Einstein?" Fourteen of those interviewed answered correctly, the rest incorrectly. Since 70 percent of the sample group were able to answer correctly, we might leap to the conclusion that 70 percent of the population—i.e., of all students at this university —would be able to answer correctly. But suppose the editor assigned two reporters to such interviews, and Reporter Number Two interviewed 20 students and obtained only eight correct answers (40 percent). What do we conclude now with regard to the population? A number of questions arise:

(a) Is the difference between the two samples due merely to chance?
(b) If the two samples are pooled, giving a total of 22 of 40 correct answers (55 percent), do we conclude that 55 percent of the population would be able to answer correctly? If so, how much confidence do we have in the statement?
(c) Might it be true that in fact less than half of all students could answer correctly?

This too is a statistical experiment, though obviously we will need to know more as to how each reporter picked his 20 students to be interviewed before it is possible to answer these questions.

These four examples of experiments have many aspects in common: Questions are being asked about *all* tosses of a coin, *all* temperatures, *all* travel times, *all* students at the university; yet we have only observations on a *few* tosses, a *few* temperatures, a *few* travel times, a *few* students' knowledge of Einstein.

Populations and Samples

The aim of statistical methods, as illustrated in the last paragraph, is to find information about a whole *population* when only a *sample* is observed.

A *population* (universe) is a collection of all observations of a specified kind. A population consists of observations that are quantitative or qualitative. The population of all travel times and the population of all temperatures are quantitative, i.e., numerical. The population of all coin tosses, each toss labeled heads or tails, is qualitative; so is the population of observations of all students' knowledge of Einstein, each observation labeled "yes" or "no" according to whether or not the student knows who Einstein was. A population may be concrete or conceptual. The population of all yes's and no's in Example 1.4 is concrete. Given enough time, we could interview each of the students at the university, since the number of students is finite and well-defined. If the university has 18,000 students, we would end up with 18,000 listings of yes's and no's. This collection would be the population of observations of students' knowledge of Einstein. The population of all heads and tails in Example 1.1 is conceptual. No matter how much time we are given, we cannot record all the results of tossing a coin, since given more time we could record more tosses. Thus, our population of heads and tails is unending, i.e., infinite, and it is conceptual since we can imagine an unending collection of heads and tails but we cannot write down this collection. Similarly, the populations of all travel times and all temperatures are conceptual and consist, in both cases, of infinite collections of numbers.

Note: In Examples 1.1 and 1.4, the observations almost certainly appear more than once. This fact is important and in defining or listing a population it is necessary to record the frequency of each different observation.

If a population is small, it may be feasible to observe it in total and obtain any information desired. Generally, because populations are too large, or for other reasons, such a complete survey is not feasible or may even be impossible.

A *sample* consists of those observations in the population that are actually taken in some well-defined experiment. If the sample is chosen in a suitable manner, it will yield some information about the whole population.

> *Note:* In most experiments it is quite evident that the observations taken represent a fraction of those possible and hence that the experiment is dealing with a sample from which to draw conclusions concerning the population. However in some cases the situation is ambiguous. For example, a professor obtains the heights of all members of his class. He may regard these observed heights as his population or he may regard them as a sample of all heights of the students at the University. (Might this be a rather bad sample?)

In Example 1.1, the conceptual qualitative population is the collection of all possible coin tosses, each labeled heads or tails. The sample is the ten tosses actually performed. In Example 1.4, the concrete qualitative population is the collection of all yes's and no's of all students at the *Daily* editor's university. The (combined) sample is the collection of 40 yes's and no's observed. What are the populations and samples in Examples 1.2 and 1.3?

A *statistical experiment*, then, consists of collecting a *sample* from a specified *population* and summarizing and analyzing the sample data.

Here are some more examples of statistical experiments.

Example 1.5   Sex prediction

A doctor asserts he has a method that is 80 percent accurate in determining, several months before birth, the sex of an unborn child. He is challenged to prove this claim. As a test, he predicts the sex of 20 unborn children and is right in 13 of the predictions. Here the observation is simply a qualitative one: prediction correct or prediction incorrect. The sample of 20 results may be used to infer something as to the correctness of all possible predictions by this doctor. This totality of all possible predictions is the population. Do we have any basis for supporting the doctor's claim?

Example 1.6   Are cold inoculations useful?

One inoculant was tested on a group of 60 soldiers: 30 soldiers were inoculated in September; at the same time 30 were given a dummy shot. The latter are known as the control group. Of the two groups, 14 of those inoculated and 24 of the control group contracted a cold that fall. The observation is a pair of values (14, 24). It could be set out in a table:

	Cold	No cold	Total
Inoculated group	14	16	30
Control group	24	6	30
Total	38	22	60

This seems to suggest that inoculation helps ward off colds, but again we might ask if this could be a chance difference. The doctors testing the inoculant do not want to disregard a promising preventative nor do they want to be fooled into believing they have a cure when they do not. Note the population here is the totality of all such paired observations (or the 2 × 2 table) of all similar conceivable experiments of this type pertaining to this inoculant. Why were not all soldiers inoculated? Why were the 30 uninoculated control soldiers given a dummy shot? They could simply have not been treated in any way.

Example 1.7 Marriage during college

A news magazine quotes a college dean as stating that marriage while attending college decreases a student's chance of getting a degree and that for those who do remain in college, marriage means lower grades on the average. It was not indicated in the article whether the dean had any data to back up his statement or whether he was merely following a common practice of individuals in an older generation in deploring any innovations by a younger generation and in hoping that the weight of his authority would substitute for facts. Like many of the problems discussed in the earlier examples, this is quite complex, and data to support or deny the dean's opinion are not easily obtained. It might be suggested that a sample be taken of married and single university students and their grade point averages (G.P.A.'s) compared. This would yield a double set of observations— the G.P.A.'s of the sample of single students and the G.P.A.'s of the sample of married students. We could try to determine something about the G.P.A.'s of the population of single students and those of the population of married students from these samples. However, data would not thereby be provided to support or contradict the dean. Why not?

Example 1.8 Prediction of success in a statistics course

A university statistics instructor is interested in knowing to what extent success in algebra is an indication of success in the basic statistics course that he is teaching. He obtains from each student his (letter) grade in the (prerequisite) algebra and then later tabulates against this information the (letter) grade in statistics. The results could be tabulated in a two-way table, as in Example 1.6, but we now have more categories:

		ALGEBRA GRADE				
		A	B	C	D	Total
	A or B	5	8	6	3	22
STATISTICS	C	2	8	10	5	25
GRADE	D or E	2	2	5	3	12
	Total	9	18	21	11	59

The numbers in the various classes are the random observations, which need to be analyzed to answer the instructor's question. Suppose that instead of letter grades the instructor had scores on an algebra placement test and numerical scores on the statistics course. What would his observations then represent?

Example 1.9 Effect of cigarette smoke on growth of mice

To test the effect of smoking on growth, a batch of mice are divided into equal-sized groups, and half are required to breathe through an apparatus that forces smoke into their lungs. The other half breathe through the same apparatus, but do not receive any smoke. After two months, samples of each group are weighed in sets of ten. What is the population? Are the observations quantitative or qualitative? Why are all the mice required to breathe through the same apparatus?

■ Problems

1.1 Give some other examples familiar to you of a sample and a population.

1.2 Formulate a question suitable for a public opinion survey. Interview a number of people and record their responses. Define the population and the sample. Are the observations qualitative or quantitative? What decisions might be based upon the results of the survey?

1.3 An amateur magician asserts that he can almost always "call" his toss of a coin. Suggest a test of this claim and identify the population.

1.4 Find the latest published report of a public opinion poll. Discuss the population sampled and the sample results.

1.5 Suggest sampling procedures that might be used to test the following statements. Be precise as to how the observations are to be defined and made. Discuss any problems that might arise.

(a) At least half of the men at this university expect to kiss a girl on their first date.
(b) Among all drivers under 25, university students are involved in fewer accidents than those drivers who are not attending or never attended a university.
(c) Children raised in an urban area do not weigh as much at age 16 as children raised in rural areas.
(d) Students who work up to half-time earn a better grade point average than those who do not work at all.

In each case specify the population and the sample. Distinguish between actual and conceptual populations and between qualitative and quantitative observations.

1.6 If the sampling procedure devised for Problem 1.5(d) were actually carried out and on the basis of the result the statement were affirmed, would you then infer that working part-time will improve your grades?

1.7 What proportion of listings in your local telephone directory are in a specified exchange? Pick a page at random in the directory and count the specified exchange numbers out of the total number on the page. Compare your results with those of others in the class.

1.8 What is the average age of pennies in circulation in the United States? Obtain ten pennies in circulation and list their ages as "0 year," "1 year,".... Obtain the average of the ten. Again compare your results with those obtained by others in the class.

1.9 If your university directory lists students' home addresses, suggest a procedure based on this list to estimate the proportion of out-of-state students at the university. Obviously, one could count the number in the whole directory, but this is tedious. A sampling procedure may give a satisfactory answer. The question then reduces to how to take this sample and how big it should be.

1.10 Are all digits used equally often in the final four digits of telephone numbers? How might this question be answered by sampling?

CHAPTER TWO

Discrete Random Variables and Probability Models

Random Variables and Sample Spaces

Statistical experiments deal with data that vary from observation to observation in ways that are not completely predictable. Can you predict exactly the next toss of a coin, your next travel time to the university, the result of the next student interview on Einstein? To emphasize this variability of the observations, or data, that statisticians deal with, the term *random* (or chance) *variable* is used to represent any possible outcome of a statistical experiment that can be specified in numerical form.

Throughout this text, capital letters such as X, Y, Z will denote random variables. In this connection it is important to distinguish between the random variable and any single realization of it. The random variable of interest in Example 1.1 (coin tossing) is the number of heads in ten tosses. This may take on any one of eleven possible values $0, 1, 2, \ldots, 10$. In the data referred to, this random variable had the particular realization 8. In Example 1.5 (sex prediction), the random variable is the number of correct predictions by the doctor of the sex of 20 unborn children. It may take on any one of the values $0, 1, 2, \ldots, 20$. In the data referred to, this random variable had the particular realization 13.

With any statistical experiment, there is a set of possible outcomes expressed in numerical form that the random variable may take on. This set of all possible numerical outcomes or values is called the *sample space* of the random variable, and the outcomes themselves are called *sample points*. Sample spaces are examples of sets that many students have studied in their high school algebra. Two examples of discrete sample spaces have been given above. For our purposes, *discrete sample spaces* are those where the set of possible values is a subset of the set of all rational numbers. In fact, most problems in this chapter will deal with *finite sample spaces*, i.e., sample spaces which consist of a finite number of rational numbers, usually integers. Later we will discuss problems where it is convenient to define sample spaces that are subsets of the set of all real numbers. We defer discussion of these spaces to Chapter 6.

Probability

Since erratic variation does occur between samples, how is it possible to use sample observations to draw conclusions about the whole population? Such conclusions are made possible by the fact that in repetitions of most statistical experiments there is an overall or long-run regularity. This is best illustrated by tossing a coin: the result of a single toss is quite unpredictable; yet if we toss a coin 100 times, it may be observed that in general the relative frequency of heads differs only slightly from one-half.

To utilize this long-run regularity in the evaluation of statistical experiments, the *theory of probability* is of basic importance. With any statistical experiment, the statistician tries to associate a mathematical or theoretical model. To do this, he may have to make certain assumptions about the way his data have been collected or about the population. These assumptions will have to be clearly stated and examined. This theoretical model in turn associates with each sample point of the discrete sample space, a *theoretical relative frequency or probability*.

Example 2.1   Coin tossing

If a coin is tossed once, the number of heads that appear is a random variable. It can take two possible values: 1 or 0. Many people, if asked, "What is the relative frequency with which a coin comes up heads?" would answer, "One-half." This may be true if the coin is perfectly symmetrical and all factors operate equally for heads or tails. Few, if any, such ideal coins may actually exist. Yet it is convenient to think of the idealized situation in which heads and tails are equally likely. Within this mathematical model, the theoretical relative frequency or probability of a head is one-half. If X denotes the number of heads, X is a random variable that can take on two possible values, 0 or 1, and this statement may also be written

$$P(X = 1) = \tfrac{1}{2} \quad \text{and} \quad P(X = 0) = \tfrac{1}{2}$$

to be read: The probability that X, the number of heads, takes on the value 1 when the experiment is performed is $\tfrac{1}{2}$ and the probability that X takes on the value 0 is $\tfrac{1}{2}$.

Consider now the experiment suggested in Example 1.1, in which a coin is tossed ten times and the number of heads that occur is counted. Let Y be this count. What is the sample space of the random variable Y? It is easy to identify the sample space, but are all the points in it equally likely? Why or why not? As will be seen shortly, more sophisticated methods are necessary to associate a theoretical model with this experiment.

Example 2.2   Taste testing

A common taste test is the following: The taster is presented with three drinks, two of one kind and one of a second. All three are indistinguishable in appearance, but the odd one may differ in taste and the taster is asked to pick it out. If the taster cannot distinguish the taste difference, then it is customary to assert that the taster has a probability of $\tfrac{1}{3}$ of selecting the correct odd drink. Why? There are three possibilities and only one correct choice, so that the chances of a correct choice are one out of three. This assumes that the taster is equally likely to choose any one of the three drinks, if he is unable to distinguish the taste difference.

This example illustrates the use of simple relative frequencies as a basis for calculating probabilities. The experiment consists of selecting one element from a set, all of which are "equally likely" to be selected. Workers in probability theory have long talked about urns containing balls of two colors. A ball is selected from the urn and the color noted. It is certainly reasonable to assume that if the urn contains 10 black balls and 20 white balls that are otherwise indistinguishable, then the probability of selecting a black one is $10/(10 + 20)$, i.e., $\tfrac{1}{3}$.

Similarly if an instructor has a group of class cards for his 40 students, ten of whom are girls, and if he selects a card "at random" from the

40, then it is reasonable to assume that the probability of the selected card being that of a girl student is $\frac{10}{40}$, or $\frac{1}{4}$.

> *Note:* This is an *assumption*. We have no physical proof that the balls in the urn or the class cards will so behave. However, we may check this assumption by a series of statistical experiments. In any series of repetitions of an experiment, the actual observed relative frequencies of each outcome will almost always differ from the theoretical frequencies, i.e., the probabilities. But we would expect that in a longer series of trials, the observed relative frequencies would get closer and closer to the theoretical values. If they did not, the model would be regarded as unsatisfactory. In fact, one part of statistical analysis is testing the adequacy of a theoretical model on the basis of sample data.

We now proceed to treat the "equally likely" model more formally, but before we do so we need an additional definition. An *event* is a set of possible sample points, i.e., a subset of the sample space. In Example 1.1 (coin tossing), the set {0, 2, 4, 6, 8, 10} is an event. In words, it is the event that the total number of heads is an even number. Similarly, {0, 1, 2, 3, 4} is an event, the event that the total number of heads does not exceed four. The event that occurs if the total number of heads differs from five by more than three is the set {0, 1, 9, 10}. We will denote events by the letters A, B, C, etc.

What we have done in the examples above is to apply the following:

Rule I for Calculating Probabilities Directly

If the sample space is finite (with n elements), if the random experiment consists of selecting one element from the n elements in such a way that each element has the same chance of being selected, and if m of the elements result in the occurrence of the event A, i.e., A contains m elements, then we define

$$P(A) = \frac{m}{n}.$$

That is, $P(A)$ is the number of elements in A divided by the total number of elements.

Rule I for calculating probabilities is intuitively obvious. Whether recognized or not, it was the basis of the procedures used in Example 1.4 (Who was Einstein?) and in Problems 1.7 and 1.9, among others. In general, an element is chosen *at random* in an experiment if each element has the same chance of being sampled. Hence, if there are m

elements of type A out of a total of n elements, the probability that any single element drawn at random is of type A is m/n.

Example 2.3   Sampling at random from a student directory

(a) If we know that 6,000 students of a university population of 18,000 are female, and a name is selected at random from the student directory, then the probability of that name's being a girl's name is 6,000/18,000, or $\frac{1}{3}$.

(b) Now suppose that we do not know the number of out-of-state students of the total 18,000. However, a sample of 100 names is selected and 28 prove to be out-of-state. We "guess" that 28 percent of the student body is from out of state. Note that in (a) we have information about a population and draw conclusions about the sample. In (b) the situation is just reversed. In (a) the sample considered was of size 1. What if it had been 100 as in (b)?

To deal with probabilities in such situations it is necessary to define operations with events and provide some additional rules. These operations are identical to those defined for sets, though with possibly different notation.

If A and B are events associated with an experiment, then we understand:

$A + B$ to mean either A occurs or B occurs, or both, i.e., $A \cup B$ of set theory.

AB to mean both A and B occur, i.e., $A \cap B$ of set theory.

$\bar{A}$ to mean A does *not* occur, i.e., A^c or $\tilde{A}$ of set theory.

Two events, A and B, are said to be *mutually exclusive* if the occurrence of one precludes the occurrence of the other. In this case AB contains no outcomes and is denoted by ϕ; i.e., if A and B are mutually exclusive, then $AB = \phi$. Often ϕ is called the *impossible event*, i.e., the null set of set theory.

Example 2.4   Playing cards

A card is drawn from an ordinary deck. Let A be the event that the card is an ace, B the event that the card is a spade. $A + B$ means the card is either an ace or a spade; AB means the card is both an ace and a spade, i.e., the ace of spades; $\bar{A}$ means the card is not an ace. $\bar{A}A$ is the impossible event; i.e., it is not possible to draw one card and have this card be both an ace and not an ace.

Example 2.5   Class cards

The 40 class cards of a statistics class are classified as follows:

	Male	Female	Total
Lower division students	20	7	27
Upper division students	10	3	13
	30	10	40

If a single card is drawn at random from these cards, we could let

A be the event that the sampled card belongs to a male student;
B be the event that the sampled card belongs to a lower division student.

According to Rule I:

$$P(A) = \frac{30}{40}, \qquad P(B) = \frac{27}{40}, \qquad P(AB) = \frac{20}{40}, \qquad P(\bar{B}) = \frac{13}{40}.$$

What does the event $A + B$ mean? It means that the card drawn belongs to a male student or to a lower division student. Now there are 30 males and 27 lower division students, but these involve some duplication, namely, the 20 male lower division students. Hence

$$P(A + B) = \frac{30 + 27 - 20}{40} = \frac{37}{40}.$$

Conditional Probability

Consider again the last example and suppose that lower division students' cards are colored white, while those of upper division students are gray. If a card is drawn and observed to be white and if we now ask what the probability is that the card belongs to a male student, the extra information that it is white changes the probability distribution with which we are working. By Rule I applied only to white cards (lower division students), it is calculated that P (card is of a male student, given that it is of a lower division student) $= \frac{20}{27}$, or in symbols $P(A|B) = \frac{20}{27}$. Observe that the probability $\frac{20}{27}$ is the ratio of two probabilities, that is,

$$P(A|B) = \frac{20}{27} = \frac{20/40}{27/40} = \frac{P(AB)}{P(B)}.$$

Consider now a general table when the numerical values are replaced by symbols.

	A	$\bar{A}$	Total
B	n_{11}	n_{12}	$n_{11} + n_{12}$
$\bar{B}$	n_{21}	n_{22}	$n_{21} + n_{22}$
Total	$n_{11} + n_{21}$	$n_{12} + n_{22}$	N

Observe that if an element were drawn at random from the N elements then

$$P(A) = \frac{n_{11} + n_{21}}{N}, \qquad P(B) = \frac{n_{11} + n_{12}}{N}, \qquad P(AB) = \frac{n_{11}}{N},$$

and

$$P(A|B) = \frac{n_{11}}{n_{11} + n_{12}} = \frac{n_{11}/N}{(n_{11} + n_{12})/N} = \frac{P(AB)}{P(B)}.$$

This type of analysis leads us to define the *conditional probability* of A, given B, denoted $P(A|B)$, by the equation

$$P(A|B) = \frac{P(AB)}{P(B)},$$

provided $P(B)$ in the denominator is not zero.

Example 2.6 Playing cards

A card is drawn from a complete deck of 52. What is the probability that it is a face card (A, K, Q, or J), given that it is not a 2, 3, 4, 5, or 6?

The answer can be found directly by Rule I but it is also useful to use the formula for conditional probabilities.

Since there are 32 cards in the deck from 7 to ace, of which 16 are face cards, P(face card, given not 2, 3, 4, 5, or 6) $= \frac{16}{32} = \frac{1}{2}$. To use the conditional probability formula, define

A to be the event that the card drawn is a face card, and
B to be the event that the card drawn is not 2, 3, 4, 5, or 6.

Then AB is the event that the card drawn is a face card and is not 2, 3, 4, 5, or 6. Observe that AB is the same as A, for as soon as we are told a card is a face card, we know it is not a 2, 3, 4, 5, or 6. Hence $P(AB) = P(A) = \frac{16}{52} = \frac{4}{13}$. This is, of course, the unconditional probability in a drawing from the whole deck when no additional information is available. Similarly by Rule I, $P(B) = \frac{32}{52} = \frac{8}{13}$, so that, given that the card drawn is not 2, 3, 4, 5, or 6, we find that the conditional probability of drawing a face card is

$$P(A|B) = \frac{4/13}{8/13} = \frac{1}{2}.$$

It may also be asked what the conditional probability is that the card is a face card, given that it is a spade. Here let A stand for a face card and C for a spade. Then

$$P(A|C) = \frac{4/52}{13/52} = \frac{4}{13}.$$

Note that the unconditional probability of A is also $\frac{4}{13}$. As is intuitively obvious, telling us that a card is a spade is of no help in deciding whether it is or is not a face card.

Example 2.7 Multiple choice question

A student is faced with a multiple choice question with five possible answers. He does not know the correct answer so he picks choice (i).

(a) What is the probability he will get the right answer?
(b) Suppose that he can rule out possibilities (iv) and (v) before he selects (i); what is now the probability that he gets the right answer?

If we suppose in (a) that all five possibilities are equally likely to be right, then clearly by Rule I, $P[(\text{i}) \text{ is the right answer}] = \frac{1}{5}$. Similarly, for (b), $P[(\text{i}) \text{ is right answer, given that (iv) and (v) have been ruled out}] = \frac{1}{3}$. Observe that we can denote by A the event that (i) is the right answer and by B the event that the right answer is one of (i), (ii), or (iii). Then

$$P(AB) = \frac{1}{5}, \qquad P(B) = \frac{3}{5},$$

and

$$P(A|B) = \frac{1/5}{3/5} = \frac{1}{3}.$$

Example 2.8 Contagion

(a) Of six trees in a line, two are diseased. If any of the six are equally likely to be affected, what is the probability that the diseased trees are side by side?

Let the trees (and the positions they occupy) be numbered from one to six; then the diseased trees may occur in positions 12, 13, 14, 15, 16, 23, 24, 25, 26, 34, 35, 36, 45, 46, 56. Of these 15 positions, which by assumption are equally likely, five are such that the diseased trees are adjacent (12, 23, 34, 45, 56). Hence by Rule I the required probability is $\frac{5}{15}$, i.e., $\frac{1}{3}$.

(b) Suppose we are informed that Tree 3 is diseased. What is the probability now that the diseased trees are adjacent? In this case there are five possibilities (1, 2, 4, 5, 6) for the other diseased tree and two spots (2, 4) where the other diseased tree is adjacent to Number 3. Again by Rule I, P(diseased trees are side by side, given that Tree 3 is diseased) $= \frac{2}{5}$.

Note that if the following events are defined:

A: diseased trees are adjacent,
B: Tree 3 is diseased,

then by Rule I,

$$P(AB) = P(\text{Trees 3 and 2 or 4 are diseased})$$
$$= P(\text{diseased trees in spots 23 or 34}) = \frac{2}{15}.$$

Also $P(B) = \frac{5}{15} = \frac{1}{3}$, so that

$$P(A|B) = \frac{2/15}{1/3} = \frac{2}{5}$$

as obtained by direct argument.

(c) Consider the same two problems with the six trees arranged in a circle so that Trees 1 and 6 are also adjacent. In this case six of the 15 possibilities result in the required event: diseased trees are adjacent. Again by Rule I, $P(A) = \frac{6}{15} = \frac{2}{5}$, so that the unconditional probability that the diseased trees are adjacent is $\frac{2}{5}$. Also, in this case $P(A|B) = \frac{2}{5}$ by the same direct argument as in (b), using Rule I, or by the conditional probability formula. For in the circular case, $P(AB) = \frac{2}{15}$, and $P(B) = \frac{1}{3}$ as in the straight-line case. Hence, for the circular case, $P(A|B) = P(A)$.

In the straight-line case, the fact that one diseased tree is not at the end changes the probability of the diseased trees being adjacent; in the circular case, the fact that we know Tree 3 is diseased adds no further information. Such occupancy problems incidentally have a wide variety of applications in physics, ecology, and meteorology, to mention only a few areas. The various possibilities will not in general be enumerated but determined by formulas from the theory of permutations and combinations. Thus the number of arrangements of two diseased trees in six places is easily seen to be $6(6 - 1)/2$. There are six choices for the first tree, and $(6 - 1)$ choices for a spot for the second tree; and this gives exactly double the number of arrangements, since we have pairs (12) and (21), etc.

Independence

Events A and B such that $P(A|B) = P(A)$ are of importance in probability and statistics. Such events are said to be *independent*. This equation says that knowledge of the occurrence of B does not affect the *probability* of the occurrence of A. If $P(A|B) \neq P(A)$, then A and B are . *dependent*.

> *Note:* Many beginning students in probability confuse the ideas of two events being mutually exclusive and two events being independent. If two events A and B are *mutually exclusive*, then they are necessarily *dependent*, since $P(A|B) = 0 \neq P(A)$ unless $P(A)$ is zero.

In Example 2.6, the event that the card is a face card is independent of the event that it is a spade. In Example 2.8(c), the event that the two diseased trees are adjacent is independent of the event that Tree 3 is diseased.

We will also need to make use of independence of two random variables. *Two discrete random variables X and Y are said to be independent* if the event $(X = x)$ is independent of the event $(Y = y)$ for any outcomes x and y in the sample spaces of X and Y. These definitions of independence are easily extended to more than two events or random variables.

In many situations, independence is obvious from the physical circumstances. Thus, suppose two coins are tossed. One is observed to fall heads. Most people will agree that this information is irrelevant to the outcome of the second coin tossed.

EXERCISES

1. Calculate $P(A), P(B), P(A + B), P(AB), P(\bar{B}), P(\bar{A}), P(A\bar{B}), P(\overline{A + B})$, $P(\overline{AB})$ for Example 2.4.
2. For the probabilities in Examples 2.5 through 2.8, state in words what is meant [e.g., in Example 2.5, $P(\bar{B}) = \frac{13}{40}$ can be stated in words as

follows: The probability that a class card drawn at random does not belong to a lower division student is $\frac{13}{40}$].

3. Give at least three examples of simple finite populations doubly classified as the class cards are and specify the events A, B, $A + B$, AB, $\bar{A}$. Also calculate some of the associated probabilities.

Simple considerations with such finite populations lead to rules for operations with probabilities. We want probabilities to act like relative frequencies.

Rule II for Calculating Probabilities Indirectly

II.1 Let S be the sample space. Then $P(S) = 1$.

II.1a If an event A is impossible, $P(A) = 0$.

II.2 If $A_1, A_2, \ldots, A_n$ are n mutually exclusive events such that $A_1 + A_2 + \cdots + A_n = S$, the sample space, then the sum of the probabilities of $A_1, A_2, \ldots,$ and A_n is one.

As an immediate consequence of Rule II.2 we have

II.3 $P(A) + P(\bar{A}) = 1$, or $P(\bar{A}) = 1 - P(A)$, since obviously A and $\bar{A}$ are mutually exclusive and $A + \bar{A} = S$. In words this says that an event either occurs or does not occur.

II.4 $P(A + B) = P(A) + P(B) - P(AB)$.   (Addition rule)

II.4a If A and B are mutually exclusive, then $P(AB) = 0$ and $P(A + B) = P(A) + P(B)$.

II.5 $P(AB) = P(A) \cdot P(B|A) = P(B) \cdot P(A|B)$.   (Multiplication rule)

II.5a If A and B are independent events, then $P(AB) = P(A) \cdot P(B)$.

Example 2.9 Taste testing (continued)

Consider two independent trials of the taste-testing experiment. What is the probability that a tester with no ability guesses correctly on both trials? On at least one trial?

The probability of a correct guess on any trial is $\frac{1}{3}$. By Rule II.5a, the probability of two correct guesses is $\frac{1}{3} \cdot \frac{1}{3} = \frac{1}{9}$.

It is equally easy to calculate the probability of *no* correct guesses. Since the probability of an incorrect guess is $1 - \frac{1}{3} = \frac{2}{3}$, by the same reasoning as above, the probability of two incorrect guesses is $(\frac{2}{3})^2 = \frac{4}{9}$.

Now a correct guess on at least one trial is the complementary event to two incorrect guesses. Therefore, by Rule II.3, $P(\text{at least one correct guess}) = 1 - P(\text{both guesses are incorrect}) = 1 - \frac{4}{9} = \frac{5}{9}$.

Some students may be helped by a diagrammatic representation of events (or sets) A, B and their union, intersection, etc. (Such diagrams are known as Venn diagrams, although Euler used them before Venn.) The sample space may be represented by points in a geometrical figure, usually a rectangle, as in the Venn diagram shown. Events are sets of sample points, represented in the Venn diagram by other geometrical figures contained in the total figure. Events A and B are represented by ellipses. The student can verify that if a point is chosen at random, then $P(A) = \frac{6}{25}$, $P(B) = \frac{5}{25}$, $P(AB) = \frac{2}{25}$, $P(A + B) = \frac{9}{25}$, $P(A|B) = \frac{2}{5}$, $P(B|A) = \frac{2}{6}$, and hence check the addition and multiplication rules.

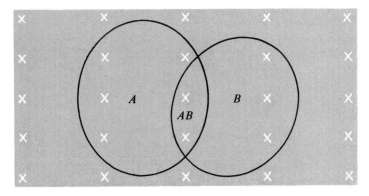

FIGURE 2.1   *A Venn diagram.*

Observe that figure $A + B$ contains the points in A and in B. Thus, if the probability of $A + B$ is to be computed and one adds the probability of each point in A to the probability of each point in B, then the probability of each point in AB has been counted twice. Hence it can be seen that the addition rule works. Further, one sees that the multiplication rule is another form of the conditional probability formula. What does saying A and B are mutually exclusive say in terms of these figures? What does independence of A and B say in terms of these figures?

Example 2.10   Experiments with two outcomes

Consider any experiment that has only two outcomes, labeled (for convenience) success or failure. Let X be the random variable that takes on the value 1 if a success is observed and 0 if a failure is observed.

Let $P(X = 1) = p$, where $0 \leq p \leq 1$. Then, by Rule II.3, $P(X = 0) = 1 - p$, so the complete probability distribution of X is

x	$P(X = x)$
0	$1 - p$
1	p
Total	1

Success might be the choice of the ace of spades (event AB in Example 2.4), in which case $p = \frac{1}{52}$. Success might be making the correct choice of the odd drink in the taste-testing experiment (Example 2.2); if the taster has no tasting ability $p = \frac{1}{3}$, but if the taster has ability, p may or may not be known. Success might be the correct prediction by a doctor of the sex of an unborn child (Example 1.5). A large number of the experiments can be fitted into this model. The reader should think up some in his own area of interest.

Probability Distributions and Probability Models

Example 2.10 has introduced a new concept: the set of outcomes of the experiment (or points in the sample space) and the associated probabilities under specified assumptions. The set of probabilities associated with all points in a sample space is known as a *probability distribution*. It is usual to tabulate these probabilities according to increasing values of the sample points, when these sample points are integers. A *probability model* is the representation of a statistical problem in an idealized fashion. It includes the sample space, the probability distribution, and the assumptions by which the probability distribution is generated. Examples 2.11 through 2.13 below show additional simple probability models.

Example 2.11   Unprepared students

In a university class, four students have been warned to be ready to give oral reports but it is known that only two will be called upon. Two of the four students prepare; two do not. Let X be the number of prepared students called. Observe that X may take on the values 0, 1, 2. To find the probability distribution of X, it is assumed that initially each student is equally likely to be called upon and then each of the three remaining is equally likely to be called.

Then

$$P(X = 2) = \text{probability that the first student called is prepared}$$
$$\text{and the second student called is prepared,}$$
$$= \tfrac{2}{4} \cdot \tfrac{1}{3} = \tfrac{1}{6} \qquad \text{(by Rules I and II.5)}.$$

Similarly,

$$P(X = 0) = \tfrac{2}{4} \cdot \tfrac{1}{3} = \tfrac{1}{6}.$$

The event $\{X = 1\}$ is more complicated. It may occur if the first student is prepared and the second unprepared, or vice versa.

Now,

P(first student called is prepared and second is unprepared)
$$= \tfrac{2}{4} \cdot \tfrac{2}{3} = \tfrac{1}{3} \qquad \text{(by Rules I and II.5)}.$$

Similarly,

P(first student called is unprepared and the second is prepared)
$$= \tfrac{2}{4} \cdot \tfrac{2}{3} = \tfrac{1}{3}.$$

How are these probabilities combined? The two events are mutually exclusive and therefore their probabilities are added. Hence

$$P(X = 1) = \tfrac{1}{3} + \tfrac{1}{3} = \tfrac{2}{3} \qquad \text{(by Rule II.4a)}.$$

Finally, the three outcomes and the associated probabilities are tabulated below.

x	$P(X = x)$	
0	$\tfrac{1}{6}$	
1	$\tfrac{2}{3}$	
2	$\tfrac{1}{6}$	
Total	1	(Check; see Rule II.2.)

This is the probability distribution for the model specified.

This example might have been formulated as follows: In a lot of four articles, two are defective. Two of the four are sampled. What is the probability distribution of the number of good articles in the sample? In this formulation the problem is of economic importance in quality control, in manufacturing, and in sampling inspection, though usually the lot size and often the sample size will be much larger than the numbers used here.

Examples 2.10 and 2.11 illustrate how the same theoretical model may be applicable to quite different real-life situations, a fact of great importance in both statistical theory and applications.

Example 2.12 Finding a defective machine

A repairman enters a statistics laboratory in which there are five identical calculating machines, one of which is defective. He selects a machine at random and examines it. If it is defective, he repairs it and leaves; otherwise he sets it aside and repeats the process. Let X denote the number of machines he examines. It is a random variable because it depends on how soon the defective machine is found.

The sample space of X is the set of integers 1, 2, 3, 4, 5. What probability model is reasonable for this random variable? If we assume that at each stage the repairman is equally likely to choose any of the unexamined machines, then the various probabilities are easily calculated by using Rules I and II.

Observe that $\{X = 1\}$ means that the first machine examined is the defective one. Hence,

$P(X = 1) =$ probability that the first machine examined is defective $= \frac{1}{5}$ (by Rule I).

$P(X = 2) =$ probability that the first machine examined is in good order and the second machine examined is defective $= \frac{4}{5} \cdot \frac{1}{4} = \frac{1}{5}$ (by Rule I and Rule II.5).

Similarly, it may be shown that

$$P(X = 3) = \tfrac{1}{5}, \qquad P(X = 4) = \tfrac{1}{5}, \qquad P(X = 5) = \tfrac{1}{5}.$$

It is useful to tabulate these results as follows:

x	$P(X = x)$	
1	$\frac{1}{5}$	
2	$\frac{1}{5}$	
3	$\frac{1}{5}$	
4	$\frac{1}{5}$	
5	$\frac{1}{5}$	
Total	1	(Check; see Rule II.2.)

This again is a theoretical model that is applicable in any searching situation where the outcomes are equally likely and searching stops when a particular outcome is achieved. See Experiment 2.2 at the end of this chapter as well as the problem set.

Many probability distributions can be derived by working with permutations and combinations. These are of importance in some areas of mathematical statistics but are infrequently encountered in statistical methodology. One such example is given here and another in the problems. In both cases the numbers are chosen sufficiently small that all possibilities may be written out, though those students familiar with permutations and combinations will prefer to use such knowledge to obtain the desired results more quickly.

Example 2.13 Runs

Events such as head or tail, boy or girl (in birth records), right or wrong are often summarized simply by noting the number of each category. The sequence of such events may also be of interest. We will construct a probability model that will apply to any of the above examples as well as others where there are two outcomes. For convenience we can think of the sequence of boys and girls (B and G) in birth records. Suppose we count the number of "runs" in each such sequence; e.g., the sequence B GG B has three runs (underlined). Let X = number of runs in a sequence of length four, with two of one kind and two of the other. What probability model is reasonable for this random variable? It is simple here to write out the various possibilities.

	Number of runs		Number or runs
B B G G	2	G B B G	3
B G B G	4	G B G B	4
B G G B	3	G G B B	2

The runs or sequences of the same kind are underlined. Assuming that these six sequences are equally likely, then the probability distribution of X is easily written down as follows:

x	$P(X = x)$
2	$\frac{1}{3}$
3	$\frac{1}{3}$
4	$\frac{1}{3}$
Total	1

(Check; see Rule II.2.)

Given a population and a procedure for selecting from the population, we can set up the probability model. It is then a mathematical problem (often beyond our present ability to solve) to find the probability distribution associated with the probability model. What the statistical analyst wants to do is to go in the opposite direction, i.e., from the observed sample to the unknown population.

Expectation and Standard Deviation

A probability distribution gives a complete picture of the behavior of a random variable but it is often too large and unwieldy. We need to summarize the data in a probability distribution just as we do any set of numerical data. Many ways of summarizing the information contained in a probability distribution are possible. The two most widely used in statistical analysis are the mean and a measure of the variability of the probability distribution.

The *mean* of a probability distribution is a weighted average of the various points in the sample space. This is an extension of the common concept of average or arithmetic mean and it is often given a new name, *expectation*. In particular, we refer interchangeably to the mean of the distribution of a random variable X or the expectation of X, and denote this by μ or by $E(X)$.

Formally, for finite sample spaces

$$\mu = E(X) = \sum x \cdot p(x),$$

where the sum is taken over all points x in the sample space, and $p(x)$ represents an abbreviated form of $P(X = x)$.

$E(X)$ may be interpreted as the long-range average of a large number of observations of the random variable X, or more precisely as the limiting value of the average of n observations of X as n goes to infinity. This statement is formalized in textbooks on the mathematical theory of probability and is known as the *Law of Large Numbers*. When in later chapters, we refer to events occurring in 95 percent of all experiments on the average, we are using average in this sense of long-run average.

[*Note:* For finite sample spaces, the definition of $E(X)$ is adequate and the ideas are simple and intuitive; later the definitions will be extended to more complex situations. For the situations dealt with in this text and in most elementary real-life problems, such extensions cause no difficulty. The reader should be warned, however, that there are some complex situations in which a more sophisticated treatment is necessary or else difficulties may arise. In fact, there are random variables X for which $E(X)$ or expected values of functions of X cannot be defined at all.]

Example 2.14   Matching pennies

Suppose you "match" for pennies. If X represents the gain on any "match," X is then a random variable with two possible values, $+1$ and -1. If each of these has probability $\frac{1}{2}$, i.e., if we assume "fair" coins, then

$$E(X) = (+1)\tfrac{1}{2} + (-1)\tfrac{1}{2} = 0.$$

On the average, or in the long run, one expects to break even, or win a zero amount. (The term expectation originated in this way in gambling games.) We note two useful results:

THEOREM 2.1(a)   *The expectation of a sum of random variables is the sum of the expectations; that is,*

$$E(X + Y) = E(X) + E(Y).$$

THEOREM 2.1(b)   *The expectation of a random variable multiplied by a constant is the expectation multiplied by the same constant; that is,*

$$E(aX) = aE(X).$$

Example 2.15   Roulette

What is the expected gain of a gambler who bets \$1.00 on Number 13 on each of 100 successive spins of a roulette wheel at Reno?

As Nevada roulette wheels are usually set up, the gambler gains $+\$35$ if his number turns up and $-\$1$; i.e., he loses \$1 if any other number turns up. A roulette wheel has numbers 1 to 36 plus a 0 and a 00 and if we assume that each of these 38 possibilities is equally likely, then the situation is as follows in any single spin of the wheel:

x	$p(x)$	$x \cdot p(x)$
$+35$	$\frac{1}{38}$	$\frac{35}{38}$
-1	$\frac{37}{38}$	$-\frac{37}{38}$

$$E(X) = -\tfrac{2}{38} = -\tfrac{1}{19} = -0.05 \qquad \text{(5 cents approximately)}.$$

Now Theorem 2.1 enables us to calculate the "gain" in 100 games, for the expectation of the sum is simply $(-\frac{1}{19}) + (-\frac{1}{19}) + (-\frac{1}{19}) + \cdots$ (repeated 100 times), i.e., $-\frac{100}{19}$ or $-\$5.26$. The average or expected "gain" over 100 games is $-\$5.26$; i.e., the player will lose $5.26, on the average. Observe that this is the *expected* result—the average of the conceptual population of all such gains on 100 plays. What happens in a single set of 100 trials may be quite different—the player could lose every time and hence lose $100. It is also possible (although extremely improbable) that he might win every time and hence win $3,500. From $-\$100$ to $+\$3,500$ is a wide range, and clearly it is important to have more precise knowledge about the variability.

One measure of this variability that is widely used is the *standard deviation*. This is defined as the *square root of the expectation of squares of deviations from the mean*, or in symbols,

$$\sqrt{\sum (x - \mu)^2 \cdot p(x)},$$

where again the summation is over all points x in the sample space. The standard deviation is denoted by S.D.(X), or by σ_X, or, if no confusion is likely to arise, by σ alone.

While the mean or expectation has a natural intuitive appeal, the same cannot be said for the standard deviation, for which there is no simple intuitive explanation. The range or difference between the largest and smallest values in the sample space might seem to be a simpler measure of variability. To show that the range is of limited use and at the same time to illustrate the value of the standard deviation, we consider six symmetrical probability distributions on the three points -1, 0, 1. For each, the range is two. Since each distribution is symmetrical, each has expectation zero, so that the standard deviations are easily calculated (Table 2.1).

Figure 2.2 makes explicit in a very elementary way the fact that the

TABLE 2.1

x	$P(X=x)$	y	$P(Y=y)$	z	$P(Z=z)$	u	$P(U=u)$	v	$P(V=v)$	w	$P(W=w)$
-1	0.0	-1	0.1	-1	0.2	-1	0.3	-1	0.4	-1	0.5
0	1.0	0	0.8	0	0.6	0	0.4	0	0.2	0	0.0
1	0.0	0	0.1	1	0.2	1	0.3	1	0.4	1	0.5
$\sigma_X = 0$		$\sigma_Y = 0.447$		$\sigma_Z = 0.632$		$\sigma_U = 0.775$		$\sigma_V = 0.894$		$\sigma_W = 1$	

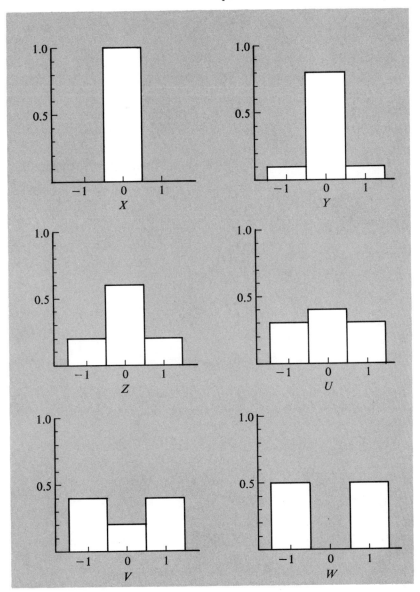

FIGURE 2.2 *A comparison which shows how the standard deviation measures the variability of probability distributions on a given sample space.*

distribution of X is concentrated at zero, that of Y is nearly as concentrated, while at the other extreme V and W are random variables that take on minimum or maximum values most or all of the time.

As the distributions progress from being as concentrated as possible to being as variable as possible, σ increases from its minimum value 0 to the value 1. One is the largest value σ can have for random variables on the sample space $-1, 0, 1$. In general, however, it is not possible to find an upper limit on σ without knowing something more about the distribution.

*Chebyshev's Inequality†

A more general way of showing how the standard deviation characterizes the variability of a distribution is seen from the following theorem:

THEOREM 2.2   CHEBYSHEV'S INEQUALITY.   *For any random variable X with mean μ, standard deviation σ, and any real number $k > 1$,*

$$P\left(\frac{|X - \mu|}{\sigma} \geq k\right) \leq \frac{1}{k^2},$$

or

$$P(\mu - k\sigma < X < \mu + k\sigma) \geq 1 - \frac{1}{k^2}.$$

In words, this theorem states that all but the fraction $1/k^2$ of any distribution must lie within plus or minus k standard deviations of the mean.

The idea of measuring *from the mean* and in *units of the standard deviation* is an important one. It is worthwhile to give this a special symbol. Define

$$Z^* = \frac{X - \mu}{\sigma},$$

so that Z^* has expectation 0 and standard deviation 1 (see Problem 2.36). Z^* is called a *standardized random variable*. In terms of Z^*, Theorem 2.2 says that

$$P(|Z^*| \geq k) \leq \frac{1}{k^2}.$$

It is helpful to put in some simple numerical values for k in Theorem 2.2; for example, if we put $k = 2$, we observe that

$$P(-2 < Z^* < 2) = P(\mu - 2\sigma < X < \mu + 2\sigma) \geq 1 - \tfrac{1}{4} \quad \text{or } 0.75;$$

---

† Starred sections may be omitted without loss of continuity.

if we put $k = 3$, we observe that

$$P(-3 < Z^* < 3) = P(\mu - 3\sigma < X < \mu + 3\sigma) \geq 1 - \tfrac{1}{9} \quad \text{or } 0.89;$$

if we put $k = 4$, we observe that

$$P(-4 < Z^* < 4) = P(\mu - 4\sigma < X < \mu + 4\sigma) \geq 1 - \tfrac{1}{16} \quad \text{or } 0.94.$$

Note: For the theorem to be true, k need not be an integer.

Variance

While the standard deviation is a simple measure characterizing the spread of a distribution or variability of a random variable for many purposes it is often more convenient to work with its square; i.e., we do not take the square root. This squared quantity is called the *variance of X*. It will be abbreviated to $V(X)$, or σ_X^2. As before, if no confusion is likely to arise, we drop the reference to X and write σ^2. We noted that the expectation of a sum is a sum of expectations. Does the same hold for the standard deviation? *No*, but there is a similar theorem for the variance, for which an additional condition must be imposed. The result is:

THEOREM 2.3(a) *The variance of a sum of* independent *random variables equals the sum of the variances.*

The variance of a sum of random variables which are *not* independent may not equal the sum of the variances (see Problem 5.27). Theorem 2.1(a) is true without such an assumption.

THEOREM 2.3(b) *For any constant a, $V(aX) = a^2 \cdot V(X)$.*

Combining Theorems 2.3(a) and 2.3(b) yields

$$V(aX + bY) = a^2 \cdot V(X) + b^2 \cdot V(Y),$$

when X and Y are independent.

An extension of Theorems 2.1 and 2.3 to more than two random variables is immediate. (For a precise formulation of these, see Chapter 6, Theorems 6.1 and 6.2.)

Example 2.16   Finding a defective machine (continued)

In this problem we defined the random variable X as the number of machines examined by a repairman in finding one defective machine among five. Recall that $P(X = 1) = P(X = 2) = \cdots = P(X = 5) = \tfrac{1}{5}$.

What are the expectation and variance of X, i.e., $E(X)$ and $V(X)$? The following table is useful for calculating $E(X)$ and $V(X)$:

x	$p(x)$	$x \cdot p(x)$	$x - \mu$	$(x - \mu)^2 \cdot p(x)$
1	$\frac{1}{5}$	$\frac{1}{5}$	-2	$\frac{4}{5}$
2	$\frac{1}{5}$	$\frac{2}{5}$	-1	$\frac{1}{5}$
3	$\frac{1}{5}$	$\frac{3}{5}$	0	0
4	$\frac{1}{5}$	$\frac{4}{5}$	1	$\frac{1}{5}$
5	$\frac{1}{5}$	$\frac{5}{5}$	2	$\frac{4}{5}$
Totals	1	$\mu = \frac{15}{5} = 3$		$\sigma^2 = \frac{10}{5} = 2$

Hence, $\mu = E(X) = 3$; $V(X) = 2$; S.D.$(X) = \sqrt{2} = 1.414$.

Example 2.17   Roulette (continued)

What is the standard deviation of the random variable, the gain on 100 one-dollar bets at roulette?

Solution: Earlier we observed that this random variable could be studied by examining the gain on one bet and using Theorem 2.1 to extend this to 100 bets. Recall that if X is the gain on one bet, we had

x	$p(x)$	$x - \mu$	$(x - \mu)^2 \cdot p(x)$
$+35$	$\frac{1}{38}$	35.0526	32.3338
-1	$\frac{37}{38}$	-0.9474	0.8739
Total			$\sigma^2 = 33.2077$

Hence, $\mu = -\frac{1}{19} = -0.0526$; $V(X) = 33.21$; S.D.$(X) = 5.76$.

If G is the gain in 100 bets, then G is the sum of 100 random variables, which are independent and have the same distribution as X. By Theorem 2.3(a), $V(G) = 33.21 + 33.21 + \cdots$ (one hundred times) $= 3,321$, so that S.D.$(G) = \$57.65$. Recall that $E(G) = \$5.26$. [*Note:* From Theorem 2.2 with $k = 2$, we may conclude that

$$P(-\$5.26 - 2(\$57.65) < G < -\$5.26 + 2(\$57.65)) \geq 0.75;$$

that is,

$$P(-\$120.56 < G < \$110.04) \geq 0.75,$$

or in words, that at least three-fourths of the time, the "gain" from playing 100 games will fall between $-\$120.65$ and $\$110.04$. While Theorem 2.2 yields some information, we will discover in Problem 6.42 that by studying this distribution more carefully, much more precise statements can be made about the distribution of G.]

Example 2.18 Experiments with two outcomes (continued)

x	$p(x)$
0	$1 - p$
1	p
Total	1

$$\mu = E(X) = 0(1 - p) + 1p = p,$$
$$\sigma^2 = V(X) = (0 - 1)^2 \cdot (1 - p) + (1 - p)^2 \cdot p = p(1 - p).$$

Functions of Random Variables

Example 2.19 Roulette (continued)

In this example, the random variable X takes on the two values -1 and $+35$. A gambler might, however, record only the number of times he wins, in which case we could think of a random variable Y defined by this experiment as follows:

$$Y = 0 \quad \text{if the gambler loses.}$$
$$Y = 1 \quad \text{if the gambler wins.}$$

It is easy to compute the probability distribution of Y as well as its expectation and variance. They are

y	$p(y)$
0	$\frac{37}{38}$
1	$\frac{1}{38}$

so that $E(Y) = \frac{1}{38}$ and $V(Y) = 0.0256$. It can also be observed that Y and X are linearly related; in fact, $Y = \frac{1}{36}(X + 1)$.

More generally, if Y is functionally related to X and X is a random variable, Y is a random variable also. The probability distribution of

X determines the probability distribution of Y, and in simple cases the latter probability distribution can be expressed in tabular form by direct computations. In general, the expectation and variance of Y can be obtained from its probability distribution and the basic definitions. However, if $Y = g(X)$, then $E(Y) = E[g(X)] = \sum g(x)p(x)$, where the summation is over all points x in the sample space of X.

Occasionally it is useful to think of a "random" variable that takes on only one value, say, a; in formal language this is expressed as $P(X = a) = 1$. Obviously for such a random variable $E(X) = a$, and $V(X) = 0$. (See Problem 2.34.) Thus any constant can be thought of as a random variable in this sense, and one can meaningfully refer to the expectation or variance of a constant. Further, it is intuitively obvious that a constant is independent of any random variable.

When Y is linearly related to X, the expectation and variance of Y can be obtained directly by means of Theorems 2.1 and 2.3 and the remarks in the preceding paragraph. Thus, for the random variable Y defined in Example 2.19, by Theorems 2.1(a) and (b),

$$E(Y) = E\left[\frac{1}{36}(X + 1)\right] = \frac{1}{36}[E(X) + E(1)]$$

$$= \frac{1}{26}\left[-\frac{1}{19} + 1\right] = \frac{1}{36}\left(\frac{18}{19}\right) = \frac{1}{38},$$

and

$$V(Y) = V\left[\frac{1}{36}(X + 1)\right] = \frac{1}{36^2}[V(X) + V(1)]$$

$$= \frac{1}{1,296}[33.21 + 0] = 0.0256.$$

These agree with the values computed directly.

The concept of a function of a random variable is often useful in simplifying the computation of a variance. For, by letting $g(X) = (X - \mu)^2$, it is seen that

$$V(X) = E(X - \mu)^2.$$

Since

$$(X - \mu)^2 = X^2 - 2X\mu + \mu^2,$$

then

$$\begin{aligned}
V(X) &= E(X^2 - 2X\mu + \mu^2) \\
&= E(X^2) + E(-2X\mu) + E(\mu^2) \quad \text{(by Theorem 2.1(a))} \\
&= E(X^2) - 2\mu E(X) + \mu^2 \quad \text{(by Theorem 2.1(b))} \\
&= E(X^2) - 2\mu \cdot \mu + \mu^2 \\
&= E(X^2) - \mu^2.
\end{aligned}$$

The formula $V(X) = E(X^2) - \mu^2$ is often referred to as the computing formula for the variance of a random variable.

Example 2.20   Finding a defective machine (continued)

Letting $U = X^2$, we have the following probability distribution for U:

u	$p(u)$	$u \cdot p(u)$
1	$\frac{1}{5}$	$\frac{1}{5}$
4	$\frac{1}{5}$	$\frac{4}{5}$
9	$\frac{1}{5}$	$\frac{9}{5}$
16	$\frac{1}{5}$	$\frac{16}{5}$
25	$\frac{1}{5}$	$\frac{25}{5}$
		$E(U) = \frac{55}{5} = 11$

Hence, as computed directly in Example 2.16,

$$E(X^2) = 11 \quad \text{and} \quad V(X) = E(X^2) - \mu^2 = 11 - 9 = 2.$$

Example 2.21   Experiments with two outcomes (continued)

Let $U = X^2$. Then the probability distribution of U is

u	$p(u)$	$u \cdot p(u)$
0	$1 - p$	0
1	p	p
		$E(U) = p$

Hence, as computed directly in Example 2.18,

$$E(X^2) = p$$

and

$$V(X) = E(X^2) - [E(X)]^2 = p - p^2 = p(1 - p).$$

EXERCISES

1. If $P(A) = \frac{1}{2}$, $P(B) = \frac{1}{4}$, $P(AB) = \frac{1}{4}$, calculate $P(A + B)$, $P(\bar{A})$, $P(A|B)$, $P(B|A)$. Are A and B independent?

2. If X has the following probability distribution:

x	$p(x)$
0	$\frac{1}{2}$
1	$\frac{1}{3}$
2	$\frac{1}{6}$

find $E(X)$, $V(X)$, $P(X$ is positive$)$, $P(X$ is odd$)$.

3. A cross tabulation of names in a faculty directory shows the following:

	Professor	Associate Professor	Assistant Professor	Other	Total
Male	159	120	210	107	596
Female	21	15	25	29	90
Total	180	135	235	136	686

(a) What is the probability that a name drawn at random from the directory is that of (i) a male, (ii) an associate professor, (iii) a female assistant professor?

(b) Given that the name drawn is a female name, what is the conditional probability that the name is that of an assistant professor?

(c) Let A be the event that the name drawn is that of a male,

B_1 be the event that the name drawn is that of professor,

B_2 be the event that the name drawn is that of an associate professor,

B_3 be the event that the name drawn is that of assistant professor,

B_4 be the event that the name drawn is that of other ranks.

Calculate

(i) $P(A|B_1)$, $P(A|B_2)$, $P(A|B_3)$, $P(A|B_4)$,

(ii) $P(A|B_1 + B_2 + B_3 + B_4)$,

(iii) $P(B_1|A)$, $P(B_2|A)$, $P(B_3|A)$, $P(B_4|A)$,

(iv) $P(A|B_1 + B_2)$, $P(B_1)$.

(d) Is $P(B_2) = 1 - P(B_1 + B_3 + B_4)$?

4. (a) For each of the random variables X, Y, Z, U, V, W, the distributions of which are given in Table 2.1, calculate the probability that the random variable is greater than or equal to one in absolute value. [*Note:* $P(|X| \geq 1) = P(X \leq -1 \text{ or } X \geq 1)$ and similarly for the others.]

★(b) For each random variable except X, define k so that $k\sigma = 1$;

hence calculate the bound as derived from Theorem 2.2 for the probability calculated in (a). For example,

$$P(|Z| \geq 1) = P(Z \leq -1 \text{ or } Z \geq 1) = 0.2 + 0.2 = 0.4.$$

Now $\sigma_Z = 0.63$, so if $k\sigma_Z = 1$,

$$k = \frac{1}{0.63} = 1.587, \qquad \frac{1}{k^2} = 0.40,$$

so by Theorem 2.2

$$P(|Z| \geq 1) = P\left(\frac{|Z|}{\sigma_Z} \geq \frac{1}{0.63}\right) \leq 0.40.$$

It is seen that for each of the variables Y, Z, U, V, W we have an equality rather than an inequality.

5. (a) Consider a new set of probability distributions as follows:

x	$p_1(x)$	$p_2(x)$	$p_3(x)$	$p_4(x)$	$p_5(x)$	$p_6(x)$
-1	0.5	0.4	0.3	0.2	0.1	0
$-\frac{1}{2}$	0	0.1	0.1	0.2	0.2	0
0	0	0	0.2	0.2	0.4	1
$\frac{1}{2}$	0	0.1	0.1	0.2	0.2	0
1	0.5	0.4	0.3	0.2	0.1	0

It is easily seen that in all cases the mean is zero; find the variance and standard deviation of each distribution. Calculate the exact probability that $|X_i|$ is greater than or equal to 0.5.
★(b) For each case calculate the bound derived by Theorem 2.2.

■ Experiments

2.1 From an ordinary deck of cards, take two red cards and two black cards and shuffle them. Draw two cards from the population of four. Count the number of red cards. This is a random variable: It is in fact an actual realization of one similar to that of Example 2.11. Repeat this 25 times and note the observed relative frequencies of the three points in the sample space. Be careful to shuffle well between each observation.

2.2 From an ordinary deck of cards, take four aces and a king and shuffle these five cards. Turn them over until the king is exposed and count the number of cards turned. This is a random variable: again a realization of the same random variable as that in Example 2.12

(finding a defective machine). Repeat this 25 times and calculate the observed relative frequencies of the five points in the sample space 1, 2, 3, 4, 5. Be careful to shuffle well between each "observation."

2.3 Open an ordinary telephone directory and select at random a number from each of the right- and left-hand pages (use only the last four digits). Allocate a score of $+1$ if the right-hand number exceeds the left-hand number and -1 in the contrary case. Ignore ties and resample. Repeat the experiment four times and let X be the sum of the scores. Obtain ten observations on X. (See Problem 2.27 for theoretical results.)

■ Problems

2.1 A rocket is composed of three components, A, B, C. It is known that the probability of A's failing is 0.50, of B's failing is 0.3, and of C's failing is 0.20. The rocket fails if any component fails. What is the probability the rocket fails, if we assume that the three components behave independently?

2.2 State the assumptions necessary and compute the probability that in a family of four children there is at least one girl. Exactly one girl.

2.3 Two dice, one red and one white, are thrown. What is the probability that the sum of the numbers showing on the top faces is seven? What is the probability that the sum of the numbers is six, given that the number showing on the red die is three. Are the events "three on the red die" and "seven for the total" independent? Consider the same problem for the events

(a) "two on the red die" and "two for the total,"
(b) "one on the red die" and "two for the total."

2.4 (Playoff series) Playoffs in some sports are determined by a three-game series, which terminates when either team has won two games. Assume Teams A and B are competing, that the teams are evenly matched, so that the probability of A's winning any game is $\frac{1}{2}$, and that outcomes of different games are independent. Find the probability that

(a) A wins the series;
(b) A wins the first game and the series;

(c) A wins the series, given that A wins the first game; show that the events "A wins the series" and "A wins the first game" are dependent.

(d) Are the events "A wins the first two games" and "B wins the series" mutually exclusive? dependent? Give reasons.

2.5   The reliability of a complex device, e.g., any of the rockets used in space exploration, depends on the reliability of many component parts. Suppose that such a device is composed of 1,000 vital parts each of which has the probability 0.999 of working properly under operational conditions. Assume that the total device works properly only if each part works, and also that failures of different parts are independent events; calculate the probability that the device works. (In this and the following problem we disregard the possibility of wear-out, i.e., that the probability of failure changes over time. Such change makes problems of reliability more complicated. However, there are many situations where the operation is of short duration and thus wear-out may be disregarded.)

2.6   (a) Consider a device with only three component parts; suppose that each has a probability of failure equal to 0.01. What is the probability that the device works? (Make the assumptions as in the last problem.)

(b)   One way to improve reliability of a complex device is to increase the reliability, i.e., the probability of working, of each component part. Another way is to provide the device with "spares," which take over automatically in case a part fails.

Now assume that each part has a duplicate that takes over in the case of failure of the initial part. Assume that the duplicates have the same probability of failure and that all failures are independent events in calculating the new probability that the whole device works.

2.7   (a) Two individuals are placed in a room with a single mosquito until one person is bitten. The experiment is repeated. Denote by p_1 the probability that Person Number 1 is bitten in any single trial. What is the probability that different individuals are bitten in two independent trials? Hence calculate the probability that the same person is bitten in two trials.

(b) Consider the same experiment with three persons involved; denote by p_1, p_2, and p_3 their respective probabilities of being bitten (so that $p_1 + p_2 + p_3 = 1$). Calculate the probability that in three independent trials all three individuals are bitten; that the same individual is bitten three times. What do these reduce to when $p_1 = p_2 = p_3$? when $p_1 = 0.6$, $p_2 = 0.3$, and $p_3 = 0.1$?

2.8 Identical twins, since they result from a single fertilized egg, are necessarily of the same sex; fraternal twins may be of either sex. If the probability of twins' being identical is $\frac{1}{3}$, and the probability of a fraternal twin's being male is $\frac{1}{2}$ (in actuality it is slightly greater than $\frac{1}{2}$), calculate the probability that the members of a pair of twins are of the same sex. To calculate the probability that twins of a pair are both female, one other piece of information is needed. What is it?

2.9 According to a National Safety Council study in 1960–1962 the passenger death rate per 100 million passenger miles traveled by railroad was 0.13; by bus, 0.16; in scheduled air transport plane, 0.57; and in passenger automobiles, 2.2. Assume that the same probabilities hold now, and calculate the probability of your surviving a flight across the country (3,000 miles) and return by private car (4,000 miles). Calculate the same probability, using the same distances, for railroad trip across and return by bus. What assumptions are made in these calculations?

2.10 A deck contains four cards (two aces and two kings). Two cards are drawn. Let A be the event that the first card is an ace, B be the event that the second card is an ace. Assume that at each draw, any card in the deck at that draw is equally likely to be drawn.

(a) If the first card is not replaced before the second is drawn, show that A and B are dependent events.
(b) If the first card is replaced before the second is drawn, show that A and B are independent events.

2.11 What is the random variable in each of Examples 1.1, 1.5, and 1.6? In Example 1.4 find three different random variables. What is the sample space associated with each of the random variables in all of these examples?

2.12 In the experiments or sampling procedures suggested by you in answer to Problems 1.3 and 1.5 (a) and (b), what are the random variables involved? What are the sample spaces?

2.13 For Example 2.2 (taste testing), let $X = 1$ if the taster is correct and let $X = 0$ otherwise. Find $E(X)$ and $V(X)$. [*Note:* You may obtain these from the definitions or by applying the results contained in Example 2.18.]

2.14   Find the probability distribution of X, the number of defectives, in a sample of size 2 from a population with five elements, two of which are defective. Do the same for a sample of size 3. In both cases, obtain $E(X)$ and $V(X)$ (the latter both from the definition and the computing formula).

2.15   Let X denote the number of games in the playoff series of Problem 2.4. What is the sample space of X? Make the same assumptions and calculate the probability distribution of X, $E(X)$, and $V(X)$ (the latter both from the definition and the computing formula).

2.16   Find the probability distribution of X, the number of machines inspected by a repairman in circumstances similar to the example given, if there are four machines originally in the laboratory. Also find $E(X)$ and $V(X)$ (the latter both from the definition and the computing formula).

2.17   An electronic calculating machine has to select one correct channel out of five. The procedure it goes through is as follows: Channels are selected at random until the correct one is found. The machine does not make a wrong selection twice. Let Y denote the number of *wrong* selections the machine makes.
(a) What possible values can Y take on?
(b) Determine the probability distribution of Y.
(c) Find $E(Y)$ and $V(Y)$.
(d) There is a functional relationship between Y and the random variable X of Example 2.12. What is it?
(e) Suppose ten machines are operating simultaneously and independently, each making such a selection. Let T be the total number of wrong selections of all ten. Find $E(\text{T})$ and $V(\text{T})$.

2.18   In an oyster experiment, an oyster predator is placed in the center of a tray with two oysters and two of other prey nearby. The experimenter notes the order of the preying on the oysters—for example, if the predator preys upon the two oysters first, the order would be 1, 2; if on the oysters last, it would be 3, 4. Let X denote the sum of the orders of preying on the two oysters. Find the probability distribution of X under the assumption that the predator chooses randomly among its available prey at each state. (Note that after preying upon an animal, that animal is killed, so it is not involved at the next choice stage.) Also find $E(X)$ and $V(X)$.

2.19   In an experiment to test associations, a biologist places two animals in a rectangular tank marked into three equal sections. At specified time intervals, the biologist notes the "distance" X between the animals. This may be zero (if the animals are in the same section); one, if the animals are in adjacent sections; or two, if they are at opposite ends of the tank. Find the probability distribution of X, if it is assumed that each animal behaves independently of the other and is equally likely to be in any section. Also find $E(X)$ and $V(X)$.

2.20   A student has a matching problem on a test. After doing the matches he knows, he finds himself left with three about which he is completely ignorant. He decides to guess on these three. Let X be the number of these he gets right. X is a random variable.
(a) What values may it take on?
(b) Three things (A, B, C) may be arranged in six orders, ABC, ACB, BAC, BCA, CAB, CBA. Assume each of these is an equally likely guess on the part of the student and calculate the probabilities that $X = 3$, $X = 2$, $X = 1$, $X = 0$. Write these in tabular form.
(c) Calculate $E(X)$ and S.D. (X).

2.21   In a multiple choice test, there are 11 questions. Questions 1 through 5 have five choices; Questions 6 through 11 have six choices, and these are given double weight. Let $X =$ total score of a student on the test. [*Note:* X can take values from 0 to 17.] Assume that a student guesses independently on each question. Find $E(X)$ and $V(X)$.

2.22   A true–false test of 20 questions is scored so that $S =$ (number right minus number wrong). What is the mean and variance of S for a student who just guesses on each question?

2.23   Find the probability distribution of X, the number of runs in five tosses of a coin in which occur three heads and two tails. Find $E(X)$ and $V(X)$.

2.24   What would be the sample space, the probability distribution, $E(X)$, and S.D. (X) in Problem 2.20 if the student had to guess on four questions instead of three.

2.25   Five cards are drawn simultaneously from a deck of 52. Let X be the number of aces in these five cards. Find the probability distribution of X.

2.26 Find the probability distribution of X, the number of calculating machines inspected by a repairman in circumstances similar to those of Example 2.12 if two of the five machines are defective and he is told to repair both. Find $E(X)$ and $V(X)$.

2.27 Two pairs engage in a tennis match in which each player of one pair meets each opponent of the other pair in a singles match. Each player gets a score of $+1$ if he wins; -1 if he loses. The team score X is the sum of the individual scores, so that the maximum team score is 4, the minimum team score is -4. What is the probability distribution of team scores if all players are equal and ties do not occur? Find the expectation and variance of X. Experiment 2.3 was a realization of the same random variable as that in this problem.

2.28 What is the expected number of machines to be examined by the repairman in two trips to the laboratory if it is assumed that
(a) in each case one of the five machines is defective?
(b) in the second case the machine repaired on trip one is not defective and is not examined?
Define a random variable for each case, state what its sample space is, and find its variance.

2.29 Consider nine repetitions of the taste-testing experiment. Assume they are independent and let Y be the total number of correct calls. Find $E(Y)$ and $V(Y)$.

2.30 In a multiple choice test a student guesses at the answer. Suppose there are m answers from which he guesses. What is the probability he guesses correctly? Let X be a random variable that equals one if the answer is correct and zero otherwise. Find $E(X)$ and $V(X)$. (See note to Problem 2.13.)

★2.31 Consider ten such multiple choice questions. Suppose that the student guesses on each and the questions are independent. If Y equals the number of correct answers, find $E(Y)$ and $V(Y)$. Evaluate these for $m = 5$, $m = 2$.

★2.32 Of ten trees arranged in a circle, three are diseased. What is the probability that all three are adjacent if all are equally likely to be diseased? More generally, if n trees are arranged in a circle and k are diseased, what is the probability the k are adjacent, if we assume all arrangements are equally probable? Check that the general formula gives the correct result for $n = 10$, $k = 3$; $n = 6$, $k = 2$.

2.33 In an experiment, a group of trees is set out in an ell with 5 trees in each arm plus the common corner tree (for a total of 11). The corner tree is artificially infected with a fungous disease. If each of the remaining trees has the same chance of being infected, what is the probability that the next tree affected will be adjacent to the corner? That the next two trees affected will be adjacent to each other and the corner tree or on either side of the corner tree?

2.34 Verify that if $X = a$ with probability one, then $E(X) = a$ and $V(X) = 0$, using the definitions.

2.35 (a) Find the probability distribution for the standardized random variable $Z*$ in Example 2.12 (finding a defective machine); i.e., find the sample space and the probability distribution of $Z = (X - 3)/(1.414)$, where X is the number of machines examined.

(b) Verify from the definitions that $E(Z*) = 0$ and $V(Z*) = 1$.

*2.36 Prove that $E(Z*) = 0$ and $V(Z*) = 1$ for any standardized random variable $Z*$ by using Theorems 2.1(b) and 2.3(b).

*2.37 Use Theorem 2.2 to find an upper bound for the probability that the student referred to in Problem 2.31 answers either all the ten questions correctly or all ten questions incorrectly, when $m = 2$. The exact probability is 0.002 (as the reader will verify in Problem 3.35).

*2.38 Use Theorem 2.2 to find a lower bound for $P(0 < Y < 6)$, when Y is the random variable in Problem 2.29. The exact probability of this event is 0.931 (as the reader will verify in Problem 3.35). [*Hint:* $(0 < Y < 6) = (|Z*| < 2.13)$, where $Z* = (Y - 3)/\sqrt{2}$.]

2.39 An automatic weather-reporting buoy frequently misses due to bad radio reception. The buoy is due to report at noon; because of the chance of failure it is also set to report at 10 and 11 A.M. and 1 and 2 P.M. If the weather report comes in at noon, or if one or more morning and one or more afternoon signals come in, the transmission is acceptable. If the probability of failure on any hour is 0.5, and if failures at different hours are independent events, what is the probability we have an acceptable transmission?

2.40 Eight trees are arranged on two concentric circles, four on an inner circle, four on an outer one. An infected tree is placed at the center. What is the probability that the first four of the original trees to be infected are all on the inner circle if it is assumed that all trees are equally likely to be infected?

CHAPTER THREE

The Binomial Probability Model

Introduction

A number of probability distributions play a major role in statistical analysis because they occur so frequently. One of the simplest of these is the *binomial probability distribution*, which is introduced by four examples, each a special case of Example 2.10.

Example 3.1 Coin tossing

A fair coin is tossed three times. Denote by X the number of heads. X is a random variable, which may take on the values 0, 1, 2, 3. What is its probability distribution? The possibilities can easily be enumerated as follows:

First toss	Second toss	Third toss	X
H	H	H	3
H	H	T	2
H	T	H	2
T	H	H	2
H	T	T	1
T	H	T	1
T	T	H	1
T	T	T	0

Since the coin is fair and the tosses are assumed to be independent, Rule II.5a implies that each of the eight possibilities is equally likely and hence that

$$P(X = 0) = \tfrac{1}{8}, \quad P(X = 2) = \tfrac{3}{8},$$
$$P(X = 1) = \tfrac{3}{8}, \quad P(X = 3) = \tfrac{1}{8}.$$

Example 3.2 Class cards (continued)

Recall the 40 class cards in Example 2.5. Let the experiment consist of drawing two of them, replacing the first before the second is drawn. Let X be the number of class cards selected that belong to male students. X can take on the values 0, 1, or 2. We have assumed that the selection was at random. This is taken to mean that the probability of getting a class card of a male is $\frac{30}{40}$, i.e., $P(A)$ in the earlier example. Now what can happen with two drawings? We could get one of these:

First draw	Second draw	X
Male	Male	2
Female	Male	1
Male	Female	1
Female	Female	0

Hence,

$$P(X = 2) = \left(\tfrac{30}{40}\right)\left(\tfrac{30}{40}\right) = 0.5625 \quad \text{(Rule II.5a)},$$
$$P(X = 1) = \left(\tfrac{30}{40}\right)\left(\tfrac{10}{40}\right) + \left(\tfrac{10}{40}\right)\left(\tfrac{30}{40}\right) = 0.3750$$
$$\text{(Rules II.4a and II.5a)},$$
$$P(X = 0) = \left(\tfrac{10}{40}\right)\left(\tfrac{10}{40}\right) = 0.0625 \quad \text{(Rule II.5a)},$$
$$\text{Total} = 1.0000 \quad \text{(Check, Rule II.2)}.$$

EXERCISES

1. Suppose three cards are drawn with replacement, as in Example 3.2. Find the probability distribution of X, the number of class cards drawn that belong to male students.

2. Find the probability distribution of Y, the number of lower division class cards if two are drawn with replacement as in Example 3.2.

3. Let X be the number of heads in two tosses of a fair coin. What is the probability distribution of X? Compare it with Example 3.2. Find $E(X)$ and $V(X)$.

4. Recall Example 2.2 (taste testing); suppose such a taste-testing experiment is done twice. Let X be the number of correct judgments in the two experiments. What is the sample space of X? Find its probability distribution. (See also Example 2.9.)

5. What two assumptions did you make in the above four exercises about the various trials in order to find the probability distributions?

Example 3.3 Traffic lights

The first traffic light on your route to the university is green for 20 seconds out of its 60-second cycle. Assume a probability of $\frac{1}{3}$ of "hitting the intersection on the green" on any particular day; what is the probability that you get the green light every day for a week (five days)? (Is the assumption likely to be strictly correct?) To calculate this probability another assumption must be made, namely, that the occurrence of the event on any one day does not affect what happens on the other days. (Is this reasonable?)

Applying Rule II.5a, we obtain

$$P(5 \text{ successes}) = \tfrac{1}{3} \cdot \tfrac{1}{3} \cdot \tfrac{1}{3} \cdot \tfrac{1}{3} \cdot \tfrac{1}{3} = \tfrac{1}{243}.$$

If X denotes the number of successes in five days, X is a random variable with possible values 0, 1, 2, 3, 4, or 5. The above statement may be written, $P(X = 5) = \frac{1}{243}$. What is $P(X = 4)$? Four successes and one failure or four greens and one red may happen in any of the following ways:

Mon.	Tues.	Wed.	Thurs.	Fri.
r	g	g	g	g
g	r	g	g	g
g	g	r	g	g
g	g	g	r	g
g	g	g	g	r

The probability of any one of these can be evaluated by Rule II.5a as $\tfrac{1}{3} \cdot \tfrac{1}{3} \cdot \tfrac{1}{3} \cdot \tfrac{1}{3} \cdot \tfrac{2}{3} = \tfrac{2}{243}$. Observe that a probability of $\frac{1}{3}$ of getting a green light implies a probability of $\frac{2}{3}$ of getting a red or amber light— Rule II.3. Now each of the events enumerated are mutually exclusive so that Rule II.4a can be applied to get

$$P(X = 4) = \tfrac{2}{243} + \tfrac{2}{243} + \tfrac{2}{243} + \tfrac{2}{243} + \tfrac{2}{243} = \tfrac{10}{243}.$$

Verify that

$$P(X = 3) = \tfrac{40}{243}, \qquad P(X = 1) = \tfrac{80}{243},$$

$$P(X = 2) = \tfrac{80}{243}, \qquad P(X = 0) = \tfrac{32}{243}.$$

Use Rule II.2 as a check on the arithmetic here.

Example 3.4 Gene inheritance

It is well known that the Mendelian theory of inheritance is based on the existence in any plant or animal of many pairs of genes. When bisexual reproduction takes place, each offspring receives one gene of each pair from each parent. Further, according to Mendelian principles, each of the two genes in any pair of the parents' sets is equally likely to be inherited; the genetic characters inherited from each parent by an individual offspring are independent events, and the genetic characters inherited by different offspring of the same parent are independent events.

Consider the M–N blood types in humans, which are apparently inherited according to this mechanism. An individual that has inherited both M genes will be denoted an M blood type; an individual with both N genes, an N blood type; while those who possess one M and one N gene are M–N blood types.

(a) What is the probability that an offspring of two M–N parents will be also M–N?

The probability asked for in (a) can be obtained very simply from the basic Rules I and II. For example, the offspring is M–N if and only if he inherits an M gene from the father and an N gene from the mother, or the converse. Now these are mutually exclusive events, so that we have

P(offspring is of blood type M–N)

$\quad = P[(\text{M gene obtained from father}) \ (\text{N gene obtained from mother})] + P[(\text{N gene obtained from father}) \ (\text{M gene obtained from mother})]$ (Rule II.4a)

$\quad = \frac{1}{2} \cdot \frac{1}{2} + \frac{1}{2} \cdot \frac{1}{2}$ (Rules I and II.5a)

$\quad = \frac{1}{2}.$

Observe that this is exactly the same probability as that of getting a head and tail in a toss of two fair coins and is derived by the same rules and calculations.

(b) What is the probability of four offspring of M–N parents being all M–N?

This is calculated in exactly the same way as the probability of five successes in the example on traffic lights, i.e., by the product

$$\frac{1}{2} \cdot \frac{1}{2} \cdot \frac{1}{2} \cdot \frac{1}{2} = \frac{1}{16}.$$

(c) What is the probability that of four offspring of M–N parents, two will be M–N and two not M–N?

Denote the four offspring by A, B, C, D; the two M–N offspring may be AB, AC, AD, BC, BD, or CD. There are six mutually exclusive possibilities. Now the probability that A and B are M–N blood types and C, D are not is $\frac{1}{2} \cdot \frac{1}{2} \cdot \frac{1}{2} \cdot \frac{1}{2} = \frac{1}{16}$.

Observe that the rule for independent events (Rule II.5a) is used here as applying to the independent inheritance of genetic characters.

Finally, since the other five probabilities (that AC are M–N types, etc.) are exactly the same, the required answer is

$$6 \cdot \frac{1}{16} = \frac{3}{8}.$$

Note that the six mutually exclusive possibilities are obtained by considering all possible combinations of A, B, C, D, taken two at a time.

Any of these problems could be changed by varying the number of trials. But it is also apparent they have something in common. They deal with trials in which an event (called success in Example 2.10) does or does not occur. The different trials do not affect one another. Finally, the probability of the occurrence of a success is the same from trial to trial. The trial may be the toss of a coin, the drawing of a card, or the reaching of an intersection. The successes referred to in these trials are (respectively) heads, obtaining the card of a male student, or "getting the green light."

Or the trial may be predicting the sex of an unborn child, a taste test, or an examination of an industrial product. In these cases success might be "correct prediction," "correct answer," or "defective product." One family of probability distributions serves to treat these diverse experiments—this is the strength of the statistical method. We proceed to derive that family of distributions.

General Formula for the Binomial Probability Distribution

Consider now n trials or experiments in each of which an event A (called success) may or may not occur. Assume that:

(1) the probability of A's occurring in any single trial is p.
(2) the different trials are unrelated, i.e., independent.

Let $T = $ the total number of occurrences of A in these n independent trials (the total number of successes in n trials), T is a random variable, which may take on values 0, 1, 2, 3,..., n.

We call T a *binomial random variable*, and proceed to find $P(T = t)$, i.e., the probability of t occurrences of the event A in n trials. Before we begin, we recall that $n! = n(n - 1)(n - 2) \cdots 3 \cdot 2 \cdot 1$ and that the number of arrangements of a indistinguishable things of one kind and b indistinguishable things of another kind is $[(a + b)!]/(a! \, b!)$. With the convention that $0! = 1$, this formula holds even for the case when $a = 0$ or $b = 0$.

Now consider the event

$$\underset{t \text{ times}}{A \, A \, A \cdots A} \qquad \underset{n - t \text{ times}}{\bar{A} \, \bar{A} \cdots \bar{A}}.$$

By Rule II.5a, the probability of this sequence's occurring is

$$\underset{t \text{ times}}{p \, p \, p \cdots p} \cdot \underset{n - t \text{ times}}{(1 - p)(1 - p) \cdots (1 - p)}.$$

Now this is only *one order* that gives rise to t occurrences of A. There are many such orders—in fact $n!/[t! \, (n - t)!]$, the number of arrangements of n things of which t are alike of one kind and $n - t$ are alike of another kind, according to the formula cited above with $a = t$, $b = n - t$. All of these orders are mutually exclusive and each means t occurrences of A. Hence, by Rule II.4a, we get the *binomial probability formula*

$$P(T = t) = \frac{n!}{t! \, (n - t)!} \, p^t (1 - p)^{n-t} \qquad \text{for } t = 0, 1, 2, \ldots, n.$$

EXERCISE

Check that the general formula gives the same results already obtained in the previous examples and exercises.

Example 3.5   Seed germination

About 70 percent of certain kinds of seeds sold on the retail market germinate when planted under normal conditions. Suppose that one package contains ten seeds. If these are planted, what is the probability of t of them germinating? Let T = the total number of germinations. T is a random variable taking values from 0 to 10. We want $P(T = t)$. To calculate this, we assume that

(a) the probability of any single seed's germinating is 0.7.
(b) the ten different seeds are independent; i.e., the germination of one seed does not affect the behavior of another.

Under these assumptions T is a binomial random variable with $n = 10$ and $p = 0.7$. Then

$$P(T = t) = \frac{10!}{t!\,(10 - t)!}\,(0.7)^t(0.3)^{10-t}.$$

This can be evaluated for different values of t by the use of logarithms. The arithmetic is facilitated by observing that for any number of trials n

$$P(T = t + 1) = \left(\frac{p}{1-p}\right)\left(\frac{n-t}{t+1}\right)\cdot P(T = t) \quad \text{for } t = 0, 1, \ldots, n - 1.$$

This is known as the *binomial probability recursion formula*. Thus, once $P(T = 0)$ is calculated, the remaining terms of the distribution are obtained by simple multiplications. In Example 3.5, $P(T = 0) = (0.3)^{10} = 0.000005905$. Using the binomial recursion formula with $p = 0.7$ and $n = 10$, one gets

$$P(T = 1) = \left(\frac{0.7}{0.3}\right)\left(\frac{10 - 0}{0 + 1}\right)(0.000005905) = 0.0001378.$$

Similarly,

$$P(T = 2) = \left(\frac{0.7}{0.3}\right)\left(\frac{10 - 1}{1 + 1}\right)(0.0001378) = 0.00145,$$

$$P(T = 3) = \left(\frac{0.7}{0.3}\right)\left(\frac{10 - 2}{2 + 1}\right)(0.00145) = 0.00902,$$

$$P(T = 4) = \left(\frac{0.7}{0.3}\right)\left(\frac{10 - 3}{3 + 1}\right)(0.00902) = 0.0368,$$

$$P(T = 5) = \left(\frac{0.7}{0.3}\right)\left(\frac{10 - 4}{4 + 1}\right)(0.0368) = 0.103.$$

However, because of their importance, the probabilities of the binomial distribution have been tabulated† for many values of n and p. A table of binomial probabilities for small values of n is provided in Appendix 2 (Table A2.1). This should serve for most of the problems in the text that involve binomial probabilities. Thus, from this

---

† See the following: *Tables of the Binomial Probability Distribution*, Applied Mathematics Series 6, National Applied Mathematics Laboratories of the National Bureau of Standards, (Washington, D.C.: U.S. Government Printing Office, 1950); Harry G. Romig, *50–100 Binomial Tables* (New York: John Wiley and Sons, Inc., 1955); *Tables of the Cumulative Binomial Probability Distribution*, Harvard University Computation Laboratory (Cambridge, Mass.: Harvard University Press, 1955).

table it is seen that for $n = 10$, $p = 0.7$, $P(T = 8) = 0.234$, $P(T = 9) = 0.121$, etc.

These tables enable us to calculate probabilities of the form $P(a \leq T \leq b)$, $P(T \leq b)$, and $P(T \geq a)$ by simple addition. For example, for $n = 20$, $p = 0.2$,

$$P(3 \leq T \leq 6) = P(T = 3) + P(T = 4) + P(T = 5) + P(T = 6)$$
$$= 0.205 + 0.218 + 0.175 + 0.109$$
$$= 0.707,$$
$$P(T \geq 8) = 0.022 + 0.007 + 0.002 + 0.001 = 0.032.$$

The binomial probability distribution defined by the binomial probability formula depends on both n, the number of trials, and p, the probability of success on a single trial. Often n is known to us and requires no further study. On the other hand, p is often unknown and the statistician's interest is focused on it. For each possible value of p (between 0 and 1), there is a corresponding probability distribution. The general formula gives rise to a whole family of distributions, each of which is binomial. For each value of p, between 0 and 1, there is a different binomial distribution. The binomial probability distribution is determined by the values of n and p. Such numbers and other characteristics of distributions are called *parameters*. The binomial distribution has two parameters, n and p.

Characteristics of the Binomial Distribution

In general, binomial probabilities are small for small t, rise steadily to a maximum (which may be small if n is large) near np and then decrease steadily. This behavior of the binomial distribution is exemplified by Figure 3.1.

The expectation and variance of the binomial distribution can be calculated by applying the basic definitions, but they will be derived here by an approach that makes use of the fact that the binomial random variable T is the total number of successes on n independent trials and hence can be written as the sum of n independent variables of the type discussed in Examples 2.10 and 2.18 (experiments with two outcomes). Let X_i = number of successes on trial i, so that

$$P(X_i = 1) = p, \qquad P(X_i = 0) = 1 - p.$$

It was shown in Example 2.18 that $E(X_i) = p$, and $V(X_i) = p(1 - p)$. Since X_i counts the number of successes on trial i, $\sum_{i=1}^{n} X_i$ counts the

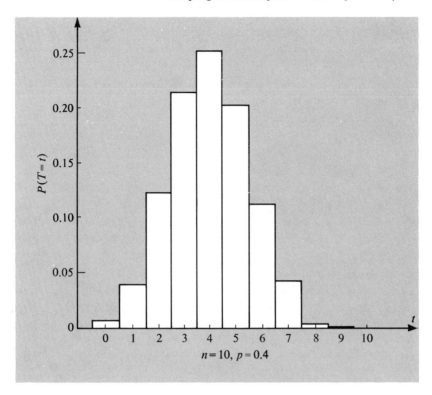

FIGURE 3.1   *A binomial histogram.*

number of successes in the n trials, i.e., $T = \sum_{i=1}^{n} X_i$. Now we have by Theorems 2.1 and 2.3 that

$$E(T) = \sum_{i=1}^{n} p = np,$$

$$V(T) = \sum_{i=1}^{n} p(1 - p) = np(1 - p).$$

Observe that the mean and variance of a binomial random variable are functions of the parameters of the distribution.

Sampling at Random from a Finite Population

The term *random sampling* implies that each element in the population has the same chance of appearing in the sample. However, if the population is finite and the sample is drawn without replacement, the population is seen to change slightly as the sampling proceeds. For example, if a card is drawn from a deck of 52 cards, the probability that it is red is 0.5. If a second card is drawn from the remaining 51 cards, the probability is not exactly 0.5 but depends on the result of the first draw. If the first card drawn is red, the conditional probability that the second is red is now $\frac{25}{51}$. If the first card is black, the conditional probability of the second one's being red is $\frac{26}{51}$.

Now consider a sample from a "deck" of 18,000 cards, which might be punch cards of students at a university. Suppose 13,000 of these are cards for male students. The probability that a card selected at random belongs to a male is 13,000/18,000 or 0.7222222. The conditional probability that a second card is that of a male student is either 12,999/17,999 or 13,000/17,999, depending on whether the first card belonged to a male or not. These two are 0.722206 and 0.722261 respectively; that is, they are essentially unchanged from the initial probability. In a sample of size 50, the conditional probabilities that the 50th card drawn belongs to a male are at least 12,951/17,951 and at most 13,000/17,951, that is, between 0.7215 and 0.7242.

Random sampling of this type from a finite population when the elements are drawn without replacement gives rise to a *hypergeometric*

TABLE 3.1   *Comparison of the Hypergeometric (Exact) and Binomial (Approximate) Probability Distribution for $N = 1,000$, $n = 20$, $p = 0.7$*

	PROBABILITIES	
t	$P(T = t)$ (exact)	$P(T = t)$ (approximate)
7	0.001	0.001
8	0.004	0.004
9	0.012	0.012
10	0.030	0.031
11	0.065	0.065
12	0.115	0.114
13	0.165	0.164
14	0.193	0.192
15	0.179	0.179
16	0.130	0.130
17	0.071	0.072
18	0.027	0.028
19	0.007	0.007
20	0.001	0.001
Total	1.000	1.000

distribution. It has been extensively studied and tabled.† However, if the sample size is small relative to the population size (a convenient rule is 5 percent or less), the binomial distribution with p constant may be used as a satisfactory approximation to this slightly more complex hypergeometric distribution. We shall use this here.

For example, consider a population of 1,000, which contains 700 males and 300 females. The exact distribution of the number of males in a sample of size 20 drawn without replacement is shown in Table 3.1 and compared with the binomial approximation.

The alert reader will realize that a number of hypergeometric distributions have already been discussed: Example 2.11, Experiment 2.1, Problems 2.1 and 2.25. The methods of these examples and problems can be used for sampling from very small populations. More generally, for hypergeometric probabilities a formula can be given, similar to the binomial formula but involving several additional factorials.

■ Experiments

3.1   Draw from a student directory a random sample of about 1 percent of the population. (If the number of listings exceeds 2,000, make the sample size 20.)   Specify the rule for drawing the random sample.   Count the number of male students listed.   Estimate the number of male students in the college.   Let T = number of male students in the sample. What kind of a random variable is T? What is the distribution of T, if p, the proportion of males on the campus, is 0.7, 0.8, 1.0?

3.2   How would you obtain a random sample of the residents of a city, of a county, of the school children in a city?

3.3   Toss a die five times and record the number of times it falls with one or two spots showing face up.   Denote by T the number of times this event occurs.   Note that T may be 0, 1, 2, 3, 4, or 5.   Repeat this experiment 25 times and record the observed frequencies of possible values of T. What is the probability distribution of T? What assumptions are necessary to calculate the probability distribution? In this experiment, 25 realizations of the same random variable studied in Example 3.3. (traffic lights) are obtained.

Such an experiment is a simulation study of the binomial model with $n = 5, p = \frac{1}{3}$.   Simulation studies, or Monte Carlo studies as they

---

† See Gerald Lieberman and Donald B. Owen, *Tables of the Hypergeometric Probability Distribution* (Stanford, California: Stanford University Press, 1961).

are often called, are an important tool in the analysis of statistical models. Such simulation studies can be accomplished with dice as here, or tables of random numbers (see Experiment 4.1), or more usually with high-speed electronic computers.

■ **Problems**

3.1 Each week during the football season, the *Times* has a contest that involves predicting the 20 winners of 20 specified football games on the following Saturday. If one guesses randomly the winner of each of the 20 games, and if there are no tie results that weekend, what is the probability that all games will be guessed correctly?

3.2 Write down the probability of hitting the green light t times in n independent trials if the probability of success on any occasion is 0.4. Evaluate this for $t = 3$, $n = 10$. What are $E(T)$ and $V(T)$?

3.3 For ease of computation, assume that the sex ratio at birth is unity. This is simply another way of saying that half the children born are male and half are female. (In actual fact, the proportion of males in single births is slightly more than one-half.)

(a) At Doctors' Hospital, eight single births occurred yesterday. What is the probability distribution of T, the number of males? Find $E(T)$ and $V(T)$.
(b) Refer to your own local newspaper and count the number of male babies among all single births—in one hospital or in all those reported. What is the probability distribution of the number of males for the n you observed? Does your observation appear to be consistent with the hypothesis that girls and boys are born in about equal numbers?

3.4 Refer to Example 1.5 (sex prediction).

(a) What is the probability of the event exactly 13 correct predictions and the probability of the event 13 or more correct predictions if the method is 80 percent accurate?
(b) What is the probability of the same two events if the method is equivalent to guessing?

3.5 (a) What is the probability that in families of six children, there is at least one girl? Is this the same as the probability of exactly one girl? (b) State the two assumptions that are made to calculate the probabilities in (a).

3.6 (a) What is the probability that in a taste test similar to that of Example 2.2 a person who is just guessing will get: (i) exactly five right in ten trials? (ii) five or more right? (b) If the taster has some ability so that his probability of a correct call on any trial is 0.8, what is the probability he will get: (i) exactly five right in ten trials? (ii) five or more right?

3.7 Do people usually begin walking on their right foot or their left foot? Sixteen people are observed and the number who start on their right foot is noted. Call this T.

(a) What is the sample space of T?
(b) Assuming that the choice of starting foot is equally likely to be left or right, find $E(T)$.
(c) What additional assumption do you need to calculate $V(T)$? With this additional assumption what is the distribution of T?
★(d) If $V(T) = 4$, could $P(T > 12) = 0.40$?

3.8 A professional baseball player has a batting average of 0.250 (i.e., his probability of getting a hit is $\frac{1}{4}$). Find the probability that he gets four hits in four times at bat. What assumptions are required? What is the expected number of hits in four times at bat? the variance?

3.9 It is claimed that the favorite horse (the one bet on most heavily) wins 30 percent of the time. On one race day with eight races, no favorite won. Comment on the event by calculating the probability of the event.

3.10 In a multiple choice test, there are five possible choices for each question. Let T denote the number of correct answers in a test of ten questions. What is the sample space of T? Is it possible to write down the probability distribution of T? Assume that a student just guesses each answer. What is the probability that he gets any single question correct? What is the probability distribution of T with this additional assumption? If five is a passing score, what is the probability that a person who just guesses on each question still passes?

3.11 (a) What is the probability that 18 or more seeds germinate out of 20 planted if the probability p of any single seed's germinating is 0.7? (b) Is this probability increased or decreased as p increases from 0.7 to 0.9? How much?

3.12 Refer to Example 1.4 (Who was Einstein?). If the proportion of the population knowing who Einstein was is 0.70, what is the probability distribution of students answering the *Daily* survey correctly (in a sample of 20)? (This is an example of sampling from a finite population, where we assume that the sample is small relative to the population, so that the binomial distribution is a satisfactory approximation.) How often would 14 or more answer correctly if in fact only 50 percent of the population know the answer?

*3.13 (a) A biologist is studying the sex ratio of a population at all stages of the season. Samples of size 10 are taken every day. Let T be the number of males in a sample. If the sex ratio is actually $\frac{1}{2}$, i.e., half are males, what is the probability distribution of T?

(b) Each day that T exceeds eight or falls below two, the biologist takes a second sample as a check. What is the probability of taking a second sample when the number of males has increased to $\frac{6}{10}$ of the population?

*3.14 A gillnet has a probability of $\frac{1}{3}$ of catching fish above 400 cm in length. What is the probability that two fish escape when six fish of this size pass through the gillnet area?

3.15 A drug laboratory puts out a smallpox vaccine. In one preparation, poor mixing results in 20 of the 100 doses being over-strength and 20 under-strength. The rest are satisfactory. If a sample of five is selected (with replacement), find the probability that: (a) all are satisfactory; (b) none are over-strength.

3.16 A standard insecticide kills 80 percent of houseflies exposed to it under laboratory conditions. A new insecticide is claimed to kill 90 percent under such conditions. Find the probability for each insecticide of killing: (a) 15, (b) 15 or more, (c) 20 out of 20.

3.17 Four students on a campus are sampled at random and asked if they have had Asian flu. Ten percent of all students on campus have (up to the present time) had Asian flu. Let $T =$ number of students who have had Asian flu among those interviewed.
(a) Work out the probability distribution of T.
(b) Calculate $E(T)$ and $V(T)$.
(c) What do you interpret "sampled at random" in the first sentence of this problem to mean?
(d) What would the probability distribution of T be if 20 students were so sampled?

3.18 A storage warehouse contains 100,000 boxes of apples, of which 10,000 are spoiled. A sample of ten boxes is taken from the warehouse. What is the probability distribution of T, the number of spoiled boxes in the sample? Find $E(T)$ and $V(T)$.

3.19 A parachute factory manufactures parachutes in lots of 1,000. Samples of five are tested: If all are satisfactory, the lot is passed. Let p be the proportion of defective parachutes in the lot.

(a) What assumptions must be made in order that T, the number of defective parachutes in the sample, has a binomial distribution?
(b) If T is binomial, write down $P(T = 0)$ as a function of p. Work this out for $p = 0.1, 0.2, 0.3, 0.4, 0.5$.
(c) If you were a parachute buyer, would you regard this as a satisfactory testing procedure?

3.20 Suppose 10 percent of the cars in Los Angeles are Cadillacs. If you stand on the corner of Wilshire Boulevard and Western Avenue and watch the north–south traffic, what is the probability that

(a) you will have to see three cars go by before the fourth, a Cadillac, passes?
(b) the fourth car that passes is a Cadillac?
(c) at least one of the first four cars is a Cadillac?

Assume that the corner in question is representative of the City of Los Angeles and that cars pass independently.

3.21 If 20 percent of male university students are married, how many married students would you expect in a random sample of ten? What is the probability that a sample of ten would have five or more married students? Would you regard as unusual such an event?

3.22 In a mail survey, questionnaires are sent out on blue forms and white ones; of the first 20 forms returned 16 are blue. If an equal number of blue and white forms were sent out, it seems reasonable to assume that in any batch of returns the probability of a returned form's being blue is $\frac{1}{2}$, and that different returns are independent events.

(a) Calculate the probability that of 20 returns, 16 are blue.
(b) Calculate the probability that of 20 returns, 16 or more are blue.
(c) Calculate the probability that of 20 returns, the difference in the numbers of blue and white returns is 12 exactly; 12 or more.

★(d) Denote by T the number of blue-form returns (out of 20). Define Z^*, the standardized random variable, and express the results of (c) in terms of probability statements about Z^*.

3.23 Consider an X-ray test for tuberculosis. Suppose that an individual's X-ray plate is read by five technicians, each of whom has a probability 0.90 of diagnosing correctly a positive case, i.e., one where the individual being tested has tuberculosis. Denote by T the number of positive diagnoses for a positive individual. Assume readings are independent and tabulate the probability distribution of T. In particular, determine the probability of no positive diagnosis by any technician. What is the increase in the probability of no positive diagnosis if each technicians' chance of error on a single reading increases from 0.10 to 0.20?

★3.24 The technique known as bioassay involves the use of biological responses to measure, i.e., "assay," the potency of drugs, viruses, etc. For example, dosages of a drug may be injected into mice or other experimental animals. Such experiments are made to compare two drugs or to establish the dosage level at which it is expected that 50 percent of the animals will respond, or to determine the dosage level at which 95 percent will respond, etc. To achieve such information usually requires use of several dosage levels and testing of several animals at each level. A full treatment of such problems is a specialized topic beyond the level of this course, but the problems below touch on some aspects of the area.

Consider a situation involving four dosage levels, which may conveniently be identified as 1, 2, 3, and 4. Suppose that at these dosage levels the probabilities of response are 0.10, 0.40, 0.75, and 0.95 respectively and that ten animals are tested at each level.

(a) What is the probability that none respond at Level 1?
(b) What is the probability that none respond at Level 2?
(c) What is the probability that all respond at Level 3?
(d) What is the probability that all respond at Level 4?
(e) What is the probability that more respond at Level 2 than at Level 1?
(f) Let $X_1 =$ the proportion of animals responding at Level 1, and $X_2 =$ the proportion of animals responding at Level 2. Find $E(X_2 - X_1)$ and $V(X_2 - X_1)$.
(g) Define X_3 and X_4 in the same way and calculate $E(X_4 - X_3)$ and $V(X_4 - X_3)$.

*3.25 Graph $P(T > 15|p)$ as a function of p when T is a binomial random variable, $n = 20$, and $p = 0, 0.1, 0.2, 0.3, 0.4, 0.5, 0.6, 0.7, 0.8, 0.9, 1$.

*3.26 If T is a binomial random variable with $n = 4$ and $p = \frac{1}{2}$, find and tabulate the distribution of

$$Z^* = \frac{T - E(T)}{\text{S.D.}(T)}.$$

Verify that $E(Z^*) = 0$ and $V(Z^*) = 1$.

*3.27 If T is a binomial random variable with $n = 16$ and $p = \frac{1}{2}$, define

$$Z^* = \frac{T - E(T)}{\text{S.D.}(T)};$$

compare the exact probability that Z^* is greater than or equal to 2 with the bound determined by Theorem 2.2.

*3.28 A quality-control laboratory tests ten items out of each large lot produced in a factory. If two or more are defective the whole lot is examined for defects. Let p be the proportion of defective items in the lot. Using the binomial approximation, and denoting the number of defectives in the sample by T, we see that

$$P(\text{whole lot is examined}) = P(T \geq 2) = 1 - P(T = 0) - P(T = 1)$$
$$= 1 - (1 - p)^{10} - 10p(1 - p)^9.$$

(a) Plot this probability as a function of p; that is, calculate, or find from tables, the required probability for $p = 0, 0.05, 0.1, 0.2, 0.3, 0.4, 0.5$, etc., and graph these probabilities.

(b) The company is considering changing its test procedure to the following procedure: sample five items and pass the lot only if all five are good. (In other words, the whole lot is examined if one or more defectives are found in the sample of five.) Write down the probability that the whole lot is examined and graph this as a function of p.

(c) Write down the probability that the lot is passed without examination and graph this as a function of p.

*3.29 In Problem 2.5 it was noted that the reliability of a complex device can be increased by providing spares that automatically take over when there is a failure. Consider a device with five essential components A, B, C, D, E, each with reliability 0.9. For each component three spares are provided in addition to the original element.

If the spares have the same reliability as the original and all failures are independent events, what is the probability that A or one of its spares operates satisfactorily? The whole device works only if each component operates, i.e., if A or one of its spares works, B or one of its spares works, etc. Find the probability that the device *fails*.

⋆3.30   In Problem 3.29, we assumed that the components were not interchangeable, so that the spares for A were useful only if A failed, B's spares would serve only the B component, etc. An alternative possibility in some devices is a situation similar to that which holds for automobile tires when one spare can be used to replace a failure of any one of the four operating tires. Of course, tires are subject to wear, so that the probability of failure changes with the usage of the tires. Consider, however, a situation where wear is disregarded; assume that there are n interchangeable components, of which k must function for the device to work. If failures of the components are independent events and the probability of failure is p, find the probability that the device works. Evaluate this probability for $n = 20$, $k = 15$, $p = 0.1$; $n = 20$, $k = 10$, $p = 0.2$; $n = 5$, $k = 4$, $p = 0.1$.

⋆3.31   In some blood tests for a pathological condition that occurs rarely, e.g., syphilis, it is cheaper to pool samples from many individuals and make a test on the combined sample. If all individuals are negative, the combined sample is negative and no further testing is necessary. If one or more individuals are positive, it is necessary to make a separate additional test for each individual. Suppose blood samples from ten individuals are combined; the individuals are sampled at random from a population with a proportion p of positives.

(a) Calculate the probability that no further testing is necessary if $p = 0.001, 0.01, 0.05, 0.10$.
(b) The number of tests made is a random variable that takes on two values—one when the combined sample is negative and eleven if retesting is necessary. Find its expected value and variance for each of the values of p listed in (a).

3.32   If T is a binomial random variable with $n = 10$ and $p = 0.4$, check that

$$P(T = 5) = \left(\frac{6}{5}\right)\left(\frac{0.4}{0.6}\right)P(T = 4)$$

and thus verify for this special case the binomial recursion formula given in the chapter.

*3.33 The recursion formula provides an easy way to find the value of t that maximizes $P(T = t)$ for fixed values of n and p. For as long as $(n - t)/(t + 1) \cdot p/(1 - p)$ is larger than one, $P(T = t + 1)$ is larger than $P(T = t)$; when $(n - t)/(t + 1) \cdot p/(1 - p)$ becomes less than one, $P(T = t + 1)$ is smaller than $P(T = t)$. Hence, the maximum probability for the binomial distribution occurs at the first integer t for which $(n - t)/(t + 1) \cdot p/(1 - p)$ is less than or equal to one.

(i) If $(n + 1)p$ is an integer,
$$P[T = (n + 1)p - 1] = P[T = (n + 1)p]$$
and these are the maximum probabilities.

(ii) If $(n + 1)p$ is not an integer, the maximum probability occurs when t is equal to the integer just below but closest to $(n + 1)p$.

(a) Verify that the statements made are correct for $n = 20$ and $p = 0.1, 0.2, 0.3, 0.4, 0.5, 0.6, 0.7, 0.8, 0.9$.

(b) If $(n + 1)p$ is less than one, the maximum occurs when $t = 0$; verify this for the distribution with $n = 10$ and $p = 0.05$.

(c) If $n(p + 1)$ is greater than n, the maximum occurs when $t = n$; verify this for the distribution with $n = 10$ and $p = 0.95$.

3.34 What two assumptions must be made about the various trials in each of the problems in this chapter so that the binomial probability formula is correct; i.e., the random variable in each problem is binomial? In some problems these assumptions are not justified. What fact enables us to use the binomial model as a satisfactory approximation?

3.35 (a) Using Table A2.1, verify that the exact probability of the event described in Problem 2.37 is 0.002. (b) Using Table A2.1, verify that the exact probability of the event described in Problem 2.38 is 0.931.

CHAPTER FOUR

Point Estimation and Hypothesis Testing for the Binomial Distribution

Introduction

In Chapter 3 we studied the theoretical probability distribution of the binomial random variable, i.e., the random variable recording the number of successes in n binomial trials. If the population parameters n and p are specified, the probability of 4 successes in 10 trials, 19 successes in 20 trials, etc., can be computed. In this chapter we study binomial trials from the opposite point of view. An experimenter performs n binomial trials, i.e., trials which are independent, each of which results in success or failure and for which the probability of success remains constant. He observes the number of successes T and knows n but does not know the other parameter p. He wishes to use the number of successes T to draw conclusions about p.

Example 4.1 Thumbtacks

A thumbtack is tossed 20 times, and 14 successes are observed, success being the result that the tack lands point up. We assume that the number of successes is a binomial random variable with $n = 20$, p unknown. What is the probability p of success on any one trial?

Example 4.2 Who was Einstein? (continued)

In Example 1.4, the campus survey to determine student knowledge of Einstein was discussed. If we assume that the students in the survey were chosen at random and that the total university population is sufficiently large so that sampling without replacement can be approximated by the sampling with replacement model, then the model for this experiment is the binomial probability distribution (with $n = 20$ in each of the two separate surveys and $n = 40$ in the combined survey). The proportion p of students who know who Einstein was is unknown and is the parameter of interest the surveyor wishes to determine.

Example 4.3 Evaluation of extrasensory perception

An experimenter selects a card from a standard deck and notes the color (red or black). A subject, who does not see the card, attempts to "read the experimenter's mind" and call the correct color. This experiment is repeated ten times, the deck being shuffled before each trial, and the subject makes seven correct identifications. Can we agree to the subject's claim that he has extrasensory perception (E.S.P.)?

Example 4.4 Evaluation of a long-range weather forecast

A meteorologist has a new long-range weather-forecast procedure, which he hopes will be useful in predicting seasonal rainfall for power and irrigation purposes. The forecasts are of five classes: much above normal, above normal, normal, below normal, much below normal. These five classes are defined so that they occur on the average with equal frequency. The meteorologist tests his procedure by making 20 independent forecasts from data taken over the past 20 years and finds that he predicts correctly in ten forecasts. Can we accept the meteorologist's claim that his procedure is of value?

Point Estimation

The answer to the problems posed in the first two examples is very simple. Although it is possible for any p between zero and one to give rise to 7 successes in 10 trials or 22 successes in 40 trials, most people would intuitively suggest that p be estimated by the proportion of successes, e.g., by 0.7 in Example 4.1 and by 0.55 from the combined samples of Example 1.4. These are sample proportions, but we are suggesting that they be used as values for the population parameters. Since samples are variable, these answers are most unlikely to be exactly right. Nevertheless most of us have the intuitive feeling that if the sample size is large enough, it gives reasonable information about the population. It is certainly true that if the sample is equal to the population then the sample proportion must equal the population proportion. On the other hand, the sample may be quite large and still not be very satisfactory if it is not properly chosen. For example, a university might have 13,000 male students and 5,000 females; a sample might consist of the 4,000 engineering students in the university. This is clearly a large sample and yet the sex ratio in the sample would almost certainly be quite different from that of the university as a whole.

Consequently, the intuitive acceptance of the fact that large samples give us useful information about populations is correct only if the samples are chosen in such a way that there is an appropriate correspondence between the real-life sampling and some probability model.

If the sampling is performed at random, and if the sample is sufficiently large, then the Law of Large Numbers (mentioned in Chapter 2 for general random variables), when applied to the binomial situation, implies that the sample proportion is arbitrarily close to the population proportion with an arbitrarily high probability.

This law does not tell us how large the sample size should be to achieve any prescribed degree of accuracy. Theorem 2.2 can be used to determine a conservative sample size that will certainly achieve any degree of accuracy (i.e., closeness of the sample proportion T/n to the population proportion p) with prescribed probability, though further results about the binomial probability model (to be given in Problem 6.43) will enable us to achieve the same accuracy with a much smaller sample size.

The Law of Large Numbers permits us to believe that large samples chosen at random will give useful information about populations. More generally, we must attempt to generalize from samples to populations, regardless of the sample size. This is a proper procedure provided we have reason to believe that the sampling corresponds to a probability model, as, for example, the binomial model, studied in the last chapter.

If T successes are observed in n binomial trials, we shall estimate p by $\hat{p} = T/n$ = sample proportion of successes. This random variable $\hat{p}$ is called a *point estimator* of p. Some properties of $\hat{p}$ are cited and proved in Chapter 6.

In Examples 4.1 through 4.4, we estimate p by 0.7, 0.55, 0.7, and 0.5, respectively. We do not expect these numbers to be exactly correct, but we have reason to believe that they will be close to the actual values of p. What can be said about the closeness of $\hat{p}$ to p will be discussed in Chapter 8.

Hypothesis Testing

In Examples 4.3 and 4.4, although point estimates of p can be obtained, an essentially different problem has been posed. Let us concentrate on Example 4.3. We begin with the assumption that the number of correct predictions is a binomial random variable with $n = 10$, p unknown. Since most people are skeptical about E.S.P., we have a prior belief in the value of p. If a subject has no E.S.P. and is merely guessing, then p should be $\frac{1}{2}$. A prior belief that specifies a value for a parameter associated with a random variable is called a *hypothesis*. A decision to accept or reject a hypothesis on the basis of experimental results is called a *test of the hypothesis*. The study of hypotheses and tests of hypotheses concerning unknown parameters p associated with binomial random variables T will concern us for the rest of this chapter.

We have hypothesized that p is $\frac{1}{2}$ in Example 4.3. We write this more compactly as

$$H : p = \tfrac{1}{2},$$

where p is the probability, on any trial, of choosing the right color.

We wish to find a "good" test of this hypothesis. It is clear, even after the experiment has been completed and the value of T obtained, that the hypothesis may be true or false, for values of p other than $\frac{1}{2}$ may have given rise to the value of T obtained. Thus, no matter whether we decide to accept or reject the hypothesis, we may be wrong. This uncertainty is inherent in every statistical problem and cannot be avoided. All we can try to do is to keep the chances of errors as small as possible. Again, intuition comes to our aid. Since T is usually near its expected value, if the subject has no E.S.P., T should be near 5; say, 4, 5, 6, or possibly 3 or 7. If the subject has E.S.P., T should be large, say, 8, 9, or 10. That is, it is intuitive that we should reject $H : p = \frac{1}{2}$ if T is large and accept it if T is small. Formally, we reject $H : p = \frac{1}{2}$ if $T \geq c$ and accept it if $T < c$, where c is an integer (close to 10). What remains is to choose c so as to minimize the chances of error. Presumably the scientific community would not wish, very often, to make the mistake of saying a person has

E.S.P. (rejecting H), when in fact he has none (H true).† Putting this formally, we want

$$P(\text{rejecting } H | H \text{ true}) = P(T \geq c | p = \tfrac{1}{2})$$

to be "small." What value should be attached to "small"? This is always a problem for beginners in statistics. The answer to this question cannot be given by the statistician, and moreover, it varies from problem to problem. For example, the hypothesis that $p = \tfrac{1}{2}$ in Example 4.1 can presumably be rejected when it is true without the error's being too serious. However, in Example 4.4, to reject the hypothesis and to claim the procedure has value when it really does not may have serious consequences. We would want "small" to be much smaller in the latter case than in the former. In each problem, the error involved in rejecting H when H is true must be investigated, and the allowable probability of making this error chosen accordingly. The maximum probability decided upon is called the error probability,‡ usually denoted by α. When expressed as a percentage, i.e., 100α percent, we use the alternative terms, *test level* or *significance level*. For example, if $\alpha = 0.05$, it is convenient to refer to a *test at the 5 percent level* or an observation that is *significant at the 5 percent level*. In practice, statisticians usually use percentage values of 10, 5, 2, 1, or 0.1 as the test levels, often picking one of them arbitrarily. Let us assume that we have chosen an error probability of 0.05 in Example 4.3. Putting the above discussion together, we see that we wish to choose c so that $P(T \geq c | p = \tfrac{1}{2}) \leq 0.05$. From Table A2.1 we have

$$P(T \geq 10 | p = \tfrac{1}{2}) = 0.001,$$
$$P(T \geq 9 | p = \tfrac{1}{2}) = 0.011,$$
$$P(T \geq 8 | p = \tfrac{1}{2}) = 0.055.$$

Since the last probability is greater than 0.05, we see that $c = 9$ is the smallest integer such that $P(T \geq c | p = \tfrac{1}{2}) \leq 0.05$. Thus, our test rule is: Reject H at the 5 percent level if $T = 9$ or 10. The smallest integer c (9 in this example) such that H is rejected if $T \geq c$ is known as the *critical level*.

Another interpretation of this rule is the following. If we observe $T = 9$ or 10, then either a rare event has occurred or H is false. We

---

† Ideally, one could wish never to make this mistake but this is impossible, as pointed out above, unless we use the following test rule: Always accept H regardless of the experimental results. This is clearly an impractical rule in real life. (Also read the discussion on Type I and Type II errors later in Chapter 4.)

‡ More precisely, the Type I error probability. This concept is elaborated later in Chapter 4.

choose to believe the latter, knowing that on the average, we will make the mistake of rejecting H when it is really true no more than 5 percent of the time over many experiments.

To summarize Example 4.3, we first choose an error probability, 0.05, that we feel we can risk. Assuming that T is a binomial random variable, we then obtain the test rule: Reject H at the 5 percent level if $T \geq 9$, i.e., accept the subject's claim that he has E.S.P. (with a 5 percent chance of error) if he makes nine or ten correct responses. In more advanced texts, it is shown that the test outlined is the "best" possible.

To answer the question posed in Example 4.3, we see that $T = 7$, so we cannot reject H at the 5 percent level; i.e., we cannot accept the subject's claim of having E.S.P. The result $T = 7$ is compatible with the hypothesis that $p = \frac{1}{2}$. Since the subject did do better than average we may not want to discard him immediately. The experimenter might wish to undertake a new experiment with this subject with a larger sample size.

[*Note:* The experimenter will be tempted to add the results from several such repetitions. An unsophisticated approach to this can be dangerous. A partial analysis of the problems involved is contained in Problem 7.44.]

Applying the same procedure to Example 4.4, we first assume that the number of correct forecasts is a binomial random variable T. Then we decide on a hypothesis for the p associated with this random variable. Using the standard argument that a procedure must prove itself before we believe in it, our hypothesis is that the procedure is of no value (one could predict as well by guessing). Putting this compactly and using Rule I yields

$$H : p = \tfrac{1}{5},$$

where p is the probability of a correct prediction on each trial. Next we choose an error probability we are willing to risk, say, 0.01. Intuitively, our test rule is: Reject H at the 1 percent level if $T \geq c$, where

$$P(T \geq c | p = \tfrac{1}{5}) \leq 0.01.$$

From Table A2.1, we have

$$P(T \geq 12 | p = \tfrac{1}{5}) = 0.000,$$
$$P(T \geq 11 | p = \tfrac{1}{5}) = 0.001,$$
$$P(T \geq 10 | p = \tfrac{1}{5}) = 0.003,$$
$$P(T \geq 9 | p = \tfrac{1}{5}) = 0.010,$$
$$P(T \geq 8 | p = \tfrac{1}{5}) = 0.032.$$

Hence, choosing the smallest c so that $P(T \geq c|p = \frac{1}{5}) \leq 0.01$, we see that the critical level is 9, and our test rule is: Reject H at the 1 percent level if $T \geq 9$; i.e., decide that the forecasting method has merit (with a 1 percent chance of error) if it predicts correctly nine or more times in the 20 trials.

Putting it differently, if we observe nine or more correct predictions, either a rare event has occurred or H is false. We choose to believe the latter, knowing that on the average we will make the error of rejecting H when it is true no more than 1 percent of the time over a large number of experiments. In any one experiment we do not know whether we have correctly rejected H (when we do reject) but we feel confident that we are correct in the sense described above.

To answer the question posed in Example 4.4, since $T = 10$, we reject H at the 1 percent level and accept the forecaster's claim that the procedure is of merit.

It should be emphasized that in Examples 4.3 and 4.4, we came to a decision. In each example the decision we made may have been right or wrong. It is only in the long run that we are confident that we have chosen the correct decision with some specified probability.

One-Sided Alternatives

In Examples 4.3 and 4.4., the hypothesis is that p is a special value ($\frac{1}{2}$ or $\frac{1}{5}$). If the hypothesis is rejected, the alternative accepted is *one-sided*, namely, that p is larger than the hypothesized value; i.e., the probability of a correct choice or correct prediction is greater than the probability due to chance. Later two-sided alternatives will be discussed. The alternative in Example 4.3 may be written compactly as

$$A : p > \tfrac{1}{2}.$$

In Example 4.4, it may be written as

$$A : p > \tfrac{1}{5}.$$

In other problems, the hypothesis might be $H : p = p_0$ and the alternative $A : p < p_0$ for some p_0 between 0 and 1. Then the "best" test rule is: Reject H if $T \leq c$, where c is the largest integer such that

$$P(T \leq c|p = p_0) \leq \alpha,$$

where α is the predetermined error probability.

Check, by referring to tables or working out some examples or by calculus if you can, that for $p_1 < p_0$,

$$P(T \geq c|p = p_0) \geq P(T \geq c|p = p_1).$$

This says that the probability of T's falling in the right tail of the distribution, i.e., that a large number of successes occurs, becomes greater as p increases (which is intuitively obvious). Therefore, the test rule that rejects H if $T \geq c$, where c is the smallest integer such that $P(T \geq c | p = p_0) \leq \alpha$, where α is the predetermined error probability, can be used for testing $H : p \leq p_0$ against $A : p > p_0$.

Similarly, if $p_1 > p_0$,

$$p(T \leq c | p = p_1) \leq P(T \leq c | p = p_0),$$

so the test rule that rejects H if $T \leq c$ can be used, at any level, to test $H : p \geq p_0$ against $A : p < p_0$. (It does not matter if the equality sign goes with the hypothesis or the alternative.)

Summary (One-Sided Alternatives)

1. To test

$$H : p = p_0 \text{ versus } A : p > p_0$$

or

$$H : p \leq p_0 \text{ versus } A : p > p_0$$

or

$$H : p < p_0 \text{ versus } A : p \geq p_0,$$

at the 100α percent level, i.e., error probability α, the test rule is: Reject H if T, the number of successes, is greater than or equal to c, the critical level, where c is chosen to be the smallest integer such that $P(T \geq c | p = p_0) \leq \alpha$.

2. To test

$$H : p = p_0 \text{ versus } A : p < p_0$$

or

$$H : p \geq p_0 \text{ versus } A : p < p_0$$

or

$$H : p > p_0 \text{ versus } A : p \leq p_0,$$

at the 100α percent level, the test rule is: Reject H if $T \leq c$, where c, the critical level, is chosen to be the largest integer such that $P(T \leq c | p = p_0) \leq \alpha$.

Each of the above tests, corresponding to a one-sided alternative, is called a *one-tailed test*. For each such problem, if a large (or small) value of T has been observed, then either a rare event has occurred or H is false. The rule says we should believe the latter knowing that we will make the serious error of rejecting H when H is true no more than 100α percent of the time, over many experiments.

Example 4.5 Evaluation of a sex-prediction method

Recall Example 1.5 and the doctor who claimed to have invented a method, correct more than 80 percent of the time, for predicting the sex of an unborn child. To test his claim, he was asked to predict the sex of 20 babies and had 13 correct predictions. Clearly we are unwilling to accept the doctor's claim. It is reasonable to ask what number of correct predictions (out of 20) would make us willing to accept the doctor's claim.

Solution: We first assume that the number of correct predictions T is a binomial random variable with parameter p. Proceeding again with the idea that a new claim should not be accepted until it has proved itself, we have the prior belief or hypothesis that the parameter is 0.8 or is less than or equal to 0.8 (indifferently); i.e.,

$$H : p \leq 0.8,$$

and the alternative is

$$A : p > 0.8.$$

Choosing (arbitrarily) $\alpha = 0.10$, we wish to find c in order that $P(T \geq c \,|\, p = 0.8) \leq 0.10$. From Table A2.1, it is seen that

$$P(T \geq 20 \,|\, p = 0.8) = 0.012,$$
$$P(T \geq 19 \,|\, p = 0.8) = 0.070,$$
$$P(T \geq 18 \,|\, p = 0.8) = 0.207,$$

so that the critical level is 19, and we reject H at the 10 percent level, i.e., accept the doctor's claim, if $T \geq 19$. The chances of our accepting his claim when it is false are no more than 10 percent, on the average.

Example 4.6 Evaluation of drug therapy

The mortality rate within one year for a given disease after diagnosis is 40 percent (according to long previous observation). That is, a person chosen at random from the population of all people diagnosed as having the given disease has probability $p = 0.4$ of dying within one year. A doctor claims to have a drug that lowers this death rate. To test his claim, 20 patients are given the drug and T, the number who die, is recorded. For what results can we accept the doctor's claim?

Solution: We assume that T is a binomial random variable with $n = 20$ and p unknown. Following the usual practice that a new drug must prove itself, our prior belief is that $p = 0.4$ (or $p \geq 0.4$, indifferently); i.e.,

$$H : p \geq 0.4,$$

and our alternative is

$$A : p < 0.4.$$

Choosing our test level as $\alpha = 0.05$, we wish to find the largest integer c, such that $P(T \leq c | p = 0.4) \leq 0.05$. From Table A2.1,

$$P(T \leq 4) = 0.050, \qquad P(T \leq 5) = 0.125.$$

Hence the critical level is 4 and we reject H at the 5 percent level, i.e., accept the doctor's claim, if there are at most four deaths among the 20 patients. The chances of accepting his claim when it is false are no more than 5 percent, on the average.

Significance Probabilities

In the procedure outlined for testing one-sided alternatives, the reader will have noticed that the test rule is constructed without reference to the observed result of the experiment. In some of the examples, the observed result was given; in others, it was not. Of course, the decision to accept or reject H depends on the observed result but this decision is automatic once the test rule has been constructed, the experiment performed, and the result recorded. We now wish to outline an alternative procedure for hypothesis testing with one-sided alternatives, which is equivalent to the above procedure but which does not require the choice of a test level, does not state the test rule explicitly, and relies entirely on the observed outcome of the experiment.

Let us start with Example 4.3 (evaluation of extrasensory perception) in which a binomial experiment yielded 7 successes in 10 trials. The hypothesis that the subject is just guessing ($p = 0.5$) implies that the expected number of successes should be five. The observation 7 is somewhat greater than this and suggests some evidence in favor of the subject's having a probability of a correct choice p greater than one-half. Whatever evidence 7 yields toward believing that p is greater than one-half, larger outcomes (8, 9, or 10) would provide stronger evidence. Hence we calculate

$$P(T = 7 | p = \tfrac{1}{2}) + P(T = 8 | p = \tfrac{1}{2}) + P(T = 9 | p = \tfrac{1}{2})$$
$$+ P(T = 10 | p = \tfrac{1}{2}) = P(T \geq 7 | p = \tfrac{1}{2}).$$

This probability is 0.172. We define 0.172 to be the *significance probability* of the observation 7. The meaning of the significance probability of 7 being 0.172 is as follows: Either an event, namely $T \geq 7$, has occurred whose probability is 0.172 if H is true, or H is false. Whether we decide to reject H or not depends on how rare an event we are willing to accept as having happened before we give up H.

In general, suppose the hypothesis is $H : p \leq p_0$, and the alternative is $A : p > p_0$ and suppose that T is observed and takes on the value t. If t is close to n, this is evidence against accepting H and in favor of the alternative A. How can we assess the evidence? If the observation t is evidence against H, then outcomes greater than t, that is, $t + 1$, $t + 2, \ldots, n$, contain more evidence against H. Thus it seems reasonable to compute the probability, under H, of all these outcomes; i.e.,

$$P(T = t | p = p_0) + P(T = t + 1 | p = p_0) + \cdots + P(T = n | p = p_0)$$
$$= P(T \geq t | p = p_0).$$

We call this the *significance probability* of the observation t.

If the hypothesis is $H : p \geq p_0$ and the alternative is $p < p_0$, then the significance probability of the observation $T = t$ is $P(T \leq t | p = p_0)$. The significance probability of an observation is also called its p value.

The advantage in giving the significance probability of the observation rather than constructing the test rule lies in the following. In many experiments, the choice of error probability will vary from one experimenter to another because different experimenters attach different degrees of importance to the error of rejecting H when it is true. By reporting the significance probability of each observation as part of the summary of the experiment, each reader of the report is allowed to draw his own conclusion as to whether he would or would not reject H. Additionally, a single experimental outcome may be only part of the evidence to affect the experimenter's decision; he may have additional qualitative information or other experimental outcomes bearing on the problem. Significance probabilities are useful in combining results of different experiments into a single answer. Thus, in Example 4.4, $P(T \geq 10 | p = \frac{1}{5}) = 0.003$, so that the significance level of 10 is 0.003. Anyone who allows an error probability as large or larger than 0.003, e.g., 0.01 or 0.05, will reject H, but anyone who requires an error probability less than 0.003, e.g., 0.001, will not reject H.

Similarly, in Example 4.5, if the doctor makes 17 correct predictions, the significance probability is 0.412. In Example 4.6, if two patients die, the significance probability is 0.003. In each example, anyone who can allow an error probability as large or larger than the significance probability reported will reject H. Those who require a lower error probability will not reject H.

Note: It should be firmly understood that one does not compute $P(T = t | p = p_0)$ to find the significance probability. This is because our test rules are of the form $T \geq c$ or $T \leq c$, and it is the probability of this kind of event that gives the significance probability.

Alternatively, suppose $T = t$ and the alternative is $A : p > p_0$. If H were rejected on the basis of the observation $T = t$, it would certainly be rejected on the basis of the outcomes $T = t + 1$, $T = t + 2, \ldots$, $T = n$. Thus, if one decides to reject H when $T = t$, the probability of making the error of rejecting H when H is true is at least

$$P(T = t | p = p_0) + P(T = t + 1 | p + p_0) + \cdots + P(T = n | p = p_0)$$
$$= P(T \geq t | p = p_0).$$

(It is at least this because H might also be rejected for values of T less than observed t.) Thus, $P(T \geq t | p = p_0)$ is the smallest probability of making the error of rejecting H when H is true if H is rejected when $T = t$. This is another interpretation of significance probabilities.

Either one can decide on an error probability and construct a test, or, if one does not wish to decide on an error probability, one can report the significance probability of the observed result.

Example 4.7   Evaluation of taste testing (continued)

To evaluate whether an individual has tasting ability, an experiment similar to the E.S.P. experiment can be performed. Suppose that the individual is given 20 taste tests and makes the correct choice in 12. Do we conclude that he has tasting ability?

Solution: Let T be the number of correct choices. We assume T is a binomial random variable with $n = 20$ and p, the probability of the taster making the correct choice at any trial, unknown. As above, we begin with the simplest or minimal assumption, which is that the individual has no tasting ability, or that $p = \frac{1}{3}$. This is the hypothesis —such a hypothesis is often referred to as the *null hypothesis* because it specifies *no* ability, etc. This can be written as

$$H : p = \tfrac{1}{3},$$

and the alternative is

$$A : p > \tfrac{1}{3}.$$

The significance probability of the observation 12, which is $P(T \geq 12 | p = \frac{1}{3})$ is found from Table A2.1 to be 0.013. The experimenter can now draw whatever conclusion he wishes depending on the error probability he can accept and possibly other factors.

Before continuing, let us stop and discuss the philosophy underlying the tests we have constructed. In most practical problems, a new product (procedure, method, etc.) is claimed to be better than an old product (procedure, method, etc.), or it is claimed to be better than chance. Following the argument that such claimants be required to furnish (statistical) proof before we believe them, we set up the null hypothesis that the claim is false. However, we may hope, and the claimant certainly does, that the evidence will be such as to allow us to reject this null hypothesis and accept the claim. Our emphasis is on rejecting H. We have chosen our tests so that we will not reject H (accept the claim) unless the evidence is very strong. Rejection of H, then, is a major decision and we can feel confident that we will not reject H very often when H is true. Suppose that the observation recorded is such that we cannot reject H. What should we do? Here the answer is less clear. In Example 4.3, we could not reject $H : p = \frac{1}{2}$ at the 5 percent level. Yet seven correct choices in ten trials lend some weight to the claim. Perhaps we should continue to experiment and hope for a more definitive result rather than stop and accept the hypothesis that the subject has no E.S.P. On the other hand, if the subject made only three correct choices, we might be willing to accept the hypothesis immediately. It seems that in the situation where we cannot reject H, the best answer is not to accept H uncritically, but rather to phrase the answer in the statistical report as follows: On the basis of the evidence, one cannot reject H at the 100α percent level. In other words, because rejection of H requires strong evidence, non-rejection of H does not lead immediately to acceptance of H. The evidence should be examined carefully to see whether more experimentation might not lead to a more definitive result, or whether the hypothesis should be accepted. The experimenter who reports the significance probability associated with the outcome of the experiment thus provides useful information to guide the user faced with deciding on the action to take when the null hypothesis is not rejected. Such action may be to perform further experiments, to act as if H were true, to combine the evidence from this experiment with that of other related experiments, or possibly to take other actions which may be available.

Summary on Significance
Probabilities (One-Sided Alternatives)

1. When testing $H : p \leq p_0$ versus $A : p > p_0$, the significance probability of the observation $T = t$ is $P(T \geq t | p = p_0)$.
2. When testing $H : p \geq p_0$ versus $A : p < p_0$, the significance probability of the observation $T = t$ is $P(T \leq t | p = p_0)$.

Two-Sided Alternatives

Until now, our alternatives have been one-sided. We now turn to the problem of two-sided alternatives. For this chapter only, we will restrict the hypothesis to $H : p = \frac{1}{2}$. When $p = \frac{1}{2}$, the binomial distribution is symmetric, e.g., $P(T = 0) = P(T = n)$, $P(T = 1) = P(T = n - 1)$, etc.

Example 4.8 Evaluation of color preference in babies

A psychologist wishes to test for color preference in babies. To each baby to be tested he offers two balls, one red and one green but otherwise indistinguishable, on each of 20 separate occasions. Let $T =$ number of occasions that a particular baby chooses the red ball. What conclusion can be drawn from this experiment with respect to this baby?

Solution 1: We assume that T is a binomial random variable with $n = 20$ and with a constant probability on each occasion that the baby will choose the red ball; denote this probability by p. If we have no previous knowledge concerning color preference, there is no reason to believe either will be preferred. Then our hypothesis is

$$H : p = \tfrac{1}{2}.$$

On the other hand, if there is a color preference we do not know if the preference will be for red or green, so p may be greater than $\frac{1}{2}$ or less than $\frac{1}{2}$; i.e., as an alternative to H we write

$$A : p \neq \tfrac{1}{2}.$$

By use of our intuition again, it is clear that values of T near 10 lend weight to the hypothesis, whereas values near 0 or 20 suggest the truth of the alternative. Our test rule is: Reject H if $T \geq c_1$ or $T \leq c_2$ (where c_1 is an integer near 20 and c_2 is an integer near 0). This is a *two-tailed test.* To find c_1 and c_2, we choose an error probability, say 0.05, and require

$$P(T \le c_1 \text{ or } T \ge c_2 | p = \tfrac{1}{2}) \le 0.05.$$

In general, one can choose c_1 and c_2 in more than one way to satisfy this equation. But, when $p = \tfrac{1}{2}$, the binomial distribution is symmetric. In the case under consideration here, where $n = 20$, this means that $P(T = 0) = P(T = 20)$, $P(T = 1) = P(T = 19)$, and in general $P(T = t) = P(T = 20 - t)$. Thus, if one rejects when $T = 20$, one should also reject when $T = 0$. If one does not reject H when $T = 14$, it is reasonable not to reject H when $T = 6$. Thus, it is reasonable to require $P(T \le c_1 | p = \tfrac{1}{2}) = P(T \ge c_2 | p = \tfrac{1}{2})$, and the problem of finding c_1, c_2 such that $P(T \le c_1 \text{ or } T \ge c_2 | p > \tfrac{1}{2}) \le 0.05$ is reduced to finding c_1 such that

$$P\left(T \le c_1 | p = \frac{1}{2}\right) \le \frac{0.05}{2} = 0.025.$$

The integer c_2 is determined from the symmetry property; that is, $c_2 = n - c_1$. From Table A2.1, $c_1 = 5$. By symmetry $c_2 = 20 - 5 = 15$. The test rule is: Reject H at the 5 percent level if $T \le 5$ or $T \ge 15$. The integers c_1 and c_2 are called the *lower and upper critical levels*.

The conclusions to be drawn from the experiment are as follows: If $T \ge 15$ or $T \le 5$, we assert that there is a color preference. We understand that we may have made a mistake in doing so but we are. confident in the sense that we will make this error no more than 5 percent of the time over many experiments. If $6 \le T \le 14$, we assert that the evidence is not sufficient (at the 5 percent level) to reject $H : p = \tfrac{1}{2}$; i.e., we do not have sufficient evidence to claim that there is a color preference.

Solution 2: Alternatively, one can use the significance-probability approach. If $T = 6$, the significance probability of the observation 6 is $2P(T \le 6 | p = \tfrac{1}{2}) = 0.116$. The reason for doubling the probability is based on an argument similar to the one that suggests (in the one-sided case) calculating the probability of all outcomes as likely or less likely under the hypothesis and more likely under the alternative. When the alternative is two-sided, this includes the outcomes in both tails that are farther or as far from the expected value as the observed outcome.

Alternatively, this can be explained in terms of rejecting the hypothesis. If H is rejected when $T = 6$, it will certainly be rejected if $T = 5, 4, 3, 2, 1, 0$. H will also be rejected, on the basis of symmetry, when

$T = 14, 15, 16, 17, 18, 19, 20$. Therefore the significance probability is $P(T \le 6 | p = \frac{1}{2}) + P(T \ge 14 | p = \frac{1}{2})$ or $2P(T \le 6 | p = \frac{1}{2})$. Anyone who can tolerate an error probability as large or larger than 0.116 will reject H, when $T = 6$ is observed. Others who prefer an error probability smaller than 0.116 would assert that H is not rejected when $T = 6$. In Solution 2, the experimenter gives the significance probability of the observation recorded.

In Example 4.8, we have studied a procedure to decide on one aspect of color preference of one baby who is tested on 20 occasions, and have suggested that the psychologist might wish to test this for a number of babies. Obviously he might perform the experiment of presenting a choice of a green or red ball to many babies and count the total number of red choices. This would be exactly the same problem as Example 4.8, provided it is appropriate to assume that the *probability of a baby's choosing the red ball is constant for all babies over all occasions of the testing.* It is possible to test separately whether this is so; this test will be studied in Chapter 11. (In particular, see Problem 11.29.)

Example 4.9 Sex ratios of young salmon

A biologist samples a population of young salmon throughout the season to determine whether the sex ratio is constantly 1:1. The procedure he adopts is to examine 20 salmon each day. He does not wish to assert that the sex ratio has changed unless he has strong evidence that this is so. What test rule should he use if he is prepared to tolerate an error probability of 0.01?

Solution: Let T = number of males on any one day. Assume that T is a binomial random variable with $n = 20$ and p unknown, where p is the probability of sampling a male. Here $H : p = \frac{1}{2}$ and $A : p \ne \frac{1}{2}$. $\alpha = 0.01$ so that $\alpha/2 = 0.005$, and c_1 is such that $P(T \le c_1 | p = \frac{1}{2}) \le 0.005$. The lower and upper critical levels are $c_1 = 3$ and $c_2 = 20 - 3 = 17$, and the test rule is: Reject H at the 1 percent level if $T \ge 17$ or $T \le 3$.

If the biologist observes 15 males in one day's sampling what is the significance probability of this observation?

Solution: The significance probability of 15 is $2[P(T \ge 15 | p = \frac{1}{2})] = 0.042$. Hence, H is rejected for any $\alpha \ge 0.042$. Otherwise, H cannot be rejected.

Note: Most beginning students in statistics have trouble in deciding whether the alternative in a given problem should be one-sided or two-sided. There are no rules that can be given. But one warning is in order. The alternative should be chosen before the experiment is performed (or at least before the results are studied). In Example 4.9, if one finds 15 male salmon in the sample of size 20, one may jump to the conclusion that the alternative should be one-sided, namely, $A : p > \frac{1}{2}$. This is incorrect, for if we study the original problem we see that our prior knowledge is that the sex ratio is $1:1$. If it has changed, we have no reason for believing the change will favor males or females. Hence, the correct alternative here is $A : p \neq \frac{1}{2}$. Perhaps the closest that one can come to a rule is the following: Unless the acceptance of a particular one-sided alternative is desired (before the data are studied), one should generally use a two-sided alternative.

Summary (Two-Sided Alternatives)

1. To test $H : p = \frac{1}{2}$ versus $A : p \neq \frac{1}{2}$ at the 100α percent significance level, i.e., error probability α, the test rule is: Reject H if T is less than or equal to c_1, or greater than or equal to c_2, the *lower and upper critical levels*, where c_1 is chosen to be the largest integer such that $P(T \leq c_1 | p = \frac{1}{2}) \leq \alpha/2$ and $c_2 = n - c_1$.

2. For testing $H : p = \frac{1}{2}$ versus $A : p \neq \frac{1}{2}$, the significance probability of the observation $T = t$ is

$$
\begin{array}{ll}
2P(T \leq t | p = \frac{1}{2}) & \text{if } t < np, \\
2P(T \geq t | p = \frac{1}{2}) & \text{if } t > np, \\
1 & \text{if } t = np.
\end{array}
$$

*Type I and Type II Errors; O.C. Curves

In the preceding discussion, all of the decision rules were chosen so as to keep small the probability of making the error of rejecting H when H is true. For example, over many trials we would very seldom say a subject has E.S.P. when he did not; or claim that a forecasting procedure had merit when it did not. It is clearly possible to reduce this chance of error to zero, if the null hypothesis is always accepted, i.e., if we deny the existence of E.S.P. no matter what experimental evidence is brought forth, or if we assert that the forecasting procedure always is no better than chance. The latter example points out the fallacy of this extreme attitude; obviously we want to have a reasonable expectation of detecting a forecasting method that is even partially successful. Similarly the psychologist wishes to learn something about babies' color preference; he does not want to hold stubbornly to the view that no color preference exists, whatever the experimental outcome.

Hence, as the perceptive reader has been aware, an experiment is usually designed, not to confirm what is now believed to be true, but to find out something new. Thus, the experiment and the decision procedure should have some chance of detecting this something new. If a subject has E.S.P. even in some limited degree or if a forecasting method is better than chance, the experimenter wants to be made aware of this. Failure to detect such phenomena is a second type of error, one that has been so far neglected. In Example 4.3, this error consists in saying a subject has no E.S.P. when, in fact, he has E.S.P.; in Example 4.4, it consists in saying a forecasting procedure has no value when, in fact, the procedure has value. Although these errors may not be as serious as the ones whose probability we have controlled, they are errors, and we would like our tests to keep the probability of these errors small. Even though a subject agrees that he does not wish to claim extrasensory perception when, in fact, he does not have such perception, still he would also like the chances to be small of the test's saying he has no E.S.P. when he does have E.S.P. Similarly, the meteorologist, while agreeing that the more serious error consists of saying the procedure is of value when it is not, would like the chances to be small that the test says his procedure is of no value when, in fact, it is of value. The object of this section is to investigate the size of these secondary errors.

In general, once the hypothesis has been chosen, there are two possibilities. The hypothesis is either true or false. After the experiment has been performed, there are two possibilities. The test rule may reject H or not reject H. These possibilities give rise to four possible situations:

1. H is true and, on the basis of our observations, we do not reject H.
2. H is false and, on the basis of our observations, we reject H.
3. H is true and, on the basis of our observations, we reject H.
4. H is false and, on the basis of our observations, we do not reject H.

In situations 1 and 2, we have made the right decision. In situations 3 and 4, we have made an error. Since the truth or falsity of H is not known to us, in any individual experiment we may make the right decision or the wrong decision. It is customary to call the error in 3 the *Type I error* and the error in 4 the *Type II error*. The above discussion can be summarized neatly in a two-by-two table as follows:

HYPOTHESIS

DECISION		True	False
	Reject *H*	Type I error	✓
	Do not Reject *H*	✓	Type II error

While it is true that in any single experiment we cannot know whether the decision we reach is right or wrong, we can calculate the probabilities of reaching a right decision or, looked at from the opposite direction, the probabilities of making a Type I or Type II error. This is exactly the same as in a trivial coin-tossing problem. Before a toss of a fair coin, a statistician has no way of knowing if it will land heads. Yet he is perfectly willing to assert that in a large number of repeated tosses, the coin will land heads approximately half the time.

We have chosen our tests so that the probability of a Type I error is kept below some preassigned level, the *significance level*. What can be said about the probability of a Type II error? We will see in individual examples that this probability may be high.

If the experimenter wishes to reduce the Type II error probability he has two choices—he can increase either the significance level or the sample size. It is generally true that for a fixed sample size, the Type II error probability decreases as the significance level is increased. The Type I and Type II errors might be thought of as two players on a seesaw: As one goes up the other goes down.

Note: The beginner should be cautioned that the relationship is not linear. For example, the sum of the two error probabilities is seldom one. See the examples following to confirm this. On the other hand if the experimenter increases the number of observations, i.e., the sample size, he reduces the Type II error probability while keeping the Type I error level fixed.

Before a discussion of the Type II error probability in detail and a demonstration of how it can be calculated, it is important to emphasize that the test rule depends only on the significance level and on the general class of alternatives, i.e., one-sided or two-sided. Hence, our earlier discussion did not need to introduce the Type II error.

Example 4.10   Evaluation of extrasensory perception (continued)

We start our discussion of the Type II error probability by referring to the E.S.P. problem. Here, the Type II error consists in accepting the hypothesis of no E.S.P. when the subject has E.S.P. What does it mean to say a subject has E.S.P.? It might mean that the subject could call each card's color correctly. This would mean that p, the probability of a correct call, is one. In such a situation every trial would result in a success and the statistician would have only a trivial problem. But the real world is not so simple as this. Few would make the claim that those with E.S.P. can achieve perfect scores in such a test; rather the claim is made that those with E.S.P. will have some ability and will discern the right color perhaps 60 percent of the time or 70 percent or even 90 percent. In other words, there is a whole family of possible alternatives. In terms of our binomial model, these are possible values of p, the probability of success, and they represent possible alternatives to the hypothesis, $p = 0.5$.

Recall that the decision rule of Example 4.3 was: Whenever T is less than or equal to eight, H is not rejected; i.e., the experimenter will remain skeptical about the claimed E.S.P. But if p is *greater* than 0.5 and eight or fewer successes are achieved, so that H is not rejected, this is an error, a Type II error. Thus, to calculate the Type II error probability in this example, it is necessary to calculate $P(T \leq 8|p)$ for each p greater than one-half. It is impossible to compute this for every p. Generally, the probability is computed for a few selected values in the family of alternatives. Also available from the steps of setting up the test decision rule is the probability of not rejecting H for the value of p specified by the hypothesis. These values are plotted on a graph and the other values are found by joining the plotted points in a smooth curve. This curve is called the *operating characteristic curve of the test (O.C. curve)*.

In the present example, from Table A2.1,

$$P(T \leq 8|p = 0.5) = 0.989,$$
$$P(T \leq 8|p = 0.6) = 0.954,$$
$$P(T \leq 8|p = 0.7) = 0.851,$$
$$P(T \leq 8|p = 0.8) = 0.625,$$
$$P(T \leq 8|p = 0.9) = 0.264,$$
$$P(T \leq 8|p = 1.0) = 0.000.$$

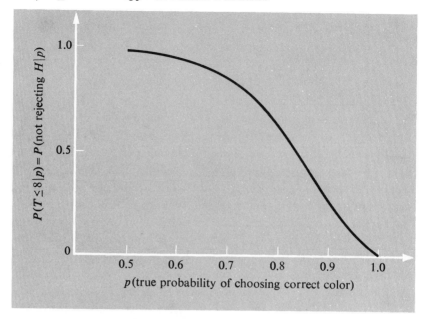

FIGURE 4.1   *The O.C. curve for Example 4.10.*

Plotting these probabilities and drawing a smooth curve, one gets the O.C. curve shown in Figure 4.1.

The complete answer to Examples 4.3 and 4.10 may now be given as follows:

Assumption: T = number of correct choices is a binomial random variable with $n = 10$, p unknown.

$$H : p = 0.5 \text{ versus } A : p > \tfrac{1}{2}.$$

Test rule (at 5 percent significance level): Reject H if $T \geq 9$. The O.C. curve is as given in Figure 4.1.

What the O.C. curve tells the investigator is that if he is sampling a population that has a high degree of E.S.P. as measured by p (say $p = 0.9$), then a screening test based on only ten trials would fail to detect 26.4 percent of this population. On the other hand, if the sample is drawn from a population that has a low degree of E.S.P. (but some ability, say $p = 0.6$), the ten trials' test procedure would be wrong 95.4 percent of the time. As pointed out earlier, the Type II error probability may be rather high, though the investigator might assert that he has no interest in an individual whose E.S.P. ability is such that he can only call the correct color 60 percent of the time.

However, if the sample is drawn from a population with moderate E.S.P. ability ($p = 0.8$) the test would still err 62.5 percent of the time. To make these error probabilities smaller, one could raise the significance level, or, better still, increase the sample size.

The Type II error probability can also be read from the graph for other values of p in the family or set of alternatives.

Example 4.11 Evaluation of a long-range weather forecast (continued)

In Example 4.4, the Type II error consists in accepting the hypothesis that the forecast procedure has no value when, in fact, it has value. As in Example 4.3, to say the procedure has value does not mean it will predict correctly all the time, i.e., $p = 1$. Rather it means that the procedure will have some predictive value and will choose the correct forecast perhaps 40, 60, or even 80 percent of the time. Thus, the family of alternatives consists of all possible values of p greater than $p = 0.2$.

Whenever T, the number of correct predictions in 20 trials, is less than or equal to eight, the experimenter does not reject the hypothesis; that is, the method is regarded as no better than chance. But, if p, the probability of a correct prediction, is greater than 0.2, this is a Type II error. Thus, there is a Type II error probability given by $P(T \leq 8|p)$ for every p greater than 0.2. As in Example 4.10, we construct the *operating characteristic curve* (O.C. curve) by plotting a few values of the Type II error probability and joining these by a smooth curve.

From Table A2.1,

$$P(T \leq 8|p = 0.2) = 0.990,$$
$$P(T \leq 8|p = 0.3) = 0.887,$$
$$P(T \leq 8|p = 0.4) = 0.595,$$
$$P(T \leq 8|p = 0.5) = 0.252,$$
$$P(T \leq 8|p = 0.6) = 0.057,$$
$$P(T \leq 8|p = 0.7) = 0.005,$$
$$P(T \leq 8|p = 0.8) = 0.000.$$

Thus, one obtains the O.C. curve as in Figure 4.2.

This graph gives the values of the Type II error probabilities for all values of p greater than 0.2. If $p = 0.2$, H is true and there is no possibility of Type II error, though a Type I error may occur. This

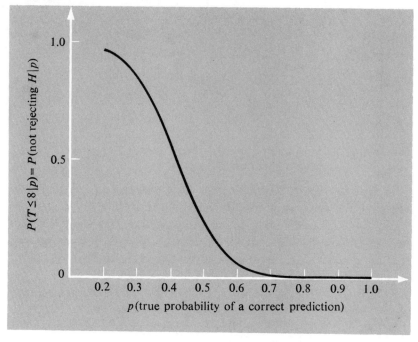

FIGURE 4.2   *The O.C. curve for Example* 4.11.

may also be read from the graph: Since the ordinate corresponding to $p = 0.2$ gives the probability of accepting H when true, the Type I error is found by subtracting the value of this ordinate from one. The complete solution to Examples 4.4 and 4.11 may now be given as follows:

Assumption: $T =$ number of correct predictions in 20 trials is a binomial random variable with $n = 20$ and p unknown.

$$H : p = 0.2 \text{ versus } A : p > 0.2.$$

Test rule (at the 1 percent significance level): Reject *H* if $T \geq 9$. The O.C. curve is constructed as in Figure 4.2 and this shows how well the test does when one of the family of alternatives is true. Observe that the O.C. curve descends more quickly to zero in Example 4.11 than in Example 4.10. This can be attributed to the larger sample size; here $n = 20$ rather than $n = 10$, as in Example 4.10.

   In summary then, the procedure for determination and evaluation of a test is as follows:

1. Set up the probability model and the hypothesis to be tested.
2. Prescribe the significance level (Type I error probability) and the general class of alternatives.

3. Determine the test rule, assuming that the hypothesis is true.
4. Consider the family of alternatives and for this family (or suitable members of the family) calculate the probability of Type II error.

Note that at step 3 the statistician is asking himself what will happen if H is true. On this basis, a test rule is determined. At step 4 he turns around and asks what will happen if he uses this rule when, in fact, H is not true but some alternative hypothesis is.

Schematically, the steps are as follows:

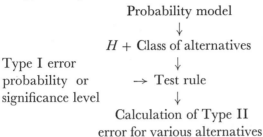

Note that the Type I error probability comes in as outside information or through an arbitrary choice by the experimenter or the statistician.

The hypothesis H usually falls out of the model automatically as the null hypothesis, though in a few situations this may not be the case. In such rare cases the experimenter decides which type of error is more serious and chooses H, so that this error becomes the Type I error (*which he is able to control*).

EXERCISES

1. For Example 4.4, find and evaluate a decision rule that keeps the probability of the Type I error below 0.05.
2. Set up 2 × 2 tables for the specific situations in Examples 4.10 and 4.11.

These examples, as stated before, have one-sided alternatives to which one-tailed tests correspond. Similarly, we constructed two-tailed tests for two-sided alternatives. These tests again kept the Type I error below some preassigned level. We can use the O.C. curve to evaluate how well these tests do in keeping the Type II error probability low.

Example 4.12 Evaluation of color preference in babies (continued)

Recall that in this example the probability model assumed that T, the number of choices of the red ball, is a binomial random variable with $n = 20$, p unknown. The hypothesis specified $p = \frac{1}{2}$ against the unrestricted alternative $p \neq \frac{1}{2}$, where p denotes the probability of choosing a red ball.

The test rule (with significance level 5 percent) was: Reject H if $T \leq 5$ or $T \geq 15$. In other words, do not reject H if $6 \leq T \leq 14$; i.e., T lies between 6 and 14 inclusive.

Now we turn around and proceed to calculate what will happen if $p \neq \frac{1}{2}$ and this test rule is used. We have to calculate $P(6 \leq T \leq 14|p)$ for various values of p. Using Table A2.1, we find

$$P(6 \leq T \leq 14|p = 0.0) = 0.000,$$
$$P(6 \leq T \leq 14|p = 0.1) = 0.011,$$
$$P(6 \leq T \leq 14|p = 0.2) = 0.195,$$
$$P(6 \leq T \leq 14|p = 0.3) = 0.583,$$
$$P(6 \leq T \leq 14|p = 0.4) = 0.874,$$
$$P(6 \leq T \leq 14|p = 0.5) = 0.958,$$
$$P(6 \leq T \leq 14|p = 0.6) = 0.874,$$
$$P(6 \leq T \leq 14|p = 0.7) = 0.583,$$
$$P(6 \leq T \leq 14|p = 0.8) = 0.195,$$
$$P(6 \leq T \leq 14|p = 0.9) = 0.011,$$
$$P(6 \leq T \leq 14|p = 1.0) = 0.000,$$

so that the O.C. curve is as in Figure 4.3.

What Figure 4.3 tells us is as follows: Suppose there are various subpopulations of babies, each subpopulation being identified by a color preference probability. For example, one group of babies may prefer the red ball and choose it 80 percent of the time. For babies drawn from this group and tested, the experimenter would correctly reject H (no color preference) 80.5 percent of the time, but he would not reject H 19.5 percent of the time; i.e., he would make a Type II error 19.5 percent of the time. Other values of the O.C. curve can be interpreted similarly. The complete solution to Examples 4.8 and 4.12 is as follows:

Assumption: $T = $ number of red balls chosen is a binomial random variable with $n = 20$ and p unknown.

$$H : p = 0.5 \text{ versus } A : p \neq 0.5.$$

Test rule (at the 5 percent significance level): Reject H if $T \geq 15$ or $T \leq 5$. The O.C. curve is constructed as in Figure 4.3 and it shows how well the test does when the alternative is true.

Note: At this stage, a student may be concerned over two problems: whether it is permitted to exceed the significance level slightly, e.g., to accept 0.051 or 0.053 for 0.05, and how to juggle the total Type I error

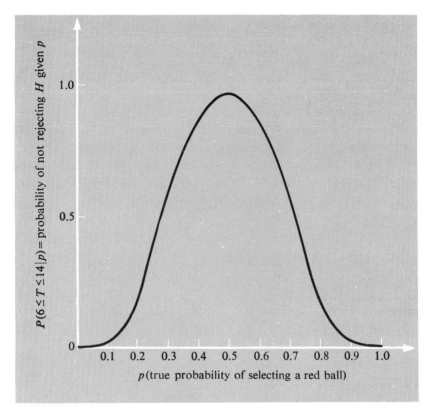

FIGURE 4.3   *The O.C. curve for Example* 4.12.

probability between the two tails of a two-sided test if the hypothesis is other than $p = \frac{1}{2}$. These problems arise in part because of the discrete nature of the binomial distribution. For larger values of n, they diminish because the steps between successive probabilities are smaller. In later chapters these problems will vanish. For the moment, in setting up test rules the upper bound imposed by the significance level should be strictly observed. And all two-tailed tests should be made symmetrical with respect to the expected value.

Summary on Hypothesis Testing

1. Each problem is translated into a mathematical model involving a random variable, in this chapter the binomial model.
2. A hypothesis is a prior belief in the value of a parameter of this model, in this chapter specifically a prior belief concerning the parameter p of a binomial probability distribution.

3. A test of a hypothesis is a decision rule to accept or reject the hypothesis based on experimental observations of the random variable; alternatively, a test is the calculation of the significance probability of the observed value under the assumption that the hypothesis is true.
4. Rejecting the hypothesis when it is true is a Type I error.
5. A test rule is chosen so that this Type I error probability is held below a preassigned level, called the significance level.
6. The test rule is evaluated by the O.C. curve which tells how well the test does in rejecting the hypothesis when the hypothesis is false, i.e., in keeping the Type II error probability low.

■ Experiments

4.1   Binomial experiments are easy to perform with coins, dice, cards, or *tables of random numbers.* The latter are essentially what the name implies. A table of random numbers could be constructed by throwing a die with ten faces and writing down the results. At present they are usually constructed by machine, which may fail to produce "ideal" random numbers. For this reason an alternative designation is "pseudo-random numbers." For our purposes such deviations from ideal randomness may be disregarded. A small table of random numbers is given in Table A2.2.† To obtain a binomial observation with, say, $n = 20$, $p = 0.13$, enter the table at any arbitrary starting point selecting 20 pairs of numbers in a horizontal or vertical direction as desired. Numbers from 00 to 12 are called "success" and numbers from 13 to 99 "failure." The number of successes is the observation of the binomial random variable. The following experiments are a simulation of the E.S.P. example by Monte Carlo methods, i.e., using random number tables.

(a) Make 25 observations of a binomial random variable with $n = 10$, $p = 0.5$. This is the random variable of the extrasensory perception experiment when the subject has no ability or is just guessing. Note particularly the number of times that $T = 9$ or $T = 10$. In these cases the hypothesis $p = 0.5$ would be rejected incorrectly. A Type I error would be committed.

★(b) Make 25 observations each of a binomial random variable with $n = 10$, $p = 0.6$, $p = 0.8$, $p = 0.9$. Record the number of times

---

† One of the largest tables is *A Million Random Digits,* published by the Free Press for the Rand Corporation.

that $T = 9$ or $T = 10$ for each of these. Plot on a graph against p the observed relative frequency with which $H : p = \frac{1}{2}$ is accepted. Compare this graph with the O.C. curve of Figure 4.1. Your graph is based on 25 observations. How well does it compare with the theoretical relative frequencies that would result from a very large number of trials, i.e., the O.C. curve for Figure 4.1?

4.2 Much of the data collected in earlier experiments may be made the basis of tests of hypotheses. For example, use the data you obtained for Problem 3.2 on the number of males out of all single births reported in a local newspaper to test the hypothesis that p, the probability of a single birth's being male, is 0.5.

4.3 Another experiment that is easy to conduct is to count the number of cars that approach an intersection from the east–west direction and the number that approach from the north–south during a given time period. Test the hypothesis that traffic is equally heavy in the two directions. Both of these experiments may give rise to a total number of trials n, for which binomial probabilities are not available in Table A2.1. In this case, you may wish to refer to more complete tables of binomial probabilities, cited on page 51.

You might also try to count the number of cars that reach an intersection "on the green" (from one direction). It is also easy to determine the proportion of the light cycle that the light is green for this direction and test a hypothesis similar to that of Example 3.3. However, the number of cars counted successively reaching the intersection on the green is not likely to be a binomial random variable. Why not?

4.4 The probability p of getting one pair (exactly) in five cards is 0.423. Deal out 20 hands of five cards (replacing the cards and shuffling the deck between each deal). Count the number of hands with exactly one pair and test the hypothesis that p is in fact 0.5.

4.5 Record the number of males among siblings of all class members. Test the hypothesis that p, the proportion of males, is one-half.

4.6 Find the proportion of male students on campus. Test the hypothesis that the members of the class are a random sample from the student body in respect to sex distribution. (Note that this is sampling from a finite population and hence involves the same approximation discussed in Chapter 3 under Sampling at Random.)

■ Problems

4.1   In the E.S.P. experiment considered in Example 4.3, a subject guesses the correct color 13 times in 20 trials. Find the significance probability of this observation. Do you conclude that the subject has E.S.P.? Take the error probability to be 0.05.

4.2   For the E.S.P. experiment, construct the decision rule for $n = 20$ and significance level 10 percent.

4.3   In the *Times* football prediction contest (see Problem 3.1) a contestant selects 14 winners in 20 games (disregarding ties). Write out, in mathematical terms, the hypothesis that the contestant is only guessing. What is the proper family of alternatives? Find the significance probability of the observation. Is the observation consistent with the hypothesis? Test at the 5 percent significance level.

4.4   What would be the test rule in Example 4.8 if n were 16 rather than 20?

4.5   Refer to Example 1.4 (Who was Einstein?). On the basis of the first sample, test the hypothesis that half or less of the students on campus know who Einstein was by finding the significance probability of the observation. Use a 5 percent significance level.

4.6   Twenty births were recorded at a local hospital, among which 14 were boys. What is the proper family of alternatives to the hypothesis that boys and girls are equally likely? Find the significance probability of the observation. Is the observation consistent with the hypothesis? Test at the 5 percent significance level.

4.7   A wheat-grower conducts an experiment to determine the percentage of wheat seeds that will germinate. The experiment consists of planting 20 seeds and counting the number that germinate. Set up a decision rule for $H : p = 0.7$ versus $A : p > 0.7$, where p is the probability that any given seed germinates. Use a 5 percent significance level.

4.8   Thirty meteorological observations are classified according to whether the last digit is or is not 0 or 5. If each digit is "equally likely," 20 percent of the observations should end in 0 or 5, and we could use such observations to test the hypothesis that p, the proportion of observations which end in 0 or 5, equals 0.2 versus the alternative that p is greater than 0.2. What is the test rule? Use a 5 percent significance level.

4.9 A "fishpond" operator at a county fair gives a prize to each contestant who catches a red "fish." He advertises that half of the "fish" in the pond are red. The Lone Stranger, always alert in maintaining law and order in the old West, has his faithful Indian friend, Pronto, check on the operator. Pronto reports that he has watched 20 customers play the game and only two have caught a red "fish." Write out, in mathematical terms, the hypothesis and proper family of alternatives concerning p, the proportion of red "fish." Find the significance probability of the observation. Can the Lone Stranger take action, 99 percent confident that the operator's advertisement is false?

4.10 In an experimental tank, fish swimming "upstream" have to make a choice between two channels, A and B. The channels are identical except that in Channel B there is a large amount of dissolved carbon dioxide. Each fish makes the choice independently of the others. The experimenter observes the number of fish that choose Channel B among 16 fish tested. He wishes to use his observation that five fish out of 16 select Channel B to test the hypothesis that the dissolved carbon dioxide makes no difference to the fish in their choices. Set this up as a statistical test; i.e., name the random variable used, give its parameters, and state the hypothesis, the family of alternatives, and the decision rule. Use a 5 percent significance level. Also find the significance probability of the observation.

4.11 Sample 30 digits from a telephone directory. Test the hypothesis that even and odd numbers occur in the directory in the same proportion. Use a 5 percent significance level.

4.12 Does the home team have an advantage? A sample of 18 football games shows that the home team was the winning team 13 times. The hypothesis is that p, the probability of the home team's winning, is $\frac{1}{2}$. What should be the family of alternatives here? Find the significance probability of the observation. Set up a test of the hypothesis using a 5 percent significance level. Is the test one-tailed or two-tailed?

4.13 Does repeating a calculation on a computing machine speed up or slow down the operation? An experimenter tries to test this by doing 12 problems twice. He notes that in three of these paired trials the first calculation is performed more quickly, while in the remaining nine the second calculation is the faster one. Are these data consistent with the hypothesis that there is no difference between the first and second trials? What assumptions are requisite for this problem to be one in which the random variable of interest is binomial? What does p represent? What is the hypothesis in terms of p? What is the family of alternatives? Find the significance probability of the observation. Construct the test rule for this problem if the significance level is 10 percent. Use the observation to decide whether or not the hypothesis should be rejected.

4.14   Entering students now receive forecasts of their university grade point average (G.P.A.). In a class of 16, it is found that 13 have achieved G.P.A.'s below their forecast, three above their forecast. Is this consistent with the hypothesis that the forecasts err equally frequently in either direction? Test at the 5 percent level.

4.15   In an experiment with polarized light, subjects are tested as follows: A triangle and a square are flashed on a viewer almost instantaneously and the subject is asked to state whether the triangle preceded the square or the converse occurred. Five subjects were tested 12 times each; in the 60 trials there were 38 correct responses.

(a) What must you assume if you wish to test the hypothesis that the probability of a correct response in these trials is 0.5?
(b) Suppose that you are now informed that one respondent obtained 12 correct responses, the others 4, 7, 7, 8. What is your judgment as to the correctness of the assumptions listed in (a)?
(c) Set up the test rule to decide whether a particular individual has or has not discriminatory ability; i.e., determine the decision rule to test $H : p = 0.5$ with $n = 12$ trials. Use a significance level of 1 percent.

4.16   Recall Problem 3.7, which dealt with which foot people usually begin walking on. Let p denote the probability that people begin walking on their right foot. What assumptions must be made to test the hypothesis that $p = \frac{1}{2}$? What are reasonable alternatives? What is the decision rule for $n = 16$? What is the significance probability associated with the observation $T = 12$ if $n = 16$? Discuss the precautions that would be necessary if this experiment involved 16 trials on four different individuals, each observed four times. (Recall Example 4.8, color preference in babies.)

4.17   In a multiple choice test of 20 questions, in each of which there are five choices, a student gets four right. What is the significance probability of this observation, on the assumption that he was just guessing? Have you proven that he was just guessing?

4.18   In Problem 3.13(b), a decision rule was proposed based on samples of the size 10. The rule was: Take a second sample if $T \leq 2$ or $T \geq 8$. What is the hypothesis tested and the error probability associated with this rule?

4.19   Problem 3.16 dealt with the testing of an insecticide. Denote by T the number of insects killed by the new insecticide. What must be assumed about T to test the hypothesis that the new insecticide's probability of killing is 0.80 or less. What is the alternative here? Why do we test the hypothesis that the probability of killing is 0.80, when the new insecticide is claimed to do better than this? What is the test rule when $n = 20$, $\alpha = 0.05$? What is the probability that H is rejected when, in fact, the probability of killing is 0.90?

4.20   Problem 3.17 dealt with sampling of students to determine whether they have had Asian flu. Suppose you suspect the sampler has tried to get into the sample students who had flu and you wish, therefore, to test whether p, the proportion who have had Asian flu, equals 0.1 against $p > 0.1$. What is the significance probability of the observation $T = 4$ if $n = 4$?

4.21   Recall Problem 3.18. Suppose, as is almost certainly true in real life, that the number of defective boxes in the warehouse is unknown, but in the sample of ten there is one defective; what would be your estimate of the proportion defective in the population? Do you think an estimate based on a sample of size ten is likely to give a reliable estimate of p? Compare the variance of T/n when $n = 10$, $p = 0.1$ with that for $n = 100$, $p = 0.1$.

4.22   In Problem 3.21 ten male university students were classified according to whether or not they were married. What null hypothesis is it reasonable to test here? Assume that the alternative of concern to the investigator is that the probability of sampling married students is greater than of sampling single students. What is the significance probability of the observation that the sample of ten contained five married students?

4.23   Using the data of Problem 3.22 test the hypothesis that $p = \frac{1}{2}$ against $p \neq \frac{1}{2}$, where p is the probability that a returned form is blue. Take $\alpha = 0.10$.

4.24   Recall Problem 2.39, the automatic weather-reporting buoy. The probability of an acceptable transmission is $\frac{25}{32}$. Yet in actual usage in the first 32 days there are only 16 acceptable transmissions. Is this "too few"? Discuss statistically.

4.25   Trout are raised in two different hatcheries and released with a mark to distinguish from which one they came. Of the first 18 returns, only four are from Hatchery Number One. Is there a significant difference in returns from the two releases? The releases were made in equal numbers. Test at the 5 percent level. What assumptions are involved in this test?

*4.26   Construct the O.C. curve for the E.S.P. problem, i.e., the test of $H : p = \frac{1}{2}$ versus $A : p > \frac{1}{2}$, for $n = 10$ and $n = 20$ and for significance levels 1 percent and 5 percent. What appears to happen as n increases? As the significance level decreases?

*4.27   Construct and compare the O.C. curves for the salmon sex ratio, i.e., the test of $H : p = \frac{1}{2}$ versus $A : p \neq \frac{1}{2}$, for $n = 20$ and significance levels 1 percent and 5 percent.

*4.28   Evaluate the O.C. curve for the test rule found in Problem 4.2 and compare it with those found in Problem 4.26.

*4.29   Evaluate the O.C. curve for the test rule found in Problem 4.4.

*4.30   In Problem 3.25, $P(T > 15|n = 20)$ was calculated for various values of p. These probabilities may be interpreted as the probabilities of rejecting $H: p = \frac{1}{2}$ for various alternatives. What is the significance level? Plot the O.C. curve of the test.

*4.31   A psychologist tests 16 persons to compare their reaction speed before and after eating. Suppose that 80 percent of the population being tested have a faster reaction before eating. What is the probability that the psychologist will reject the null hypothesis that the proportion of the population with a faster reaction before eating is one-half? He tests this null hypothesis at the 5 percent level.

*4.32   In the ordinary development of oyster larvae, 10 percent are abnormal. A higher percentage may occur if their water supply is polluted. This may be used as a test of the water condition. As a routine check, twenty larvae are placed in a sample of water. If five or more of the larvae show abnormality, pollution is suspected. This procedure may be thought of as a test of a hypothesis.

(a) What is the hypothesis and what is the alternative? What is the significance level and what assumptions are involved?

(b) Suppose the water has deteriorated to the point that the probability of an abnormal larva is one-half. What is the probability that pollution will be detected by this routine test?

Random Sampling, Sampling Distributions, Summarization of Data, and Estimation of Parameters

Random Sampling

In Chapter 3 we studied the binomial random variable which arises from a series of binomial trials. We obtain this from a random variable X that may take on two values: 1 with probability p, and 0 with probability $1 - p$. We observe n independent repetitions of X, obtaining $X_1, X_2, \ldots, X_n$, where X_i $(i = 1, 2, \ldots, n)$ is the random variable representing the outcome on the ith trial.

> *Note:* Since we have not actually performed any experimental trials, we write $X_1, X_2, \ldots, X_n$ to represent the sample. If the trials were actually performed, we would obtain a set of n numbers, each a 1 or a 0. Different people, performing the n trials independently of each other, would obtain varying sets of numbers. Unless we list the outcomes of actual experimentation, we will always use capital letters to indicate that we are dealing with random variables that represent the possible outcomes on each trial.

We usually are not so much interested in $X_1, X_2, \ldots, X_n$ as in the sample total, $T = X_1 + X_2 + \cdots + X_n$ which is a binomial random variable with parameters n and p. T is a function of the sample $X_1, X_2, \ldots, X_n$ so that its probability distribution is also called a sampling distribution.

In this chapter, we study random sampling, a generalization of binomial sampling in that X may now be any random variable. We also study functions of the random sample and their probability distributions, called *sampling distributions*.

More precisely, $X_1, X_2, \ldots, X_n$ *is said to be a random sample on X if*

1. A series of n experiments is performed, on each of which a possible outcome of the random variable X is observed, and each outcome obtained is recorded. X_i is the random variable representing the outcome obtained on the ith trial $(i = 1, 2, \ldots, n)$.
2. Each of $X_1, X_2, \ldots, X_n$ is a random variable having the same probability distribution as X.
3. The trials are independent, so that knowledge of the outcome on any one trial does not affect the probabilities of the various outcomes on other trials.

Example 5.1   Binomial sampling

If X is a random variable such that $P(X = 1) = p$ and $P(X = 0) = 1 - p$ and $X_1, X_2, \ldots, X_n$ is a random sample on X, then we have binomial trials and $T = X_1 + X_2 + \cdots + X_n$ is a binomial random variable with parameters n and p.

Example 5.2   Telephone calls

Let X be the number of telephone calls received at a company's switchboard on Monday between 9 A.M. and 10 A.M. Let $X_1, X_2, \ldots, X_{10}$ be the number of calls on ten successive Mondays. If it can be assumed that the conditions under which the ten experiments are performed are essentially unchanged and if the result on any Monday does not influence the probability of the result on any other Monday, then $X_1, X_2, \ldots, X_{10}$ is a random sample of size 10 on X.

Example 5.3   Los Angeles schoolchildren's I.Q.'s

Let X be the I.Q. of a schoolchild chosen at random from all schoolchildren in Los Angeles. Let $X_1, X_2 \ldots, X_{20}$ be the result of 20 such choices. If on each trial, each child has the same probability of being chosen and if the result on any trial does not change the probability of the result on any other trial, then $X_1, X_2, \ldots, X_{20}$ is a random sample of size 20 on X.

Example 5.4   Movie attendance in Toronto

Let X be the number of movies seen by a randomly chosen resident of Toronto in the month of December. A team of interviewers is sent out to obtain this information from 50 residents; i.e., each interviewer obtains such observations on 50 randomly chosen residents. The results obtained by one interviewer would be a set of 50 numbers, $X_1, X_2, \ldots, X_{50}$, which would be a random sample of size 50 on X.

Although X_i represents the outcome observed on the ith trial, $X_1, X_2, \ldots, X_n$ are properly called random variables in each example, since in theoretical discussions that occur before experimentation their values are not known. And, if the experimenter were to repeat all n trials more than once, or if more than one experimenter were to perform the n trials, it is very likely that a different set of n numbers would be observed for each set of n trials performed.

We have discussed examples of random variables X and random samples on such X. Samples often come from a finite population, as in Examples 5.3 and 5.4 and as was discussed in Sampling at Random, Chapter 3. Here, let X be a randomly chosen numerical observation from such a population. We speak interchangeably in this situation of the *probability distribution of the random variable X* or of the *population frequency distribution*. In order to obtain a random sample on X, as defined in this section, it is necessary and sufficient that after each trial the outcome observed be replaced in the population and be available as a possible outcome on the next trial. In Example 5.3, the population consists of the I.Q.'s of all Los Angeles schoolchildren. $X_1, X_2, \ldots$, X_{20} is a random sample on X if and only if after each trial the I.Q. actually observed is replaced in the population and is one of the possible outcomes on the next trial. Sampling from a finite population in which the outcome of each trial is replaced in the population before the next trial is called *sampling with replacement*.

Sampling Without Replacement

Usually, it is more convenient not to replace the outcome of any trial and indeed it is often impossible to do so. For example, if one has a finite population of light bulbs, and the experiment consists of drawing a bulb at random and measuring its lifetime until it burns out, this bulb cannot be used again. In such situations, the sampling is said to be *sampling without replacement*. For sampling without replacement, the definition of a random sample given at the beginning of this chapter does not apply, and a slightly different definition is required. *A sample drawn from a finite population without replacement is said to be a random sample* if, at each trial, the outcome is chosen at random from all those outcomes remaining in the population.

In either type of random sampling, we let X_i be the random variable that represents the outcome observed on trial i. Then $X_1, X_2, \ldots, X_n$ is the set of random variables representing the outcomes of the n trials. (The sample size n is necessarily less than or equal to the population size if the sampling is done without replacement.) In both types of random sampling, X_i has the same probability distribution as that of X. This is obvious when the sampling is with replacement, but the method of proof is more difficult if the sampling is without replacement. In random sampling with replacement, the various random variables are independent, while in random sampling without replacement they are not. This is again obvious since knowledge of the outcome on the first trial, for example, will not affect the probabilities of the other outcomes on other trials in the former case but will in the latter.

Example 5.5 A lottery

A lottery sells 500 tickets numbered 1 through 500. Five numbers are to be drawn and each of the five will receive a cash prize. Let X be the random variable recording the number chosen on any draw. Then $X_1, X_2, \ldots, X_5$ represent the five winning numbers for this lottery. If the rules of the lottery specify that no number can win two or more prizes but otherwise that the sampling is to be at random, then $X_1, X_2, \ldots, X_5$ represents a random sample without replacement from a finite population. If the rules of the lottery allow a number to win as often as it is drawn and specify that the sampling should be at random, then each number drawn is replaced before the next number is drawn and $X_1, X_2, \ldots, X_5$ represents a random sample with replacement from a finite population or, alternatively, a random sample on X.

Example 5.6 Success at university

To investigate how well freshmen do at university, a freshman class is studied. A freshman from this class is chosen at random and assigned the value 1 if he passes all his freshman courses, the value 0 if he fails one or more courses. Let X be the random variable that records 1 or 0 depending on the result of this experiment. The experiment is repeated 25 times and the results $X_1, X_2, \ldots, X_{25}$ are listed. Each of X_1 through X_{25} is a 0 or a 1. If the sampling is done with replacement (and at random), then $X_1, X_2, \ldots, X_{25}$ is a random sample on X or a random sample with replacement from a finite population. If the sampling is done without a replacement (which is more common) but otherwise at random, then $X_1, X_2, \ldots, X_{25}$ is a random sample without replacement from a finite population. Let $T = X_1 + X_2 + \cdots + X_{25}$. If there has been random sampling with replacement, then T is a binomial random variable. If there has been random sampling without replacement, then T is a hypergeometric random variable. In either case, T represents the number of freshmen in the sample who have failed no courses. As already mentioned, if the sample size is small compared to the population size, then T has much the same probability distribution under either method of sampling. This is in fact generally true for other random variables, to be studied later.

It should be pointed out that in random sampling without replacement, it does not matter if the sample is chosen one by one or all at once, provided only that if it is chosen all at once each outcome has the same probability of appearing in the sample. This, along with the fact that it is often desirable to have as many different outcomes in the sample as possible, makes random sampling without replacement more satisfactory in a great many experiments.

Sampling Distributions

A random sample on X or a random sample without replacement generates a number of random variables, and from these we can derive others which will be useful to us. The simplest example is that associated with Example 5.1 (binomial sampling) where the random variable has the distribution

x	$p(x)$
0	$1 - p$
1	p

If n such observations are made independently, and $X_1, X_2, \ldots, X_n$ represent the possible outcomes, and if we sum these to yield T, the total number of successes, then T is also a random variable and its probability distribution is given, as shown in Chapter 3, by

$$P(T = t) = \frac{n!}{t! \, (n - t)!} p^t (1 - p)^{n-t} \qquad t = 0, 1, \ldots, n.$$

As was noted earlier, this is an example of a sampling distribution.

For another example, consider again Example 5.4. If it were possible to take a complete census we could graph or tabulate the population distribution (of the number of movies seen in December by Toronto residents). It might, for example, resemble Figure 5.1.

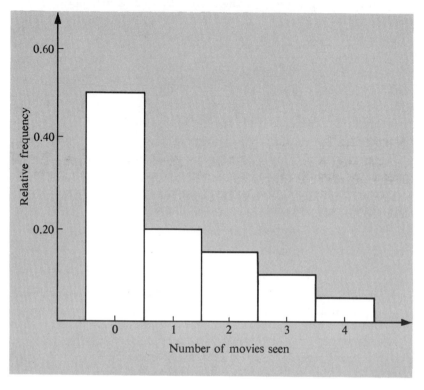

FIGURE 5.1   *The population distribution for Example 5.4.*

Now consider an interviewer who samples 50 people. He has as a result 50 observations, $X_1, X_2, \ldots, X_{50}$, which he may report, or he may simply report the total number of movies seen by all members of his sample. This total will be a random variable—another interviewer will undoubtedly find a different total. The probability distribution of such sample totals is a *sampling distribution*.

In Example 5.6, T is a random variable arising from random sampling. Its sampling distribution is binomial or hypergeometric, as the sampling is with or without replacement.

Such sampling distributions may be found by a mathematical analysis, as we did in the binomial case, or by the use of a high-speed computer. We illustrate how the computer might proceed if the population were large, and illustrate the idea of sampling distributions further by considering some rather trivial populations that can be handled without extensive computations.

Example 5.7 Random sampling from a uniform distribution

Consider the population with five elements, numbered 1 to 5, having the following frequency distribution:

x	$p(x)$
1	$\frac{1}{5}$
2	$\frac{1}{5}$
3	$\frac{1}{5}$
4	$\frac{1}{5}$
5	$\frac{1}{5}$

This is, of course, identical with the probability distribution of X, the random variable discussed in Examples 2.12 and 2.16 (finding a defective machine).

Now suppose that two elements are drawn with replacement from this population, so that two independent observations X_1, X_2 are obtained; i.e., a random sample of size 2 on X is obtained. It is easy to enumerate the 5^2 possibilities and compute, for example, the sampling distribution of $X_1 + X_2$, the total number of machines examined. These are listed in Table 5.1.

This can be carried a step further by considering three independent observations X_1, X_2, X_3 on X rather than two. The computations are more tedious but it is not hard to work out the sampling distribution of $X_1 + X_2 + X_3$ shown in Table 5.2.

Some of the work in deriving this distribution can be lessened by observing that the distribution is symmetrical about its expected value, which is 9. (What is the relationship of this expectation to $E(X)$?)

Example 5.8 The sampling distribution of the sample
mean from a uniform population

In Example 5.7, we studied the behavior of the sample total; it is more usual to look at the sample mean.

We treat again a very small finite population. Consider a population of five individuals whose ages are 32, 34, 36, 38, 40. Table 5.3

TABLE 5.1

$X_1 = x_1$	$X_2 = x_2$	$X_1 + X_2 = x$	$P(X_1 + X_2 = x)$
1	1	2	$\frac{1}{25}$
1 2	2 1	3	$\frac{2}{25}$
1 2 3	3 2 1	4	$\frac{3}{25}$
1 2 3 4	4 3 2 1	5	$\frac{4}{25}$
1 2 3 4 5	5 4 3 2 1	6	$\frac{5}{25}$
2 3 4 5	5 4 3 2	7	$\frac{4}{25}$
3 4 5	5 4 3	8	$\frac{3}{25}$
4 5	5 4	9	$\frac{2}{25}$
5	5	10	$\frac{1}{25}$

TABLE 5.2

$X_1 + X_2 + X_3 = x$	$P(X_1 + X_2 + X_3 = x)$
3	1/125
4	3/125
5	6/125
6	10/125
7	15/125
8	18/125
9	19/125
10	18/125
11	15/125
12	10/125
13	6/125
14	3/125
15	1/125

shows the distribution of an observation X drawn at random from this population.

TABLE 5.3

$X = x$	$P(X = x) = p(x)$	$x \cdot p(x)$	$(x - \mu)^2 \cdot p(x)$
32	$\frac{1}{5}$	$\frac{32}{5}$	$\frac{16}{5}$
34	$\frac{1}{5}$	$\frac{34}{5}$	$\frac{4}{5}$
36	$\frac{1}{5}$	$\frac{36}{5}$	0
38	$\frac{1}{5}$	$\frac{38}{5}$	$\frac{4}{5}$
40	$\frac{1}{5}$	$\frac{40}{5}$	$\frac{16}{5}$

By immediate computation, we see that

$$\mu = E(X) = \tfrac{180}{5} = 36,$$
$$\sigma^2 = V(X) = \tfrac{40}{5} = 8.$$

Observe that μ can be regarded as either the mean or average of the population of five ages or as the expectation of an observation X drawn randomly from this population and that a similar dual interpretation exists for the variance σ^2.

Now consider means of samples of size 2 drawn from this population *without* replacement. There are $5 \cdot 4$, or 20, possible samples, if order of the sampled individuals is taken into account. These are listed in Table 5.4.

TABLE 5.4

$X_1 = x_1$	32, 34	32, 36	32, 38	32, 40	34, 36
$X_2 = x_2$	34, 32	36, 32	38, 32	40, 32	36, 34
$\bar{X} = x$	33	34	35	36	35

$X_1 = x_1$	34, 38	34, 40	36, 38	36, 40	38, 40
$X_2 = x_2$	38, 34	40, 34	38, 36	40, 36	40, 38
$\bar{X} = x$	36	37	37	38	39

The sample means are shown below the paired samples. (It is obvious that either order gives the same value for $\bar{X}$.) Table 5.5 shows the probability distribution by direct count.

TABLE 5.5

$\bar{X} = x$	$P(\bar{X} = x) = p(x)$	$x \cdot p(x)$	$[x - E(\bar{X})]^2 \cdot p(x)$
33	$\frac{2}{20} = \frac{1}{10}$	$\frac{33}{10}$	$\frac{9}{10}$
34	$\frac{2}{20} = \frac{1}{10}$	$\frac{34}{10}$	$\frac{4}{10}$
35	$\frac{4}{20} = \frac{2}{10}$	$\frac{70}{10}$	$\frac{2}{10}$
36	$\frac{4}{20} = \frac{2}{10}$	$\frac{72}{10}$	0
37	$\frac{4}{20} = \frac{2}{10}$	$\frac{74}{10}$	$\frac{2}{10}$
38	$\frac{2}{20} = \frac{1}{10}$	$\frac{38}{10}$	$\frac{4}{10}$
39	$\frac{2}{20} = \frac{1}{10}$	$\frac{39}{10}$	$\frac{9}{10}$

By adding, one sees that $E(\bar{X}) = \frac{360}{10} = 36$ and $V(\bar{X}) = \frac{30}{10} = 3$. These calculated values of $E(\bar{X})$ and $V(\bar{X})$ illustrate the following theorems.

THEOREM 5.1   *The sampling distribution of* $\bar{X} = (1/n) \sum_{i=1}^{n} X_i$ *for samples of size n drawn randomly but* without *replacement from a population of size N with mean* μ *and variance* σ^2 *has the following properties:*

(a) $E(\bar{X}) = \mu$;

(b) $V(\bar{X}) = \frac{\sigma^2}{n} \left(\frac{N - n}{N - 1} \right).$

Proof of (a):

$$E(\bar{X}) = E\left(\frac{X_1 + X_2 + \cdots + X_n}{n}\right)$$

$$= \frac{1}{n} E(X_1 + X_2 + \cdots + X_n) \qquad \text{by Theorem 2.1(b) since } n \text{ is a constant}$$

$$= \frac{1}{n} [E(X_1) + E(X_2) + \cdots + E(X_n)] \qquad \text{by Theorem 2.1(a)}$$

$$= \frac{1}{n} \underbrace{[\mu + \mu + \cdots + \mu]}_{(n \text{ times})} = \frac{n\mu}{n} = \mu.$$

The variance part of the theorem is more difficult to prove because the successive observations are *not* independent and Theorem 2.3 does not apply. Verify that for Example 5.8, $\sigma^2 = 8$, $n = 2$, and $N = 5$ so that $V(\bar{X}) = 3$ as derived directly.

If the sample mean $\bar{X}$ comes from a random sample on X (or if the sampling is with replacement), the successive observations are independent and the formula for $V(\bar{X})$ simplifies, as shown in Theorem 5.2 below.

THEOREM 5.2 *The sampling distribution of $\bar{X}$ for samples of size n drawn at random on X, or drawn at random with replacement from a finite population with mean μ and variance σ^2, has the following properties:*

(a) $E(\bar{X}) = \mu$;

(b) $V(\bar{X}) = \dfrac{\sigma^2}{n}$.

Proof:

(a) This is proved as in Theorem 5.1(a).

(b) $$V(\bar{X}) = V\left[\frac{(X_1 + X_2 + \cdots + X_n)}{n}\right]$$

$$= \frac{1}{n^2} V(X_1 + X_2 + \cdots + X_n) \qquad \text{by Theorem 2.3(b)}$$

$$= \frac{1}{n^2} (V(X_1) + V(X_2) + \cdots + V(X_n)) \qquad \text{by Theorem 2.3(a)}$$

$$= \frac{1}{n^2} \underbrace{(\sigma^2 + \sigma^2 + \cdots + \sigma^2)}_{(n \text{ times})} = \frac{n\sigma^2}{n^2} = \frac{\sigma^2}{n}.$$

Example 5.9 The sampling distribution of the sample mean from a uniform population (continued)

To illustrate Theorem 5.2(b), consider the same population as in Example 5.8 above except that the samples are drawn *with* replacement. The $5 \cdot 5$, or 25, possible samples are: 32, 32; 32, 34; 34, 32; 32, 36; 36, 32; 32, 38; 32, 32; 32, 40; 40, 32; 34, 34; 34, 36; 36, 34; 34, 38; 38, 34; 34, 40; 40, 34; 36, 36; 36, 38; 38, 36; 36, 40; 40, 36; 38, 38; 38, 40; 40, 38; 40, 40. We list next the $\bar{X}$ associated with these 25 samples: 32, 33, 33, 34, 34, 35, 35, 36, 36, 34, 35, 35, 36, 36, 37, 37, 36, 37, 37, 38, 38, 38, 39, 39, 40.

TABLE 5.6

$\bar{X} = x$	$P(\bar{X} = x) = p(x)$	$x \cdot p(x)$	$[x - E(\bar{X})]^2 \cdot p(x)$
32	$\frac{1}{25}$	$\frac{32}{25}$	$\frac{16}{25}$
33	$\frac{2}{25}$	$\frac{66}{25}$	$\frac{18}{25}$
34	$\frac{3}{25}$	$\frac{102}{25}$	$\frac{12}{25}$
35	$\frac{4}{25}$	$\frac{140}{25}$	$\frac{4}{25}$
36	$\frac{5}{25}$	$\frac{180}{25}$	0
37	$\frac{4}{25}$	$\frac{148}{25}$	$\frac{4}{25}$
38	$\frac{3}{25}$	$\frac{114}{25}$	$\frac{12}{25}$
39	$\frac{2}{25}$	$\frac{78}{25}$	$\frac{18}{25}$
40	$\frac{1}{25}$	$\frac{40}{25}$	$\frac{16}{25}$

By adding, one sees that $E(\bar{X}) = \frac{900}{25} = 36$ and $V(\bar{X}) = \frac{100}{25} = 4$. Note $V(\bar{X}) = 4$, i.e., $\sigma^2/2$, as it should according to the formula. By listing the 125 samples of size 3 (taken *with* replacement) it can be shown that in this case $V(\bar{X}) = \frac{8}{3}$.

These examples illustrate the sampling distribution of the total and sample mean; of interest also are the sample range, the sample standard deviation, and the largest observation in the sample. In theory, we can study any function of the sample observations. We are most interested in the sample mean and sample variance because they can be used to give information about the population mean and variance.

Summarization of Data

In real life, the n trials may be observed only once. That is, the experimenter sets up an experiment that involves the recording of some number. He performs the experiment n times under identical conditions (or as nearly so as possible) and in such a way that the result of one trial does not influence the results of other trials (if the sampling is done with replacement). He finally has at his disposal a collection of n numbers. For example, the results of Example 5.2 might be as follows: 10, 4, 6, 8, 12, 9, 4, 10, 4, 7. In Example 5.3, the results might be as follows: 103, 95, 110, 125, 89, 105, 93, 97, 115, 117, 100, 97, 125, 87, 95, 106, 103, 131, 112, 101.

What should be done with this mass of raw data? In the case of Examples 5.1 and 5.7, we added all the observations together and recorded only the total, e.g., the number of successes in Example 5.1. This is a very useful and very obvious summarization of the n separate observations and it has a simple interpretation, whereas a large collection of 1's and 0's might be quite difficult to interpret. The problem of summarizing more complex sets of observations to facilitate their analysis is more difficult, though clearly very desirable.

Given a set of observations, we can arrange these into a *sample frequency distribution*. The frequency distribution shows the frequency of different sample values in increasing order. For example, the sample frequency distribution of Example 5.2 whose outcomes are listed above is shown in Table 5.7.

TABLE 5.7

Value of observation	Frequency
3 or less	0
4	3
5	0
6	1
7	1
8	1
9	1
10	2
11	0
12	1
13 or more	0
Total	10

In such a sample frequency distribution, we may record the data exactly as measured, as in Example 5.2, or only by classes or groups.

For example, the data of Example 5.3, given at the beginning of this section, may be summarized into classes as in Table 5.8.

TABLE 5.8

Class	Class midpoint	Frequency
85–89	87	2
90–94	92	1
95–99	97	4
100–104	102	4
105–109	107	2
110–114	112	2
115–119	117	2
120–124	122	0
125–129	127	2
130–134	132	1
		Total 20

When calculations have to be done without a machine the latter reduction may be very helpful, but with the ever increasing availability of computers it is becoming less and less important. When data are grouped, in calculation of $\bar{X}$, it is assumed that the average value in each class is the midpoint of that class; to calculate s^2 it is necessary to assume that all values in each class fall at the class midpoint. Thus grouping introduces some errors. If grouping is performed extensively, elaborate rules may be prescribed as to the number of groups, the length of the class intervals, the location of the class boundaries, etc. If the observations are graphed, it is usual to show grouped data. Graphs which plot frequencies against class midpoints or class intervals are called *histograms*. (See Appendix 1 for a more formal definition.) The reader who wishes to study grouping and graphical representation more thoroughly is referred to this appendix. In this chapter, we will deal only with arithmetical summaries.

Sample Mean and Sample Standard Deviation

The frequency distribution conveniently records all the data. This distribution may still be too unwieldy for much analysis, particularly if there are many observations. Sample frequency distributions may be summarized, as probability distributions were. Of the many possible ways of doing this, two *statistics* have been computed most frequently (a *statistic* is a function of the observations). These are the *sample mean* and *sample variance*, denoted by $\bar{X}$ and s^2, respectively. These correspond to the population quantities $E(X) = \mu$ and $V(X) = \sigma^2$, computed from the population probability distribution of X.

Just as μ and σ^2 yield much information about the probability distribution of X, $\bar{X}$ and s^2 yield much information about the frequency distribution of the random sample.

The formulas for the sample mean are

$$\bar{X} = \frac{1}{n} \sum_{i=1}^{n} X_i \qquad \text{for ungrouped data}$$

and

$$\bar{X} = \frac{1}{n} \sum_{i=1}^{k} f_i X_i \qquad \text{for grouped data,}$$

where k is the number of classes, X_i is the midpoint of the ith class $(i = 1, 2, \ldots, k)$, f_i is the frequency of the ith class, and $n = \sum_{i=1}^{k} f_i =$ the total number of observations. (Note that sample frequency distributions show absolute frequencies, not relative frequencies, as probability distributions do; hence, the final division by n.)

The formulas for the sample variance are

$$s^2 = \frac{1}{n-1} \sum_{i=1}^{n} (X_i - \bar{X})^2 = \frac{1}{n-1} \left[\sum_{i=1}^{n} X_i^2 - n(\bar{X})^2 \right] \qquad \text{for ungrouped data,}$$

and

$$s^2 = \frac{1}{n-1} \sum_{i=1}^{k} f_i (X_i - \bar{X})^2 = \frac{1}{n-1} \left[\sum_{i=1}^{k} f_i X_i^2 - n(\bar{X})^2 \right] \qquad \text{for grouped data.}$$

The *sample standard deviation* s is the (positive) square root of s^2.

EXERCISES

1. Show that $\sum_{i=1}^{n} (X_i - \bar{X}) = 0$.
2. Show that $\sum_{i=1}^{n} X_i^2 = (n-1)s^2 + n\bar{X}^2$. This equation relating the sample statistics is the analogous equation to $E(X^2) = \sigma^2 + \mu^2$ for the population quantities.

Estimation of μ, σ^2

It is important to understand that $\bar{X}$ and s^2 are random variables. When the experiment is performed just once, the observations are recorded, and from these $\bar{X}$ and s^2 can be computed. But if the whole experiment is done again, different values of $\bar{X}$ and s^2 will almost invariably result. We know in fact that $\bar{X}$ has a sampling distribution; an example of such a distribution was calculated in Example 5.8. Moreover, if we have random sampling with or without replacement, Theorems 5.1 and 5.2 show that $E(\bar{X}) = \mu$, which states that while $\bar{X}$ varies from sample to sample, on the average it will yield the right value of μ, the population mean. These results justify the use of $\bar{X}$, the sample mean, as an estimator of μ, the population mean, providing the sampling is done at random.

Moreover, Theorems 5.1 and 5.2 give additional information, namely, the fact that $V(\bar{X}) = \sigma^2/n[(N - n)/(N - 1)]$ (sampling without replacement) and that $V(\bar{X}) = \sigma^2/n$ (sampling with replacement). In either case, it is seen that $\bar{X}$ tends to vary less about its expected values μ than does X, on the average. These formulas also show that, as n becomes large, $V(\bar{X})$ tends to zero, or, in other words, with probability arbitrarily close to one, $\bar{X}$ is arbitrarily close to μ; i.e., the Law of Large Numbers holds.

[*Note:* Theorem 5.2 of this chapter and Theorem 2.2 can be used to prove the Law of Large Numbers though, of course, to make this proof complete we need proofs also for Theorems 2.2 and 2.3.

The student who takes further courses in mathematical statistics will encounter random variables for which the variance $V(X)$ is not defined. The Law of Large Numbers still holds if $E(X)$ is defined, though obviously another method of proof is required. We will not concern ourselves with such random variables in this text, but only consider ones for which $E(X)$ and $V(X)$ are defined.]

Now consider s^2, the sample variance, and its relationship to the population variance. The first formula for the sample variance is, in each case, the definition formula. The second, which can be derived from the first algebraically, is simpler for computation. The definition formulas for the sample variance look like the corresponding formula for the population variance σ^2, *except for the divisors*. By analogy with the formula for $\bar{X}$ you might expect the divisor to be n. Formerly s^2 was defined with divisor n, but modern statisticians use the divisor $n - 1$. Why?

The estimator of the mean has the property that $E(\bar{X}) = \mu$; we would like s^2 to have a similar property. If s^2 is defined with divisor $n - 1$, then $E(s^2) = \sigma^2$, if there is random sampling or random sampling with replacement from a finite population. We see that $E(s^2) \doteq \sigma^2$ even if the random sampling is without replacement from a finite population. Why is $E(s^2)$ equal to σ^2 in the case of random sampling? The population variance is an average of squared deviations from the *population mean*. We do not measure deviations from the population mean μ but from the *sample mean* $\bar{X}$. The expected square deviations $E(X_i - \bar{X})^2$ are, on the average, slightly smaller than those of $E(X_i - \mu)^2$, but the division by $n - 1$ rather than n in the definition of s^2 fortunately just compensates for this. Since $E(s^2) = \sigma^2$ and since the Law of Large Numbers holds for s^2, that is, s^2 is arbitrarily close to σ^2 with probability arbitrarily close to 1 when n is large, we use s^2 as an estimator of σ^2.

Estimators that have the properties of $\bar{X}$, s^2, i.e., that are right on the average or for which $E(\bar{X}) = \mu$ and $E(s^2) = \sigma^2$, are called *unbiased*. In general, an estimator $\hat{\theta}$ of a parameter θ is said to be *unbiased* if $E(\hat{\theta}) = \theta$.

Although it is fairly easy to show that $E(s^2) = \sigma^2$, so that s^2 is an unbiased estimator of σ^2, it is often extremely difficult to compute $E(s)$. Even when $E(s)$ can be obtained (as for the normal population distribution, to be discussed in Chapter 6), it is most often the case that $E(s) \neq \sigma$, so that s is not an unbiased estimator of σ in general. Nevertheless, statisticians continue to estimate σ by s, since it is convenient to compute.

Application to the Binomial Probability Distribution

If X takes on the values 1 with probability p and 0 with probability $1 - p$, we have binomial trials. Then $\mu = E(X) = p$; $V(X) = p(1 - p)$; and $\bar{X} = (1/n) \sum_{i=1}^{n} X_i = T/n = \hat{p}$. Thus, for binomial trials $\bar{X}$ reduces to $\hat{p}$, which was used in Chapter 4 to estimate p; this estimation of p by $\hat{p}$ is a special case of the general rule that μ is estimated by $\bar{X}$.

Since $E(T)$ was shown to be np, it follows by Theorem 2.1 that $E(T/n) = E(\hat{p}) = p$, confirming for this example what has been stated to be true for $\bar{X}$ in general.

Further, $\sigma^2 = V(X) = p(1 - p)$ is estimated by

$$s^2 = \frac{1}{n-1} \left(\sum_{i=1}^{n} X_i^2 - n\bar{X}^2 \right).$$

Now for binomial trials $X_i = 1$ or 0 and $\sum_{i=1}^{n} X_i^2 = \sum_{i=1}^{n} X_i = n\hat{p}$ since $\hat{p} = (1/n) \sum_{i=1}^{n} X_i$.

Thus s^2 reduces to

$$\frac{1}{n-1} \left(\sum_{i=1}^{n} X_i^2 - n\bar{X}^2 \right) = \frac{n\hat{p} - n\hat{p}^2}{n-1} = \frac{n}{n-1} \hat{p}(1 - \hat{p}).$$

Now

$$V(\hat{p}) = V\left(\frac{T}{n}\right) = \frac{p(1 - p)}{n},$$

so that an unbiased estimator of $V(\hat{p})$ is $\hat{p}(1 - \hat{p})/(n - 1)$.

Coded Calculations

The formulas given above for $\bar{X}$ and s^2 are not always the most convenient to use. It may be simpler to "*code*" the data, i.e., in the intermediate stages to work with a different origin and different units. *We can choose any working origin and unit we wish, provided we convert back at the end of the calculations.* It is convenient to choose the working origin near the center of the data and the units equal to the length of the class intervals (when the data are grouped). Recall that working with grouped data requires all observations in a group to be assigned to the midpoint of the class interval. The procedure of coding is best described by examples as below.

DECODING RULE   If the working origin is d and the units are of length c, then to convert back to original units,

$$\bar{X} \text{ (decoded)} = c\bar{X} \text{ (coded)} + d,$$

$$s^2 \text{ (decoded)} = c^2 s^2 \text{ (coded)}.$$

We exemplify this by considering the data of Examples 5.2 and 5.3.

Example 5.2 (continued)

Find $\bar{X}$ and s^2 directly (Table 5.9) and by coding (Table 5.10).

TABLE 5.9

X_i	f_i	f_iX_i	$f_iX_i^2$
4	3	12	48
5	0	0	0
6	1	6	36
7	1	7	49
8	1	8	64
9	1	9	81
10	2	20	200
11	0	0	0
12	1	12	144
Total	10	74	622
$n = 10$		$\sum f_iX_i = 74$	$\sum f_iX_i^2 = 622$

Hence,

$$\bar{X} = \frac{74}{10} = 7.4,$$

$$s^2 = \frac{1}{9}\left[622 - \frac{(74)^2}{10}\right] = 8.27.$$

To code, we choose a value near the middle, say 8. The coded data are as follows. (Since the observations are in whole numbers, there is no need to change the units.)

TABLE 5.10

X_i (coded)	f_i	f_iX_i		$f_iX_i^2$
-4	3	-12		48
-3	0	0		0
-2	1	-2		4
-1	1	-1		1
0	1	0	subtotal	0
			-15	
1	1	1		1
2	2	4		8
3	0	0		0
4	1	4	subtotal	16
			9	
Total	10	-6		78
		$\sum f_iX_i = -6$	$\sum f_iX_i^2 = 78$	

$$X \text{ (coded)} = \frac{-6}{10} = -0.6$$

$$X \text{ (decoded)} = 1(-0.6) + 8 = 7.4,$$

$$s^2 \text{ (coded)} = \frac{1}{9}\left(78 - \frac{(-6)^2}{10}\right) = \frac{74.4}{9} = 8.27,$$

$$s^2 \text{ (decoded)} = 1^2(8.27) = 8.27.$$

The results of the two methods are identical, as indeed they must be.

Example 5.3 (continued)

Find X and s^2 from the grouped data in Table 5.11 using coding.

TABLE 5.11   *Uncoded Data*

Midpoint	Frequency
87	2
92	1
97	4
102	4
107	2
112	2
117	2
122	0
127	2
132	1
Total	20

Choosing a value near the middle, we take 107 as the origin and 5 as unit and get the data shown in Table 5.12.

$$X \text{ (coded)} = \frac{-4}{20} = -0.2,$$

$$X \text{ (decoded)} = 5(-0.2) + 107 = 106,$$

$$s^2 \text{ (coded)} = \frac{1}{19}\left(128 - \frac{(-4)^2}{20}\right) = \frac{127.2}{19} = 6.69,$$

$$s^2 \text{ (decoded)} = (5)^2(6.69) = 165.75.$$

TABLE 5.12   *Coded Data*

X_i (coded)	f_i	$f_i X_i$		$f_i X_i^2$
−4	2	−8		32
−3	1	−3		9
−2	4	−8		16
−1	4	−4		4
0	2	0	subtotal −23	0
1	2	2		2
2	2	4		8
3	0	0		0
4	2	8		32
5	1	5	subtotal 19	25
Total 20		−4		128

$$\sum f_i X_i = -4 \qquad \sum f_i X_i^2 = 128$$

EXERCISE

Compute $\bar{X}$ and s^2 for Example 5.3 from the ungrouped data and compare your answers with those obtained from the grouped data above. Are they sufficiently close so that you are willing to use the grouped data since it simplifies calculations? Note that while coding does not change the values obtained for $\bar{X}$ and s^2, grouping may change them; the coarser the grouping the larger changes to be expected.

Summary on Estimation

We presuppose as given a population with mean μ and variance σ^2 or, equivalently, a random variable with $E(X) = \mu$ and variance σ^2. A sample of observations is drawn at random from the population either with or without replacement.

Functions of the observations, called statistics, are used to estimate population parameters. An estimator of such a parameter is a random variable. An estimator $\hat{\theta}$ is an unbiased estimator of θ if $E(\hat{\theta}) = \theta$.

In particular, $\bar{X}$ estimates μ:

$$E(\bar{X}) = \mu,$$

$$V(\bar{X}) = \frac{N-n}{N-1} \cdot \frac{\sigma^2}{n} \qquad \text{(sampling without replacement)},$$

$$= \frac{\sigma^2}{n} \qquad \text{(sampling with replacement)};$$

and s^2 estimates σ^2:

$$E(s^2) \doteq \sigma^2 \qquad \text{(sampling without replacement)},$$

$$E(s^2) = \sigma^2 \qquad \text{(sampling with replacement)}.$$

■ Experiments

5.1 Obtain the height to the nearest inch of each member of the class and plot this information in a frequency distribution by inch intervals and by 3-inch intervals. Use 3-inch intervals so that one class is 62.5 to 65.5 in. Find $\bar{X}$ and s for the ungrouped and grouped data, both with coding and without. Compare your answers. Has grouping caused large errors?

5.2 Obtain the grade point average (G.P.A.) for each member of the class. Estimate your university mean G.P.A. by assuming that the observations taken in the class are a random sample from the university student population. Why might this not be true? Also estimate the variance of the population of grade point averages of the university.

5.3 Construct a population of 55 numbered tags with numbers distributed as follows:

X	Frequency	X	Frequency
0	10	5	5
1	9	6	4
2	8	7	3
3	7	8	2
4	6	9	1

This is a *finite* population of size 55. Find μ and σ^2. Now have each member of the class draw from this population (with replacement) ten samples of size 5. For each sample of size 5, compute the mean. The sample means from the whole class can be tabulated in a frequency distribution. What are the *expected* mean and variance of these sample means? What are the actual mean and variance for the observations made by the class? Now combine the ten samples of size 5 into two samples of size 25. What are the expected mean and variance of these sample means (means of samples of size 25)? What are the actual mean and variance of the class results?

■ Problems

5.1   Measuring is being done with a yardstick that is imperfect. Suppose that the stick is in fact 35.9 in. in length and that measurements made with it have a standard deviation of 0.1 in. Consider the distance marked out by 20 lengths of the yardstick. Is it a random variable? What are its mean and standard deviation?

5.2   Separate samples of sizes 20 and 10 are taken of the undergraduate and graduate students of the University of Washington. If the proportion of women among the undergraduates is $\frac{1}{4}$ and among graduates, $\frac{1}{5}$, what is the expected total number of women in the combined sample? What is the variance of this total? What is the variance of the number of men in the combined sample?

5.3   Fifty seeds that have germination probability 0.6 and 50 seeds that have germination probability 0.8 are planted and the number of germinations counted. What are the mean and variance of the number of germinations?

5.4   In a class of 30 students, 20 have had a cold-vaccine inoculation. Let the probability of getting a cold (in a specific period) be 0.5 for those who received an inoculation and 0.7 for those not inoculated. What are the mean and variance of the total number in the class who get a cold—if we assume that the events of catching a cold by members of the class are independent?

5.5   The weight of concrete blocks has a mean of 60 lb and a standard deviation of 2 lb. Find the expectation and variance of truckloads of such blocks if each load contains 200 blocks.

*5.6   Four independent random samples of an animal population are taken to determine the proportion of mature animals. In four samples of size n_1, n_2, n_3, n_4, the proportions of mature animals are m_1, m_2, m_3, m_4. Let

$$m = \frac{m_1 + m_2 + m_3 + m_4}{4}.$$

Find the standard deviation of m, assuming that the proportion of mature animals in the whole population is M.

5.7   Two independent forecasts are available of next year's salmon run in a river system. The forecasts F_1, F_2 are both subject to error. Suppose their variances are σ_1^2, σ_2^2. The best weighted average of the two forecasts is

$$\frac{\sigma_2^2 F_1 + \sigma_1^2 F_2}{\sigma_1^2 + \sigma_2^2}.$$

Find the variance of this weighted average.

*5.8   A group of students is assigned to work 10 problems. If the average time per problem is 1 hour and if the standard deviation of the time per problem is 15 minutes, what can be said about the total time required to work all 10 problems? Find a bound for the probability that the total time exceeds 20 hours.

5.9   The grade point averages of each class of a senior high school are shown in the table below, together with the proportion of students in each class.

Class	Subpopulation mean G.P.A.	Subpopulation standard deviation	Proportion
Sophomore	2.5	0.5	0.36
Junior	2.8	0.4	0.34
Senior	3.1	0.3	0.30

(a) Find the population mean and standard deviation of the whole high school.

*(b) Use Theorem 2.2 to find an upper bound for the probability that the G.P.A. of a randomly selected student exceeds 3.54. (For comparison it will be shown in Problem 6.23 that with additional assumptions this probability is exactly 0.057.)

5.10 Consider a population consisting of six trees with heights of 40, 45, 50, 60, 65, and 70 feet. A sample of size 2 is drawn from this population. Let H be the height of the *taller* of the two trees in the sample.

(a) Work out the probability distribution of H.

(b) Calculate $E(H)$, $V(H)$.

5.11 Consider a population of six individuals with G.P.A.'s 1.5, 2.0, 2.5, 3.0, 3.5, 4.0. Write out the sampling distribution of sample means for $n = 2$. Calculate μ, σ^2, $E(\bar{X})$, $V(\bar{X})$. Do the same for $n = 3$.

5.12 Recall Examples 2.12 and 2.16 (finding a defective machine). We studied in Example 5.7 the sampling distribution of $X_1 + X_2$, where X_1, X_2 are two realizations of such a random variable. Consider the following variation: X_1 is a random variable, the number of machines examined on the first occasion. On the second occasion the repairman does not examine the machine defective on the first occasion. What is the distribution of X_2? What is the sampling distribution of $X_1 + X_2$?

5.13 Find, by computing all possibilities, the sampling distribution of the mean of two observations on the random variable of Example 2.13 (runs).

5.14 Consider n repetitions of the experiment outlined in Example 2.11 (unprepared students). Let Y be the total number of unprepared students called. Find $E(Y)$ and $V(Y)$. Check that the formulas give the correct results for the case $n = 2$ by working out the sampling distribution in this case.

5.15 The annual precipitation for the past 20 years at a station in Washington is recorded in the frequency table below:

Precipitation (in inches)	Frequency
27.5–32.5	3
32.5–37.5	9
37.5–42.5	4
42.5–47.5	3
47.5–52.5	1

Find $\bar{X}$ and s.

5.16 The following data represent the lengths of a sample of 1,000 Alaska salmon:

Length (in inches)	Number of males	Number of females
$20\frac{1}{2}$	1	1
21	0	1
$21\frac{1}{2}$	4	2
22	6	13
$22\frac{1}{2}$	7	28
23	28	76
$23\frac{1}{2}$	55	102
24	106	134
$24\frac{1}{2}$	89	80
25	84	50
$25\frac{1}{2}$	74	13
26	31	2
$26\frac{1}{2}$	6	2
27	3	
$27\frac{1}{2}$	1	
28	0	
$28\frac{1}{2}$	0	
29	1	
Total	496	504

(a) Find $\bar{X}$ and s for the male-salmon-length data.
(b) Find $\bar{X}$ and s for the female-salmon-length data.

5.17 Twenty university students in a random sample have the following grade point averages (G.P.A.'s):

2.1 2.4 2.8 3.4 3.1 1.8 1.3 3.7 3.9 1.7
2.8 2.7 2.0 1.5 3.2 1.4 2.3 1.6 2.9 2.9

(a) Arrange these data in a frequency distribution.
(b) Estimate the mean G.P.A. for all students at this university.
(c) Estimate the variance of the G.P.A.'s for the students at this university.

5.18 The following data are weights (in ounces) of 20 apples sampled from deliveries to a storage plant from one orchard. Use the *fully coded method* to obtain $\bar{X}$ and s^2 to one decimal:

12 13 13 14 15 15 16 16 16 16
17 17 17 17 17 18 18 18 19 20

5.19 A group of medical students reported the following oral temperatures (taken on rising):

Temperature	Frequency	Temperature	Frequency
98.1	1	98.6	6
98.2	0	98.7	6
98.3	3	98.8	4
98.4	9	98.9	5
98.5	4	99.0	2

Find $\bar{X}$ and s^2.

5.20 The following are observations of the diameter of Saturn's rings made by Bessel in the years 1829 to 1831.

38.91	38.93	39.17	39.57	39.30
39.35	39.14	39.29	39.40	39.28
39.41	39.36	39.42	39.41	39.43
39.02	38.86	39.21	39.60	39.45
39.32	39.31	39.04	39.46	39.03
39.25	39.47	39.32	39.33	39.62
39.40	39.20	39.30	39.43	39.36
39.01	39.51	39.17	39.54	39.72

Calculate $\bar{X}$ and s^2.

5.21 The following data show counts of yeast cells in 20 squares of a hemacytometer (a device used to count blood cells and other microscopic objects) (data from W. S. Gossett):

1, 4, 1, 5, 6,   4, 3, 7, 4, 4,   8, 10, 6, 3, 3,   5, 5, 3, 3, 4.

Estimate the mean number of cells per square from this sample of observations. Estimate also the population variance.

5.22 The scores on a mathematics examination are as follows:

Interval	Frequency	Interval	Frequency
0–4	1	50–54	5
5–9	1	55–59	5
10–14	1	60–64	6
15–19	1	65–69	4
20–24	2	70–74	3
25–29	2	75–79	3
30–34	3	80–84	2
35–39	3	85–89	2
40–44	4	90–94	1
45–49	4	95–99	1

Find $\bar{X}$ and s^2.

5.23 Find $\bar{X}$ and s^2 for the following data showing blood pressures of male university students (use classes starting from 99.5 to 104.5, 104.5 to 109.5, ..., 149.5 to 154.5):

150	128	113	116	108	133	113	118	135	119
119	124	121	126	112	116	115	135	101	108
116	121	117	110	116	132	138	128	114	121
119	117	125	124	114	112	123	112	125	135
105	127	103	119	122	109	121	103	142	120

5.24 If you did Experiments 2.1, 2.2, and 2.3, set up the sample frequency distributions obtained. Find $\bar{X}$ and s^2 in each case. How well do these estimate the population mean and population variance, which, for comparison purposes, are given below?

Experiment	Random variable X	$E(X)$	σ_X^2
Sampling two cards from four (unprepared students)	Number of red cards	1	$\frac{1}{3}$
Sampling from five cards until king is exposed (finding a defective machine)	Number of cards turned	3	2
Numbers from a telephone directory	Sum of scores of right-hand-page numbers	0	4

5.25 Select a book at random from your own library and estimate the number of words in the book, indicating the procedure used. What is the estimated variance of your estimate?

5.26 Drop a thumbtack on the table 20 times and count the number of times it falls point up. Estimate the probability that a tack when dropped will fall point up. What can you say about the accuracy of your estimate? [*Hint:* Estimate $V(\hat{p})$.]

*5.27 Example 2.11 (unprepared students) can be used to illustrate that Theorem 2.3 may not hold if the variables are not independent. Define X_1 = number of prepared students on the first selection of a student and X_2 = the number of prepared students in the second selection of a student. Calculate the probability distribution of X_1, its expectation, and its variance. If the result of the first sampling is unknown to us, X_2 has the same distribution as X_1. Also $X_1 + X_2 = X$, the number of unprepared students in Example 2.11. Show that $E(X_1) + E(X_2) = E(X_1 + X_2) = E(X)$, but that $V(X_1) + V(X_2) \neq V(X_1 + X_2) = V(X)$.

*5.28 The value, $\frac{1}{3}$, of $V(X)$ in Example 2.11 can be derived from Formula (b) of Theorem 5.1 together with the result of Theorem 2.3. Show how this is done.

5.29 In Example 1.4 (Who was Einstein?) two samples each of size 20 were taken. Let T_1 denote the students knowing who Einstein was in Sample 1, and T_2, the same random variable for the second sample. As can be formally proved, but which is also intuitively reasonable, T, the combined total of T_1 and T_2, is binomial if T_1 and T_2 are binomial random variables with the same parameter p. The expectation and variance of T are easily derived from Theorems 2.1 and 2.3. Derive them.

CHAPTER SIX

Continuous Distributions, the Normal Probability Model, and Approximations

Continuous Distributions

The random variables studied in Chapters 2, 3, and 4 were discrete; i.e., they could only take on rational values. If the random variable is a measurement, e.g., a length, a weight, a time of survival, a distance, etc., it is still true that the values observed are rational. But as the measuring device is made more accurate, measurements become more accurate. It is conceivable in theory, and very useful in practice, to think of measurements that are accurate to any desired degree of accuracy. For random variables that can be so measured, the sample space is a line segment (possibly infinite). In Example 1.3 we discussed the time taken to travel to the university. This random variable has for its sample space all real numbers between 0 and some upper bound, perhaps 2 hours. In Example 1.9 we discussed the weights of mice. This random variable has for its sample space all real numbers between 0 and some upper bound, say 16 ounces.

Example 6.1 Catching a bus

A city bus is scheduled to arrive at its terminal at 20-minute intervals. We assume first that the bus is never late or early (an assumption never satisfied in real life). A person who knows nothing about the schedule of this bus arrives at the terminal and catches the bus as soon as it arrives. Let X be the time, measured in minutes, that he must wait until he catches the bus. Assuming that the time can be measured to any degree of accuracy, the sample space of X is the line segment consisting of all real numbers between 0 and 20.

Various questions can be asked about the probability distribution of X. For example, what is the probability that the person has to wait at least 10 minutes; i.e., what is $P(X \geq 10)$? We might answer this question by saying $P(X \geq 10) = \frac{10}{20} = \frac{1}{2}$. Why? What assumption is involved? Using the same assumption, we find that $P(5 \leq X \leq 10) = \frac{5}{20} = \frac{1}{4}$, $P(X \leq 4) = \frac{4}{20} = \frac{1}{5}$, etc.

Let x be any real number between 0 and 20. What is $P(X = x)$? This is more difficult to answer. If instead we choose an interval of length L, centered at x and contained in the interval between 0 and 20, and ask for the probability that X falls in the interval, then $P(X$ is in an interval of length L centered at $x) = L/20$. Now $0 \leq P(X = x) \leq P(X$ is in an interval of length L centered at $x) = L/20$ for any length L. If we let L become smaller and smaller, we see that the answer to our first question must be $P(X = x) = 0$ for *any* x between 0 and 20.

The random variable X studied in Example 6.1 is a continuous random variable. Formally, a *continuous random variable* X is one whose sample space is a line segment (possibly infinite) and for which $P(X = x) = 0$ for *each* real number x.

> *Note:* The beginner is often troubled by a probability model that assigns probability zero to each point. This is due partly to the fact that discrete probability models, with which he is most familiar, assign positive probabilities to each possible point. Only the impossible event has probability zero. From one view, positive probabilities are possible only because the number of points in a discrete probability model is not "too large" (at most, countably infinite, for those who are familiar with the term). Hence, one explanation of the fact that continuous probability models assign probability zero to each point is that the number of points in the sample space has become "too large" (uncountably infinite). Alternately, one can interpret $P(X = x) = 0$ to mean not that $(X = x)$ is impossible (for clearly, each time X is observed, some point must occur) but that the relative frequency of the event $(X = x)$ for each real number x approaches 0 as the number of observations of X tends to infinity.

Thus, in studying continuous random variables X, we are interested in the probability that X lies in an interval (a line segment) rather than in the probability that X equals some point. These probabilities give the probability distribution of X. Since $P(X = x) = 0$ for any real number x, when X is a continuous random variable, it follows that

$$P(a < X < b) = P(a \leq X < b) = P(a < X \leq b)$$
$$= P(a \leq X \leq b).$$

Thus, in dealing with continuous random variables, it does not matter whether any inequality is strict or not. The reader should understand that these statements do *not* hold for discrete random variables.

Example 6.2   Raindrops

Consider a square (12 inches by 12 inches), marked out on a horizontal slab of concrete placed outdoors, which is watched until hit by a raindrop. If the square is marked out in a coordinate system with origin at the lower left-hand corner, then we can define (X, Y) to be the coordinates of the point on which the first raindrop falls. Both X and Y are continuous random variables with the same sample spaces, namely, all real numbers between 0 and 12. We can ask many questions concerning the probability distribution of X or of Y or of (X, Y). For example, what is $P[(X, Y)$ is in the upper right-hand quarter of the square]? One possible answer is $\frac{1}{4}$. Why? What assumption is involved? Similarly we can compute, using the same assumption that $P[(X, Y)$ is in a rectangle of area s square inches contained in the square] $= s/144$, $P(0 \le X \le 6) = \frac{1}{2}$, $P(3 \le Y \le 4) = \frac{1}{12}$, $P[(X, Y) = (x, y)] = 0$, $P(X = x) = 0$, $P(Y = y) = 0$, etc.

Both of the above examples depend on randomness. More precisely, the underlying probability models for the random variable in Examples 6.1 and 6.2 are extensions to the line and to the plane of the distribution of Example 2.12 (finding a defective machine), which assigned equal probability to each point in the sample space. Such distributions, whether on a finite set of points, a finite line segment, or a finite rectangle in the plane, are known for obvious reasons as *uniform* distributions. The uniform distribution on a finite line segment assigns to subintervals of this line segment probabilities proportional to the subinterval's length. The uniform distribution on a finite rectangle assigns to subrectangles of the finite rectangle probabilities proportional to the subrectangle's area. The uniform distribution is perhaps the simplest of continuous probability distributions, but a far more important continuous probability model for most practical purposes is illustrated by the following example.

Example 6.3   Bus arrivals

In Example 6.1, we assumed that the bus arrived punctually at its terminal. In real life the bus usually arrives a little early or a little late. If the deviations from the scheduled time of arrival should be recorded for many occasions, it would be the case that very few deviations would

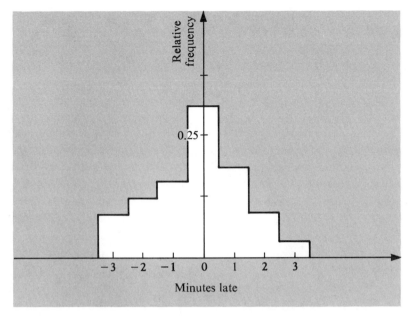

FIGURE 6.1 *A histogram for Example* 6.1.

be exactly 0 but that deviations near 0 would occur more frequently, while large deviations would occur infrequently. If these observations were grouped and graphed as a histogram, the resulting graph might look like Figure 6.1. If the number of observations were increased and the class width were decreased, the histogram might very well approach a smooth bell-shaped curve, symmetrical about 0.

Many mathematical curves have this shape. However, one family in particular has been found to fit observed data very well in many different fields. This is the normal family of curves, represented by the formula

$$f(x) = \frac{1}{\sigma\sqrt{2\pi}} e^{-(x-\mu)^2/2\sigma^2},$$

where e is the base of natural logarithms. To five-decimal accuracy, $e = 2.71828$, though it will be seen that this value is rarely needed. The graph of a typical member of the normal family of curves is shown in Figure 6.2.

Assigning particular values to μ and σ gives particular members of the family; i.e., μ and σ are parameters for the normal family as p and n were for the binomial family. For Example 6.3 (bus arrivals), μ might be 0 while σ might be 1 or 2 minutes.

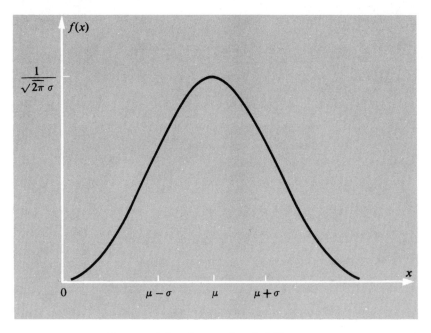

FIGURE 6.2 *A normal probability curve.*

Expectation and Variance for Continuous Random Variables

The formulas given for expectation and variance in Chapter 2 involved summations. These sums must, for continuous random variables, be replaced by integrals. While formal manipulation of the integrals is of considerable importance in mathematical statistics courses dealing with continuous random variables, it will be sufficient here to use verbal definitions. The mean μ of a continuous random variable X, also denoted $E(X)$, is a weighted (integral) average of all points in the sample space. Similarly, the variance $V(X)$ is a weighted (integral) average of all squared deviations of points in the sample space from μ or $E(X)$.

Theorems 2.1, 2.2, 2.3, 5.1, and 5.2 were stated for expectations and variances defined in terms of discrete random variables. That they still hold with the extended definition is not immediately obvious. In fact, new proofs are necessary, though in advanced probability it is usual to give a definition of expectation and variance that applies to both types of probability models, so that the proofs may be condensed. All of the theorems stated above hold for both discrete and continuous random variables, provided the expectations and variances are defined. It is useful to restate Theorems 2.1 and 2.3 for n variables rather than for two.

THEOREM 6.1 *If X_1, X_2, ..., X_n are random variables for which $E(X_1)$, $E(X_2)$, ..., $E(X_n)$ are defined, and $a_1, a_2, ..., a_n$ are constants, then*

$$E\left(\sum_{i=1}^{n} a_i X_i\right) = \sum_{i=1}^{n} a_i E(X_i).$$

THEOREM 6.2 *If X_1, X_2, ..., X_n are* independent *random variables for which $V(X_1)$, $V(X_2)$, ..., $V(X_n)$ are defined, and $a_1, a_2, ..., a_n$ are constants, then*

$$V\left(\sum_{i=1}^{n} a_i X_i\right) = \sum_{i=1}^{n} a_i^2 V(X_i).$$

If we were to set up probability models for several of the random variables considered in Chapter 5, it is likely that we would prefer to consider them as continuous random variables, e.g., the weights of Problems 5.5 and 5.18, and the precipitation of Problem 5.13, and the lengths of Problems 5.16. In fact, even for the I.Q.'s of Example 5.3 and the scores of Problem 5.22, which are obviously discrete random variables, it is often convenient and simplest to build a continuous probability model. All such continuous models are certainly abstractions of real life. Theorems 6.1 and 6.2 show that insofar as the calculation of expectations and variances of linear combinations of random variables is concerned, there is no need to worry as to whether the underlying probability models are discrete or continuous. However, for most problems we almost certainly will need to know or assume something more about the probability model than just its mean and variance. We now return to properties of the normal probability model introduced by Example 6.3.

Normal Probability Distributions

A *normal random variable* X is one whose sample space is the whole real line, and for which $P(a < X < b)$ is obtained by finding the area under some specified member of the family of normal curves and above the line segment ab placed on the horizontal axis (see Figure 6.3).

Since a member of the normal family of curves is specified by two parameters μ and σ, the probability distribution of a normal random variable is specified by the same two parameters. We will speak, interchangeably, of a *normal random variable*, a *normal probability distribution*, a *normal population*, the *probability distribution determined by a normal curve*, or a *normally distributed random variable*.

The parameters of the family of normal distributions have been

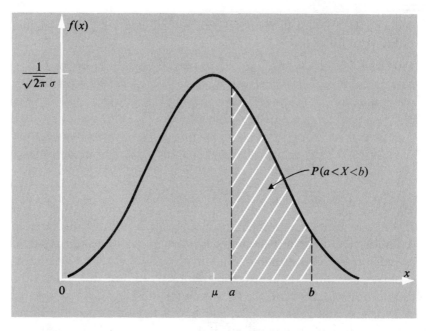

FIGURE 6.3   *The probability that a normal random variable takes on a value in the line segment ab.*

assigned the symbols μ and σ, which have been used, in general, for expectation and standard deviation. By this notation we have anticipated the result that μ is indeed the expectation, or mean, of a normal random variable and also that σ is its standard deviation. The fact that a normal distribution is completely characterized by its mean μ and its standard deviation σ (or variance σ^2) is one reason why the sample mean $\bar{X}$ and the sample standard deviation s have been used so extensively in descriptive statistics. If we can assume that a normal probability model is an appropriate one for the distribution of a random variable, and if we have a sample mean $\bar{X}$ and sample variance s^2, we have unbiased estimates of μ and σ^2, and thus we can make useful estimates about any desired aspect of the distribution.

The family of normal distributions has many important and useful properties, some of which are listed below.

1. If X is normally distributed with mean μ and standard deviation σ, then $Z = (X - \mu)/\sigma$ is *normally* distributed with mean 0 and standard deviation 1. The symbol Z, without an asterisk, will be reserved to represent the *standard normal random variable*.

2. The normal distribution is symmetrical about the mean; i.e., $P(X < \mu - x) = P(X > \mu + x)$; thus, $P(Z < 0) = P(Z > 0) = \frac{1}{2}$.

3. If $X_1, X_2, \ldots, X_n$ are normally distributed and independent, then any linear function of these X's is normally distributed; i.e., for any constants $a_1, a_2, \ldots, a_n$, $\sum_{i=1}^{n} a_i X_i$ is normally distributed.

Combining the results of Theorems 6.1 and 6.2 and property (3), we have

THEOREM 6.3 *If $X_1, X_2, \ldots, X_n$ are normally distributed, independent, random variables, then $\sum_{i=1}^{n} a_i X_i$ is also normally distributed with expectation $\sum_{i=1}^{n} a_i E(X_i)$ and variance $\sum_{i=1}^{n} a_i^2 V(X_i)$. In particular, if the X's have the same expectation μ and variance σ^2, then $\bar{X} = (1/n)(\sum_{i=1}^{n} X_i)$ is normally distributed with expectation μ and variance σ^2/n.*

The last statement in Theorem 6.3 gives the exact sampling distribution of $\bar{X}$ when the random sample is on a normal random variable X with mean μ and variance σ^2. This is one example in which the sampling distribution of $\bar{X}$ belongs to the same family of distributions as the original random variable X does.

Many tables exist that enable us to obtain normal probabilities. In Table A2.3 $P(0 < Z < z)$ is tabulated, where Z is the standard normal random variable. Thus,

$$P(-1 \leq Z \leq 0) = P(0 \leq Z \leq 1) \quad \text{from property (2)}$$
$$= 0.34.$$
$$P(Z > 1.96) = 0.5 - P(0 \leq Z \leq 1.96)$$
$$= 0.5 - 0.475$$
$$= 0.025.$$

Using Table A2.3 and properties (1) and (2) of the normal distribution, we can evaluate probabilities such as $P(X \leq x)$ where X is a normal random variable with known mean μ and known standard deviation σ as shown in Examples 6.3 to 6.5.

Example 6.3 (continued)

If it is known that deviations of the arrival time of the bus from the scheduled time are normally distributed with mean 0 and standard deviation two minutes, then it is possible to compute the probability that its arrival time deviation will fall in any specified interval. For example, what is the probability it will arrive after the scheduled time of arrival but not more than one minute late?

Solution: Let X be the bus-arrival-time deviation, i.e., the difference between the arrival time and the scheduled time. For convenience, the minus sign will be attached to deviations when the bus arrives ahead of time. This problem asks for the probability that X falls between 0 and 1, in symbols $P(0 \leq X \leq 1)$. To use Table A2.3, we must convert X to Z; i.e., we write $Z = (X - \mu)/\sigma$, or for this example $Z = (X - 0)/2$; now $(0 \leq X \leq 1)$ is equivalent to

$$\left(\frac{0}{2} \leq \frac{X}{2} \leq \frac{1}{2}\right) \quad \text{or} \quad \left(0 \leq Z \leq \frac{1}{2}\right),$$

so

$$P(0 \leq X \leq 1) = P(0 \leq Z \leq \tfrac{1}{2}),$$

and the latter probability is found in Table A2.3 as 0.1915. That is, the probability that the bus arrives late but not later than one minute behind schedule is 0.19.

Example 6.4   Heights of men

The Army has a vast quantity of data on male measurements. From such data they have determined the frequency distribution of heights by area, age, race, etc. If males, aged 18, inducted in California are assumed to be normally distributed with mean height 69 in. and standard deviation 2.8 in., what proportion of these men fall below 63 in. in height? what proportion above 72 in.?

Solution: What is being asked for is the proportion of the population below 63 in., or, in probability terms, $P(X < 63)$, where X is the height of a man chosen at random from the specified population. If we assume a normal distribution, this probability is computed by converting X to a standard normal variable by the operations of subtracting out the mean and dividing by the standard deviation. Thus,

$$P(X < 63) = P\left(\frac{X - \mu}{\sigma} < \frac{63 - 69}{2.8}\right)$$

$$= P(Z < -2.14)$$

$$= P(Z > +2.14) \quad \text{by symmetry of the normal distribution}$$

$$= 0.5 - P(0 \leq Z \leq 2.14)$$

$$= 0.5 - 0.4838$$

$$= 0.0162.$$

The proportion falling below 63 in. is 0.0162, i.e., 162 in 10,000. Similarly,

$$P(X > 72) = P\left(\frac{X - \mu}{\sigma} \geq \frac{72 - 69}{2.8}\right)$$

$$= P(Z \geq 1.07)$$

$$= 0.5 - P(0 \leq Z \leq 1.07)$$

$$= 0.5 - 0.3577$$

$$= 0.1423.$$

The proportion falling above 72 in. is 0.1423, i.e., 1,423 in 10,000. [*Note:* The solution to Example 6.4 (heights of men) depends very strongly on the assumption of normality of the population. If nothing were assumed as to the form of the distribution, then it would be necessary to use Theorem 2.2. For example,

$$P(X \leq 63) = P\left(\frac{X - \mu}{\sigma} \leq -2.14\right).$$

Now

$$P\left(\left|\frac{X - \mu}{\sigma}\right| \leq 2.14\right) > 1 - \frac{1}{(2.14)^2} \qquad \text{by Theorem 2.2}$$

$$> 1 - 0.218$$

$$> 0.782,$$

and

$$P\left(\frac{X - \mu}{\sigma} \leq -2.14\right) < P\left(\left|\frac{X - \mu}{\sigma}\right| \geq 2.14\right) < 1 - 0.782 = 0.218.$$

In words, what is being said is that the probability in the center (between -2.14 and $+2.14$) exceeds 0.782. Therefore, the probability in both tails (and hence certainly in one tail) is *less than* $1 - 0.782$, i.e. 0.218. In fact, in this example, the upper bound of 0.218 given by Chebyshev's inequality (Theorem 2.2) compares badly with the probability 0.0162, assuming normality. Chebyshev's inequality is important in the theory of probability but is rarely useful in applied problems.]

Example 6.5   Salmon lengths

In an experiment to determine the effect of gillnets of different meshes on a salmon population, it is necessary first to find the proportion of the population in different size classes. Use the fact that the mean length of these salmon is 645 mm with a standard deviation of 25.2 mm (determined from several thousand measurements), and assume that their lengths are normally distributed. Find the expected proportion in each of the size classes: 550 to 575; 575 to 600; 600 to 625; . . . ; 725 to 750.

Solution: Let X = length in mm of a salmon chosen at random from this population. $E(X) = \mu = 645$; S.D.$(X) = 25.2$.

$$P(550 < X \le 575) = P\left(\frac{550 - 645}{25.2} < \frac{X - \mu}{\sigma} \le \frac{575 - 645}{25.2}\right).$$

(As usual, the first step is to get a standard normal variable by subtracting the mean and dividing by the standard deviation.)

$$
\begin{aligned}
P(550 < X \le 575) &= P\left(\frac{-95}{25.2} < Z \le \frac{-70}{25.2}\right) \\
&= P(-3.77 < Z \le -2.78) \\
&= P(2.78 < Z \le 3.77) \\
&= 0.4999 - 0.4973 \\
&= 0.0026.
\end{aligned}
$$

Then this procedure is repeated for the next class interval.

$$
\begin{aligned}
P(575 < X \le 600) &= P\left(\frac{575 - 645}{25.2} < \frac{X - \mu}{\sigma} \le \frac{600 - 645}{25.2}\right) \\
&= P\left(\frac{-70}{25.2} < Z \le \frac{-45}{25.2}\right) \\
&= P(1.78 < Z \le 2.78) \\
&= 0.4973 - 0.4625 \\
&= 0.0348.
\end{aligned}
$$

It is apparent that this can be simplified.

Class boundary

c	$c - \mu$	$(c - \mu)/\sigma$	$P[(c - \mu)/0 < Z < 0]$
550	-95	-3.77	0.4999
575	-70	-2.78	0.4973
600	-45	-1.78	0.4625
625	-20	-0.79	0.2852

c	$c - \mu$	$(c - \mu)/\sigma$	$P[0 < Z < (c - \mu)/\sigma]$
650	5	0.20	0.0793
675	30	1.19	0.3830
700	55	2.18	0.4854
725	80	3.17	0.4992
750	105	4.17	0.5000

Finally, the various probabilities are obtained by successive subtraction except for the interval that straddles the mean. Here, the two probabilities are added to get the total $P(625 < X \leq 650) = 0.3645$. Hence we finally have

Class interval	Probability or expected proportion
550–575	0.0026
575–600	0.0348
600–625	0.1773
625–650	0.3645
650–675	0.3037
675–700	0.1024
700–725	0.0138
725–750	0.0008

Examples 6.4 and 6.5 illustrate how a table of probabilities for the standard normal probability distribution can be used to obtain probabilities for arbitrary normal random variables. Examples 6.6 and 6.7 illustrate how Table A2.3 and Theorem 6.3 can be used to calculate probabilities for sums and averages of independent, normally distributed random variables.

Example 6.6   Truck overloading

The van of a truck can hold 30 containers (identical in size). If the weight of a container is assumed to be a normal random variable with mean 125 lb and standard deviation 15 lb, what is the probability that 30 containers will overload the truck if it can safely carry 4,000 lb?

Solution: Let X_i be the weight of container i $(i = 1, 2, \ldots, 30)$. We assume these random variables are normal and *independent*. Then, by Theorem 6.3, $S = X_1 + X_2 + \cdots + X_{30}$ is a normal random variable with mean 3,750 lb and standard deviation $15\sqrt{30}$ lb. The required probability is then

$$P(S > 4,000) = P\left(\frac{S - 3,750}{15\sqrt{30}} > \frac{250}{15\sqrt{30}}\right)$$
$$= P(Z > 3.04)$$
$$= 0.0012.$$

The probability of overloading is 0.0012 or, alternatively, the truck will be overloaded 12 times in every 10,000 on the average.

Note: The student should be alert to see that the standard deviation of S in Example 6.7 is obtained in the following way: The variance of each X_i is 15^2. Thus by Theorem 6.3 the variance of S is $15^2 \cdot 30$. Then the standard deviation of S is $15\sqrt{30}$ lb.

**Example 6.7 Los Angeles schoolchildren's I.Q.'s
(continued)**

Consider the I.Q.'s of the children discussed in Example 3.3. If we assume that the I.Q. of a Los Angeles schoolchild chosen at random from the population of all Los Angeles schoolchildren is a normal random variable with mean 100 and variance 144, what is the probability that a class of 20 will have an average I.Q. of at least 105?

Solution: Let X_i be the I.Q. of individual i $(i = 1, 2, \ldots, 20)$ in the class. We assume that these random variables are normal and *independent*. Then, by Theorem 6.3, $\bar{X} = \frac{1}{20}\sum_{i=1}^{20} X_i$ is a normal random variable with mean 100 and variance $144/20 = 7.2$ or standard deviation $\sqrt{7.2}$. The required probability is

$$P(\bar{X} = 105) = P\left(\frac{\bar{X} - 100}{\sqrt{7.2}} \geq \frac{105 - 100}{\sqrt{7.2}}\right)$$
$$= P(Z \geq 1.87) = 0.5 - P(0 \leq Z \leq 1.87)$$
$$= 0.5 - 0.4693 = 0.0307.$$

If the members of this particular class are indeed a random sample from all Los Angeles schoolchildren, then the class average I.Q. has probability 0.0307 of being at least 105.

The alert reader will have observed that we are using a probability model with a continuous random variable for finite populations, e.g., heights of Army inductees, lengths of salmon, etc. Necessarily then, the model cannot be a faithful representation of the real-life situation. Even worse, the function given by the equation

$$f(x) = \frac{1}{\sqrt{2\pi}\,\sigma}\, e^{-(x-\mu)^2/2\sigma^2}$$

takes on values from $-\infty$ to $+\infty$. Does this mean the model assigns positive probabilities to heights of less than *minus* four feet, to bus delays of more than 14,167 years, etc.? The answer is *yes* but the probabilities assigned are so small that they are zero to four decimal places or more and can be ignored in practice. We must emphasize that the normal probability model is an abstraction; no observations in nature have been found that fit it *exactly*, yet many random variables turn up in nature that are approximately normally distributed, and the approximation is adequate for many practical purposes.

Why this should be so is explained at least in part by a mathematical theorem, called the Central Limit Theorem. More precisely, one form of this theorem is:

THEOREM 6.4 *If $X_1, X_2, \ldots, X_n$ are independent random variables having a common probability distribution, a common mean μ, and a common variance σ^2, then the probability distribution of $(\bar{X} - \mu)/(\sigma/\sqrt{n})$ is arbitrarily close to that of a standard normal random variable for sufficiently large n.*

In fact, even if the random variables have different distributions with different means and variances, their sum or mean may be approximately normally distributed, though some slight additional restrictions are now needed. Many variables we observe in nature, e.g., the height of an individual, the length of a fish, etc., are the resultant of many factors, e.g., heredity, environment, etc. If the resultant observation is in some manner a linear combination of many independent variables, then it is reasonable to expect it to be approximately normally distributed.

The mathematical theorem does not say how large "sufficiently large" is and it cannot, for the closeness of the probability distribution of $\bar{X}$ to a normal probability distribution for a specified sample size n depends on the parent distributions, i.e., the distributions of the components $X_1, X_2, \ldots, X_n$. If the X's have distributions which are symmetrical and bell-shaped, then means of samples of size 2 or 3 may already be approximated by a normal distribution.

Normal random variables are sometimes generated by computers by averaging a number of uniform random variables and in general an average of eight has been found to be satisfactory. This says that probability statements about means of random samples of size 8 from a uniform probability distribution are adequately approximated by the normal distribution. While many sampling experiments have been done to explore this problem for various distributions, no hard and fast rule can be given, since it is certainly possible to create distributions for $X_1, X_2, \ldots, X_n$ such that the distribution of $\bar{X}$ is far from normal even for samples of several hundred. Such pathological distributions appear rarely in nature, leading many experimenters to believe that every random variable they encounter is normal. This is not so. See Problem 6.4. We suggest that students be aware of the assumptions made in the examples and problems in Chapters 6 to 12, but be prepared to accept them for a while. Methods of testing the assumption of normality and methods of avoiding the assumption are given later.

An Application of the Central Limit Theorem to the Binomial Random Variable

As a practical example of how the Central Limit Theorem works, we apply it to the binomial random variable. We saw, in Example 5.1, that the binomial random variable T, with parameters n and p, can be written as

$$T = X_1 + X_2 + \cdots + X_n,$$

where X_i is 1 or 0 according as the ith trial results in success or failure. Since $X_1, X_2, \ldots, X_n$ each have expected value p and variance $p(1 - p)$ and are independent, then $(\bar{X} - p)/\sqrt{p(1 - p)/n} = (T - np)/\sqrt{np(1 - p)}$ has for sufficiently large n a distribution arbitrarily close to that of the standard normal distribution. In practice, this mathematical limit theorem is used as an approximate method for obtaining binomial probabilities. For example, to compute $P(4 \leq T \leq 10)$, given that T is a binomial random variable with parameters $n = 20$, $p = \frac{1}{2}$, we have

$$P(4 \leq T \leq 10) = P\left(\frac{4 - 10}{\sqrt{5}} \leq \frac{T - 10}{\sqrt{5}} \leq \frac{10 - 10}{\sqrt{5}}\right)$$

$$\doteq P(-2.69 \leq Z \leq 0) = 0.4965.$$

The exact probability is 0.587 (see Table A2.1).

EXERCISE

Use the normal approximation to find the following binomial probabilities approximately.

$$P(T \geq 11 | n = 20, p = 0.4),$$
$$P(T \leq 5 | n = 40, p = 0.36),$$
$$P(T \geq 30 | n = 36, p = 0.75),$$
$$P(4 \leq T \leq 16 | n = 30, p = 0.4).$$

[*Note:* There is a simple way to improve on this approximation, which can be motivated by asking for the normal approximation to $P(T = 4 | T$ is binomial with $n = 20$, $p = \frac{1}{2})$.

This is seemingly impossible until it is recognized that we are approximating the areas on a histogram of binomial probabilities by areas under the normal curve. The probability that $X = 4$ is represented geometrically by the rectangle on the base AB in Figure 6.4, i.e., by the rectangle erected on $(3\frac{1}{2}, 4\frac{1}{2})$. This area can be approximated by the area $ABCD$, i.e., by the normal probability $P(3\frac{1}{2} \leq X \leq 4\frac{1}{2})$, which is quite well defined and in fact equals

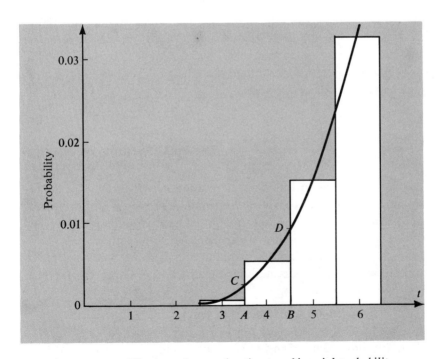

FIGURE 6.4   *The normal approximation to a binomial probability.*

$$P\left(\frac{3.5 - 10}{\sqrt{5}} \le Z \le \frac{4.5 - 10}{\sqrt{5}}\right) = P(-2.91 \le Z \le -2.46) = 0.0051.$$

More generally, $P(4 \le T \le 10)$ is represented by the rectangles on the base (3.5 to 10.5) so that a better approximation to $P(4 \le T \le 10)$ is

$$P\left(\frac{3.5 - 10}{\sqrt{5}} \le Z \le \frac{10.5 - 10}{\sqrt{5}}\right) = P(-2.91 \le Z \le 0.224) = 0.5853.$$

As a general rule, to improve the normal approximation for binomial probabilities, first change all inequalities into the form $\le$ or $\ge$; reduce integers at the lower end of the inequality by $\frac{1}{2}$ and increase those at the upper end by $\frac{1}{2}$; convert to standard random variables and use Table A2.3.

Use Table A2.1 to check that the exact probabilities are $P(T = 4) = 0.005$ and $P(4 \le T \le 10) = 0.587$, thus verifying the accuracy of the approximation.]

By using Theorem 6.4, Examples 6.6 and 6.7 can be done without the assumption of normality. If, in these examples, $X_1, \ldots, X_n$ ($n = 30$ and 20) are merely assumed to be independent and have the same probability distribution, then $(S - 30 \cdot 125)/15\sqrt{30} = (\bar{X} - 125)/(15/\sqrt{30})$ and $(\bar{X} - 100)/(12/\sqrt{20})$ are approximately normally distributed, so that 0.0012 in Example 6.6 and 0.0307 in Example 6.7 are the approximate probabilities by Theorem 6.4, even under these weaker assumptions.

The Poisson Approximation to Binomial Probabilities

It is convenient to introduce here another approximation for the binomial random variable when p is small. The reason for introducing another approximation is that the normal approximation is best when p is near $\frac{1}{2}$. When p is near 0, the normal approximation is not so accurate as the following approximation, called the Poisson approximation, after the French mathematician who developed the method.

If p is small, then

$$P(T = t) \doteq \frac{e^{-\mu}\mu^t}{t!}, \qquad \text{where } \mu = np.$$

Here are some comparisons of exact binomial probabilities and their Poisson approximations.

n	p	$\mu = np$	t	Exact probability $[n!/n!\,(n-t)!]p^t(1-p)^{n-t}$	Poisson approximation $e^{-np}(np)^t/t!$
40	0.01	0.4	0	0.669	0.670
40	0.01	0.4	1	0.270	0.268
40	0.05	2.0	0	0.129	0.135
40	0.05	2.0	1	0.271	0.271
40	0.05	2.0	2	0.278	0.271
100	0.01	1.0	0	0.366	0.368
100	0.01	1.0	1	0.370	0.368
100	0.01	1.0	2	0.185	0.184
100	0.01	1.0	3	0.061	0.061
250	0.04	1.0	1	0.001	0.001
250	0.04	1.0	2	0.006	0.005

The Poisson approximation is easier to compute directly and easier to tabulate than the binomial formula since it depends only on the expected value $\mu = np$ rather than on n and p separately.†

EXERCISE

Use the Poisson approximation to find approximate probabilities for the following binomial probabilities:

$$P(T = 4 \mid n = 100, p = 0.05),$$
$$P(T = 1 \mid n = 50, p = 0.01),$$
$$P(T \geq 1 \mid n = 100, p = 0.02),$$
$$P(T \leq 4 \mid n = 50, p = 0.04),$$
$$P(1 \leq T \leq 6 \mid n = 100, p = 0.05).$$

Example 6.8 Recessive genes

One percent of a population of Drosophila consists of individuals that are pure recessive with respect to a particular gene. A geneticist has reason to believe that in a particular subpopulation the proportion of such pure recessives will be higher than 0.01. He samples 200 individuals in the subpopulation and finds seven pure recessives; what is the significance probability of this observation?

† A small table is given in Appendix 2 (Table A2.4). A larger table is Molina's *Poisson's Exponential Binomial Limit* (D. Van Nostrand, Inc., Princeton, N.J., 1967).

Solution: The problem can be thought of as a test of

$$H : p = 0.01 \text{ versus } A : p > 0.01,$$

where p = proportion of pure recessives and where it is assumed that T, the number of pure recessives in the sample, is a binomial random variable. We need to calculate $P(T \geq 7 \mid p = 0.01)$. This is easily done by use of the Poisson approximation and Table A2.4; since $np = 2$ from this table, we derive $P(X \geq 7) \doteq 0.004$ and the significance probability is 0.004.

■ Experiments

6.1 Obtain or construct a simple spinner; such a device can be used to obtain realizations of a uniform and other random variables. For example, after each random spin one can measure the angle from the vertical line drawn from the center to the base of the spinner (so that the angle lies between 0 degrees and 360 degrees). This generates a random variable with a uniform distribution on the line segment (0, 360). Repeat this experiment 40 times: for simplicity record the quadrant in which the spinner falls; compare the frequencies of occurrence in each quadrant with that expected under the uniform distribution model.

6.2 The spinner device of Experiment 6.1 can be used to construct a quite different random variable. After the spinner comes to a stop, draw a line extending it in the downward direction until the line extension intersects the x axis (the horizontal line tangent to the base of the spinner). Denote the point of intersection as A and the signed distance OA (see Figure 6.5) by X, which is clearly a random variable. What happens to the size of X if the spinner stops in a position nearly parallel to the x axis?

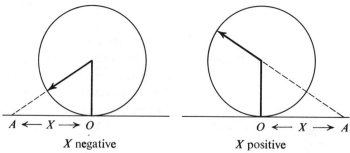

$A \longleftarrow X \longrightarrow O$ $O \longleftarrow X \longrightarrow A$

X negative X positive

FIGURE 6.5 *An example of a Cauchy random variable.*

If each member of the class obtains ten realizations of this random variable X, the total class results can be recorded in a sample frequency distribution and plotted as a histogram. It is also worthwhile to fit a normal distribution to this set of observations. It should be observed that the distribution generated has "too many" large positive and large negative values of X. This distribution is known as the Cauchy distribution and is famous in mathematical statistics. The curve from which the probabilities can be derived is superficially quite similar to the normal curve, but from a statistical and probabilistic point of view the Cauchy and normal family are very different.

6.3   Each member of the class should draw five sets of random numbers from Table A2.2, each set consisting of four two-place decimal fractions; for each set calculate $\bar{X}$; each member of the class thus obtains five realizations of an approximately normal random variable. Again it is useful to arrange the totality of all class observations in a sample frequency distribution, plot a histogram, and fit a normal distribution to the empirically derived data. This experiment is an empirical study of the Central Limit Theorem, and relates to the results stated above concerning one of the methods used by computers to obtain random normal variables. It is also worthwhile in this experiment to compare the expected and observed means and variances of the realized $\bar{X}$'s. Since the basic X's are uniform on the points 0.00, 0.01, ..., 0.99, they have mean 0.495 and variance 0.833. (Check this and note their similarity to the mean and variance of a continuous uniform random variable on $(0, 1)$, given in Problem 6.16.) Thus the $\bar{X}$'s have mean 0.495 and variance 0.208, according to the theoretical model.

Table A2.5 shows a small table of standard normal random variables (also called random normal deviates or Gaussian deviates). One of the largest tables of this type is found in the reference given in Experiment 4.1. However, in most current simulation studies involving normal random variables, these are obtained by the computer itself using uniform random variables as above or by other methods, rather than from tables. These tables will be used in simulation experiments in the next chapter.

6.4   *Poisson approximation.* Sample 100 random two-digit numbers in Table A2.2; record as a failure any number drawn that is included in 00, 01, 02, 03, or 04. Denote by T the number of failures. This is a realization of the random variable of Problem 6.30 (rocket failure). Repeat this experiment a sufficient number of times so that at least

100 realizations of T are available from the class as a whole. Compare the observed frequency of the event $(T \leq 4)$ with the approximate probability computed in Problem 6.30; do the same for the event $(T \leq 10)$.

■ **Problems**

6.1 On the basis of information given by shoe manufacturers, Army Ordnance ordered shoes for the Women's Army Corps on the assumption that women's shoe sizes are normally distributed with mean 5.05 and standard deviation 1.5. How many shoes of sizes $8\frac{1}{2}$ and 5 were ordered in the first lot of 100,000? (Observe that shoe size $8\frac{1}{2}$ actually means $8\frac{1}{4}$ to $8\frac{3}{4}$ and similarly shoe size 5 means $4\frac{3}{4}$ to $5\frac{1}{4}$.)

6.2 The acceptance limits for the diameter of ball bearings from a particular production process are 0.495 cm and 0.505 cm. If the machine is producing ball bearings according to a normal distribution with mean 0.500 cm and S.D. 0.002 cm, what proportion of its production is acceptable? What is the change in this proportion if the standard deviation increases to 0.005 cm? What is the proportion accepted if the standard deviation is 0.002 cm but the mean is 0.502 cm?

6.3 High school grade point averages in the State of Washington have a mean of 2.80 with a standard deviation of 0.24. A college that has up to now required high school students to have a 2.20 grade point average to enter is considering changing the requirements to a 2.50 grade point average. What will be the change in the proportion of high school graduates eligible to enter the college if grade point averages are assumed to follow a normal distribution?

6.4 Many random variables have an approximate normal distribution, but not all. Of the following random variables, which do you think would not even be approximately normally distributed and why? For those indicated to have a nonnormal distribution, sketch roughly the form the distribution might have: (a) incomes of families in the U.S.A.; (b) weights of men; (c) waiting times for a bus; (d) ages of employees of a large company; (e) scores on an all-state high school achievement test; (f) diameters of poplar leaves.

6.5 Assume that the length of the time period from conception to birth in humans follows a normal distribution, with a mean of 280.5 days and a standard deviation of 8.4 days. In a paternity case being contested in the courts it is proved that the length of time from the alleged time of conception to birth was at least 301 days. Discuss.

6.6 "Grading on the curve" means assigning grades according to the normal distribution. In a test, the mean was 55 with standard deviation 10. If A grades are assigned to 10 percent of the class and if the scores are normally distributed, what is the lower limit of scores that receive an A grade?

*6.7 (a) Let X be the length of time in days after midnight May 31 until a sockeye salmon moves up the Fraser River past a fishery at the mouth. Assume that X is normally distributed with mean 75.5 days and standard deviation 25.1 days. The fishery is to be closed on a date that permits at least 25 percent of the salmon to escape to the spawning area. (Assume that no fish escape through the fishery.) What should the closing date be?

(b) If the closing date were set for midnight, August 15, what proportion would escape?

(c) A late closure may be desirable economically but from some biological point of view the central section of the run should be protected. What should the closure period be so that the middle 25 percent escape?

(d) Suppose that the closure is established in advance of the season to be the period August 10–20; in actuality the run is early with the mean date being August 12 and the actual standard deviation 19.3 days. What is the actual proportion not caught by the fishery?

6.8 In Problem 5.5 the expectation and variance of a load of 200 concrete blocks were derived on the assumption that the blocks had a mean $\mu = 60$ lb and a standard deviation $\sigma = 2$ lb. Assume now that the weights are normally distributed and calculate how often a truck-load exceeds 12,100 lb in weight. The assumption that the individual weights are normally distributed is not really necessary. Why not?

6.9 An elevator has a sign saying its maximum safe load is 1,700 lb. If men's weights are assumed to follow a normal distribution with mean 165 lb and standard deviation 15 lb, what is the probability that ten men whose weights are taken to be independent will overload the elevator?

6.10 In a pilot selection program, candidates are given two tests: one mental, one physical. In both cases the test scores are normally distributed with a mean of 50; for the mental test, the standard deviation of the scores is 10; for the physical test, the standard deviation of the scores is 20. The final evaluation is based on a weighted score:

$$W = \text{physical score plus twice the mental score.}$$

Assume the two test scores are independent. Determine a cutoff point w such that $P(W < w) = 0.25$.

6.11   Professor Prompt has left for his 8:30 class at 8:15 ever since he discovered that his travel time to class is normally distributed with mean 11 minutes, standard deviation 2 minutes. This year he is moving to a new house that is another 10-minutes-drive further from the university. The standard deviation for this additional time is 1 minute. Prompt now leaves at 8:05 and he claims he won't be late as often as formerly. Prove or disprove this claim, noting any assumptions you need to make.

6.12   Men in the United States have a mean weight of 165 lb with a standard deviation of 15 lb.

(a) Find the average weight and the standard deviation of a group of 200 men on an airplane.

(b) Suppose that the group is made up of 120 men, 80 women. (Women have a mean weight of 120 lb and a standard deviation of 12 lb.) What is the average weight and standard deviation of the plane's passenger load?

6.13   Readings of barometric pressure have a standard deviation (standard error) of 0.1 millibar. What is the standard deviation (standard error) of the difference of two independent barometric pressures? How often will the difference of two readings exceed 0.5 millibars, assuming that the two readings are normally distributed?

6.14   Errors in reading an instrument or gauge are often normally distributed with mean zero. A check of pressure gauge readings show that 5 percent of the readings are in error by 1 pound or more. Calculate the standard deviation of the readings and hence determine the proportion of readings that are correct to within one-half pound of pressure.

6.15   A doctor believes that cases of appendicitis are unaffected by weather and other external factors and in fact are likely to occur randomly at any time of the year. Denote by X the time, in days, from January 1 to the occurrence of an appendicitis case. What is the assumption about the distribution of X? If the assumption is true what fraction of appendicitis cases would you expect to occur in July, August, and up to September 11? Would you be surprised if, of 100 cases, 37 occurred in a randomly selected half of the year? (Compute a significance probability.)

*6.16 In Example 6.1 (catching a bus) it was suggested that waiting times were uniformly distributed on the interval (0, 20) minutes. If so, the expected waiting time is 10 minutes. It can also be shown that the variance of waiting times is $20^2/12$. (In general, a uniform random variable on the line segment (a, b) has mean $(a + b)/2$ and variance $(b - a)^2/12$.) What is the expected average waiting time of ten people? Compare the variance of the average waiting time for the following two cases: (a) All ten arrivals are independent. (b) There are two groups of five people; all people in each group wait exactly the same time but the arrivals of the two groups are independent.

6.17 When a group of Douglas fir seedlings were planted, their average height was 1.5 ft with a standard deviation of 2 in. During the next 12 years their *annual* growth varied randomly with a mean each year of 1 ft and a standard deviation of 1 in. Assume all random variables are normally distributed and independent.

(a) At the end of this 12-year period, what proportion of the trees has a height exceeding 13.5 ft?
(b) What are the heights of the central 50 percent of the population?

6.18 A number of random temperature measurements are made at the surface and bottom of a body of water. The data are summarized in the following table:

	Number of observations	Mean temperature	Standard deviation
Surface	100	12°C	2°C
Bottom	50	5°C	1°C

Define the mean temperature gradient G as follows:

$$G = \frac{\text{Mean surface temperature} - \text{Mean bottom temperature}}{\text{Average depth}}.$$

(a) Estimate G for average depth of 28 ft.
(b) Estimate the standard error of your estimate of G.

6.19   An insect passes through two stages between egg and adult. Assume that the lengths of time in these stages are independent and normally distributed with means 2 days and 4 days, standard deviations 0.5 and 1.2 days. What length of time will be required so that one may assert that 95 percent of the insects from a given hatch have reached maturity?

6.20   A machine performs three operations in sequence. Let T_1, T_2, T_3 be the times required for these three operations. Let $S = T_1 + T_2 + T_3$; i.e., S is the sum of the times of the three operations. If T_1, T_2, T_3 are assumed to be independently normally distributed with means 10, 15, and 20 seconds respectively and standard deviations 1, 2, and 2 respectively, find the value s such that $P(S \le s) = 0.99$.

6.21   The index of runoff in a river system has been observed to be related to the precipitation in the river's drainage area for the past three years in the following manner:

$$Y = 3(0.7X_1 + 0.2X_2 + 0.1X_3),$$

where

X_1 = yearly precipitation in the area in the current year,
X_2 = yearly precipitation in the area in the previous year,
X_3 = yearly precipitation in the area in the year two years previous,
Y = index of runoff.

If the X's are normal with mean 33.3 and standard deviation 5.5, what is the probability that the index of runoff will fall below 90? Assume also that the amounts of precipitation in different years are independent.

*6.22**   Using the data from Example 6.5 (salmon lengths), what bound could be placed on the proportion differing from the mean by more than 50 mm, if only Theorem 2.2 is used (i.e., normality is not assumed)? Compare this with the exact probability derived assuming normality.

6.23   Verify the probability statement in Problem 5.9 under the assumption that the G.P.A.'s of students at the high school are normally distributed.

6.24   In a salmon hatchery it is the aim of the superintendent to release only those lots of fish that have mean weight above 30 grams. To achieve this, samples of size 10 are taken from the lot and weighed.

If the sample 10 have a total weight exceeding 300 grams, the lot of fish is released; otherwise it is retained.

(a) How often will this decision rule result in release of a lot with $\mu = 29.0$, $\sigma = 2$?

(b) How often will a lot be retained with $\mu = 31.0$, $\sigma = 2$?

(c) What assumption did you make about salmon weights to answer parts (a) and (b)?

*6.25 In Problem 3.24 the technique of bioassay was outlined. Recall that in a bioassay experiment animals are tested at different dosage levels. In one model for these experiments it is suggested that the probability of a response at level x is equal to the proportion of animals whose tolerance X (which is a random variable) is less than x. If tolerances X are normally distributed with mean 2.5 and standard deviation 1.2, find the probability of response to dosage levels 1, 2, 3, and 4.

6.26 A factory manufactures machine parts that are expected to have a tolerance (error) of no more than 0.1 in. Its test program consists of selecting ten parts from each large lot and measuring the tolerance. If all ten meet the standard the lot is passed. Suppose that in fact the parts in the lot are normally distributed with a mean error of 0 but a standard deviation of 0.1 in. What proportion of the parts has an error exceeding 0.1 in.? Hence calculate the probability that a lot is passed.

6.27 If, in Example 4.3 (extrasensory perception), the subject is asked to select the correct color 100 times, what is the (approximate) probability that he will make 60 or more correct choices if he is guessing, i.e., $p = \frac{1}{2}$? What is the (approximate) significance probability of the observation 60? Would you reject $H : p = \frac{1}{2}$ versus $A : p > \frac{1}{2}$ at the 5 percent level if the subject made 60 correct choices?

6.28 If, in Example 4.8 (color preference in babies), the choice of balls was offered to a tested baby 50 times, what is the (approximate) probability that 28 or more times the baby chose a red ball if there is no color preference, i.e., $p = \frac{1}{2}$? Using the normal approximation, determine the significance probability of the observation $T = 28$, recalling that in this example we are testing $H : p = \frac{1}{2}$ against $A : p \neq \frac{1}{2}$.

*6.29 Construct the test rule and the O.C. curve for Problem 6.28.

6.30 A rocket has probability $p = 0.05$ of failing to fire success-fully. Use the Poisson approximation to find the probability that 4 or fewer rockets will fail to fire successfully in 100 firings. (Assume independence between firings.) Find the probability that 10 or less will fail to fire successfully in 100 firings.

6.31 The rocket manufacturing company of Problem 6.30 now claims to have improved their rockets so that the probability of failure is less than 0.05. What is the hypothesis and alternative for this problem? If 100 rockets are fired and 2 failures are observed, what is the significance probability of this observation? Would you reject the hypothesis and accept the company's claim at the 5 percent level?

6.32 Construct a test rule for testing the hypothesis against the alternative in Problem 6.31 at the 5 percent level.

*6.33 Construct the O.C. curve for the test rule found in Problem 6.32. What is the probability (as read from the O.C. curve) of reject-ing H and accepting the company's claim if, in fact, $p = 0.025$?

6.34 In the past year at the 20 exits and entrances to the Seattle Freeway there have been 145 major accidents. Of these, 24 have occurred at one exit which was previously identified as being poten-tially dangerous. Is the number of accidents at this exit significantly greater than one would expect by chance alone (test at the 5 percent level)? [*Note:* On the basis of previous information, we can set up the hypothesis and the alternative. If no such previous information existed and this exit was selected for testing only because it had the largest number of accidents, the usual test would no longer be valid. If the sample is selected because of an unusual feature in the data, we cannot assume a *random* sampling and use this sample for an ordinary significance test.]

6.35 Fit a normal curve to the male-salmon-length data of Problem 5.16 (see Example 6.4). Do the same for female-salmon lengths.

6.36 Use the results obtained in Problem 5.23 to fit a normal distribution to the blood pressure data in that problem.

*6.37 Use the Central Limit Theorem and the results of this chapter to obtain an improved 75 percent probability statement for the note following Example 2.17 (roulette).

6.38 A rare blood type occurs in 4 percent of the U.S. population. A survey team goes to Alaska and samples the Indian population there. In a sample of 100 individuals it finds that 8 of them have this blood type. If the percentage occurrence in this population is also 4 percent, what is the probability that an observation will differ from the mean in either direction by at least as much as the given observation?

6.39   A volume V of water contains M bacteria. A subvolume v of the water is sampled and placed in a test tube for culturing. Assume that the probability of the sample's containing any particular bacterium is v/V and that samplings of different bacteria are independent events. What is the probability that the sample of volume v is sterile, i.e., contains no bacteria. Suppose $M = 10,000$, $v/V = 1/10,000$; find an approximate value for this probability.

6.40   A unit volume (one bushel) of Grade 1 wheat has a mean weight of 65.0 lb with a standard deviation of 0.2 lb. If, in the grading process, samples of one bushel are first weighed and rejected for Grade 1 if their weight falls below 64.5 lb, how frequently is a true Grade 1 sample erroneously rejected? Assume that the weight of a unit volume of Grade 1 wheat is a normal random variable.

*6.41   Many decision rules to classify an individual into one of two populations depend on a classification score that, while it may depend on many variables, is usually a random variable. Moreover, the distributions of classification scores for the two populations may overlap so that there are possible errors of misclassification. This may be illustrated by grading wheat, where for simplicity we consider only the variable weight per unit volume. Assume that Grade 2 wheat has a mean weight of 64.2 lb per bushel ($\sigma = 0.30$) and that weights are normally distributed.

(a) Find a weight x such that P(a Grade 1 bushel weighs less than x) = P(a Grade 2 bushel weighs more than x), where Grade 1 wheat is as described in Problem 6.40.

(b) If such an x were the basis of classification between Grades 1 and 2, the probability of classifying Grade 1 wheat as Grade 2 would equal the probability of classifying Grade 2 wheat as Grade 1. How large are the probabilities of misclassification?

(c) What would be the decision cutoff value x be if samples of size 4, i.e., 4 one-bushel samples, were the basis of the decision? How much would this reduce the probabilities of misclassification?

*6.42   In the note following Example 2.17 (roulette), it was shown, by means of Chebyshev's inequality, that $P(-\$120.56 < G < \$110.04) \geq 0.75$, where G was the gain on 100 one-dollar roulette bets. Using the Central Limit Theorem, verify that the probability of the stated event is approximately 0.96. Again, the lower bound given by Chebyshev's inequality is quite poor.

*6.43 In the section on Point Estimation, Chapter 4, it was stated that Theorem 2.2 could be used to find a sample size that would assure any prescribed closeness of $\hat{p} = T/n$ to p with any prescribed probability. To compare the sample sizes required by the use of Theorems 2.2 and 6.4, consider the following:

(a) Use Theorem 2.2 to find the smallest n such that T/n differs from p by no more than 0.05 with probability at least 0.90; i.e., find n so that $P(|T/n - p| > 0.05) \leq 0.10$.

   Hint:

   (i) Show that $p(1 - p) \leq \frac{1}{4}$ for $0 \leq p \leq 1$.
   (ii) Show that if n is chosen as the first integer greater than or equal to $p(1 - p)/[(0.05)^2(0.10)]$, then this n will do.
   (iii) Hence, show that if n is chosen to be $1/[4(0.05)^2(0.10)] = 1,000$, this n will certainly suffice.

(b) Use Theorem 6.4 to find the smallest n such that T/n differs from p by no more than 0.05 with probability at least 0.90; i.e., find n so that $P(|T/n - p| > 0.05) \leq 0.10$.

   Hint:

   (i) Show that n must satisfy the equation

$$n = \frac{p(1 - p)(1.645)^2}{(0.05)^2}.$$

   (ii) Hence, show that if n is chosen to be the first integer greater than or equal to $(1.645)^2/4(0.05)^2$, this n will suffice.

(c) Compare your answers in parts (a) and (b) to see the saving in sample size achieved by use of Theorem 6.4.

CHAPTER SEVEN

Point Estimation and Hypothesis Testing for the Mean of a Normal Population

Estimation

In Chapter 4 we studied the problem of estimating p, the unknown probability of success in n binomial trials, and the problem of testing prior hypotheses concerning p. In this chapter, we will study the same two problems for the expected value μ of a normal population.

The problem of finding a point estimator of μ was answered in Chapter 6. If $X_1, X_2, \ldots, X_n$ is a random sample from a normal population with unknown expected value μ and variance σ^2, then the estimator of μ, denoted by $\hat{\mu}$, is

$$\hat{\mu} = X = \frac{1}{n} (X_1 + X_2 + \cdots + X_n),$$

the average of the observations.

Since $\hat{\mu}$ is a linear combination of independent normal random variables, Theorem 6.3 tells us that $\hat{\mu}$ is a normal random variable with expected value μ and variance σ^2/n. Since $V(\hat{\mu})$ decreases as n increases, the larger the sample, the greater the probability that $\hat{\mu}$ will be close to μ.

Hypothesis Testing

In testing hypotheses concerning μ, we follow the same procedure as in Chapter 4. That is, we have a prior belief (hypothesis) concerning μ and we choose an error probability (significance level), the largest probability we will risk of making the error of rejecting the hypothesis when it is true. Alternatively, we can calculate the significance probability associated with the observed sample, i.e., the probability of finding a sample differing as much from that hypothesized as the observed one.

The problem is complicated in the case of a normal population since there is a second parameter σ^2, which may or may not be known. We will treat the two cases separately, starting with the case where σ^2 is known.

Case 1 : σ^2 Known

It may well be asked how σ^2 can be known when μ is not. The answer is that more often than not, σ^2 is not known and Case 2 will be more important. We treat the less practical case first because it is simpler. On occasion, σ^2 may be known from theoretical considerations. Or both μ and σ^2 may be known in the sense that we have very accurate estimators of them based on previous observations. Our hypothesis is that μ and σ^2 will have these known values in the present experiment.

Example 7.1 Quality control of sugar packages

In industrial quality control, it is customary to sample frequently from the articles produced by a machine or a factory. For example, consider a packaging machine set to fill boxes of sugar to a weight of 1.1 lb. From a series of past records, it is observed that the weights of the boxes of sugar are normally distributed with a standard deviation of $\sigma = 0.02$ lb. Occasionally, however, the machine "slips"; i.e., the average changes from 1.1 lb to some larger or smaller value. The choice between continuing operations or stopping the process is to be made on the basis of observations of a sample from the machine; i.e., some small number from those packaged is selected and actually weighed. Let the sample size be 10.

Solution: Let X be the net weight (in pounds) of a sugar package produced by this machine. It is assumed that X is a normal random variable with parameters μ and σ^2.

The company does not wish to shut the machine down without reason. Thus, its prior belief is that the machine is operating satisfactorily. This is written compactly as

$$H : \mu = 1.1, \quad \sigma = 0.02.$$

The alternative is that the machine has slipped; i.e.,

$$A : \mu \neq 1.1.$$

The rule we choose should be such that the probability of stopping production unnecessarily (the error probability) should be small, say 0.01. As in Chapter 4, the choice of significance level varies from problem to problem and depends on the seriousness of the error.

We are now ready to choose a decision rule. Since X, the sample mean, is a good estimator of μ, we use it to construct our decision rule. If H is true, X should be close to 1.1. If H is false, X should be larger than 1.1 or smaller than 1.1; i.e., it is plausible that we should reject H if $X - 1.1$ is too large negatively or positively. To make the last statement precise, we use the probability distribution of X when H is true. Since X is a normal random variable with expected value 1.1 and standard deviation $0.02/\sqrt{10}$ when H is true, $Z = (X - 1.1)/(0.02/\sqrt{10})$ is a standard normal random variable. From Table A2.3, we find that

$$P(|Z| \geq 2.58) = P(Z \geq 2.58) + P(Z \leq -2.58) = 0.01.$$

Thus, if H is true, $(X - 1.1)/0.00633$ falls between ± 2.58 with probability 0.99, or $X - 1.1$ falls between ± 0.0163, or X falls between 1.0837 and 1.1163. Put mathematically,

$$P(-0.0163 < X - 1.1 < 0.0163 | H \text{ is true}) = 0.99$$

or

$$P(1.0837 < X < 1.1163 | H \text{ is true}) = 0.99.$$

Thus, if our observed X falls outside this range, either H is false or an event whose probability is 0.01 has occurred. We prefer to choose the former, knowing that our chance of making an error is 1 percent on the average. That is, for this particular experiment our rule may give us the correct answer or it may not, but in many performances of this experiment the machine will be shut down unnecessarily only 1 percent of the time, on the average.

To summarize, we first choose a hypothesis and an alternative

$$H : \mu = 1.1, \quad \sigma = 0.02 \quad \text{versus} \quad A : \mu \neq 1.1$$

and a significance level, $\alpha = 0.01$. Then we choose as our test rule: Reject H at the 1 percent level; i.e., shut down the machine, if X does not fall between 1.0837 and 1.1163, the lower and upper critical levels for X. Otherwise, do not reject H; i.e., assume the machine is in good working order.

EXERCISE

Find the decision rule for Example 7.1 if the sample size is (a) 5, (b) 20.

This example involves a two-sided decision rule, since slippage in either direction is undesirable. The rule, in its setting up, arbitrarily was made symmetrical (by choosing equal "rejection rails"). This choice might be modified in this "quality control" problem, though it is customary in most scientific problems to make the decision rule symmetrical. The sugar-packaging problem might also be modified by using a variable sample size or other advanced techniques, which will not be considered here.

The following example illustrates the one-sided decision rule when σ^2 is known.

Example 7.2   Light-bulb lifetimes

An electrical company has been selling a bulb it advertises as having an average life of 1,000 hours. To be more precise, assume that the lifetime of these bulbs is a normal random variable with expected value 1,000 hours and standard deviation 200 hours (known from repeated past observation). The company's research staff claims to have improved the bulb so that μ is now greater than 1,000 hours. To test this claim, 20 new bulbs are allowed to burn and their lifetimes recorded. Find a test rule, based on these 20 observations, for accepting or rejecting the research staff's claim.

Solution: Let X be the lifetime of a new bulb (in hours). It is assumed that X is a normal random variable with expected value μ and variance σ^2.

The company would not want to make the error of putting the new bulb on the market and claiming it had a longer average life when in fact it did not. Since it does not want to accept the claim unless there is strong evidence for doing so, the hypothesis is

$$H : \mu = 1{,}000, \quad \sigma = 200,$$

and the alternative of interest is

$$A : \mu > 1{,}000.$$

To keep the probability of the error described in the last paragraph small, a significance level is chosen, say, 1 percent.

From general considerations, it is observed that X should be close to 1,000 if H is true and larger than 1,000 if A is true. Thus, we reject H if $\bar{X}$ is too large. To make this statement precise, we use the fact that $\bar{X}$ is a normal random variable with mean 1,000 hours and standard deviation $200/\sqrt{20}$ when H is true. Then $Z = (\bar{X} - 1,000)/(200/\sqrt{20})$ is a standard normal random variable. From Table A2.3

$$P(Z \geq 2.33) = 0.01.$$

Thus, with probability 0.99, Z is less than 2.33; i.e., $(\bar{X} - 1,000)/(200/\sqrt{20})$ is less than 2.33, $\bar{X} - 1,000$ is less than $(2.33)(200/\sqrt{20}) = (2.33)(44.72) = 104.15$, or $\bar{X}$ is less than 1,104.15. That is,

$$P(\bar{X} < 1104.15 | H \text{ is true}) = 0.99.$$

Thus, if the observed $\bar{X}$ is greater than or equal to 1,104.15, the critical level for $\bar{X}$, then H is false, or an event whose probability is less than or equal to 0.01 has occurred. We choose to believe the former, knowing we will make an error 1 percent of the time, on the average.

To summarize, we choose a hypothesis and an alternative

$$H : \mu = 1,000, \quad \sigma = 200 \quad \text{versus} \quad A : \mu > 1,000$$

and a significance level, 1 percent. Our test rule is: Reject H; i.e., accept the claim (at the 1 percent level) if $\bar{X} \geq 1,104.15$. Otherwise, do not accept the claim. Our probability of making the serious error of putting the new bulb on the market with its claim of superiority when the new bulb is not superior is 0.01.

Note that, as in Chapter 4, when we do not reject H, it is not necessary to accept H uncritically. If $\bar{X}$ is much larger than 1,000 but less than 1,104.15, we might wish to experiment further. If $\bar{X}$ is much smaller than 1.104.15, we may be willing to believe, immediately, that the new bulb is not an improvement.

EXERCISE

Find the test rule in Example 7.2 if the sample size is (a) 5, (b) 10.

Summary of Test Procedures for a Normal Mean (σ^2 Known)

Let $X_1, X_2, \ldots, X_n$ be independent observations, i.e., independent random variables that are assumed to be normally distributed with mean μ, standard deviation σ.

Two-Sided Alternatives

$$H : \mu = \mu_0, \quad \sigma = \sigma_0 \quad \text{versus} \quad A : \mu \neq \mu_0.$$

The test is based on the sample mean $\bar{X}$, which under the hypothesis is normally distributed with mean μ_0, variance σ_0^2/n. The decision rule, such that the error probability is α, is: Reject H if

$$\frac{\bar{X} - \mu_0}{\sigma_0/\sqrt{n}} \leq -z_\alpha \quad \text{or} \quad \frac{\bar{X} - \mu_0}{\sigma_0/\sqrt{n}} \geq +z_\alpha,$$

where z_α is defined by the equation

$$P(|Z| \geq z_\alpha) = P(Z \leq -z_\alpha) + P(Z \geq z_\alpha) = \alpha.$$

The numbers $-z_\alpha$ and $+z_\alpha$ are the *lower* and *upper* critical levels for the standardized test statistic.

This rule may also be written: H is rejected at the 100α percent significance level if

$$\bar{X} \leq \mu_0 - \frac{\sigma_0 z_\alpha}{\sqrt{n}} \quad \text{or} \quad \bar{X} \geq \mu_0 + \frac{\sigma_0 z_\alpha}{\sqrt{n}};$$

i.e., H is not rejected if

$$\mu_0 - \frac{\sigma_0 z_\alpha}{\sqrt{n}} < \bar{X} < \mu_0 + \frac{\sigma_0 z_\alpha}{\sqrt{n}}.$$

The numbers $\mu_0 \pm \sigma_0 z_\alpha/\sqrt{n}$ are *critical levels* for the test statistic $\bar{X}$.

One-Sided Alternatives

1. $H : \mu \leq \mu_0, \quad \sigma = \sigma_0 \quad \text{versus} \quad A : \mu > \mu_0.$

H is rejected at the 100α percent significance level if

$$\bar{X} \geq \mu_0 + \frac{\sigma_0 z_{2\alpha}}{\sqrt{n}}.$$

2. $H : \mu \geq \mu_0, \quad \sigma = \sigma_0 \quad \text{versus} \quad A : \mu < \mu_0.$

H is rejected at the 100α percent significance level if

$$\bar{X} \leq \mu_0 - \frac{\sigma_0 z_{2\alpha}}{\sqrt{n}}.$$

The right-hand sides of these two inequalities are the *critical levels* for the test statistic $\bar{X}$.

[*Note:* The reason that $z_{2\alpha}$ is the critical level in one-sided tests is unclear to some students. Note that we have defined z_α by the equation $P(|Z| \geq z_\alpha) = \alpha$; i.e., the probability in *both* tails is α. From the symmetry of the normal distribution it follows that the probability in one tail $P(Z \geq z_\alpha) = \alpha/2$. Consequently if a one-tail probability of level α is required we see that since $P(|Z| > z_{2\alpha}) = 2\alpha$, $P(Z > z_{2\alpha})$ $= 2\alpha/2 = \alpha$. Hence rejecting in the *upper* tail when Z exceeds $z_{2\alpha}$ yields the prescribed error probability of α. The same argument applies to a test when rejection is in the lower tail only.]

Significance Probabilities

As in Chapter 4, we present an alternative approach to hypothesis testing for μ based on the significance probabilities of observed outcomes.

If the 20 observations of Example 7.2 result in the value $\bar{X} = 1,055.2$, the significance probability of this observation is the probability of observing a value of $\bar{X}$ as large or larger than 1,055.2, given that H is true. That is, the significance probability is

$$P(\bar{X} \geq 1,055.2 | H \text{ is true}) = P\left(\frac{\bar{X} - 1,000}{200/\sqrt{20}} \geq \frac{55.2}{200/\sqrt{20}}\right)$$
$$= P(Z \geq 1.23)$$
$$= 0.1093.$$

We compute the significance probability from the event $(\bar{X} \geq 1,055.2)$ since our test rule is of the form: Reject H if $\bar{X} \geq c$. In the present example, the event $(\bar{X} \geq 1,055.2)$ has occurred, whose probability is 0.1093 if H is true, or H is false. If one can tolerate an error probability as large or larger than this, one rejects H. Otherwise, one cannot reject H. The best feature of this method is that the experimenter merely reports the significance probability, letting each reader make his own decision based on the error probability he can risk. As was discussed in Chapter 4, in a statistics course it is customary to treat each experiment as the sole basis of a decision, whereas in actual-life situations there may be numerous pieces of information being brought to bear on any particular decision.

Further, the decisions may be to accept H, reject H, or continue experimentation. When the significance probability is near the significance level, more experimentation may certainly be advisable before a decision is reached.

If the physical situation permits, the experiment may be conducted in a stepwise procedure. After each observation, i.e., step, there is a formal rule to decide whether to accept *H*, to reject *H*, or to postpone decision and instead take another observation. This important method of statistical experimentation and decision making bears the name of "sequential analysis."

Example 7.3 Diet supplement

A study on diet supplements involves the observation of growth of a large number of experimental animals. The study begins by determining that animals on a standard diet starting from a standard initial weight gain 5 lb on the average in one month; further, these weight gains are approximately normally distributed with a standard deviation of 2 lb; i.e., $\mu = 5$ and $\sigma = 2$. A diet supplement is expected to increase the average weight gain. To test this possibility, 16 animals are fed their regular diet plus the supplement for one month. It is observed that the average weight gain is 6.22 lb. Does the diet supplement significantly increase weight gains?

Solution :   Let *X* be the weight gain per month (in lb) if a standard experimental animal is fed on a standard diet plus supplement. Assume that *X* is a normal random variable with expected value μ and variance σ^2. Then we have

$$H : \mu = 5, \quad \sigma = 2 \quad \text{versus} \quad A : \mu > 5.$$

Since the alternative is one-sided, the significance probability of the observation 6.22 is

$$P(\overline{X} \geq 6.22 | H \text{ is true}) = P\left(\frac{\overline{X} - 5}{2/\sqrt{16}} \geq \frac{1.22}{2/\sqrt{16}}\right)$$
$$= P(Z \geq 2.44)$$
$$= 0.0073.$$

The observation is significant at any level greater than or equal to 0.73 percent; i.e., anyone whose error probability is at least 0.0073 will reject *H*. Otherwise, he will not reject *H*. In particular, if one had set one's error probability at 0.01, he would reject *H* and accept the claim that the diet supplement increased weight gains.

EXERCISE

Find the significance probabilities of the observations 5.90 lb and 5.75 lb. Which, if any, would be significant at the 5 percent level? 1 percent level?

Example 7.4 Quality control of sugar packages
(continued)

If the ten observations result in a mean of 1.112, we can find the significance probability as follows: If $\overline{X} = 1.112$, then $z = (1.112 - 1.1)/0.02/\sqrt{10} = 1.90$. Then, $P(|Z| \geq 1.90) = 0.574$ is the significance probability of the observation 1.112. The reason that the absolute value of Z must be used is that the hypothesis is rejected if $\overline{X}$ (or Z) is too large or too small. Thus, as in the two-sided examples in Chapter 4, $P(Z \geq 1.90)$ is only half the required probability.

In this problem, the decision rule approach is more appropriate, since routine decisions are being based repeatedly on routine samples. In Example 7.3, a scientist reporting the results of such an experiment might appropriately report the significance level of the observed results of the experiment.

Examples 7.5 Grades of married students

The grade point average (G.P.A.) of all regular students in the College of Arts and Sciences of State University is 2.45, with a standard deviation of 0.5. In Example 1.7, the dean who declaims against marriage in college states that a sample of 25 married students shows their average to be 2.35. Can the dean conclude that married students have a lower G.P.A. than the general group of students in the college?

Any group of students drawn at random from the college will have a mean G.P.A. that is most likely to differ from 2.45. Some of these will lie above 2.45 and some below it. How can we distinguish between real differences and sampling error?

Solution: Let X be the G.P.A. of a student chosen at random from all regular students in the College of Arts and Sciences at State University. We assume that X has a normal distribution with mean 2.45 and standard deviation 0.5. The dean has obtained a sample of 25 and observes that $\overline{X} = 2.35$. The significance probability associated with this particular observation is found as follows:

$$z = \frac{2.35 - 2.45}{0.5/\sqrt{25}} = \frac{-0.10}{0.10} = -1.$$

Now

$$P(|Z| \geq 1) = P(Z \leq -1) + P(Z \geq -1) = 0.6826.$$

In other words, 68 percent of the time the sample mean will differ from the population mean by at least 0.10 grade points.

It is reasonable to ask: Why take $P(|Z| \geq 1)$, i.e., the absolute value, in the probability calculation? Implied though not stated in the formulation of the problem were the alternatives to H. If the true mean G.P.A. of married students is not 2.45, it may be above or below it. Hence, the hypothesis will be rejected if $\bar{X}$ is much above 2.45 or much below 2.45. A two-sided decision rule is called for, whichever way the problem is attacked.

Summary of Significance Probabilities (σ^2 Known)

Let $X_1, X_2, \ldots, X_n$ be a random sample on X, a normal random variable, with expected value μ and variance σ^2.

Two-Sided Alternatives

$$H : \mu = \mu_0, \quad \sigma = \sigma_0 \quad \text{versus} \quad A : \mu \neq \mu_0.$$

If $\bar{X} = c$, then $z = (c - \mu_0)/(\sigma_0/\sqrt{n})$ and, the significance probability of the observation c is $P(|Z| \geq |z|)$.

One-Sided Alternatives

1. $H : \mu = \mu_0, \quad \sigma = \sigma_0 \quad \text{versus} \quad A : \mu < \mu_0.$

If $\bar{X} = c$, then $z = (c - \mu_0)/(\sigma_0/\sqrt{n})$, and the significance probability of the observation c is $P(Z \leq z)$.

2. $H : \mu = \mu_0, \quad \sigma = \sigma_0 \quad \text{versus} \quad A : \mu > \mu_0.$

The significance probability of $\bar{X} = c$ is $P(Z \geq z)$, where $z = (c - \mu_0)/(\sigma_0/\sqrt{n})$.

Case 2 : σ^2 Unknown ; Student's t Distribution

In Case 2, σ^2 has to be estimated by s^2. This introduces an extra source of random variation. Thus, while $(\bar{X} - \mu)/(\sigma/\sqrt{n})$ is a standard normal random variable, $(\bar{X} - \mu)/(s/\sqrt{n})$ is not. But the distribution of $(\bar{X} - \mu)/(s/\sqrt{n})$, while not normal, has been worked out mathematically. Tables of its probabilities are available as is the case for the normal distribution.

Since the normal distribution is used to calculate probabilities, "fit" sample distributions, etc., complete tables of it are widely available. The distribution of $(\bar{X} - \mu)/(s/\sqrt{n})$, when $X_1, X_2, \ldots, X_n$ is a random sample on a normal random variable X with parameters μ and σ^2, is known as *Student's t distribution*. A table of critical levels of the distribution is given in Table A2.6.

The statistic $(\bar{X} - \mu)/(s/\sqrt{n})$ is usually denoted by the symbol t. The use of a lower-case letter for a random variable is a departure from our notation that uses capital letters for random variables and the corresponding lower-case letters for realizations. While this usage is now extensive, the use of the symbol t for the random variable $(\bar{X} - \mu)/(s/\sqrt{n})$ as defined above is both older and more widely accepted. We feel that a change here at the present time would not be beneficial to the student who expects to study statistical references in scientific literature.

The distribution of t depends on the distribution of s^2. Recall that the sample variance s^2, as defined with divisor $n - 1$, i.e.,

$$s^2 = \frac{\sum_{i=1}^{n} (X_i - \bar{X})^2}{n - 1},$$

is an unbiased estimate of σ^2.

Roughly, one may think of the sample variance as the average of squares of $n - 1$ "free" terms plus one more that is not free to vary. Why is this? The terms are of the form $X_1 - \bar{X}, X_2 - \bar{X}, \ldots, X_n - \bar{X}$. Now

$$\frac{\sum X_i}{n} = \bar{X}, \quad \text{or} \quad \sum X_i - n\bar{X} = 0, \quad \text{or} \quad \sum_{i=1}^{n} (X_i - \bar{X}) = 0.$$

In words, the *sum of the deviations from the sample mean must total zero*. Thus, we say that s^2 has $n - 1$ *degrees of freedom*. The distribution of s^2/σ^2 is entirely determined by $n - 1$ and is an example of a χ^2 probability distribution with $n - 1$ degrees of freedom. (This will be discussed in more detail in Chapter 11.) From this discussion, we note that $n - 1$ is simply a parameter for the probability distribution of s^2/σ^2. However, the usage of "degrees of freedom," abbreviated to d.f., is so prevalent in statistical literature that we continue to use it here rather than the word parameter. The argument in the last paragraph provides another reason for dividing by $n - 1$ to obtain a sample variance which is an unbiased estimate of the population variance. (See the discussion in Chapter 5 on estimation of σ^2.)

In turn, the distribution of $t = (\bar{X} - \mu)/(s/\sqrt{n})$ is said to have $n - 1$ degrees of freedom when $X_1, X_2, \ldots, X_n$ is a random sample on X, a normal random variable with mean μ and variance σ^2. The t

distribution, also known as Student's t distribution, is completely determined by the parameter $n - 1$. The t distribution is symmetric about zero as is the normal distribution; if the number of degrees of freedom is at least 2, the mean of that distribution is zero. If the number of degrees of freedom is 1, the mean is undefined, but this is of little concern since samples of size 1 or 2 are of little use in statistical inference. In fact with samples of size 1, t is not defined at all. Why?

As the degrees of freedom increase, the t distribution approaches that of the standard normal distribution. This can be checked by looking at the critical levels in Table A2.6; e.g., $t_{0.05}$ is seen to be approaching $z_{0.05}(1.96)$ as n increases. This is reasonable since with large samples s^2 is a very good estimator of σ^2, and consequently t and Z are almost identical.

Like z_α, we define t_α as

$$P(|t| \geq t_\alpha) = \alpha \qquad \text{or} \qquad P(t \leq t_\alpha) + P(t \geq t_\alpha) = \alpha.$$

The numbers $-t_\alpha$ and $+t_\alpha$ are the *lower* and *upper critical levels* for the statistic t. We are using here the symmetry of the t distribution.

The test rules are found in Case 2 exactly as in Case 1, with z_α replaced by t_α and σ by s. Significance probabilities are computed in exactly the same way, with Z replaced by t. Since the tabulations of the t distribution are not as complete as for the normal distribution, interpolation may have to be used to get an approximate answer.

Summary of Test Procedures for a Normal Mean (σ^2 Unknown)

Two-Sided Alternatives

$$H : \mu = \mu_0 \quad \text{versus} \quad A : \mu \neq \mu_0.$$

Reject H if

$$\bar{X} \leq \mu_0 - \frac{s t_\alpha}{\sqrt{n}} \qquad \text{or} \qquad \bar{X} \geq \mu_0 + \frac{s t_\alpha}{\sqrt{n}}.$$

The right-hand sides of these inequalities are the *lower* and *upper* critical levels for the test statistic $\bar{X}$.

One-Sided Alternatives

1. $H : \mu = \mu_0 \quad \text{versus} \quad A : \mu < \mu_0.$

Reject H if

$$\bar{X} \leq \mu_0 - \frac{s t_{2\alpha}}{\sqrt{n}}.$$

2. $H : \mu = \mu_0$ versus $A : \mu > \mu_0$.

Reject H if

$$\overline{X} \geq \mu_0 + \frac{s t_{2\alpha}}{\sqrt{n}}.$$

The right-hand sides of the two inequalities are called the *critical levels* for the test statistic $\overline{X}$.

Summary on Significance Probabilities (σ^2 Unknown)

Two-Sided Alternatives

$$H : \mu = \mu_0 \quad \text{versus} \quad A : \mu \neq \mu_0.$$

If $\overline{X} = c$ and $s = d$, the significance probability of $\overline{X} = c$, $s = d$ is

$$P\left(|t| > \frac{|c - \mu_0|}{d/\sqrt{n}}\right).$$

One-Sided Alternatives

1. $H : \mu = \mu_0$ versus $A : \mu < \mu_0$.

The significance probability of $\overline{X} = c$, $s = d$ is

$$P\left(t < \frac{c - \mu_0}{d/\sqrt{n}}\right).$$

2. $H : \mu = \mu_0$ versus $A : \mu > \mu_0$.

The significance probability of $\overline{X} = c$, $s = d$ is

$$P\left(t > \frac{c - \mu_0}{d/\sqrt{n}}\right).$$

Example 7.6 Reducing without dieting

A proprietary medicine is advertised as being useful in reducing without any dietary restrictions. A doctor performs an experiment with 20 medical students in which they continue their usual diet for one month, together with the advertised "reducing" medicine. The variable measured is their weight change over the month. Here are the results (weight change in pounds): -3, $+1$, -1, 0, 0, 1, -1, 0, 2, 3, -4, -2, -1, -1, 0, 1, 1, 2, -2, -1. It is calculated that $\overline{X} = -0.2$, $s^2 = 3.01$, $s = 1.735$. The null hypothesis here is $\mu = 0$, or, in other words, the mean weight change is zero. This is the normal scientific attitude of skepticism—the proprietary medicine must demonstrate clearly that it is effective. The only alternative of particular interest is $\mu < 0$. Choose the conventional 5 percent significance level. The test can be performed by setting up a rejection rule which is of the form: Reject H if

$$\bar{X} \leq 0 - \frac{(1.735)(1.729)}{\sqrt{20}},$$

i.e., if

$$\bar{X} \leq -0.671.$$

Observe that in obtaining this rule, we tacitly assumed that the weight changes came from a normal population. The value 1.729 is found in Table A2.6, corresponding to the one-tailed t value for the 5 percent significance level with 19 degrees of freedom ($n = 20$, so $n - 1 = 19$). Since $\bar{X} = -0.2$ for the observed experiment, H is not rejected. There is no conclusive or significant evidence that the proprietary medicine has an effect on reducing.

An alternative way of performing such a test is to calculate the observed t:

$$t = \frac{\bar{X} - 0}{s/\sqrt{n}} = \frac{-0.2}{1.735/\sqrt{20}} = -0.516.$$

Since $-1.729 < -0.516$, the conclusion is the same: H is not rejected. If t had fallen below -1.729, i.e., in the left-hand tail, H would have been rejected. The significance probability of $\bar{X} = 0.2$, $s = 1.735$ is $P(t < -0.516)$, which cannot be found in the abbreviated table but is clearly greater than 5 percent.

Note that when σ is unknown and the t test is used, each sample provides its own s and hence each sample will have its own rejection rule. In routine sampling where σ is known, a rejection rule can be set up once and used thereafter. More typically, in scientific experimentation this is not possible, and the significance probability approach to the problem is perhaps simpler and more common.

Example 7.7 Comparison of high schools

An education student doing a thesis project selects a number of pairs of students in John Marshall Junior High School. He chooses the pairs so that the two members are as much alike as possible, except that after completing junior high school, one member of the pair goes to Roosevelt High School, the other to Lincoln High School. At the end of one year of senior high school, all students are given an achievement test. The differences of the paired students are as follows: 8, 3, -4, 2, 0, -16, 7, -9, 3, 0, 4, -3, 12, 2, 4, 3, -8, -6. Each of these figures is the achievement score of the student who went to Roosevelt, minus the score of the student who went to Lincoln. Are the results significant at the 5 percent level?

Solution: Let X = difference in scores of any one of the pairs. X is a random variable with a mean μ unknown to the experimenter. The parameter μ is the average of such differences obtained from all possible pairs of students subject to this "treatment." The question asked is equivalent to testing the hypothesis

$$H : \mu = 0 \quad \text{versus} \quad A : \mu \neq 0.$$

Assume that X is normal. The test statistic is $t = (\bar{X} - 0)/(s/\sqrt{n})$, which has a t distribution with $n - 1$, i.e., 17 degrees of freedom (d.f.).

H is rejected at the 5 percent level if

$$\bar{X} \leq 0 - \frac{2.11(s)}{\sqrt{18}} \quad \text{or} \quad \bar{X} \geq + \frac{2.11(s)}{\sqrt{18}},$$

for $t_{0.05} = 2.11$ when t has 17 d.f.

Referring to the sample values, we can easily calculate $\bar{X}$ and s as $\bar{X} = 0.222$, $s^2 = 46.18$, $s = 6.80$. H is rejected if $\bar{X} \leq -3.38$ or $\bar{X} \geq +3.38$; the critical levels for $\bar{X}$ are ± 3.38. Since $\bar{X} = -0.222$, H is *not* rejected; i.e., the difference is *not* significant at the 5 percent level.

An alternate way of making the test is to calculate $(\bar{X} - 0)/(s/\sqrt{n})$ $= -(0.222\sqrt{18})/6.80 = -0.138$ and note that $-2.11 < -0.138 < +2.11$, so that H is *not* rejected. The significance probability of $\bar{X} = 0.222$, $s = 6.80$ is $P(|t| > 0.138)$, which is again not in the table but is much larger than 5 percent.

EXERCISES

1. If $\bar{X} = -1.01$, $s = 2.02$, $n = 16$ in Example 7.6, would you accept or reject H at the 5 percent level? Find the significance probability of the given observation.

2. If $\bar{X} = 4.21$, $s = 5.30$, $n = 12$ in Example 7.7, would you accept or reject H at the 5 percent level? Find the significance probability of the given observation.

Applications of the Central Limit Theorem

In this chapter we have developed tests of hypotheses concerning the mean μ of a normal population both when σ^2 is known and when it is unknown. For these tests to have the exact significance levels given, the underlying random variable or population must have a normal distribution. However, Theorem 6.4 (Central Limit Theorem) tells us that $\bar{X}$ is approximately normally distributed with mean μ and variance σ^2/n regardless of the underlying population distribution. Thus, in Case 1 (known variance), the tests given will serve just as well for testing hypotheses concerning the mean μ of any population provided that it is recognized that the error probability is only approximately equal to that prescribed.

In practice, it has been found that the approximation is quite close and adequate for practical purposes when the sample size is 10 or more, and hence, the assumption of normality can be relaxed in the discussion of Case 1, in such situations.

In studying Case 2 (variance unknown), the Central Limit Theorem as stated in Theorem 6.4 no longer applies. If the underlying random variable X is not normal, then $t = (\bar{X} - \mu_0)/(s/\sqrt{n})$ no longer has Student t distribution. However, by more advanced results, as n increases, the probability distribution of t still approaches that of a standard normal random variable, if H is true. Thus, in Case 2, the tests given are again applicable to hypotheses concerning the mean of any population with finite mean and variance, provided the sample size is sufficiently large. In practice, a sample of size 10 or more is generally considered to be sufficient for the error probability to be sufficiently close to the prescribed significance level. Hence, in both cases the requirement of normality can be relaxed provided the sample sizes are sufficiently large.

Some of the hypothesis testing problems of Chapter 6 made use of these facts. Before proceeding, we give two further examples to illustrate the methods involved.

Example 7.8   Taste testing (continued)

In Example 4.7, the taste tester tried to choose the odd drink in each of ten trials. Now, let us increase the number of trials to 72 and find the decision rule for testing

$$H : p = \tfrac{1}{3} \quad \text{versus} \quad A : p > \tfrac{1}{3}$$

at the 1 percent level.

Solution: Let T be the total number of correct choices in 72 trials. We assume that T is a binomial random variable with unknown parameter p, the probability of a correct choice on any trial. Since the family of alternatives is one-sided, the decision rule is one-tailed; i.e., we want to find an integer c such that

$$P(T \geq c \mid p = \tfrac{1}{3}) \leq 0.01.$$

Now,

$$P\left(T \geq c \mid p = \frac{1}{3}\right) = P\left(\frac{T - 24}{4} \geq \frac{c - 24}{4} \,\middle|\, p = \frac{1}{3}\right)$$

since $E(T) = np = 72(\tfrac{1}{3}) = 24$ and $V(T) = np(1 - p) = 72(\tfrac{1}{3})(\tfrac{2}{3}) = 16$. By the Central Limit Theorem,

$$P\left(\frac{T - 24}{4} \geq \frac{c - 24}{4} \,\middle|\, p = \frac{1}{3}\right) \doteq P\left(Z \geq \frac{c - 24}{4}\right),$$

and from Table A2.3, $P(Z \geq 2.33) = 0.01$.

Hence, $(c - 24)/4 = 2.33$ or $c = 33.32$. Technically, our decision rule is: Reject H at the 1 percent level if $T \geq 33.32$. But, since T can only take on integer values, $(T \geq 33.32) = (T \geq 34)$, and our decision rule becomes: Reject H at the 1 percent level if $T \geq 34$; i.e., conclude that the taste tester has ability if he makes 34 or more correct choices in 72 trials.

Example 7.9 Gene inheritance (continued)

Recall Example 3.4, in which gene inheritance was discussed. In 96 offspring of Aa parents, 30 are observed to be aa. Is this consistent at the 1 percent level with Mendelian theory, according to which in this situation $P(\text{offspring is } aa) = \tfrac{1}{4}$?

Solution: Let T be the total number of aa offspring in 96 observations of offspring from Aa parents. We assume that T is a binomial random variable with unknown parameter p, the probability that an offspring of such parents will be aa. The hypotheses and alternative of interest are

$$H : p = \tfrac{1}{4} \quad \text{versus} \quad A : p \neq \tfrac{1}{4},$$

since, if Mendelian theory is inappropriate to this problem, p may be either more or less than $\tfrac{1}{4}$. Because the family of alternatives is two-sided, the test is two-tailed; i.e., we wish to find c_1 and c_2 such that

$$P(T \leq c_1 \text{ or } T \geq c_2 \mid p = \tfrac{1}{4}) \leq 0.01.$$

As in Chapter 4, many choices of c_1 and c_2 will satisfy this equation.

For convenience, we will always choose c_1 and c_2 to be symmetric about the mean, $E(T) = 96(\frac{1}{4}) = 24$. This enables us to work with the absolute value of the difference $T - 24$, and hence, the problem is reduced to finding c such that

$$P(|T - 24| \geq c|p = \tfrac{1}{4}) \leq 0.01.$$

Compute that $V(T) = 18$, so that

$$P\left(|T - 24| \geq c \Big| p = \frac{1}{4}\right) = P\left(\frac{|T - 24|}{\sqrt{18}} \geq \frac{c}{\sqrt{18}} \Big| p = \frac{1}{4}\right)$$

$$\doteq P\left(|Z| \geq \frac{c}{4.242}\right)$$

by the Central Limit Theorem and $P(|Z| \geq 2.58) = 0.01$ from Table A2.3, so we see that $c/4.242 = 2.58$ or $c = 10.94$. Technically, our decision rule is: Reject H at the 1 percent level if $|T - 24| \geq 10.94$. Again, since T must be an integer, $(|T - 24| \geq 10.94) = (|T - 24| \geq 11)$, and the decision rule is: Reject H if $|T - 24| \geq 11$; i.e., reject H if T is either less than or equal to 13 or greater than or equal to 35. Since we observed $T = 30$, we find this observation consistent with Mendelian theory.

The significance probability of $T = 30$ is $2P(T \geq 30|p = \frac{1}{4})$ because the alternative is two-sided. Using the Central Limit Theorem again, we obtain

$$P\left(T \geq 30 \Big| p = \frac{1}{4}\right) = P\left(\frac{T - 24}{\sqrt{18}} \geq \frac{30 - 24}{\sqrt{18}} \Big| p = \frac{1}{4}\right)$$

$$\doteq P(Z \geq 1.41) = 0.079,$$

so that the significance probability of the observation $T = 30$ is 0.158 (approximately).

[*Note:* We have not made use of the correction factor, which makes the normal approximation more accurate. The reader who wishes to get a better approximation through use of this correction factor should work his problems as in Examples 7.8 and 7.9. Then he should compute the error probability of the decision rule constructed using the correction factor. It may turn out that the critical value has to be changed by 1 to satisfy the significance-level requirement and the rule that c be the largest (smallest) integer satisfying this requirement. The correction factor can also be used in obtaining significance probabilities.]

*Type I and Type II Errors; O.C. Curves

As in Chapter 4, the reader should have been aware that in each of the previous examples, there is a second error we have so far ignored. In Example 7.1, a test was chosen so that a machine would not be shut down needlessly very often. This protected the company from losing output while a satisfactory machine was being checked out. But what of a buyer? From his point of view, he does not care how often the company's machines are shut down. His only worry is that each package contain at least 1.1 lb of sugar, on the average. For him, the serious error consists in accepting the hypothesis, when, in fact, the machine is really producing packages that weigh less than 1.1 lb on the average, i.e., when the machine has "slipped" downward.

In general, the situation is exactly the same as in Chapter 4. The prior belief or hypothesis may be true or false (and we do not know which of these prevails). On the basis of experimentation, we accept or reject the hypothesis. In either case, we may be right or we may have made an error. We can summarize this in a 2 × 2 table as in Chapter 4.

TRUE SITUATION

		H is true	H is false
	Accept H	√	Type II error
DECISION	Do not accept H	Type I error	√

In any one experiment in which a decision is made, the decision may be right or wrong. We have chosen our tests so that the error probability is small. In terms of the diagram, we have kept the Type I error probability below some level, the significance level. What can be said of the Type II error probability?

Case 1: σ^2 Known

In constructing our test rules, we only need to know the distribution of X under the assumption that the hypothesis is true. The values of μ and σ^2 are usually determined from previous experiments. If we wish to find Type II error probabilities, we have to assume that the value of σ^2 does not change in the present experiment even if the value of μ does. In Example 7.1, we assume that even if the machine has "slipped," the standard deviation has not changed. This is an assumption which may need to be justified. In Example 7.2, we assume that the standard deviation remains unchanged even if the improvement does increase the average lifetime. This assumption may be justified by arguing that the improvement acts in exactly the same way on each bulb and the variations observed are due to individual differences in the bulbs. However, this argument is *not* a proof and our assumption is still an assumption. It should, if necessary, be justified by experiment.

EXERCISE

Construct a 2 × 2 table for Example 7.1.

Example 7.10   Quality control of sugar packages (continued)

The Type II error probability in this example is the probability of accepting H when, in fact, H is false. Putting it compactly, we obtain $P(1.0837 < \bar{X} < 1.1163 | H$ is false). When H is false, it is assumed that $\bar{X}$ is a normal random variable with a standard deviation $\sigma = 0.02$ and a mean other than 1.1. It is seen, as in Chapter 4, that there is not one Type II error probability but one for each possible alternative value of μ. Since there are an infinite number of possible values, we compute only a few and, as in Chapter 4, we interpolate to sketch a curve, the *operating characteristic curve* (O.C. curve) of the decision rule. If $\mu = 1.07$, then

$$P(1.0837 < \bar{X} < 1.1163 | \mu = 1.07, \sigma = 0.02)$$

$$= P\left(\frac{1.0837 - 1.07}{0.02/\sqrt{10}} < Z < \frac{1.1163 - 1.07}{0.02/\sqrt{10}}\right)$$

$$= P(2.17 < Z < 7.33)$$

$$= 0.015.$$

That is, if the machine has really "slipped" so that $\mu = 1.07$ (and the variance has not changed), the probability of a Type II error is 0.015. This is good news for the buyer for he sees that if the machine has "slipped" downwards as little as 0.03 lb, he will receive these underweight packages only 0.15 percent of the time, on the average.

The calculations may be systematized as follows:

μ	$z_1 = \dfrac{1.0837 - \mu}{0.02/\sqrt{10}}$	$z_2 = \dfrac{1.1163 - \mu}{0.02/\sqrt{10}}$	$P(z_1 < Z < z_2)$
1.07	2.17	7.33	0.015
1.08	0.59	5.74	0.28
1.09	−1.00	4.16	0.84
1.10	−2.58	2.58	0.99
1.11	−4.16	1.00	0.84
1.12	−5.74	−0.59	0.28
1.13	−7.33	−2.17	0.015

From these values, the O.C. curve may be plotted as in Figure 7.1.

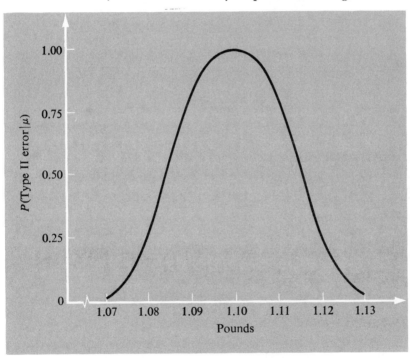

FIGURE 7.1   *The O.C. curve for Example 7.10.*

EXERCISE

1. In an earlier exercise, decision rules were found for Example 7.1 when
   the sample size was 5 and 20. Construct tables of Type II error probabilities for these two rules as in the table above.

2. Plot all three O.C. curves on the same graph. What do you surmise happens to the Type II error probabilities as the sample size increases?

It should be repeated that the tests we construct keep the Type I error probability below some preassigned test level while the Type II error probabilities may be large or small. It is important, therefore, to choose the hypothesis, whenever possible, so that the more serious error is the Type I error. With a fixed Type I error level, to decrease Type II error levels it is necessary to increase the sample size. One of the problems of experimental design is to determine what sample size reduces the Type II error level to an acceptable standard for a specified alternative.

Example 7.11 Light-bulb lifetimes (continued)

In computing the Type II error probabilities and the O.C. curve for this example, we assume that the standard deviation remains unchanged even if the mean has been increased. Then, if H is false, X is a normal random variable with mean greater than 1,000 and standard deviation of 200. There is a family of Type II error probabilities, one for each possible mean. We wish to find

$$P(\overline{X} < 1104.15 | \mu, \sigma = 200).$$

As in Example 7.10, we construct a table:

μ	$z = \dfrac{1104.15 - \mu}{200/\sqrt{20}}$	$P(Z < z)$
1,000	2.33	0.9901
1,025	1.77	0.9616
1,050	1.21	0.8869
1,075	0.65	0.7422
1,100	0.09	0.5359
1,125	−0.47	0.3192
1,150	−1.03	0.1515
1,175	−1.59	0.0559
1,200	−2.14	0.0162

From these values, the O.C. curve can be sketched as in Figure 7.2. Observe that even when $\mu = 1,100$ (an average improvement of 100 hours) there is a more than 50 percent chance of accepting H, i.e., saying $\mu = 1,000$. This shows that the test is not very good (although

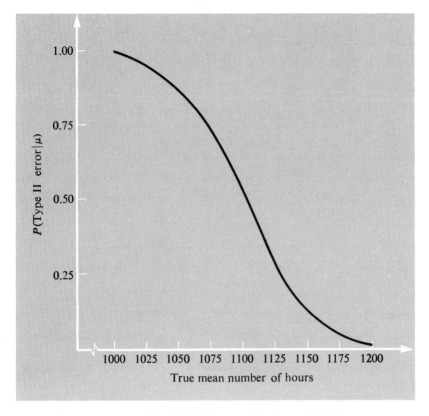

FIGURE 7.2   *The O.C. curve for Example* 7.11.

it is the best possible for the given significance level and sample size). The Type II error would decrease if the significance level were raised, or, better still, if the sample size were increased.

EXERCISES

1. In an earlier exercise, test rules were constructed for Example 7.2 when the sample sizes were 5 and 10. Construct O.C. curves for these rules, similar to the one above.

2. Plot all three O.C. curves on the same graph.

Observe that in both cases, the O.C. curve cannot be constructed until the test rule is specified. This is one good reason for using the test rule approach rather than the significance probability approach. The latter has advantages only when the Type II errors are ignored. Observe also, that the O.C. curves are quite different for one-sided and two-sided alternatives. However, O.C. curves for decision rules concerning means of normal populations are roughly of the same shape as the corresponding ones for the parameter p in Chapter 4. (Compare Figures 7.1 and 7.2 with Figures 4.2 and 4.3.)

Case 2

When X has a normal distribution with parameters μ and σ^2 and $X_1, X_2, \ldots, X_n$ is a random sample on X, $(\bar{X} - \mu)/(s\sqrt{n})$ has a t distribution with $n - 1$ degrees of freedom. If μ is not the mean of X, then $(\bar{X} - \mu)/(s/\sqrt{n})$ has neither a normal nor a t distribution. Thus, for the viewpoint of testing $H : \mu = \mu_0$, $(\bar{X} - \mu_0)/(s/\sqrt{n})$ has a t distribution when H is true, and we can construct test rules or find significance probabilities. But if H is false, $(\bar{X} - \mu_0)/(s/\sqrt{n})$ does not have a t distribution and other tables are required to find Type II error probabilities. In more advanced texts, the distribution of $(\bar{X} - \mu_0)/(s/\sqrt{n})$ is derived under the alternative A, and tables are available for finding Type II errors. Since these, unfortunately, are beyond the scope of this text, Type II errors will not be considered for Case 2.

■ Class Experiment

7.1 (a) Set up the two-sided test of the hypothesis $H : \mu = 0$, when $\sigma = 1, n = 4, \alpha = 0.10$.

(b) Members of the class should draw enough samples of size 4 from Table A2.5 (normal random variates) to obtain a total of 100 samples, calculate $\bar{X}$ for each sample, and record whether or not the hypothesis $\mu = 0$ is accepted or rejected. In 100 samples, 10 rejections are expected. How many actually occur? These rejections are erroneous since drawings from a table of random normal deviates have mean 0 and variance 1. They are Type I errors.

*(c) Calculate $P(\text{accepting } H|\mu)$ for the alternative values, μ equal to 0.5, 1.0, 1.5.

*(d) Plot the operating characteristic of the test. How are the points on the left-hand side of the origin ($\mu = 0$) determined?

*(e) Members of the class should draw enough samples of size 4 from a table of random normal deviates to obtain a total of 100 samples, add 0.5 to each observation, and then calculate $\bar{X}$. Finally, note whether $H : \mu = 0$ is now accepted or rejected. What is the observed frequency of acceptances? How does this compare with the theoretical expected frequency calculated in (c)?

★(f)   Repeat (e) but this time add 1 to each observation; repeat it again, adding 1.5 to each observation. These give empirical observations corresponding to the probability of accepting H calculated for $\mu = 0.5, 1.0, 1.5$ in (c).

■ **Problems**

7.1   The sugar-packaging machine in Example 7.1 is replaced by a new one, for which it turns out that $\sigma = 0.04$. What should the decision rule now be as to whether or not to stop the machine? It is still based on samples of size 10, with the same significance level, 1 percent.

7.2   If in Problem 7.1 the average of ten observations is $X = 1.115$ lb, find the significance probability of this observation. Is this observation significant at the 5 percent level? the 1 percent level?

7.3   What will be the decision rule for Problem 7.1 if the significance level is changed from 1 percent to 5 percent?

7.4   The machine of Example 7.1 is reset to produce packages that average 1.01 lb. What should the decision rule now be if $n = 10$, $\alpha = 0.01$, $\sigma = 0.01$?

7.5   If the packaging machine of Example 7.1 is set for an average of 1.01 and if $\sigma = 0.01$, how often does it produce packages weighing less than 1 lb when it is operating properly?

7.6   If in Problem 7.4, the ten observations yield $X = 1.00$ lb, find the significance probability of this observation. Is it significant at the 5 percent level? the 1 percent level? the 0.1 percent level?

7.7   Rephrase Problem 6.5 as a test of a hypothesis and calculate the significance probability of the observation.

7.8   Recall Problem 6.28. This problem dealt with 50 trials for color preference on the results of which would be based a test of $H : p = \frac{1}{2}$ against $A : p \neq \frac{1}{2}$. Set out the decision rule in terms of T, the number of red preferences, if a 5 percent significance level is used.

7.9   Recall Problem 6.12, where it was stated that men in the United States have a mean weight of 165 lb with a standard deviation of 15 lb. A particular insurance company checks on a group of 121 of its policyholders and finds their sample has a mean weight of 160.5 lb. Is the difference significant at the 5 percent level?

7.10 Recall the data given in Problem 5.19 on oral temperatures:

Temperature	Frequency	Temperature	Frequency
98.1	1	98.6	6
98.2	0	98.7	6
98.3	3	98.8	4
98.4	9	98.9	5
98.5	4	99.0	2

Test the hypothesis: $\mu = 98.6$ at the 5 percent level.

7.11 Recall the data of Problem 5.17. Test the hypothesis that this is a random sample from a university student population whose mean G.P.A. is 2.45 (5 percent significance level).

7.12 Experience shows that a fixed dose of a certain drug causes an average increase of pulse rate of 10 per minute. A group of nine patients given the same dose showed the following increases in pulse rate: 13, 15, 14, 10, 8, 12, 16, 9, 20. Using this information, a two-sided alternative, and a significance level of 5 percent, test whether there is sufficient evidence that this group of nine is significantly different in response to the drug. What assumptions need to be made about the random variable which measures the pulse-rate increase of a randomly chosen patient? Why?

7.13 A civil rights trial alleges discrimination against minority races in a particular county in the selection of juries; all minority races make up 24 percent of the adult population of the country. The current jury panel has 65 members of whom only 10 are of minority races. Discuss this from a statistical point of view.

7.14 In California in an experiment to evaluate whether cloud-seeding causes increased precipitation, two areas were selected, which, on the basis of previous observation, were known to receive equal precipitation. On the approach of each winter storm, a decision was made at random to seed one of the two areas. The difference in precipitation in the two areas was then recorded. Shown below are the differences for 12 storms (precipitation in the seeded area minus precipitation in the unseeded area in tenths of an inch): 4, 1, 5, 2, −2, 0, 3, 3, 2, 3, 5, −2. What conclusion can be drawn as to the effect of cloud-seeding on increasing precipitation?

7.15   For Example 7.6 (reducing without dieting), test the hypothesis in two ways at the 1 percent significance level. Is it necessary to repeat the calculations for the second method?

7.16   In Example 7.6, suppose that at the end of the experiment, the doctor finds that students 9, 10, 16, 17, 18, and 20 have not been taking the medicine as they were instructed. He drops their observations (2, 3, 1, 0, 2, 1) and analyzes the remainder. What is his conclusion now ($\alpha = 0.05$)?

7.17   Refer to the data of Example 7.5 (grades of married students). Could this sample have come from a population with $\mu = 2.45$, $\sigma = 0.5$? More precisely, test $H : \mu = 2.45$, $\sigma = 0.5$ versus $A : \mu \neq 2.45$, taking $\alpha = 0.05$. Does this agree with the result obtained in Example 7.5 by means of the significance probability?

7.18   Suppose the sample size on which the dean's data on G.P.A.'s of married students (Example 7.5) had been 100 rather than 25. Find the significance probability of the observation and the test rule ($\alpha = 0.05$). Do the two methods give the same result?

7.19   In the same university, another professor samples students and obtains the G.P.A.'s of those who smoke more than one pack of cigarettes per day. He samples 68 and finds their mean G.P.A. is 2.62. Find the significance probability of this observation. Can he conclude that smokers have a significantly different G.P.A. from those of all students (5 percent significance level)? Can he conclude that smoking improves grades? What assumption must he make about G.P.A.'s?

7.20   For the data of Example 1.2 (body temperatures), test the hypothesis that the temperatures given there have a true mean of 98.6. Use $\alpha = 0.05$. What assumption is made about the population of temperatures? Find also the significance probability of the observations.

7.21   A commuter reads a travel survey report that claims that the mean time to cross a bridge at rush hour is 8.2 minutes with a standard deviation of 2.1 minutes. He notes his time for two weeks (ten trips). His mean is 9.6 minutes. Find the significance probability of the observations summarized by this mean. Can he conclude that it is significantly different at the 5 percent level from the mean claimed by the survey? What assumptions are made about the random variable that measures the time taken to cross the bridge?

7.22   In Problem 4.13, a comparison was reported of times of calculation of a problem on first or second trials. Suppose that the actual differences in time had been recorded and that these differences (in seconds) were -3, 16, 32, 5, -26, 40, 11, -7, 8, 19, 9, 15. The random observations shown are the time for the first calculation minus the time for the second calculation.

(a) Test the hypothesis $\mu = 0$ against the alternative $\mu \neq 0$ at the 5 percent level by constructing the test rule.
(b) Find the significance probability of the observations.
(c) What are the differences between the statistical analysis used here and in Problem 4.13?
(d) What assumption is made about the differences?

7.23   Use the data of Problem 5.23 to test the hypothesis $\mu = 120$ at the 1 percent significance level. Use either method.

7.24   In Example 5.3 (Los Angeles schoolchildren's I.Q.'s), the I.Q.'s of 20 schoolchildren were obtained, from which $\bar{X} = 106$ and $s^2 = 167.75$ were calculated. The population mean I.Q. of all children in the United States is assumed to be 100. Are the observed data consistent with this assumption? Test by either method at the 5 percent significance level. Generally, I.Q.'s are considered to be normally distributed. Is this assumption necessary?

7.25   A climatologist is comparing a number of adjacent weather stations to determine whether their climates differ significantly. One comparison is based on the differences of June precipitation for 23 years. Here are the data for the period 1930 through 1952:

0.26	0.96	0.66	-0.48	0.39	0.05	0.44
-0.06	-0.83	0.06	-2.79	-0.12	1.42	-0.15
-0.45	-0.40	0.18	1.51	-0.23	-0.34	-1.08
-0.44	-1.24					

Is the difference in June precipitation significant at the 5 percent level? Use either method.

7.26   Obtain the all-university mean G.P.A. for your university and test whether the mean of the G.P.A.'s of students in the class is significantly different from this at the 5 percent level.

7.27   The Honorable Mole MacCaroney, who says, "Germs is everywhere," claims that his sanitary spray is so effective in killing germs that it reduces the weight of dirt by *at least* one-tenth of a pound per cubic foot (due to elimination of the germs?). An expert in this matter conducts the following experiment:

He weighs several samples of dirt before and after applying the sanitary spray. Here are the results:

Sample	Difference in weight before and after spraying (in tenths of lb per cu ft)
1	−1
2	0
3	1
4	0

(a) Test the hypothesis that the spray has no effect on weight.
(b) The hypothesis that the spray has no effect is not rejected. What can the Honorable Mole MacCaroney say that is valid statistically to defend his claim?
(c) What is the way to meet his objection?

7.28   The average length of all two-year-old male fur seals is 36.5 in. Forty-four tagged seals of this class were recovered in 1950. Their mean length was 36.0 in., with $s = 2.1$ in. Is there a significant difference from the mean of the whole population (at the 5 percent level)?

7.29   Recall Problem 6.27 (extrasensory perception), where we considered 100 trials of the E.S.P. experiment. The hypothesis tested is $H : p = \frac{1}{2}$ versus $A : p > \frac{1}{2}$. Set up the decision rule in terms of T, the number of correct choices if $\alpha = 0.01$.

★7.30   A study is to be conducted to determine whether a blood test yields the same results on fresh blood as on blood one day old. The plan is to take blood samples and, dividing them in half, analyze one half immediately and the other half after one day. The statistical analyst is asked whether a sample of 25 such duplicate determinations is large enough. To answer this question, he will need to know several additional pieces of information. What are they?

7.31   Evaluate the significance probability of your observation of traffic counts (Experiment 4.3) using the normal approximation to the binomial distribution.

7.32   A biologist is interested in determining the effect of a chemical spray on controlling a fungous infection that is now present in

30 percent of the trees in a forest stand. A test area of 100 trees is sprayed. Later examination shows that of these 100, 20 remain infected. State

(a) the random variable;
(b) the hypothesis and alternative of interest;
(c) the assumptions necessary to find the probability distribution of the random variable;
(d) the biologist's conclusion (1 percent significance level).

*7.33 Students at State University are given an entrance forecast of their all-college G.P.A. They are told that the differences between forecast and actual G.P.A. have a standard deviation of 0.45. A professor randomly samples 20 students on campus and compares their G.P.A.'s with their forecast G.P.A.'s. The mean difference (actual G.P.A. minus forecast G.P.A.) is 0.31.

(a) Is the difference significant at the 5 percent level? (That is, test the hypothesis $\mu = 0$ with $\alpha = 0.05$.)
(b) Find the significance probability of the observation.
(c) Is the sample size sufficient, so that the professor would have an 80 percent probability of detecting a mean difference of 0.5?
(d) The professor necessarily samples students on campus whose college career is not completed. Comment on this in regard to any conclusions he might draw.
(e) Suppose that the sample had been drawn by questioning a single class. Would this be a satisfactory random sampling procedure?
(f) If the standard deviation were unknown or if the professor believed incomplete G.P.A.'s have a different standard deviation from 0.45, could he still test the hypothesis $\mu = 0$ on the basis of the information given? What additional information is needed?

*7.34 Find the O.C. curve for the decision rule in Problem 7.1. More precisely, find the probability of accepting $H : \mu = 1.1$, $\sigma = 0.04$ when, in fact, $A : \mu \neq 1.1$, $\sigma = 0.04$ is true. Do this for alternatives $\mu = 1.09, 1.08, 1.07, 1.06, 1.05$. The Type II error probabilities for $\mu = 1.11, 1.12, 1.13, 1.14, 1.15$ can be obtained by symmetry and the O.C. curve sketched.

*7.35 Find the O.C. curve for Problem 7.3. Compare it with that of Problem 7.34.

*7.36 If, in Problem 7.5, the machine "slips" so that its average is $\mu = 0.99$ lb, how often will it produce packages weighing less than 1 lb?

*7.37 Suppose that in the sugar package example, the buyer does the sampling. His hypothesis is that $H : \mu = 1.1$, $\sigma = 0.02$, but since he is only worried about underweight packages, his alternative is $A : \mu < 1.1$, $\sigma = 0.02$. Since he does not worry so much about shutting a properly working machine down, he sets $\alpha = 0.10$. Set up his decision rule. Construct the O.C. curve for this rule. Does the rule seem satisfactory from his point of view? Compare this O.C. curve with the original O.C. curve for the two-sided alternative.

*7.38 In Problem 7.18, find the Type II error probability for $n = 100$, $\sigma = 0.5$, $\alpha = 0.05$, and $\mu = 2.25$.

*7.39 A medical research team is checking the procedure of a laboratory that makes chemical tests. Among several analyses made, one is the length of time required for a sample containing an added chemical to change color. This is a difficult analysis and is usually done in duplicate; i.e., the same analysis is made twice on separate halves of the sample, but by different technicians. Let μ denote the mean difference between the measurement of Technician No. 1 and the measurement of Technician No. 2.

(a) The research team wishes to determine whether $\mu = 0$, which it must be if the procedure is to be valid. They ask a statistician how many duplicate determinations should be sampled to determine this. He cannot answer without at least three items of further information. What are they?
(b) Assume the test of the hypothesis $\mu = 0$ is made at the 5 percent level, that the sample size is 4, and $\sigma = 5$. What is the probability that the test will detect the fact that $\mu = 10$?

*7.40 Recall Problem 6.2, which dealt with the production of ball bearings. The machine was set to produce ball bearings with a mean of 0.500 cm and a standard deviation 0.002 cm. If the machine performs correctly, then 98.8 percent of the bearings produced fall between the limits 0.495 and 0.505.

(a) Suppose that the company shifts from 100 percent inspection to a sample quality control scheme that depends on a rejection rule for μ based on $\bar{X}$. What should this rejection rule be if the sample size is 25 and the error level is 0.10?
(b) With what probability will the sample procedure and the test rule detect a machine that has slipped so that $\mu = 0.498$?

*7.41 Problem 6.39 recounted derivation of the probability that a sample of water was sterile (as determined by a biological culture test). For $M = 10,000$, $v/V = 1/10,000$, the probability is 0.36. Consider a test in which 40 samples of volume v are tested against the possibility that M has increased (in which case the probability of a sterile sample decreases). Write the test rule that you would use in this situation, taking into account that you wish with probability 0.99 to declare as unsafe water for which $M > 10,000$.

*7.42 Problem 4.15 referred to an experiment for testing visual discrimination under polarized light. The total experiment involved 60 trials. While there is some doubt that p is constant, what would the test rule be for the hypothesis $H : p = \frac{1}{2}$ versus $A : p \neq \frac{1}{2}$ if the random variable T = total number of correct responses is indeed binomial, with $n = 60$. Construct the O.C. curve for this test.

*7.43 From long experience with a process for manufacturing an alcoholic beverage, it is known that the yield is normally distributed with a mean of 500 units and a standard deviation of 100 units. A modification of the process is suggested for which it is claimed that the mean yield will increase (leaving the standard deviation unchanged). We propose, using a 5 percent level of significance, to make a test of the null hypothesis that the mean yield remains unchanged at 500 units. If the alternative hypothesis is that the mean yield is greater than 500,

(a) with 49 observations, what is the decision rule?
(b) with 49 observations, if the mean yield is actually 535 units, i.e., $A : \mu = 535$ is true, what is the probability of *rejecting* the null hypothesis?
(c) how many observations should be taken to make the probability of rejecting the null hypothesis equal to 0.90 when the true mean yield is 535 units?

*7.44 (Dangers of using cumulative results in rejected experiments.)

(a) Consider an E.S.P. experiment as in Example 4.3 with 40 trials. What is the significance probability of a score of 30?
(b) Suppose that the experimenter starts with 2,000 subjects, and tests each of them 20 times. Those with scores of 15 or greater are retained for further testing. What is the probability that of the 2,000 subjects 40 or more score 15 or greater if all are guessing? These 40 are selected for a second test of 20 trials. What is the

probability that one or more subjects scores 15 or higher (again assuming that each subject guesses)? What is the probability that both these events occur—which implies that at least one subject will have a cumulative score of 30 or greater? Compare this with the probability computed in part (a) for an experiment of 40 trials on a single randomly selected subject.

CHAPTER EIGHT

Confidence Intervals

Introduction

A sample yields some information about the population from which it is drawn. For example, the African explorer who was met by a group of seven-foot men knew that the population contained some seven-foot men. However, these might be a specially selected group chosen to intimidate strangers or perhaps they might be "runts" of the tribe forced to do unpleasant tasks. Or they might be representative of the population. The statistician naturally tries to conduct sampling experiments so that the random observations are representative of the population and so that the probability distribution of the random observations can be calculated. The observations and probability theory can then be used to draw inferences about the population. Such inferences may be used to support or deny prior hypotheses or they may be simple estimators of the population parameters.

For example, in Chapter 5 point estimators were studied and it was noted that the mean of a random sample is an estimator of the population mean. But as the student has observed, the point estimator of a parameter usually changes with every sample taken. The statistician would like to know how close the estimator is to the true value. Some information is given by the variance (or standard deviation) of the estimator if this is known.

If the variance of the estimator is not known, it may be possible to estimate it also. Thus, in many fields it is customary to affix to the estimator $\bar{X}$ of μ the *standard error of the mean*, namely, $s/\sqrt{n}$. Since the variance of $\bar{X}$ is σ^2/n, the estimated variance of $\bar{X}$ is s^2/n, and the standard error of the mean is the square root of the estimated variance of $\bar{X}$. Thus a set of data such as that presented in Problem 5.20 (Saturn's rings) might have been summarized as having a mean 39.31 ± 0.031. The figure 0.031 is the estimated standard deviation of $\bar{X}$, i.e., $s/\sqrt{n}$, and ±0.031 suggest something about the reliability of 39.31. In particular, we might feel that the true mean diameter of Saturn's rings is "probably" within ±0.031 of 39.31. As soon as we introduce the term "probably" it becomes reasonable to ask with what probability and to try to clarify exactly what is meant here. There are several problems: What is the random variable here (presumably not the true mean diameter of Saturn's rings)? How reliable is the estimator of σ^2? What can be said about the distributions of the random variables that are involved?

Confidence Intervals

Clarification of these concepts came during the 1930's, though some of the ideas of what we now call the *theory of confidence intervals* were developed earlier. The basic idea is to find a formula that associates an interval with each sample observation and each prescribed probability level. The interval is asserted to contain the true parameter value, and our confidence in the statement is that of the prescribed probability level. In other words, rather than looking for a statement about the reliability of the estimate and thus trying to evaluate the statement, we begin with a probability level and a probability statement about the random variables with which we are working. It is often easy then, by using ordinary algebra, to convert this into a statement about the unknown parameter, in particular, into a statement that the parameter lies within a certain interval. Such an interval is called a *confidence interval*. The prescribed probability is called the *confidence coefficient*.

Confidence Intervals for μ:
X Normally Distributed

Consider the probability statement that can be made about a sample mean drawn from a normal population with mean μ and variance σ^2:

$$P\left(-t_\alpha \leq \frac{\bar{X} - \mu}{s/\sqrt{n}} \leq t_\alpha\right) = 1 - \alpha.$$

We used this to find a two-tailed rejection rule for testing hypotheses about μ; i.e., we solved

$$\bar{X} - \frac{st_\alpha}{\sqrt{n}} = \pm t_\alpha$$

for $\bar{X}$, obtaining $\bar{X} = \mu \pm st_\alpha/\sqrt{n}$. The rejection rule determined in this way is: Reject the hypothesis that the mean is μ if $\bar{X} \leq \mu - st_\alpha/\sqrt{n}$ or $\bar{X} \geq \mu + st_\alpha/\sqrt{n}$.

We can also solve the above equation (or the inequalities inside the above probability statement) for μ. The result is $\mu = \bar{X} \pm st_\alpha/\sqrt{n}$ or in the form of inequalities,

$$\bar{X} - \frac{st_\alpha}{\sqrt{n}} \leq \mu \leq \bar{X} + \frac{st_\alpha}{\sqrt{n}}.$$

This pair of inequalities is strictly equivalent to the pair of inequalities inside the parentheses of the probability statement; since the first inequalities are true with probability $1 - \alpha$, the same can be said about the second inequalities. This suggests a procedure as follows.

From each random sample $X_1, X_2, \ldots, X_n$, form the interval $\bar{X} - st_\alpha/\sqrt{n}$, $\bar{X} + st_\alpha/\sqrt{n}$; then these random intervals will include the population mean μ with probability $1 - \alpha$; i.e., the proportion of times μ is included between $\bar{X} \pm st_\alpha/\sqrt{n}$ is $1 - \alpha$, on the average. The set of all possible random samples determines, by means of this rule, a set of random intervals that are confidence intervals, with confidence coefficient $1 - \alpha$, for μ, the *mean* of a normal population.

Example 8.1 Heights of university men

A random sample of 32 university male students was taken by the university medical officer in connection with a study for other purposes. In the course of the study the height of each individual was measured and the following results obtained: $\bar{X} = 68.06$, $s^2 = 14.45$ (so that $s = 3.80$).

Find a confidence interval for μ, the mean height of men at this university, assuming that heights of university men are normally distributed, and using as confidence coefficient 0.95.

Solution: From Table A2.6, interpolating for 31 degrees of freedom, we derive the probability statement $0.95 = P(-2.04 \leq t \leq +2.04)$ $= P[-2.04 \leq (\bar{X} - \mu)/(s/\sqrt{n}) \leq +2.04]$.

We can solve the two equations

$$\frac{X - \mu}{s/\sqrt{n}} = -2.04 \quad \text{and} \quad \frac{X - \mu}{s/\sqrt{n}} = +2.04$$

for μ and find that

$$\mu = X - \frac{2.04s}{\sqrt{n}} \quad \text{and} \quad \mu = X + \frac{2.04s}{\sqrt{n}}.$$

Substituting $X = 68.06$, $s = 3.80$ yields the interval $(68.06 - 1.37, 68.06 + 1.37)$ or $(66.69, 69.43)$.

We conclude with the statement that with 95 percent confidence μ, the mean height of all male students at this university, lies between 66.69 and 69.43 in.

It is important to distinguish between the use of the words probability and confidence coefficient. In Example 8.1, we *cannot* say that μ lies between 66.69 in. and 69.43 in. with probability 0.95. The mean height of all university students μ is some *fixed* but unknown number. Thus μ either does or does not lie in the interval $(66.69, 69.43)$. We say that with confidence coefficient 0.95, μ lies between 66.69 in. and 69.43 in., and we interpret this in exactly the same way that we interpreted hypothesis tests. That is, if we perform the experiment just once and obtain just one interval, we either are correct when we say that μ lies in the interval or we are wrong. But in many experiments, we will find many intervals and 95 percent of them, on the average, will contain μ. Thus in our one experiment we are confident (95 percent confident) that we are correct when we assert that μ lies in the interval.

Another way of interpreting confidence intervals is the following: If a statistician performs many experiments and constructs, for each experiment, a confidence interval for μ with confidence coefficient 0.95, in any one trial he will not know whether his interval includes μ or not but he will be confident in the sense that 95 percent of the intervals will contain μ, on the average.

EXERCISE (CLASS)

Use Table A2.5 to draw a sample of four standard normal variates. Calculate $\bar{X}$, s, and a 90 percent confidence interval for μ. Repeat this until a total of 100 such intervals have been obtained by the class. (If the class has done Class Experiment 7.1(b), the data in that experiment may be used here to make the 90 percent confidence intervals, and no new observations are required.) These random variables have true mean zero; record how many of the confidence intervals include zero. It is useful to plot these intervals on lines parallel to the x axis, as shown in Figure 8.1; variability of the intervals and the ones that fail to include $\mu = 0$ are easily observed.

The process of obtaining confidence intervals has been likened to the game of horseshoes or ringtoss. The peg is fixed; the position of the horseshoe or ring after the toss varies. On some occasions the horseshoe or ring surrounds the peg (corresponding to μ's being included within the confidence interval), and on others it fails to do so.

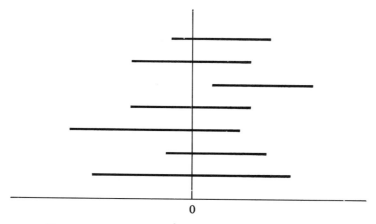

0

FIGURE 8.1 *Ninety percent confidence intervals for μ.*

In testing hypotheses, the statistician is free to choose the significance level for rejecting the hypothesis when it is true. Once the significance level has been selected for a fixed sample size, he has no further control over the probabilities of other errors. In confidence interval estimation, the statistician has at his disposal the confidence coefficient. When this has been selected, he has no control over the length of the interval.

[*Note:* In hypothesis testing, the statistician should keep in mind that he reduces the Type I error by increasing the Type II error and vice versa. In confidence interval estimation, he pays for an increased confidence coefficient with longer and presumably less useful intervals.]

EXERCISE

Verify that the 80, 90, 95, 99 percent confidence intervals for μ in Example 8.1 are as follows:

Confidence coefficient	Confidence interval (inches)
0.80	67.18–68.94
0.90	66.92–69.20
0.95	66.69–69.43
0.99	66.22–69.90

Though σ is usually not known in a problem where estimation of μ is of interest, it may occasionally happen that it is. In this case the statistician starts from the probability statement

$$P\left(-z_\alpha \le \frac{X - \mu}{\sigma/\sqrt{n}} \le z_\alpha\right) = 1 - \alpha$$

and by the same steps derives as a confidence interval

$$\left(X - \frac{\sigma z_\alpha}{\sqrt{n}}, \; X + \frac{\sigma z_\alpha}{\sqrt{n}}\right)$$

with confidence coefficient $1 - \alpha$.

These intervals have the property that their length is always the same, i.e., $2\sigma z_\alpha/\sqrt{n}$, in contrast to those given by the earlier formula in which the length was $2st_\alpha/\sqrt{n}$, a random variable. Of course, as n increases, t_α tends to z_α (check this in Table A2.6) and s tends to σ, so that for large n, the two sets of intervals must be approximately the same. Returning to the discussion on Saturn's rings, if we regard s in this example as essentially the same as σ (as was done in the 19th century by most experimenters and still is in the 20th century in some areas of application), the interval 39.31 ± 0.31 can be interpreted as the confidence interval $X \pm (1)(\sigma/\sqrt{n})$. Since $P(-1 < Z < +1) = 0.68$, it follows that 39.31 ± 0.31 is approximately a 68 percent confidence interval for μ. Also used formerly was the *probable error*, namely, $0.6745\, s/\sqrt{n}$. The interval $X \pm 0.6745\, s/\sqrt{n}$ can be given a similar interpretation. Check that $P(-0.6745 < Z < 0.6745) = 0.50$, so that this interval is approximately a 50 percent confidence interval for μ.

Another discussion of confidence intervals, based on the relationship between decision rules and confidence intervals, may be helpful. As shown in the derivation of the interval $\bar{X} \pm st_\alpha/\sqrt{n}$, the initial probability statement is the same one that led to a two-tailed test for μ. It follows that if a particular value of μ, say μ_0, is in the 95 percent confidence interval, then $H : \mu = \mu_0$ (versus $A : \mu \neq \mu_0$) would not be rejected at the 5 percent significance level. Conversely, if μ_1 is not in the 95 percent confidence interval for μ, then $H : \mu = \mu_1$ (versus $A : \mu \neq \mu_1$) is rejected at the 5 percent level. Thus we can define a confidence interval, with confidence coefficient $1 - \alpha$, as the set of values of the parameter that would not be found significant in a two-tailed test at level α.

EXERCISE

Using the data of Example 8.1, test the hypotheses

$$H_1 : \mu = 66.68,$$
$$H_2 : \mu = 66.69,$$
$$H_3 : \mu = 69.43,$$
$$H_4 : \mu = 69.44.$$

Work carefully and observe that H_1 and H_4 are just rejected, H_2 and H_3 just accepted. As pointed out above, any hypotheses specifying that μ has some value between 66.69 and 69.43 would not be rejected on the basis of this sample at the 5 percent level.

For this reason, among others, it is now customary to choose one of the confidence coefficients 0.90, 0.95, or 0.99.

Confidence Intervals for the Binomial Parameter *p*

Various charts and tables have been constructed to calculate confidence intervals for the binomial parameter, based on an observation T of the total number of successes in n independent binomial trials. These tables† are needed in the same way that special tables are needed for hypothesis testing in the binomial case for small n.

For larger n, the normal approximation to the binomial distribution, discussed in Chapter 6, is useful for obtaining confidence intervals for p. This is a straightforward application of the results of the first part of this chapter. $\bar{X}$ is replaced by $\hat{p}$, and σ^2 by an unbiased estimator of the variance on any trial, namely, $[n/(n - 1)]\hat{p}(1 - \hat{p})$.

---

† Such a table can be found in A. Hald, *Statistical Tables and Formulas* (New York: John Wiley and Sons, Inc., 1952).

Thus, a confidence interval for p, with approximate confidence co-efficient $1 - \alpha$, is

$$\hat{p} \pm t_\alpha \sqrt{\frac{\hat{p}(1 - \hat{p})}{n - 1}}.$$

Example 8.2 Who was Einstein? (continued)

Recall Example 1.4. The combined sample in the example gave a value of $T = 22$ with $n = 40$; i.e., 22 of the 40 students knew who Einstein was.

Thus $\hat{p} = 0.55$ and the confidence interval is

$$0.55 \pm 2.02 \sqrt{\frac{(0.55)(0.45)}{39}},$$

i.e., 0.55 ± 0.16 or $(0.39, 0.71)$. With approximately 95 percent confidence, it can be asserted that between 39 percent and 71 percent of the students know who Einstein was. Having calculated the confidence interval, a test of any two-sided hypothesis concerning p is immediate. For example, $H : p = \frac{1}{2}$ versus $A : p \neq \frac{1}{2}$ is not rejected at the 5 percent level, since 0.5 is within the 95 percent confidence interval.

Since such confidence intervals are only approximate, based as they are on the Central Limit Theorem, various modifications of the approximation have been given. Thus the reader may encounter confidence intervals for p calculated with t_α replaced by z_α, and with $n - 1$ by n, since the ratio $(n - 1)/n$ is close to one for values of n for which the approximation is appropriate. Still another approach is to start with the probability statement

$$P\left(-z_\alpha < \frac{\hat{p} - p}{\sqrt{p(1 - p)/n}} < z_\alpha\right) \doteq 1 - \alpha.$$

The two equations

$$\frac{\hat{p} - p}{\sqrt{p(1 - p)/n}} = \pm z_\alpha$$

can be converted into one quadratic equation in the unknown by squaring both sides. It can be shown that the two solutions of the quadratic equation are the ends of an approximate confidence interval for p with confidence coefficient $1 - \alpha$. Whether one of these approximations is better in some sense than the others is not known and we will use here only the simple procedure that is strictly analogous to that derived for the mean of a normal distribution.

Confidence Intervals for the Mean of a Second Sample

On occasion, after a sample has been taken, it is useful to ask for a confidence interval on the mean of a second sample, which has not yet been taken. For example, a computer does ten problems in an average time of 8.3 minutes. What may be said about the average time of ten more similar problems? A confidence interval for such a second sample mean can be readily deduced from a probability statement analogous to the earlier one when the underlying variables are normally distributed. If X is the first sample mean, X' the second sample mean, based on independent random samples of size n and m respectively from the same normal population, then $X - X'$ is a normal random variable with mean zero and variance $\sigma^2[(1/n) + (1/m)]$. The latter result comes from Theorem 2.3: The variance of a sum of independent variables is the sum of the variances, and any constant multipliers are squared. Hence

$$P\left(-z_\alpha \leq \frac{X - X'}{\sigma[(1/n) + (1/m)]^{1/2}} \leq z_\alpha\right) = 1 - \alpha.$$

If σ is not known, which is the usual case, it must be replaced by s, the estimated standard deviation. This comes from the first sample and hence has $n - 1$ d.f. Then the proper probability statement is

$$P\left(-t_\alpha \leq \frac{X - X'}{s[(1/n) + (1/m)]^{1/2}} \leq t_\alpha\right) = 1 - \alpha.$$

Setting

$$\frac{X - X'}{s[(1/n) + (1/m)]^{1/2}} = \pm t_\alpha$$

and solving for X' yields

$$X' = X \pm st_\alpha\left(\frac{1}{n} + \frac{1}{m}\right)^{1/2},$$

where t_α is found in Table A2.6 using $n - 1$ d.f. This is the required confidence interval. For example, if $X = 8.3$, $n = 10$, and if, in addition, we are given $s = 1.5$, then a 95 percent confidence interval for X' is

$$8.3 - (1.5)(2.26)(\tfrac{1}{10} + \tfrac{1}{10})^{1/2}, \qquad 8.3 + (1.5)(2.26)(\tfrac{1}{10} + \tfrac{1}{10})^{1/2},$$

i.e., (6.78, 9.82). In words, the second sample mean is expected to lie between 6.78 and 9.82. It is well to be clear as to what is meant in the confidence coefficient attached to this statement. If a statistician follows this rule each time he draws a *pair* of samples from a normal population, then the statements made about the second sample mean will be correct 95 percent of the time. The probability statement applies to the totality of pairs, *not the totality of second samples for a fixed observed single first sample.*

The same procedure can be used with a slight modification for a second binomial sample.

Example 8.3   Television viewers

A rating service finds that 24 of 48 television sets are tuned to Channel 8 at a particular time. What may be said of the proportion of Channel 8 viewers in a second sample of size 50, with confidence coefficient 0.95? Let $\hat{p}$ denote the observed proportion in the first sample, i.e., $\hat{p} = T/n$. Let $\hat{p}'$ denote the (to be) observed proportion in a second independent sample. For n and m sufficiently large, $\hat{p} - \hat{p}'$ is approximately normally distributed. Further, it has mean zero and variance $p(1 - p)[(1/n) + (1/m)]$.

Then an approximate confidence interval for $\hat{p}' = T'/m$ is

$$\hat{p} \pm t_\alpha \sqrt{\left(\frac{n}{n-1}\right)\hat{p}(1 - \hat{p})\left(\frac{1}{n} + \frac{1}{m}\right)}.$$

For this example, $\hat{p} = 0.50$, $t_{0.05} = 2.01$, $n = 48$, and $m = 50$ so the confidence interval is

$$0.50 \pm 2.01 \sqrt{\frac{48}{47}(0.50)(0.50)\left(\frac{1}{48} + \frac{1}{50}\right)} = 0.50 \pm 0.205$$

$$\text{or} \quad (0.295 \text{ to } 0.705).$$

That is, we can assert with 95 percent confidence that the second sample will show a proportion of Channel 8 viewers between 0.295 and 0.705.

Again the probability statement applies to all *pairs* of binomial observations. It is useful to point out that the earlier formulas provided confidence intervals for a parameter or population value. The formulas given in this section yield confidence intervals for a random variable—a second sample mean or proportion.

Summary

A confidence interval procedure is a rule that attaches to each sample an associated confidence interval with a prescribed confidence coefficient. This interval is asserted to include or contain either the unknown parameter value or a yet-to-be-observed random variable. The totality of such statements, based on all possible samples, is true with probability equal to the prescribed confidence coefficient.

Useful confidence interval formulas for the parameters and distributions indicated are:

Mean of normal population (σ known):

$$\bar{X} \pm \frac{\sigma z_\alpha}{\sqrt{n}}.$$

Mean of normal population (σ unknown):

$$\bar{X} \pm \frac{s t_\alpha}{\sqrt{n}}.$$

Mean of second sample from a normal population (σ unknown):

$$\bar{X} \pm s t_\alpha \left(\frac{1}{n} + \frac{1}{m}\right)^{1/2}.$$

Proportion in a binomial distribution:

$$\hat{p} \pm t_\alpha \sqrt{\frac{\hat{p}(1 - \hat{p})}{n - 1}}.$$

Proportion in a second sample from a binomial distribution:

$$\hat{p} \pm t_\alpha \sqrt{\frac{n}{n - 1} \hat{p}(1 - \hat{p})\left(\frac{1}{n} + \frac{1}{m}\right)}.$$

All of these have confidence coefficient $1 - \alpha$, either exactly or approximately.

The confidence coefficient is exact in the case of the normal distribution and approximate for the binomial distribution, since the probabilities from which they are derived are based on the central limit theorem and hence only approximately correct. By virtue of the central limit theorem the formulas for the confidence interval for the mean may be used for any population and will be approximately correct unless the sample is very small and the population is very unusual.

■ **Experiments**

8.1   Recall the results of Experiments 2.1, 2.2, 2.3.

(a) For Experiment 2.1, define the event E: no red card is sampled. What is a 95 percent confidence interval for p, the probability that no red card is sampled, based on the 25 observations made? Test $H : p = \frac{1}{6}$ versus $A : p \neq \frac{1}{6}$ at the 5 percent level either directly or using the confidence interval method.

(b) For Experiment 2.2, define the event E: the king is exposed in one or two trials. Let p be the probability of this event and find a 99 percent confidence interval for p based on the observations made. Test $H : p = \frac{1}{2}$ versus $A : p \neq \frac{1}{2}$ at the 1 percent level.

(c) For Experiment 2.3, define the event E: each right-hand page number is larger than corresponding left-hand page number. (This occurs if and only if the score is $+4$.) Find a 95 percent confidence interval for p, the probability that $X = 4$. Test $H : p = \frac{1}{6}$ versus $A : p \neq \frac{1}{6}$ at the 5 percent level.

8.2   Confidence intervals may be determined for the probabilities of any of the experiments of Chapter 4. Determine such intervals and use the intervals obtained to test the hypothesis that was indicated in the experiment.

8.3   Recall the data obtained in Problem 5.26. Find a 95 percent confidence interval for the probability p that a tack when dropped will fall point up.

■ **Problems**

8.1   Find a 99 percent confidence interval for the G.P.A. of the university from which the sample of Problem 5.17 was drawn.

8.2   (a) Use the data of Problem 5.19 to state what may be said with 95 percent confidence about the mean oral temperature of the population of medical students referred to. (b) Find a 90 percent confidence interval for the mean of a second sample of ten oral temperatures taken on rising.

8.3   Using the data of Problem 7.33, find a 90 percent confidence interval for the mean difference (actual G.P.A. minus forecast G.P.A.).

8.4   Use the result given in Problem 4.12 to determine a 95 percent confidence interval for the probability of a home team winning.

8.5 How is the length of a confidence interval for μ related to sample size?

(a) Compare the confidence intervals for μ if $X = 10$, $s = 5$ when $n = 20$, 40, 80.

(b) In the binomial case, compute confidence intervals for the following cases: $n = 20$, $T = 10$; $n = 40$, $T = 20$; $n = 80$, $T = 40$. Calculate the length of the interval in each case. Note that, as in part (a), the third interval length is approximately half the first, the second interval length is about $1/\sqrt{2}$ times the first.

8.6 A random sample of 100 students from the student directory shows 24 to be from out of state.

(a) Find a 95 percent confidence interval for the proportion of out-of-state students.

(b) Give also a 95 percent confidence interval for the proportion in a second sample (of 100) from this population.

8.7 A sample of 22 fish has mean length 23.5 cm with a standard deviation of 5.4 cm. Find a 95 percent confidence interval for a single additional individual from this population.

8.8 A test of 25 electronic tubes yields the following results concerning their length of life (X): $X = 1{,}118$ hours, $s = 50$ hours. Find a 90 percent confidence interval for μ, the mean length of life of the whole population of electronic tubes.

8.9 (a) Could the intervals obtained by the rule $X \pm (s t_\alpha / \sqrt{n})$ be shorter than those obtained using the rule $X \pm (\sigma z_\alpha / \sqrt{n})$ based on the same data?

(b) Refer to the data of the class exercise following Example 8.1. In this experiment, samples of size 4 were drawn from a normal population with variance 1. The length of a 95 percent confidence interval, if we make use of the known variance, is $2(1.96)(1/\sqrt{4})$, i.e., 1.96. How many of the intervals obtained in this experiment exceed 1.96 in length? How many are less than 1.96 in length?

(c) Why do the intervals based on the formula $X \pm (s t_\alpha / \sqrt{n})$ tend to be longer on the average than those using the known variance? Does this have any connection with the t distribution replacing the normal distribution? How do the tails of the t distribution compare with the tails of the normal distribution?

8.10 The average weight of 100 randomly selected ten-year-old Seattle boys is 80.5 lb.

(a) What additional information, if any, do you need to calculate a 99 percent confidence interval for μ, the mean weight of all Seattle ten-year-old boys?

(b) Suppose you have calculated a confidence interval for the mean weight of Seattle ten-year-old boys and found it to be 78.3 to 82.7 lb. Does this mean that no ten-year-old boy in Seattle weighs less than 78.3 or more than 82.7 lb? If not, what does it mean?

(c) Compute a 99 percent confidence interval for the weight of an individual boy to be selected from this population. [*Hint*: First use the information in (b) to calculate s.]

8.11   In a particular county, the proportion of unemployed workers in the population of all employable individuals is unknown. A statistician of the Bureau of Labor Statistics wishes to determine a 95 percent confidence interval for the proportion of unemployed workers in the population. He would like his confidence interval for this proportion to be no *longer* than 0.2.

(a) If he randomly samples 100 employable individuals and finds 20 unemployed, will his requirement be satisfied?

(b) What is the random variable in this problem and what distribution does it have?

(c) What is the connection between this distribution and the confidence interval?

(d) Define what you mean by a confidence interval in this problem.

8.12   Find a confidence interval for the number of words in the book that you sampled in Problem 5.15.

8.13   The following frequency table shows for 20 American statisticians (listed in the directory of the Institute of Mathematical Statistics) the length of time (in years) between completion of their bachelor's degree and the listed date of their Ph.D.

Years	Frequency
4	5
5	4
6	2
7	3
8	2
9	1
10	1
12	1
17	1

(a) Find a 90 percent confidence interval for the mean length of time between a bachelor's degree and a Ph.D. for the population from which this sample is drawn.

(b) Specify carefully what the population is.

(c) The 95 percent confidence interval is (5.33, 8.37). Does this mean that only 5 percent of the population have elapsed times (from bachelor's degree to Ph.D.) of less than 5.33 years?

8.14   (a) A student entering university receives a G.P.A. prediction of 2.80. He is also told that these predictions are correct on the average, but that the variance of the errors of prediction is 0.25. Can he set up a 95 percent confidence interval for his expected university G.P.A.?

(b) The mean G.P.A. prediction for this freshman class of 4,068 is 2.73. What is a 95 percent confidence interval for the expected mean university G.P.A. for this class?

8.15   What is the relationship of the point estimate of μ and the confidence interval estimate for μ? Of the point estimate of p and the confidence interval estimate for p?

*8.16   You have some sample data on G.P.A.'s of students at the university and wish to calculate a confidence interval for the mean G.P.A. of all students.

(a) $\bar{X} \pm (st_\alpha/\sqrt{n})$ and $\bar{X} \pm (\sigma z_\alpha/\sqrt{n})$ are both confidence intervals for μ, the mean of a normal population. How do you decide which to use?

(b) The confidence intervals $\bar{X} \pm (1.83 \, s/\sqrt{n})$ determined from a sample of size 10 will fail to include μ, the true mean, on occasion. How frequently will this be, on the average?

(c) You may decide your confidence interval is too long. Name two things you might do to obtain a shorter confidence interval.

(d) Your 95 percent confidence interval turns out to be (2.2, 2.6). Can you now go up to any student and say to him with 95 percent confidence, "Your G.P.A. lies between 2.2 and 2.6"? Why or why not?

8.17   (a) The mean length of time spent in the pupa stage by a sample of nine moths is 49 hours. The standard deviation of the sample is 10 hours. Find a 95 percent confidence interval for the population mean.

(b) In (a), a 95 percent confidence interval was asked for. This means, on the average, in 5 percent of such experiments the confidence limits do not include the population mean and a false statement is made. Can I cut down on this probability of making a false statement, and if so, what do I lose instead?

*8.18 What happens to the length of the confidence interval for a mean as n tends to infinity? What happens to the length of a confidence interval for a second sample mean of size m (fixed) as n tends to infinity? What happens to the length of a confidence interval of a second sample mean, if the second sample m tends to infinity but n remains fixed?

8.19 Use the data on male salmon given in Problem 5.16 to find a 95 percent confidence interval for the mean length of the male population; do the same for the female salmon. Many people are tempted to use these separate intervals to make a comparison between the mean of the male and female populations. This is not valid though it is possible to use the sample estimated difference $\bar{X}_m - \bar{X}_f$ to find a confidence interval for $\mu_m - \mu_f$, where the subscripts m and f refer to males and females respectively. For large samples, as in Problem 5.16, this is quite simple since the Central Limit Theorem certainly holds; for smaller samples, assumptions must be made not only about the form of the distribution but the relative magnitudes of the population variances. (See Problem 12.23.)

8.20 Compare the 10, 25, 80, 90, 95, and 99 percent confidence intervals for μ, the mean diameter of Saturn's rings. Use the data of Problem 5.20 and the normal approximation.

8.21 In Problem 5.8 the information was given that the mean time to work certain problems was 1 hour (standard deviation 15 minutes). Assume that the times are normally distributed and compute the probability that the time to work ten problems is between 9 and 11 hours. [*Note:* Distinguish this from a confidence interval problem.]

8.22 (a) Refer to the data of Example 7.5 (grades of married students). Recall that the G.P.A. of the 25 married students sample was 2.35, and that it was assumed that $\sigma = 0.5$; use these data to obtain a confidence interval for the G.P.A. of married students. Use the confidence interval to test the hypothesis $\mu = 2.45$ against the alternative $\mu \neq 2.45$.

(b) If the actual 25 grades had been given, a different confidence interval could have been computed. This would have involved one less assumption. (Which one?) How would the interval be obtained?

8.23   Find a 90 percent confidence interval for μ in Example 7.6 (reducing without dieting), and use this to test $H : \mu = 0$ at the 10 percent significance level against $A : \mu \neq 0$.

8.24   Use the data of Example 1.2 (body temperature) (see also Problem 7.20) to calculate a confidence interval for mean body temperature. Use $\alpha = 0.05$. From the results of Problem 7.20 can you say in advance whether 98.6 will lie inside or outside the interval?

8.25   In Problem 7.22 data were given on the difference in times of calculations of a problem on first and second trials. Calculate a 90 percent confidence interval for μ, the mean difference, and show that $\mu = 0$ is rejected at the 10 percent level. (Recall that $\mu = 0$ was not rejected at the 5 percent level.) What is the relationship between these two results and the significance probability of the observations?

8.26   In the last three weeks of the *Times* Football Guessing Contest, out of a total of 60 possible guesses, a contestant has gotten 38 right. Assume that the results of the different guesses are independent and that he has the same probability of being right throughout.

(a) Find a 95 percent confidence interval for p, the probability of guessing any single game result correctly.
(b) Is he doing significantly better than chance (at the 5 percent significance level)?

*8.27   A recent issue of *Science* reports on a radar determination of the radius of Venus: It is stated that the most recent estimate by this method is $6,053.7 \pm 2.2$ kilometers. Assume that the number 2.2 represents the standard error of the observations, that is, $s/\sqrt{n}$.

(a) What other information is needed to work out a 95 percent confidence interval for μ, the radius of Venus?
(b) Though the information required is missing, it is possible to find the widest and narrowest possible 95 percent confidence intervals for μ, still assuming normality of the observations. Obtain those intervals.

8.28   The length of time needed to grow a new variety of wheat (from time of planting to time of harvesting) is 98.4 days. This is the average for 12 years. The standard deviation of those 12 observations is 4.1 days.

(a) Estimate the growing time for next year.
(b) Indicate in some appropriate manner the reliability of this estimate.

*8.29 A biochemist, investigating the birth weight of rats whose mothers have been on a protein-deficient diet, reports on an experiment that gave a mean weight of 4.46 ± 0.22 grams ($n = 31$). A repetition of this experiment yields the results for the mean 4.28 ± 0.34 grams ($n = 18$). Compute a combined estimate of μ and of σ^2 and use this to find a 95 percent confidence interval for μ, mean birth weight. [*Note:* Since the variance of X is inversely proportional to sample size, the best (minimum variance unbiased estimate) of μ based on two sample means X_1, X_2 is $(n_1 X_1 + n_2 X_2)/(n_1 + n_2)$, where n_1, n_2 are the respective sample sizes. Similarly it may be shown that the best combined estimate of σ^2 is

$$\frac{(n_1 - 1)s_1^2 + (n_2 - 1)s_2^2}{(n_1 - 1) + (n_2 - 1)}.]$$

*8.30 A candidate for elective office has a sample poll made in his electoral district. A random sample of 432 persons who expect to vote show the following division: for candidate, 217; for opponent, 169; undecided, 46.

Find 95 percent confidence intervals for p = proportion of votes supporting this candidate,

(a) under the assumption that all undecided voters will vote for the candidate;
(b) under the assumption that all undecided voters will vote for the opponent;
(c) under the assumption that the undecided voters will not vote.

*8.31 Consider the 386 decided votes of Problem 8.30; the candidate would like to know if he can be 95 percent sure of at least half the votes of the decided voters. Can he use the confidence interval of 8.30(c) to answer this question? Why or why not? If not, how can he proceed to answer the question?

*8.32 In Theorem 5.1, it was noted that the variance of the sample mean X of a sample taken without replacement from a finite population of size N is $(\sigma^2/n)[(N - n)/(N - 1)]$. The factor in brackets is referred to as the finite population correction and can and should be used when the sampling fraction n/N is known and is not negligibly small.

(a) A sample of 100 farms out of a total of 400 in Grant County was taken to determine the mean wheat acreage per farm in the county. If $\bar{X}$ = mean acreage on sampled farms = 645 acres, s = 121 acres, find a 90 percent confidence interval for μ = mean acreage per farm, taking into account the finite population correction.

(b) After determining the mean acreage per farm, since the number of farms is known, it is easy to determine the confidence interval for the total number of acres in wheat. Do so for this example with confidence coefficient 0.95.

*8.33   An educational testing agency tests a language examination on what it believes to be a random sample of the graduate student population. A group of 854 students obtain a mean score of 285 with a standard deviation of 55. The maximum possible score is 500. Assume that scores are normally distributed and estimate what range of scores will be obtained by the top 5 percent of students in this population.

*8.34   A pollution study is conducted for 25 days and it is found that a major city in the United States has an average midday concentration of carbon monoxide of 12.3 parts per million (standard deviation 4.4 parts). Will the 95 percent confidence interval for μ, mean concentration of carbon monoxide, be less than 1 part per million in length? If not, estimate how many observations should be made to achieve this. The population mean μ is the average over a long period of time, and it is assumed that this is unchanged though of course there are day-to-day fluctuations that are assumed to be normally distributed. The required sample size is an estimate, i.e., random variable. Why?

*8.35   Age determinations are to be made on a random sample of animals taken from a population to determine the mean age of the population.

(a) What will be the estimate of the population mean?
(b) How can we determine the reliability of this estimate? The biologist asks that the sample be sufficiently large that, with 99 percent confidence, the statement can be made that the estimate differs from the true value by less than ± 0.20.
(c) This is a requirement on the confidence interval. What is the requirement?
(d) If σ is known to be 2, what is the required sample size?

*8.36   Recall Example 1.3 (travel times). A student notes the following ten travel times (in minutes) from home to university in the

two-week period (he leaves home at approximately 9 A.M. each time):
21, 25, 30, 24, 23, 22, 23, 45, 24, 20. Construct a 95 percent confidence
interval for the mean μ of all possible travel times. What assumptions
do you need to make concerning such travel times in order to obtain
the confidence interval? Is there anything in the data that might lead
you to believe the assumptions needed are invalid?

CHAPTER NINE

Joint Probability Models

Introduction

In Chapters 2 through 8, we studied a single random variable or random samples on such a variable, that is, independent repetitions of the same random variable. Many examples come to mind in which two or more random variables need to be studied during one experiment. We will restrict our study to two random variables for the most part, the extension to more than two random variables being handled in obvious ways.

Example 9.1   An experiment with two outcomes and a number of runs

In Example 2.13 we considered the number of runs in four births, two of each sex. We might be interested in both the number of males and the number of runs. Consider four independent births in which it is assumed that either sex is equally likely on each birth. Let X be the number of males and Y the number of runs.

The probability distribution of X is binomial with $n = 4$, $p = \frac{1}{2}$, and hence:

$$P(X = 0) = \tfrac{1}{16},$$
$$P(X = 1) = \tfrac{4}{16},$$
$$P(X = 2) = \tfrac{6}{16},$$
$$P(X = 3) = \tfrac{4}{16},$$
$$P(X = 4) = \tfrac{1}{16}.$$

Now, *given* X, we find it easy to write down the possible orders, as in Example 2.13 (where $X = 2$). If $X = 0$ or 4, then only one run is possible, i.e., $P(Y = 1 | X = 0) = P(Y = 1 | X = 4) = 1$.

If $X = 1$, then we have these possibilities:

Outcome	Number of runs
G G G $\overline{\text{B}}$	2
G G $\overline{\text{B}}$ $\overline{\text{G}}$	3
$\overline{\text{G}}$ B $\overline{\text{G}}$ $\overline{\text{G}}$	3
$\overline{\text{B}}$ $\overline{\text{G}}$ $\overline{\text{G}}$ G	2

so $P(Y = 2|X = 1) = \frac{1}{2}$ and $P(Y = 3|X = 1) = \frac{1}{2}$. The same results hold if $X = 3$.

For $X = 2$, we have already computed that $Y = 2$, 3, or 4, with probabilities $\frac{1}{3}$. We can now put these results together in a table, using Rule II.5 of Chapter 2. Let $p(x, y) = P(X = x$ and $Y = y) = P(\{X = x\}\{Y = y\}) = P(X = x, Y = y)$. Then, for example,

$$p(2, 3) = P(X = 2 \text{ and } Y = 3)$$
$$= P(X = 2) \cdot P(Y = 3|X = 2) \quad \text{(by Rule II.5, Chapter 2)}$$
$$= \frac{6}{16} \cdot \frac{1}{3} = \frac{2}{16}.$$

Thus, in the table below, the entry corresponding to $X = 2$ and $Y = 3$ is $\frac{2}{16}$, the probability that *both* these events occur.

x \ y	1	2	3	4	Total
0	$\frac{1}{16}$	0	0	0	$\frac{1}{16}$
1	0	$\frac{2}{16}$	$\frac{2}{16}$	0	$\frac{4}{16}$
2	0	$\frac{2}{16}$	$\frac{2}{16}$	$\frac{2}{16}$	$\frac{6}{16}$
3	0	$\frac{2}{16}$	$\frac{2}{16}$	0	$\frac{4}{16}$
4	$\frac{1}{16}$	0	0	0	$\frac{1}{16}$
Total	$\frac{2}{16}$	$\frac{6}{16}$	$\frac{6}{16}$	$\frac{2}{16}$	1

Verify that $p(x, y)$ when summed over all possible values (x, y) has total 1.

Jointly Discrete Probability Distributions

The random variables X and Y of Example 9.1 are examples of finite random variables, as defined in Chapter 2. The entries within the table of Example 9.1 form a probability distribution on the joint sample space of X and Y, the pairs of values to which probabilities are assigned. To emphasize that there is more than one random variable and more than one probability distribution, it is customary to call this probability distribution the *joint probability distribution of X and Y*. Example 9.1 is an example of what are called jointly discrete random variables. Formally, X and Y are *jointly discrete random variables* if their joint sample space consists of pairs of rational numbers and each possible pair is assigned a nonnegative probability such that the sum over all possible pairs is one. These probabilities make up the *joint probability distribution*. Most of our examples and problems on jointly discrete random variables will have joint sample spaces which consist of only a finite number of pairs of sample points, these pairs usually being integers. When the number of pairs is finite, we again use the term *finite sample space*. Observe that when X and Y are jointly discrete random variables, then both X and Y are, individually, discrete random variables.

The marginal totals on the right-hand side of the table in Example 9.1 are familiar, since they are the binomial probabilities associated with the random variable X. To distinguish these from the joint probability distribution of (X, Y), it is convenient to refer to them for obvious reasons as the *marginal probability distribution* of X. What are the column totals at the bottom of the table? These are the marginal probabilities of Y, and thus this line yields the *marginal probability distribution* of Y. Thus we see that the marginal distribution of Y in more usual form is

y	$p_Y(y)$
1	$\frac{1}{8}$
2	$\frac{3}{8}$
3	$\frac{3}{8}$
4	$\frac{1}{8}$
Total	1

EXERCISES

1. Find $E(Y)$ and $V(Y)$.
2. Find the probability distribution of the random variable, $Z = Y - 1$. This distribution is identical with that of what random variable that has been studied earlier?

More formally, if X and Y are jointly discrete random variables, the *marginal probability that $X = x$*, denoted by $p_X(x)$, is

$$p_X(x) = \sum_y p(x, y),$$

where $p(x, y) = P(X = x \text{ and } Y = y)$ and the sum is taken over all sample points y in the sample space of Y. A similar definition holds for $p_Y(y)$, the marginal probability that $Y = y$.

Discrete Conditional Probability Distributions

In Chapter 2, a definition was given of conditional probability, which, in fact, was used in obtaining the entries for the table in Example 9.1. It is useful to define the conditional probability distribution of Y, given X (or of X, given Y) when X and Y are jointly discrete random variables. In terms of the joint probability distribution and the marginal probability distribution of X, the *conditional probability that $Y = y$, given $X = x$*, denoted by $P(Y = y | X = x)$ is

$$P(Y = y | X = x) = \frac{p(x, y)}{p_X(x)}.$$

Thus, given $X = 2$, the conditional distribution of Y is

y	$P(Y = y \| X = 2)$
2	$\frac{1}{3}$
3	$\frac{1}{3}$
4	$\frac{1}{3}$
Total	1

This is clearly quite different from the conditional distribution of Y, given $X = 1$, which is

y	$P(Y = y \| X = 1)$
2	$\frac{1}{2}$
3	$\frac{1}{2}$
Total	1

In Chapter 2 the independence of two random variables X and Y was defined in terms of events. Now we can give an equivalent definition in terms of joint probability distributions. Two jointly dis-crete random variables are said to be independent if $P(X = x, Y = y) = P(X = x) \cdot P(Y = y)$ for all pairs (x, y) in the joint sample space. The reader can verify that this is equivalent to $P(X = x | Y = y) = P(X = x)$ for all pairs (x, y) for which $P(Y = y) > 0$ or to $P(Y = y | X = x) = P(Y = y)$ for all pairs (x, y) for which $P(X = x) > 0$, so that knowledge of the value of Y (of X) does not affect the probability of any value of X (of Y). In Example 9.1, X and Y are easily seen to be dependent.

Since the marginal distributions are identical with those defined in Chapter 2, it is not necessary to redefine the means and variances. We can also work with *conditional means* and *conditional variances*; e.g.,

$$E(X|Y = y) = \sum_{x} xP(X = x | Y = y),$$

where the summation is over all points x in the sample space of X, and

$$V(X|Y = y) = \sum_{x} [x - E(X|Y = y)]^2 P(X = x | Y = y),$$

where the summation is over all points x in the sample space of X. $E(X|Y = y)$ is to be read as the conditional mean of X, given $Y = y$, and the symbol $V(X|Y = y)$ is similarly to be read as the conditional variance of X, given $Y = y$.

Note: For a fixed value y in the sample space of Y, $P(X = x | Y = y)$ is a probability distribution for X as x ranges over all points in the sample space of X, and $E(X|Y = y)$ and $V(X|Y = y)$ are simply the mean and variance of this distribution. The latter two quantities are functions of y only. Similar statements may be made concerning Y for each fixed x in the sample space of X.

It is useful to define one new summarizing concept, *the covariance of X and Y*, denoted by Cov (X, Y) or σ_{XY}, defined as follows for finite sample spaces.

$$\text{Cov}(X, Y) = \sum_{x} \sum_{y} (x - EX)(y - EY)p(x, y),$$

where the summation is over all points (x, y) in the joint sample space of X and Y.

Example 9.2 An experiment with two outcomes and a number of runs (continued)

We illustrate the concepts of conditional mean, conditional variance, and covariance by studying the random variables in Example 9.1. In tabular form, we have the following conditional probability distributions for X for each given possible value of Y.

x	$P(X=x|Y=1)$	$P(X=x|Y=2)$	$P(X=x|Y=3)$	$P(X=x|Y=4)$
0	$\frac{1}{2}$	0	0	0
1	0	$\frac{1}{3}$	$\frac{1}{3}$	0
2	0	$\frac{1}{3}$	$\frac{1}{3}$	1
3	0	$\frac{1}{3}$	$\frac{1}{3}$	0
4	$\frac{1}{2}$	0	0	0

Thus,

$$E(X|Y = 1) = 0 \cdot \tfrac{1}{2} + 1 \cdot 0 + 2 \cdot 0 + 3 \cdot 0 + 4 \cdot \tfrac{1}{2} = 2,$$

and

$$V(X|Y = 1) = (0 \cdot 2)^2 \cdot \tfrac{1}{2} + (1 - 2)^2 \cdot 0 + (2 - 2)^2 \cdot 0 + (3 - 2)^2 \cdot 0$$
$$+ (4 - 2)^2 \cdot \tfrac{1}{2}$$
$$= 4.$$

The reader should verify that $E(X|Y = 2) = 2$, $V(X|Y = 2) = \tfrac{2}{3}$, $E(X|Y = 3) = 2$, $V(X|Y = 3) = \tfrac{2}{3}$, $E(X|Y = 4) = 2$, and $V(X|Y = 4) = 0$.

One may interpret $E(X|Y = 2) = 2$ intuitively as follows. If the experiment described in Example 9.1 is performed a great many times and the value of X is recorded only on these trials for which $Y = 2$, then the long-run average of such values will be 2.

To facilitate the computation of Cov (X, Y), we write down a table with possible values of $x - E(X)$ and $y - E(Y)$ along the edges. [Verify that $E(X) = 2$ and $E(Y) = 2\tfrac{1}{2}$.]

		$y - E(Y)$			
		$-1\frac{1}{2}$	$-\frac{1}{2}$	$\frac{1}{2}$	$1\frac{1}{2}$
	-2	$\frac{3}{16}$	0	0	0
	-1	0	$\frac{1}{16}$	$-\frac{1}{16}$	0
$x - E(X)$	0	0	0	0	0
	1	0	$-\frac{1}{16}$	$\frac{1}{16}$	0
	2	$-\frac{3}{16}$	0	0	0

For each value of $x - EX$ and $y - EY$ the corresponding entry in the table is $(x - EX)(y - EY)p(x, y)$. By adding all the entries in the table, it is immediately observed that Cov $(X, Y) = 0$.

While the covariance is a measure of the dependence of X and Y, it is only in special cases that Cov $(X, Y) = 0$ implies X and Y are independent. On the other hand, what if X and Y are independent? Then,

$$\text{Cov }(X, Y) = \sum_x \sum_y (x - EX)(y - EY)p(x, y)$$

$$= \sum_x \sum_y (x - EX)(y - EY)p_X(x)p_Y(y)$$

$$= \left[\sum_x (x - EX)p_X(x)\right]\left[\sum_y (y - EY)p_X(y)\right].$$

But

$$\sum_x (x - EX)p_X(x) = \sum_x xp_X(x) - \sum_x EXp_X(x)$$

$$= EX - EX \sum_x p_X(x)$$

$$= EX - EX$$

$$= 0,$$

since $\sum_x p_X(x) = 1$. Hence, Cov $(X, Y) = 0$, and we have the important result for finite sample spaces.†

THEOREM 9.1 *If X and Y are independent random variables, then* Cov $(X, Y) = 0$.

To emphasize it once more the converse is not necessarily true, as the previous example shows.

Example 9.3 Finding two defective machines

Consider the same search problem as in Example 2.12, modified as follows. Two machines of the five are known to be defective.
Let

X = number of machines examined in finding the first defective,

Y = number of machines examined after the first defective is found, in the search for the second defective.

Both X and Y include, in their total, the defective machine.
Check that

$$P(X = 1) = \tfrac{4}{10},$$
$$P(X = 2) = \tfrac{3}{10},$$
$$P(X = 3) = \tfrac{2}{10},$$
$$P(X = 4) = \tfrac{1}{10}.$$

---

† The theorem can be extended to any random variables for which the covariance can be defined.

Check that

$$P(Y = 1|X = 1) = P(Y = 2|X = 1) = P(Y = 3|X = 1)$$
$$= P(Y = 4|X = 1) = \tfrac{1}{4},$$

$$P(Y = 1|X = 2) = P(Y = 2|X = 2) = P(Y = 3|X = 2) = \tfrac{1}{3},$$

$$P(Y = 1|X = 3) = P(Y = 2|X = 3) = \tfrac{1}{2},$$

$$P(Y = 1|X = 4) = 1.$$

For example, $P(X = 2) = P[(\text{first machine examined is good})(\text{second machine is defective})] = \tfrac{3}{5} \cdot \tfrac{2}{4} = \tfrac{6}{20} = \tfrac{3}{10}$, and $P(Y = 2|X = 2) = P[(\text{first machine examined in the second search is good})(\text{second machine examined in search is defective})] = \tfrac{2}{3} \cdot \tfrac{1}{2} = \tfrac{1}{3}$. This follows since the event $(X = 2)$ implies that there remains a total of three machines, of which two are good, one defective. Thus, the joint probability distribution of (X, Y) is as in the table below.

x \ y	1	2	3	4	Total
1	$\tfrac{1}{10}$	$\tfrac{1}{10}$	$\tfrac{1}{10}$	$\tfrac{1}{10}$	$\tfrac{4}{10}$
2	$\tfrac{1}{10}$	$\tfrac{1}{10}$	$\tfrac{1}{10}$	0	$\tfrac{3}{10}$
3	$\tfrac{1}{10}$	$\tfrac{1}{10}$	0	0	$\tfrac{2}{10}$
4	$\tfrac{1}{10}$	0	0	0	$\tfrac{1}{10}$
Total	$\tfrac{4}{10}$	$\tfrac{3}{10}$	$\tfrac{2}{10}$	$\tfrac{1}{10}$	1

EXERCISES

1. Find $E(X)$, $E(Y)$, $V(X)$, $V(Y)$, and Cov (X, Y) for Example 9.3.
2. For each possible value y of Y find the conditional probability distribution of X, $E(X|Y = y)$, and $V(X|Y = y)$ for Example 9.3.

Related to the covariance is the *correlation coefficient*, denoted by ρ_{XY} (or simply ρ if no confusion will arise) and defined as

$$\rho_{XY} = \frac{\sigma_{XY}}{\sigma_X \cdot \sigma_Y}.$$

The Cov (X, Y) of a given pair of random variables X and Y may take on positive or negative values of any magnitude. The correlation coefficient ρ_{XY} is simply the standardized covariance, and it can be shown that $-1 \leq \rho_{XY} \leq +1$ for any two random variables X and Y. More explicitly, if one defines $X^* = [X - E(X)]/\sigma_X$ and $Y^* = [Y - E(Y)]/\sigma_Y$; i.e., if X^* and Y^* are the standardizations of X and Y, then

$$\rho_{XY} = \text{Cov}\ (X^*, Y^*) = \rho_{X^*Y^*}.$$

Check that $\rho_{XY} = -0.5$ for Example 9.3.

The Multinomial Probability Distribution

Experiments with two outcomes, in which separate trials are independent and in which the probability of the two outcomes labeled success and failure remain fixed from trial to trial, are of importance in probability and statistical analysis. The total number of successes T in n such trials has a binomial distribution. However, there are many such series of independent trials in which the number of possible outcomes is more than two. Such trials are called *multinomial trials*. In multinomial trials, it is necessary to record the number of occurrences of each outcome, and hence we have more than one random variable. These random variables are called *multinomial random variables*. Example 1.8 (prediction of success in a statistics course) is an example of multinomial trials in which there are 12 possible outcomes. Other examples are easily found. In an experiment to test a cold vaccine, subjects might be classified as having no cold, one cold, or more than one cold during the experimental period, in which case there are three possible outcomes. Most public opinion polls classify respondents into five categories, e.g., strongly in favor, in favor, neutral, opposed, or strongly opposed to a particular issue or individual. In analyzing a multiple-choice test with four choices for each question, a psychologist might prefer to consider the frequency of each of the four responses rather than simply the number right or wrong. An evaluation of a weather forecast may classify it as correct, practically correct, or incorrect. Each of these is an example of multinomial trials with (respectively) 12, 3, 5, 4, and 3 multinomial random variables.

Example 9.4   Gene inheritance (continued)

Recall Example 3.4 (gene inheritance). In Example 3.4, we discussed very briefly the principles of Mendelian theory in regard to inheritance of a single gene combination, e.g., MN. The genotypes of several offspring of an MN–MN mating may be MM, MN, or NN with probabilities $\frac{1}{4}, \frac{1}{2}, \frac{1}{4}$. Consider four offspring and assume that the inheritances of their genes are independent events. What is the probability that one is MM, two MN, one NN?

Let

$$X = \text{the number of MM genotypes,}$$

$$Y = \text{the number of MN genotypes,}$$

$$Z = \text{the number of NN genotypes.}$$

We are asking for $P(X = 1, Y = 2, Z = 1)$. Clearly $X + Y + Z = 4$. Now suppose the first offspring is MM, the next two, MN, and the last, NN. The probability of this event is $\frac{1}{4}(\frac{1}{2})^2\frac{1}{4}$ by Rule II.5a. This is one of the possible orders. Label this order *abbc*; the possible orders can be obtained by counting. For example, the possibilities are

abbc	*babc*	*bbca*	*cabb*
abcb	*bacb*	*bcab*	*cbab*
acbb	*bbac*	*bcba*	*cbba*

that is, 12. All of these orders are mutually exclusive and have probability $\frac{1}{4}(\frac{1}{2})^2\frac{1}{4}$ or $\frac{1}{64}$; by Rule II.4a of Chapter 2, the probability of the desired event is $\frac{12}{64}$ or, symbolically,

$$P(X = 1, Y = 2, Z = 1) = \tfrac{12}{64}.$$

In general, four letters, one of one kind, two of another, and one of a third, may be arranged in $4!/(1!\,2!\,1!)$ ways. Check that $4!/(1!\,2!\,1!) = 12$.

The general formula for the probability distribution associated with multinomial random variables is deduced in the same manner as the binomial probability formula was. For example, given n independent trials, each of which results in one of the events E_1, E_2, or E_3 with probabilities p_1, p_2, and p_3 $(p_1 + p_2 + p_3 = 1)$, denote by T_1, T_2, and T_3 the number of occurrences of E_1, E_2, and E_3 respectively. It can be shown that

$$P(T_1 = t_1,\ T_2 = t_2,\ T_3 = t_3) = \frac{n!}{t_1!\,t_2!\,t_3!}\,p_1^{t_1}p_2^{t_2}p_3^{t_3},$$

provided that t_1, t_2, and t_3 are nonnegative integers such that $t_1 + t_2 + t_3 = n$. This formula can be extended in a rather obvious way to experiments with more than three outcomes.

Properties of the Multinomial Distribution

For multinomial trials with three outcomes, it can be shown by the same method as that used for the binomial distribution that

$$E(T_1) = np_1, \qquad E(T_2) = np_2, \qquad E(T_3) = np_3$$

and

$$V(T_1) = np_1(1 - p_1), \qquad V(T_2) = np_2(1 - p_2),$$
$$V(T_3) = np_3(1 - p_3).$$

New results for the multinomial distributions are

$$\sigma_{T_1 T_2} = -np_1 p_2, \qquad \sigma_{T_1 T_3} = -np_1 p_3, \qquad \sigma_{T_2 T_3} = -np_2 p_3.$$

Hence, deduce that

$$\rho_{T_1 T_2} = -\sqrt{\frac{p_1 p_2}{(1 - p_1)(1 - p_2)}}, \dots$$

Distributions of Jointly Continuous Random Variables

All of the concepts set out in detail for discrete random variables can be extended to continuous random variables.

If a pair of random variables X and Y have for their joint sample space a two-dimensional rectangle (possibly infinite) and if $P(X = x, Y = y) = 0$ for each pair of real numbers x, y, then (X, Y) are *jointly continuous*.

Since the joint probability of any pair of real numbers is zero, we begin our study of jointly continuous probability distributions by asking for the joint probability that (X, Y), when observed, will take on a value in some subrectangle in the joint sample space. This is the analogue of what was done for a continuous random variable in Chapter 6. Given the joint probabilities of rectangles, one can compute the joint probability that (X, Y) will take on a value in any simple geometrical figure—the only probabilities needed in elementary problems. Further, knowledge of the joint probabilities of rectangles will yield the marginal probability distributions of X and Y. Moreover, independence or dependence of X and Y can be determined by the probabilities assigned to rectangles. To be precise, *continuous random variables X and Y are independent* if for any four real numbers a, b, c, d,

$$P(a < X < b, c < Y < d) = P(a < X < b)P(c < Y < d).$$

[*Note:* If X and Y are jointly discrete random variables, then X is a discrete random variable (as is Y). However, it is not necessarily the case that if X and Y are jointly continuous random variables then X is a continuous random variable. But, in this text, the jointly continuous probability distributions studied will always be such that the marginal probability distributions are continuous.]

Example 6.2 (raindrops) is, in fact, an example of a model for a two-dimensional continuous random variable. From physical considerations we assume that X and Y are independent in this example.

Example 9.5   Catching a bus

In Example 6.1 we discussed the random variable generated by waiting times for a bus, assuming that such waiting times were uniformly distributed on the time interval between buses (0 to 20 minutes). Consider now two people independently arriving to catch the bus. Let their waiting times be X_1, X_2.

Now define

$$X = \text{maximum of } X_1 \text{ and } X_2,$$
$$Y = \text{minimum of } X_1 \text{ and } X_2,$$

so that X is the longer waiting time and Y the shorter waiting time. Now,

$$P(X \leq 10) = P(\text{both } X_1, X_2 \leq 10) = P(\{X_1 \leq 10\}\{X_2 \leq 10\})$$
$$= P(X_1 \leq 10)P(X_2 \leq 10)$$
$$(\text{since } X_1, X_2 \text{ are independent})$$
$$= \tfrac{1}{2} \cdot \tfrac{1}{2} = \tfrac{1}{4} \quad (\text{by definition of the uniform}$$
$$\text{distribution}).$$

More generally, for any real number x between 0 and 20

$$P(X \leq x) = P(\text{both } X_1, X_2 \leq x)$$
$$= P(\{X_1 \leq x\}\{X_2 \leq x\})$$
$$= P(X_1 \leq x)P(X_2 \leq x)$$
$$= \left(\frac{x}{20}\right)^2$$

and

$$P(X \leq 5, Y \geq 3) = P(\text{both } X_1, X_2 \text{ lie between 3 and 5})$$
$$= P(3 \leq X_1 \leq 5) \cdot P(3 \leq X_2 \leq 5)$$
$$= \tfrac{1}{100}.$$

EXERCISES

1. Show that

$$P(Y \geq 5) = \left(\frac{1}{4}\right)^2$$

and

$$P(Y \geq y) = \left(\frac{20 - y}{20}\right)^2$$

for any real number y between 0 and 20.

2. Use Exercise 1 and Example 9.5 to show that

$$P(X \leq 5) \cdot P(Y \geq 3) = \frac{1}{16} \cdot \frac{289}{400} = 0.045 \neq 0.01$$

and hence show by use of the definition of independence that X and Y are dependent variables. (This is obviously true since knowledge of X gives information about the values Y may take on.)

It is possible to define conditional probability distribution functions for jointly continuous random variables though the fact that $P(X = x, Y = y) = 0$ means that a more sophisticated approach is necessary. It will not be given here. However, the concepts of covariance and correlation are easily extended to the case of continuous random variables with sums replaced by integrals. Theorem 2.3 can now be extended to cover all random variables for which variances are defined. In particular for two random variables we have:

THEOREM 9.2 *For any random variables X and Y for which $V(X)$ and $V(Y)$ are defined and for any constants a and b,*

(a) $V(aX + bY) = a^2 V(X) + b^2 V(Y) + 2ab \, \text{Cov}(X, Y)$.
(b) *In particular,* $V(X + Y) = V(X) + V(Y) + 2 \, \text{Cov}(X, Y)$;
$$V(X - Y) = V(X) + V(Y) - 2 \, \text{Cov}(X, Y).$$
(c) $\text{Cov}(X, X) = V(X)$.

Equation (b) follows from (a) by letting $a = 1$ and $b = +1$ in the first line and $b = -1$ in the second line. Equation (c) follows from (b) by letting $Y = X$ in (b) to get

$$V(X - X) = V(X) + V(X) - 2 \, \text{Cov}(X, X)$$

or

$$0 = 2V(X) - 2 \, \text{Cov}(X, X).$$

Theorems 2.3 and 6.2 are seen to be special versions of Theorem 9.2 obtained by setting $\text{Cov}(X, Y) = 0$, which is correct for independent random variables.

EXERCISE

Check that Theorem 9.2 holds for the random variables defined in Example 9.2.

There are generalizations of Theorem 2.3 and 9.2 that relate the covariances of sums. One such theorem, which may easily be generalized to any finite number of summands, is as follows.

THEOREM 9.3 *Let X_1, X_2, Y_1, and Y_2 be random variables for which* Cov (X_i, Y_j) *exist* $(i = 1, 2; j = 1, 2)$, *and let* a_1, a_2, b_1, *and* b_2 *be any constants. Then*

$$\text{Cov } (a_1X_1 + a_2X_2, b_1Y_1 + b_2Y_2)$$
$$= a_1b_1 \text{ Cov } (X_1, Y_1) + a_1b_2 \text{ Cov } (X_1, Y_2)$$
$$+ a_2b_1 \text{ Cov } (X_2, Y_1) + a_2b_2 \text{ Cov } (X_2, Y_2).$$

Jointly Normal Probability Distributions

The most commonly used model for two jointly continuous random variables is a generalization of the normal probability model. The joint normal probability model for two random variables X and Y is characterized by *five* parameters: $\mu_X = E(X)$, $\mu_Y = E(Y)$, $V(X) = \sigma_x^2$, $V(Y) = \sigma_y^2$, and $\rho_{XY} = \rho$.

Probabilities for the normal distribution (one variable) are represented by areas under a curve that is bell- or hat-shaped. Probabilities for a joint normal distribution (bivariate) are represented by volumes under a hat. The hat has its maximum height at the point with coordinates (μ_X, μ_Y). The cross section of the hat obtained by slicing the hat with any plane perpendicular to the hat's base is a normal curve as defined in Chapter 6. The cross section of the hat obtained by slicing it with a plane parallel to its base is an ellipse. The ellipse is a circle with center (μ_X, μ_Y) if and only if $\sigma_X^2 = \sigma_Y^2$ and $\rho = 0$.

If X and Y are independent random variables, then $\rho = 0$. It is an important property of *joint normal* random variables X and Y that if $\rho = 0$ then X and Y are independent; i.e., covariance zero implies independence for jointly normal random variables.

Note: As emphasized earlier, this is not true in general, but because it is true for the often-used model of joint normality, many beginners tend to be confused and assume that $\rho = 0$ means independence in general.

Tables are available to obtain standardized joint normal probabilities, i.e.,

$$P\left(\frac{X-\mu_X}{\sigma_X} \le x, \quad \frac{Y-\mu_Y}{\sigma_Y} \le y\right).$$

These depend on ρ. Such tables are not given in this text.

One other property of the joint normal distribution will be used later, namely, the fact that the conditional expectations of normal variables are linear and the conditional variances constant. Specifically, if X and Y are joint normal random variables with means μ_X, μ_Y, variances σ_X^2, σ_Y^2, and correlation coefficient ρ, then

$$E(Y|X) = \mu_Y + \frac{\rho\sigma_Y}{\sigma_X}(X - \mu_X) \qquad \text{(this is linear in } X\text{)}.$$

$$E(X|Y) = \mu_X + \frac{\rho\sigma_X}{\sigma_Y}(Y - \mu_Y) \qquad \text{(this is linear in } Y\text{)}.$$

$$V(Y|X) = \sigma_Y^2(1 - \rho^2) \qquad \text{(this does not depend on } X\text{)}.$$

$$V(X|Y) = \sigma_X^2(1 - \rho^2) \qquad \text{(this does not depend on } Y\text{)}.$$

The equations for $E(Y|X)$ and $E(X|Y)$ are known as regression equations, and statistical analysis of such equations will be discussed in Chapter 10. The last two equations give some insight into ρ^2. For, writing the equation for $V(Y|X)$ in the form $V(Y|X)/\sigma_Y^2 = 1 - \rho^2$ and recalling that $0 \le \rho^2 \le 1$, it is seen that the conditional variance of Y, given X, is no greater (and is usually strictly less) than the unconditional variance of Y. In other words, knowledge of X decreases the variance of Y. Since, for jointly normal random variables, the conditional variance of Y is independent of X, the decrease in variance is always the same and is measured by $\sigma_Y^2 - V(Y|X)$. The proportional decrease, as a proportion of the unconditional variance, is

$$\frac{[\sigma_Y^2 - V(Y|X)]}{\sigma_Y^2} = 1 - \frac{V(Y|X)}{\sigma_Y^2}$$

$$= 1 - (1 - \rho^2)$$

$$= \rho^2.$$

That is, ρ^2 measures the proportional decrease in the variance of Y due to the additional information contained in the knowledge of X. If $\rho = 0$, there is no decrease in variance, which is not surprising since $\rho = 0$ implies (for jointly normal random variables) that X and Y are independent and hence that knowledge of X does not yield any information concerning Y. If $\rho = \pm 1$, it follows that $V(Y|X) = 0$ and hence in this case knowledge of X completely determines Y. Now $\sigma_Y^2 = [\sigma_Y^2 - V(Y|X)] + V(Y|X)$ where both terms on the right are non-negative. Since the first term represents the reduction in variance due to the knowledge of X, the second term $V(Y|X)$ is often called the *residual variance of* Y and ρ^2 can be interpreted as the proportion of the variance of Y which is *attributable* to X. Since a similar argument could be used on the equation $V(X|Y) = \sigma_X^2(1 - \rho^2)$, ρ^2 is also the proportion of the variance of X which is *attributable* to Y.

For example, consider an adult population. Define (X, Y) to be the height and weight of a randomly selected member of the population and assume (X, Y) to be jointly normal. Heights and weights are both quite variable so that σ_X^2 and σ_Y^2 are relatively large. Now consider the weights of all males in the population whose height is 70 in. The variance of this subpopulation, that is, $V(Y|70)$, may be much less than σ_Y^2. The reduction in variance is measured by ρ^2. If ρ^2 is, for example, 0.99, then knowing X gives nearly complete information about Y; if $\rho^2 = 0.50$, then half the variation in Y is attributable to X; or, in symbols, $V(Y|70) = \frac{1}{2}\sigma_Y^2$. If $\rho^2 = 0$, then X and Y are independent, so that information about X yields no information concerning Y.

Since the binomial distribution becomes approximately a normal distribution as n, the number of trials, increases, it is to be expected that the same will be true of the multinomial distribution, and this is in fact so. As n, the number of trials, increases, the standardized multinomial random variables have a joint probability distribution that tends to a joint normal distribution with means zero and variances unity. Since the multinomial random variables are dependent, the limiting joint normal distribution, in general, has correlation coefficients that are different from zero.

■ Experiments

9.1   Take five cards of which three are kings, two aces; shuffle and draw cards until both aces are drawn. Record the number of cards drawn until the first ace is exposed, the number of cards drawn after this until the second ace is exposed (in both cases the ace is counted as one of the cards drawn). Repeat this 100 times, shuffling well between each trial. Record the results in a two-way table, giving the frequency of the various outcomes. What is the expected frequency of the various outcomes? What is the expected frequency of each possible outcome? (This is a simulation of the random variable discussed in Example 9.3.)

9.2 Draw five cards from an ordinary deck of cards and record the number of cards of each suit. Repeat this 100 times and compare the expected frequency with that actually observed. What is the probability of getting only hearts? Only black cards? How often are these events observed? This experiment is a simulation of the random variable defined in Problem 9.13.

9.3 Draw 30 triples of random normal deviates; define $X =$ the sum of the first and second observations and $Y =$ the sum of the first and third observations. Retain these results for Experiment 10.4. Observe that $X = Z_1 + Z_2$ and $Y = Z_1 + Z_3$, where Z_1, Z_2, Z_3 are independent standard normal random variables. Use Theorems 2.1 and 9.2 and 9.3 of this chapter to compute $E(X)$, $E(Y)$, σ_X^2, σ_Y^2, σ_{XY}, ρ_{XY}. This is the basis of dependence of some of the random variables observed in nature—they have a common part.

9.4 Consider the random variables obtained by throwing two ordinary dice and defining X as the larger number facing upward and Y as the smaller number. What is the joint sample space of (X, Y)? [*Hint:* It has 21 points.] Work out the probability distribution of (X, Y). Throw the dice 100 times and record the observed frequencies. Test whether the sample mean of X differs significantly from $E(X)$; do the same for Y. [*Note:* To make a simultaneous comparison of $\bar{X}$ with $E(X)$ and $\bar{Y}$ with $E(Y)$ is beyond the level of this course.]

■ Problems

9.1 Consider four trials of the taste-testing experiment (Example 2.2), where p, the probability of a correct choice, is $\frac{1}{3}$. Let X be the number of successes and Y the number of runs in the sequence of successes and failures. Work out the joint probability distribution of (X, Y), $E(X)$, $E(Y)$, $V(X)$, $V(Y)$, and ρ_{XY}.

9.2 In Example 9.3, calculate $E(Y|X)$ for each X and show that these lie on a line. Graphically or analytically find the equation of this line. Is $V(Y|X)$ constant?

9.3 Again refer to Example 9.3 (finding two defective machines). Define X as in Example 9.3 and Z as the total number of machines examined. Find the joint probability distribution of X and Z. Is $E(Z|X)$, the *regression of Z on X*, linear as a function of X?

*9.4 Consider, in Example 9.4 (gene inheritance), 20 offspring whose inheritances of genes may be regarded as independent events. Denote by T_1 the number of types MM; by T_2, the number of types MN; and by T_3, the number of type NN.

(a) Calculate $E(T_1)$, $E(T_2)$, $E(T_3)$, $V(T_1)$, $V(T_2)$, $V(T_3)$, $\rho_{T_1 T_2}$, $\rho_{T_1 T_3}$, and $\rho_{T_2 T_3}$.

(b) Calculate $P(T_1 = 10, T_2 = 10, T_3 = 0)$, $P(T_1 = 10, T_2 = 5, T_3 = 7)$. [*Hint:* Use Table A2.1 for the first of these.]

9.5 In a multiple choice questionnaire each question has four possible answers. Assume that a student guesses independently on each question. What is the probability that in five questions he guesses exactly two a's, one b, one c, and one d? (Do not work out.) Find the expected number of answers in each category.

9.6 Consider a multiple choice questionnaire where each question has five possible responses. The educator who set the test has characterized the responses as right, nearly right, wrong, absurd, absurd. Of 100 responses to our question, there are 44 right, 26 nearly right, and 20 wrong, while 10 picked one of the two absurd answers. Estimate the probability of a right answer and find a 95 percent confidence interval for this probability.

9.7 Suppose, in Problem 9.6, that the answers are scored as follows:

Right	$+1$
Nearly right	$\frac{1}{2}$
Wrong	0
Absurd	-1

What is the expected score of a person who just guesses in 100 questions? (Recall that there are two absurd answers.) What is the variance of this score?

9.8 In a study on the spread of a rumor, a large population is sampled randomly to determine the proportion p of the population who know the rumor. In a sample of size n let T_1 be the number who know the rumor and T_2 be the number who do not know the rumor. Find Cov (T_1, T_2) and $\rho_{T_1 T_2}$.

9.9 A random sample is made of n families; the observation made is the number of children per family. Let p_0 be the probability that a family has no children and in general p_i be the probability that a family has i children $(i = 1, 2, \ldots)$. Also let T_i = the number of families with i children $(i = 0, 1, \ldots)$. Let k be the maximum number of children. Define $X = T_1 + 2T_2 + \cdots + kT_k$; it is seen that X is the number of children in the families sampled. Assume $T_0, T_1, \ldots, T_k$ are multinomial random variables, and calculate $E(X)$, $V(X)$. Work this out for $p_0 = 0.15$, $p_1 = 0.30$, $p_2 = 0.40$, $p_3 = 0.15$, $n = 100$. Since $\sum_{i=0}^{3} p_i = 1$, it is tacitly being assumed that $k = 3$, which is not true in real life but is being assumed here for convenience.

9.10   Assume that scores on the verbal (V) and mathematical (M) parts of a scholastic aptitude test are jointly normally distributed with means 500, standard deviations 100, and correlation coefficient $\rho = 0.89$. Let $X = V + M$. What are the mean and variance of X? X is also normally distributed. Find values x_0, x_1 such that $P(X < x_0) = P(X > x_1) = 0.025$. Is (x_0, x_1) a 95 percent confidence interval for $E(X)$?

9.11   A book publisher samples 20 pages of a book in press and finds 18 completely correct, one with minor errors, and one with major errors. Major errors will involve resetting the page at a cost five times as great as the cost for corrections needed for a page with minor errors. Assume that the cost for corrections to a page with minor errors is \$15 and estimate the total cost of corrections in this 1,000-page book. What is the variance of this estimate?

9.12   A college bases its freshman admission actions on the assumption that 80 percent of male applicants it accepts will in fact enroll while 60 percent of the female applicants it accepts will enroll.

(a) If it accepts 800 men and 500 women, what will be its expected freshman enrollment?

(b) Calculate the difference in the variance of the freshman enrollment according to three assumptions:

  (i) Male and female acceptances are independent events.
  (ii) If X = male enrollment and Y = female enrollment, $\rho_{XY} = \frac{1}{2}$.
  (iii) With X and Y as in (ii) but $\rho_{XY} = -\frac{1}{2}$.

  What other assumptions are you making in the calculations of the variance?

★9.13   A research experiment is conducted to compare four varieties of grain. The experiment is conducted on a field divided into five rows of four plots each. In each row a plot is selected randomly *for each* variety. Denote by T_i the number of plots planted to variety i, in the first column ($i = 1, 2, 3, 4$).

(a) Write down the joint distribution function of T_1, T_2, T_3, T_4.
(b) Find $E(T_1)$ and $P(T_1 = t | T_4 = 4)$ for appropriate t.

9.14   In a test for tuberculosis, sputum samples are put on slides and diagnosed as positive, doubtful, or negative. The probabilities of these three diagnoses are 0.8, 0.15, and 0.05 for samples from persons known to have tuberculosis and 0.15, 0.15, and 0.70 for samples from persons diagnosed as free of tuberculosis. The test is applied to a population containing 900 tuberculosis-free individuals and 100 with tuberculosis. What is the expected number of positive, doubtful, and negative diagnoses. Calculate the variance of these numbers.

9.15   The joint distribution of (X, Y) is given by the following table:

x \ y	0	1	2
0	$\frac{1}{6}$	$\frac{1}{6}$	$\frac{1}{6}$
1	$\frac{1}{6}$	$\frac{1}{6}$	0
2	$\frac{1}{6}$	0	0

(a) Work out the conditional distribution of X, given Y.
(b) Determine ρ_{XY}.

*9.16   Three students are doing a multiple choice test which consists of 20 questions, each of which has five choices. Let X denote the score of A, who is just guessing; let Y denote the score of B, who knows the first ten and gets them right but guesses on the second ten questions; and let Z denote the score of C, who copies A's first ten answers but guesses his own answers on the second ten.

(a) Find the expectation and variance of X, Y, Z.
(b) Find the expectation and variance of $X + Y + Z$.
(c) Which of the pairs (X, Y), (X, Z), (Y, Z) consist of independent random variables?

*9.17   Let X be the number of heads in the first and second tosses of a coin, Y the number of heads in the first and third tosses of a coin. Find the joint probability distribution of (X, Y), the marginal distributions, and the conditional distributions. Are (X, Y) independent?

*9.18 Three balls are distributed randomly in three cells. Let X_i be the number of cells containing exactly i balls ($i = 0, 1, 2, 3$). Determine the joint sample space of X_0, X_1, X_2, X_3. Write down the joint distribution of X_0, X_1, X_2, X_3. Are the variables independent?

*9.19 A lot of articles contains two defective and three good articles. From the lot, a sample of three articles is taken and inspected. A second inspector subsamples two of the three and inspects them also. Let X = number of defectives in the first sample of three, Y = number of defectives in the subsample of two. Find the joint distribution of (X, Y). Are (X, Y) independent?

*9.20 An (Aa, Aa) cross produces n offspring. Let X = number of AA offspring, Y = number of Aa offspring, Z = number of aa offspring. Find the joint probability distribution of (X, Y, Z); the marginal distributions of X, Y, Z; and the conditional distributions of $Y|X$ and $Z|Y$. Are X, Y, Z independent?

9.21 Of five machines in a laboratory two are defective. A repairman examines them until he finds the two defective. Let X = number of machines examined *before* he finds the first defective, Y = number of machines examined *after* he finds the first defective but *before* he finds the second. Find the joint, marginal, and conditional distributions. Relate these random variables to those of Example 9.3.

CHAPTER TEN

Regression and Correlation

Regression

In Chapter 9 we studied probability models involving more than one random variable. In this chapter, we turn to the study of statistical problems involving two variables, at least one of which is random. In the first part of the chapter we will study the relationship between the variables; the purpose of this may be to obtain better estimators, predictors, confidence intervals, etc., for parameters associated with one of the random variables, or the existence of a relationship may be of interest. In the seeking of improved estimators or predictors, knowledge of the other variable will be of use.

Example 10.1   Weight loss and calorie intake

Let Y be the weekly weight loss in pounds of a dieter chosen at random from the population of adult American male dieters. Such loss is a random variable that is of importance to many people, e.g., dieters, doctors, health food specialists, etc. It is quite possible to obtain a random sample of dieters and measure their weight losses; in more technical language, we have obtained a random sample on Y. The sample mean $\bar{Y}$ estimates μ_Y, the average weight loss. $\bar{Y}$ would give us some idea of the weight loss to be expected if a male from the given population dieted for a week. But it is likely that with some additional information we could more accurately predict the weight loss. There are many variables that affect weight loss during dieting. We will consider here only one obvious one, namely the number of calories per day in the diet. Let X be this number. This variable X changes from diet to diet, but it is not generally considered to be random. Rather it is set by the diet, the dieter, or the doctor before the dieting starts. If told that one diet contains 900 calories per day, we feel that the weight loss will be greater than if the diet contains 1,500 calories per day. Whether the diet contains 900 or 1,500 calories, the weight loss is a random variable, but it is reasonable to expect that the lower the number of calories, the greater the weight loss. One of the tasks in this chapter is to formulate a method for making the last statement more precise.

Example 10.2 Baseball attendance and forecast temperature

Let Y be the number of persons attending a randomly chosen week-day baseball game at Yankee Stadium. Y is a random variable of importance to many people associated with the stadium. For example, the program distributor would like to have some idea of the value that Y will take on so that he neither runs out of programs nor has a large surplus. A simple way of estimating Y for any future occasion could be found as follows. We observe a random sample on Y and estimate μ_Y, the average number of customers, by $\bar{Y}$. If the distributor accepted $\bar{Y}$ as his predictor for the future and so based his program order on this predictor every day, he would very often have a large surplus and he would very often run short. If he were to have some additional information, he might do a better job of estimating the number of customers, and hence the number of programs to be printed. There are many variables that affect attendance. We will consider only one, forecast temperature. Let X be the forecast temperature in degrees Fahrenheit at Yankee Stadium on a randomly chosen weekday. X is a *random variable*, knowledge of which will aid the distributor. For example, if the forecast temperature is 40 deg, the distributor expects that there will be fewer customers than if the temperature is forecast to be 85 deg. Even when $X = 40$ or 85 deg, Y is still a random variable, but it is reasonable to assume that the higher X is, the larger Y will be. The distributor will consequently print fewer programs on cool days than on warm days. What attendance to associate with a given predicted temperature is one of the problems to be discussed in this chapter.

In both examples, Y is a dependent random variable depending on another independent variable X, which may or may not be random. In Example 10.1, X is not random but in Example 10.2 it is. Other examples in which the independent variable is fixed by the experimenter and the other variable is random but dependent are the following: A biologist wishes to determine the effect, if any, that temperature has on the rate of growth of a plant; a physiologist may set up an experimental study to measure the effect of alcohol consumption on delay in responses of humans. Other examples in which both the dependent and independent variables are random are the following: A psychologist may wish to predict university grades on the basis of high school grades; a hydrologist may wish to predict the maximum height of a river during spring runoff based on the amount of snow that fell on the river's watershed during the previous winter.

In each of the examples, the reader should be able to think of other variables that affect the dependent random variable and hence see the need for studying three, four, or more variables at once. In this book, however, we restrict ourselves to two variables. The method used can be extended to more variables and the interested reader can find the details in more advanced texts.

Because the dependent variable is random, it can never be predicted with complete accuracy. We therefore fix our attention on the expected value of the dependent random variable and seek to find its relationship with the independent variable. We try to see how the average baseball crowd depends on temperature or how the average weekly weight loss depends on the daily number of calories. In general, the relationship may be of any form. To simplify matters, we *assume that the relationship is linear.* (Recall Example 9.3 and Problem 9.2 as illustrations of such a linear relationship.) There are several reasons for making this assumption. First, if X and Y are both random variables it is quite possible that they are jointly normally distributed, in which case, as stated in Chapter 9, the assumption is satisfied. Since many pairs of random variables in nature are approximately jointly normally distributed, the assumption holds for these. Second, many relationships that are not linear are approximately linear over some range. Hence, the assumption of linearity is a good approximation over this range. Third, the assumption of linearity leads to an easy mathematical theory. If neither of the other reasons put forward can be justified, this latter reason by itself is perhaps justification enough for studying the theory in an elementary course, since the methods used when the relationship is linear can be used in many situations when the relationship is nonlinear. However, the results in the latter situations are generally more complicated.

It is sometimes helpful to think of the two variables as cause and effect, as in the examples on plant growth or alcohol-caused delays in human responses. In other examples, they do not have to be cause and effect; e.g., high school grades and college grades may both be associated with other factors (effort, intelligence, environment, etc.) rather than one's directly causing the other. The interpretation of cause-and-effect relationships must be handled with care.

It should be reemphasized that we are *assuming* that the expected value of the dependent random variable is a linear function of the independent variable. Whether or not the assumption is correct or even an adequate approximation is a more difficult question with which we cannot deal.

Example 10.3 Grade prediction

The following data show high school and freshman year G.P.A.'s for ten students who entered the College of Arts and Sciences at State University directly from high school:

Student	1	2	3	4	5	6	7	8	9	10
High school G.P.A.	2.0	2.1	2.3	2.4	2.6	2.8	3.0	3.1	3.2	3.5
Freshman year G.P.A.	1.5	2.2	2.5	1.6	2.0	1.8	2.0	2.6	3.4	2.4

These are plotted in the graph (called a scatter diagram) in Figure 10.1. This is typical of much biological and sociological data. Data from experiments in physics and chemistry tend to show less scatter, so that in these areas it is sometimes possible to fit a line to experimental results "by eye." With more scattered data, this approach is unsatisfactory and we present here a more objective method. There are several analytic procedures to "fit a line," but the most common in use is that which goes under the name of "least squares."

Formally, we have a dependent random variable Y and an independent variable X, which may be random or may be fixed by the experimenter. If $E(Y|X)$ denotes the expected value of Y for a given value X, then we make *Assumption 1*: $E(Y|X) = \alpha + \beta X$.†

This is the formula for a straight line with X on the horizontal axis and the expected value of Y on the vertical axis. This statement is the mathematical equivalent of the assumption made earlier in this section. The straight line is called the *regression line of Y on X*.

We must also make an assumption concerning the variance of Y. If $V(Y|X)$ denotes the variance of Y for a given value X, then we make *Assumption 2*: $V(Y|X) = \sigma^2_{Y|X} = \sigma^2_1$, a constant independent of X; i.e., the conditional variance of Y, given X, is independent of X.

---

† The α in this equation bears no relation to the 100α percent significance level used in previous chapters.

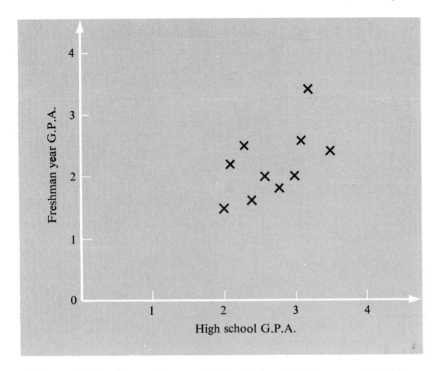

FIGURE 10.1 *Scatter diagram of high school and freshman year G.P.A.'s.*

These assumptions are satisfied whenever X and Y are jointly normally distributed, as pointed out in Chapter 9. The import of these two assumptions is that for each value of X there is a population of Y's having expected value $E(Y|X)$ and variance σ_1^2.

The constants α, β, and σ_1^2 are fixed in any one problem but may vary from problem to problem; i.e., they are parameters associated with Y. The vertical intercept is α, and β is the slope of the regression line. In any given problem these parameters are unknown and we wish to obtain estimates of them. To do this, we take n pairs of measurements, (X_1, Y_1), (X_2, Y_2), ..., (X_n, Y_n). If both variables are random, the pairs are assumed to be a random sample on (X, Y). If the X values are fixed by the experimenter, it is assumed that Y_1, Y_2, ..., Y_n are independent random variables. By assumption, their means are $\alpha + \beta X_1$, $\alpha + \beta X_2$, ..., $\alpha + \beta X_n$, and they have a common variance σ_1^2.

The observations $(X_1, Y_1) \cdots (X_n, Y_n)$ can be arranged in a joint (sample) frequency table, which may be grouped or not as convenient. If the data of Example 10.3 were grouped by intervals of one-half grade point (1.25–1.75; 1.75–2.25; 2.25–2.75; 2.75–3.25; 3.25–3.75), the table would have the following appearance.

		Y = freshman year G.P.A.				
x	y	1.25–1.75	1.75–2.25	2.25–2.75	2.75–3.25	3.25–3.75
	1.75–2.25	1	1	0	0	0
X = high	2.25–2.75	1	1	1	0	0
school G.P.A.	2.75–3.25	0	2	1	0	1
	3.25–3.75	0	0	1	0	0

Additionally it is informative to plot the points on a graph showing X on one axis and Y on the other. Such a plot of random observations is called a *scatter diagram*. See Figure 10.1 for a scatter diagram of ungrouped data. The scatter diagram enables the experimenter to check very roughly whether the data are consistent with the assumptions $E(Y|X) = \alpha + \beta X$ and $V(Y|X) = \sigma_1^2$.

Regardless of whether or not a scatter diagram is plotted, the observations are used to estimate the true regression line.

This estimated line is called the *sample regression line of Y on X* and its formula is

$$\widehat{E(Y|X)} = \hat{\alpha} + \hat{\beta} X,$$

where

$$\hat{\beta} = \frac{\sum_{i=1}^n (X_i - \bar{X})(Y_i - \bar{Y})}{\sum_{i=1}^n (X_i - \bar{X})^2} = \frac{\sum_{i=1}^n X_i Y_i - (1/n)(\sum_{i=1}^n X_i)(\sum_{i=1}^n Y_i)}{\sum_{i=1}^n X_i^2 - (1/n)(\sum_{i=1}^n X_i)^2}$$

and

$$\hat{\alpha} = \bar{Y} - \hat{\beta} \bar{X}.$$

This line is the best estimator, in the sense of least squares, of the assumed (but unknown) straight line $E(Y|X) = \alpha + \beta X$. By this is meant that among all possible straight lines, the sample regression line is the one which minimizes the sums of the squares of the deviations of the observed Y's from the sample regression line; i.e.,

$$\sum_{i=1}^n [Y_i - (a + bX_i)]^2$$

is minimized with respect to all choices of a and b, when a and b are chosen as $\hat{\alpha}$ and $\hat{\beta}$, as defined above. This line also has the property that the random estimators $\hat{\alpha}$ and $\hat{\beta}$ are unbiased; i.e., $E(\hat{\alpha}) = \alpha$ and $E(\hat{\beta}) = \beta$.

It should be observed that one can rewrite the sample regression line as

$$\widehat{E(Y|X)} = \bar{Y} + \hat{\beta}(X - \bar{X}).$$

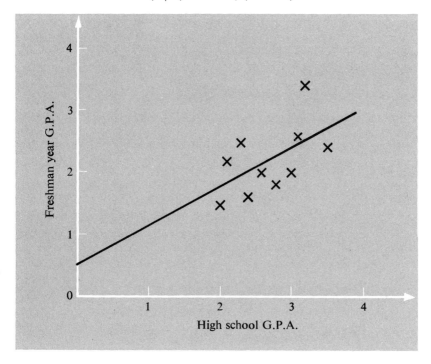

FIGURE 10.2   *Sample regression line of freshman year G.P.A.'s on high school G.P.A.'s.*

This form is often preferred, since it shows that the sample regression line is the straight line with slope $\hat{\beta}$ that passes through $(\bar{X}, \bar{Y})$. σ_1^2 is estimated by

$$
\begin{aligned}
s_{Y|X}^2 &= \frac{\sum\limits_{i=1}^{n} (Y_i - \hat{\alpha} - \hat{\beta}X_i)^2}{n-2} \\[2ex]
&= \frac{\sum\limits_{i=1}^{n} [(Y_i - \bar{Y}) - \hat{\beta}(X_i - \bar{X})]^2}{n-2} \\[2ex]
&= \frac{\sum\limits_{i=1}^{n} Y_i^2 - (1/n)\left(\sum\limits_{i=1}^{n} Y_i\right)^2 - \hat{\beta}\left[\sum\limits_{i=1}^{n} X_iY_i - (1/n)\left(\sum\limits_{i=1}^{n} X_i\right)\left(\sum\limits_{i=1}^{n} Y_i\right)\right]}{n-2}
\end{aligned}
$$

(computing formula).

This is clearly an analogue to $s^2 = \sum_{i=1}^{n} (X_i - \bar{X})^2/(n-1)$ [which might also be written $\sum_{i=1}^{n} (X_i - \hat{\mu})^2/(n-1)$ in Chapter 6]. In the single variable problem, $\bar{X}$ is the estimate of the population mean, and the terms $(X_i - \bar{X})$ are deviations from this estimated mean. Here $\hat{\alpha} + \hat{\beta}X$ is the estimated mean (line) and the

$$[Y_i - \widehat{E(Y|X_i)}] = [Y_i - \hat{\alpha} - \hat{\beta}X_i]$$

are the deviations from it. The divisor $n - 2$ calls for comment. In the simple case, one parameter was estimated, and to get an unbiased estimate it was necessary to reduce the divisor from n to $n - 1$. Here two parameters are estimated and the estimate of σ_1^2 is unbiased if the divisor is $n - 2$.

The subscript $Y|X$ will be used with this estimate to distinguish it from s_Y^2, which is $\sum (Y_i - \bar{Y})^2/(n-1)$, i.e., the sample variance of the Y's if the X's were disregarded. There is also $s_X^2 = \sum (X_i - \bar{X})^2/(n-1)$, the variance of the X's with Y's disregarded. This does not have to be a sample variance, for the X's do not have to be random— they may represent a set of values chosen by the experimenter. However, it is still useful to use the symbol s_X^2 and the term variance.

Example 10.4 Grade prediction (continued)

If a relationship exists between high school and university grades, it should be useful as a tool in predicting the grades of other students entering the university from this population. The simple linear relationship is assumed as a starting point. In other words, if Y denotes freshman G.P.A., and X, high school G.P.A., it is assumed that

(a) $E(Y|X) = \alpha + \beta X$;

(b) $\sigma_{Y|X}^2$ is a constant σ_1^2.

That is, for any given high school G.P.A. X, the corresponding university freshman G.P.A.'s are randomly distributed with this mean and variance. α, β, and σ_1^2 may be estimated by the formulas given. The data and calculations are outlined in the table on the next page.

It is straightforward to compute

$$\bar{X} = 2.70, \qquad \bar{Y} = 2.20,$$

$$\beta = \frac{60.79 - \frac{1}{10}(27.0)(22.0)}{75.16 - \frac{1}{10}(27.0)^2} = 0.615$$

X	Y	X²	Y²	XY	Ŷ	$(Y - \hat{Y})^2$
2.0	1.5	4.00	2.25	3.00	1.770	0.073
2.1	2.2	4.41	4.84	4.62	1.832	0.136
2.3	2.5	5.29	6.25	5.75	1.954	0.298
2.4	1.6	5.76	2.56	3.84	2.016	0.173
2.6	2.0	6.76	4.00	5.20	2.139	0.019
2.8	1.8	7.84	3.24	5.04	2.262	0.213
3.0	2.0	9.00	4.00	6.00	2.385	0.148
3.1	2.6	9.61	6.76	8.06	2.446	0.024
3.2	3.4	10.24	11.56	10.88	2.508	0.796
3.5	2.4	12.25	5.76	8.40	2.692	0.085
27.0	22.0	75.16	51.22	60.79	22.004	1.965

so that the sample regression line is

$$\widehat{E(Y|X)} = 2.20 + 0.615(X - 2.70),$$

though it is usual to write simply

$$\hat{Y} = 2.20 + 0.615(X - 2.70)$$
$$= 0.615X + 0.54$$

as the prediction equation showing the estimated $\hat{Y}$ corresponding to any X. For example, if $X = 2.0$, then

$$\hat{Y} = 0.615(2.0) + 0.54$$
$$= 1.230 + 0.54 = 1.770.$$

In words, this says that 1.77 is the estimated mean freshman G.P.A. of all students entering with a high school average of 2.0. Similarly, for $X = 3.0$, $\hat{Y} = 0.615(3.0) + 0.54 = 2.385$. From two such points, the estimated regression line can be drawn. However, the computing table shows the $\hat{Y}$ corresponding to all observed X. The reason for this is discussed in the next paragraph.

Turning to σ_1^2, this parameter is estimated by $s_{Y|X}^2$, which can be computed directly from the computing formula so that

$$s_{Y|X}^2 = \frac{1}{8}\left\{51.22 - \frac{(22.0)^2}{10} - (0.615)\left[60.79 - \frac{1}{10}(27.0)(22.0)\right]\right\}$$

$$= \frac{1.965}{8} = 0.25.$$

The computing formula hides to a large extent what is really involved. To illustrate the real nature of $s_{Y|X}^2$, two columns have been added to the basic calculation tables. These are for $\hat{Y}$ and $(Y - \hat{Y})^2$. As noted above, $\hat{Y}$ is the value of Y estimated from the prediction equation for each given X; hence $(Y - \hat{Y})^2$ is the squared deviation of estimated values from observed values. Thus, it is alternatively seen that

$$s_{Y|X}^2 = \frac{1}{n-2} \sum_{i=1}^{n} (Y_i - \hat{Y}_i)^2 = \frac{1}{8} (1.965) = 0.25$$

in this example.

In the previous example, the sample regression line was used to predict values of Y corresponding to values of X. Care must be taken in such predictions. For example, one can formally set $X = 0$ into the equation and obtain $\hat{Y} = 0.54$. This says that a high school G.P.A. of zero will correspond to an estimated freshman average of 0.54. This is clearly nonsense since anyone whose high school G.P.A. is zero will not enter college. The assumed straight-line relationship is adequate only over a limited range, and prediction outside this range is dangerous. At the other end, if $X = 4$, then $\hat{Y} = 3.00$ but since we had no data for X greater than 3.5, use of the regression for $X = 4$ has doubtful validity. In both cases, we have extrapolated, i.e., predicted values outside the range of plotted values. This is dangerous and, in general, one should be content to interpolate, i.e., predict within the range of observed values.

EXERCISES

1. If the sample regression line in Example 10.1 is $\hat{Y} = 5.9 - 0.002X$, with X the calories per day and Y the weight loss in pounds, predict the average weekly weight loss if $X = 1,200$ calories; 600 calories; 0 calories. Comment.

2. If the sample regression line in Example 10.2 is $\hat{Y} = 400X - 16,000$, where $X =$ forecast temperature, $\hat{Y} =$ number attending the baseball game, predict the average crowd when $X = 80°$; $60°$; $20°$. Comment.

Tests and Confidence Intervals for
α and β

To get additional information concerning α, β, and σ_1^2 we add *Assumption 3*: Y is normally distributed for each X.

Beta is estimated by $\hat{\beta}$, a linear function of the Y's. Since these are independent normal random variables by Theorem 6.3, $\hat{\beta}$ is normally distributed with mean β and variance

$$\sigma_1^2 \left[\sum_{i=1}^{n} (X_i - \bar{X})^2 \right]^{-1}.$$

[*Note:* To derive $V(\hat{\beta})$, we observe that

$$\hat{\beta} = \frac{\sum_{i=1}^{n} (X_i - \bar{X})(Y_i - \bar{Y})}{\sum_{i=1}^{n} (X_i - \bar{X})^2} = \frac{\sum_{i=1}^{n} (X_i - \bar{X}) Y_i}{\sum_{i=1}^{n} (X_i - \bar{X})^2} - \frac{\bar{Y} \sum_{i=1}^{n} (X_i - \bar{X})}{\sum_{i=1}^{n} (X_i - \bar{X})^2}$$

$$= \frac{\sum_{i=1}^{n} (X_i - \bar{X}) Y_i}{\sum_{i=1}^{n} (X_i - \bar{X})^2}$$

since

$$\sum_{i=1}^{n} (X_i - \bar{X}) = 0.$$

Thus,

$$V(\hat{\beta}) = \frac{\sum_{i=1}^{n} (X_i - \bar{X})^2 \sigma_1^2}{[\sum_{i=1}^{n} (X_i - \bar{X})^2]^2} = \frac{\sigma_1^2}{\sum_{i=1}^{n} (X_i - \bar{X})^2}.]$$

Since σ_1^2 is generally unknown, it is replaced by $s_{Y|X}^2$, and

$$\frac{(\hat{\beta} - \beta) \sqrt{\sum_{i=1}^{n} (X_i - \bar{X})^2}}{s_{Y|X}}$$

is a t random variable with $n - 2$ degrees of freedom. This statistic can be used to test hypotheses concerning β or to find confidence intervals for β. For example, using Table A2.6 with $n - 2$ d.f., we can find t_ϵ such that

$$P\left[-t_\epsilon < \frac{(\hat{\beta} - \beta) \sqrt{\sum_{i=1}^{n} (X_i - \bar{X})^2}}{s_{Y|X}} < t_\epsilon \right] = 1 - \epsilon.$$

From this probability statement, one obtains by algebraic manipulation, as in Chapter 8, that a confidence interval for β with confidence coefficient $1 - \epsilon$ is

$$\hat{\beta} \pm \frac{s_{Y|X} t_\epsilon}{\sqrt{\sum_{i=1}^{n} (X_i - \bar{X})^2}}.$$

Perhaps the most important hypothesis concerning β is $H : \beta = 0$. If H is true, then $E(Y|X) = \alpha$, and knowledge of X does not help in predicting the value of Y. The alternative to this hypothesis may be one-sided or two-sided; i.e., the alternative may be $A : \beta > 0$, or $A : \beta \neq 0$. One-sided alternatives are appropriate when prior knowledge is sufficient to state that $\beta \geq 0$, e.g., in studies of heights and weights, or $\beta \leq 0$, e.g., in studies of weight loss and calorie intake. In other problems, two-sided alternatives are appropriate. In any case, if $H : \beta = 0$ can be rejected using the test statistic

$$\frac{(\hat{\beta} - 0)\sqrt{\sum_{i=1}^{n}(X_i - \bar{X})^2}}{s_{Y|X}},$$

then we are confident that knowledge of X aids in predicting the average value of Y.

The implications of the rejection or nonrejection of the hypothesis $\beta = 0$ are often confused. If the assumption $E(Y|X) = \alpha + \beta X$ is in fact true, then rejection of $H : \beta = 0$ implies that the average value of Y does vary with X. If $\beta = 0$ is not rejected, then the data are consistent with the possibility that the average value of Y does not depend on X.

On the other hand, in many problems the investigator calculates the linear regression and tests the hypothesis $\beta = 0$ without an adequate check of the assumption of linearity. If, in fact, $E(Y|X)$ is not linearly related to X, it is possible that we might have a relationship such as that pictured in Figure 10.3.

If linearity were assumed in this situation, the hypothesis $\beta = 0$ would seldom be rejected, even though there is clearly a relationship between $E(Y|X)$ and X.

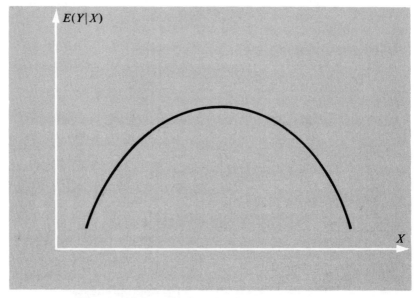

FIGURE 10.3 *An example of nonlinear regression.*

While such a situation can happen, usually the experimenter has enough information to rule this out and can make the inferences suggested above based on the results of the test of the hypothesis $\beta = 0$. Or the experimenter can test the hypothesis that $E(Y|X) = \alpha + \beta X$ against some alternative. This test, which is not discussed here, is known as a test of linearity.

Although α is usually of lesser importance than β, similar results allow us to obtain confidence intervals for α or tests of hypotheses concerning α. The parameter α is estimated by $\hat{\alpha} = \bar{Y} - \hat{\beta}\bar{X}$, a linear function of the Y's. Since these are independent normal random variables, $\hat{\alpha}$ is normally distributed with mean α and variance

$$\frac{\sigma_1^2(\sum_{i=1}^n X_i^2)}{n[\sum_{i=1}^n (X_i - \bar{X})^2]}.$$

[*Note:* When the X's are not random, $V(\bar{Y} - \hat{\beta}\bar{X})$ can be derived from Theorem 6.3 by use of the fact that $\bar{Y}$ and $\hat{\beta}$ are independent. That they are independent is proved in mathematical statistics textbooks but is beyond the level of this book. Making use of this, we have

$$V(\bar{Y} - \hat{\beta}\bar{X}) = V(\bar{Y}) + (\bar{X})^2 V(\hat{\beta}).$$

Replacing $V(\hat{\beta})$ by the formula found on page 239, the student can verify that $V(\hat{\alpha})$ is as given above.

If the X's are also random, then the probability distributions, expected values, and variances must be considered as conditional and the same arguments then apply.]

Replacing σ_1^2 by $s_{Y|X}^2$, the statistic

$$\frac{(\hat{\alpha} - \alpha)\sqrt{n \sum_{i=1}^n (X_i - \bar{X})^2}}{s_{Y|X} \sqrt{\sum_{i=1}^n X_i^2}}$$

is a t random variable with $n - 2$ d.f. This statistic can be used to test any hypothesis about α and, as with β, the two numbers

$$\hat{\alpha} \pm \frac{s_{Y|X} t_\epsilon \sqrt{\sum_{i=1}^n X_i^2}}{\sqrt{n \sum_{i=1}^n (X_i - \bar{X})^2}}$$

yield a confidence interval for α with confidence coefficient $1 - \epsilon$.

Example 10.5 Grade prediction (continued)

In the problem of estimating the regression line of freshman G.P.A.'s, 95 percent confidence intervals for α and β are found as follows: $\hat{\alpha} = \bar{Y} - \hat{\beta}\bar{X} = 2.20 - (0.615)(2.70) = 0.54, \quad \hat{\beta} = 0.615,$

$\sum X_i^2 = 75.16$, $\sum (X_i - \bar{X})^2 = 2.26$, $n = 10$, $s_{X|Y} = 0.5$, and $t_{0.05} = 2.306$ (8 d.f.). A 95 percent confidence interval for α is

$$0.54 \pm \frac{(2.31)(0.5)\sqrt{75.16}}{\sqrt{10(2.26)}} = 0.54 \pm 2.10 \quad \text{or} \quad (-1.56, 2.64).$$

A 95 percent confidence interval for β is

$$0.615 \pm \frac{(2.31)(0.5)}{\sqrt{2.26}} = 0.615 \pm 0.77 \quad \text{or} \quad (-0.155, 1.385).$$

Using the relationship between hypothesis testing and confidence intervals, we see that the hypothesis $H : \beta = 0$ versus $A : \beta \neq 0$ would not be rejected at the 5 percent level. However, the sample size is small and zero is close to one end of the interval. Thus, we should not uncritically accept $H : \beta = 0$ but probably try to obtain a larger sample size.

Confidence Intervals for Predictions

The above were simple extensions of confidence interval formulas to regression parameters. However, there are other confidence statements that may be of interest. In the grade prediction problem, it is of importance to assign some confidence statement to a prediction (i.e., to a $\hat{Y}$ corresponding to a given X). For example, what is a confidence interval for the predicted mean G.P.A. of all students entering the College of Arts and Sciences at State University with a 2.0 high school G.P.A.? Or an individual student may wish to know what confidence can be placed in his prediction—this is the problem of determining a confidence interval for a second sample mean from a first set of observations. For an individual student, the second sample is of size 1, i.e., $m = 1$.

To find a confidence interval for $E(Y|X_0)$ for a fixed X_0, it is observed that

$$\hat{Y}_0 = \widehat{E(Y|X_0)} = \hat{\alpha} + \hat{\beta}X_0 = \bar{Y} + \hat{\beta}(X_0 - \bar{X})$$

is a linear combination of the Y's. Since these are independent normal random variables, $\hat{Y}_0$ is normally distributed. Its mean is $\alpha + \beta X_0$ and its variance is

$$\frac{\sigma_1^2}{n} + \frac{(X_0 - \bar{X})^2 \sigma_1^2}{\sum (X_i - \bar{X})^2}.$$

Thus,

$$\frac{\hat{Y}_0 - E(Y|X_0)}{s_{Y|X}\sqrt{(1/n) + [(X_0 - \bar{X})^2/\sum (X_i - \bar{X})^2]}}$$

has a t distribution with $n - 2$ d.f. so that the two numbers

$$\hat{Y}_0 \pm s_{Y|X} t_\epsilon \sqrt{\frac{1}{n} + \frac{(X_0 - \bar{X})^2}{\sum_{i=1}^{n} (X_i - \bar{X})^2}}$$

yield a confidence interval for $E(Y|X_0)$ with confidence coefficient $1 - \epsilon$. Let (X_{10}, Y_{10}), (X_{20}, Y_{20}), ..., (X_{m0}, Y_{m0}) be a second random sample and let $\bar{X}_0$ and $\bar{Y}_0$ denote, respectively, the sample average of these X's and Y's. Then $\bar{Y}_0 - \hat{Y}_0 = \bar{Y}_0 - \hat{\alpha} - \hat{\beta}X_0$ is a normal random variable with mean zero and variance

$$\sigma_1^2 \left[\frac{1}{n} + \frac{1}{m} + \frac{(X_0 - \bar{X})^2}{\sum_{i=1}^{n} (X_i - \bar{X})^2} \right].$$

The variance of $\hat{Y}_0$ is

$$\frac{\sigma_1^2}{n} + \frac{(X_0 - \bar{X})^2 \sigma_1^2}{\sum_{i=1}^{n} (X_i - \bar{X})^2};$$

the extra term σ_1^2/m comes from the variance of $\bar{Y}_0$ as in the similar problem in Chapter 8. Hence, the two numbers

$$\hat{Y}_0 \pm s_{Y|X} t_\epsilon \left[\frac{1}{m} + \frac{1}{n} + \frac{(X_0 - \bar{X})^2}{\sum_{i=1}^{n} (X_i - \bar{X})^2} \right]^{1/2}$$

yield a confidence interval for $\bar{Y}_0$ with confidence coefficient $1 - \epsilon$. The commonest application is when $m = 1$, in which case $\bar{Y}_0$ can be written simply Y_0.

Example 10.6 Grade prediction (continued)

Find 95 percent confidence intervals for the average freshman G.P.A. of all students who enter with a high school G.P.A. of 3.0 and the predicted freshman G.P.A. of an individual student entering with a high school G.P.A. of 3.0.

Solution: From earlier computations, we have $X_0 = 3.0$, $\hat{Y}_0 = 2.385$, $\bar{X} = 2.70$, $s_{\hat{Y}|X}^2 = 0.25$, $\sum (X_i - \bar{X})^2 = 2.26$, $n = 10$, $t_{0.05} = 2.31$ (8 d.f.) and $X_0 - \bar{X} = 0.3$.

Thus, a 95 percent confidence interval for the average freshman G.P.A. of all students who enter with a high school G.P.A. of 3.0 is $2.385 \pm (2.31)(0.50) \sqrt{\frac{1}{10} + (0.3)^2/2.26} = 2.385 \pm 0.432$ or $(1.953, 2.813)$.

A 95 percent confidence interval for the predicted freshman G.P.A. of an individual who enters with a G.P.A. of 3.0 is

$$2.385 \pm (2.31)(0.50)\sqrt{1 + \frac{1}{10} + \frac{(0.3)^2}{2.26}} = 2.385 \pm 1.233$$

or $(1.152, 3.618)$.

Note that the last confidence interval is rather wide and probably not too valuable for prediction. Again, a larger sample size usually produces smaller intervals. For, as n increases, the terms $1/n$ and $\bar{X}^2/\sum_{i=1}^{n}(X_i - X)^2$ decrease so that the confidence intervals for α, β, and $E(Y|X_0)$ tend to width zero. On the other hand, the confidence interval for an individual prediction Y_0 does not tend to zero as the sample size increases. This happens because of the first term under the square root of the second half of the expression for the confidence interval for Y_0. This term is of course unaffected by the sample size n.

In other words the variance of an individual prediction depends on three factors—the variability associated with the estimation of α (the intercept) and of β (the slope), and the individual variability. The former terms become small as sample size increases; the latter term is independent of the sample size.

EXERCISE

Find 95 percent confidence intervals for the average and individual freshman G.P.A.'s of students whose high school G.P.A. is 2.7.

Example 10.7 Egg counts of herring

In a California herring investigation, the following data were obtained on the number of eggs of four-year-old herring, classified according to length:

Length (mm)	Number of eggs
163	14,083
168	10,985
168	16,380
171	15,135
172	13,526
176	15,052
193	25,294
194	24,309

(a) Is the regression significant? In other words, test the hypothesis $\beta = 0$ at the 5 percent significance level.

(b) Another four-year-old herring of length 182 mm taken in a different haul was reported as having 33,859 eggs. Is this reasonable? Test at the 5 percent significance level.

Solution: By direct computation,

$$n = 8 \qquad \sum X_i = 1{,}405 \qquad \sum Y_i = 134{,}764$$

$$\sum X_i^2 = 247{,}703 \qquad \sum Y_i^2 = 2{,}456{,}603{,}036$$

$$\sum X_i Y_i = 24{,}054{,}246$$

$$\bar{Y} = 16{,}845.5$$

$$\hat{\beta} = \frac{24{,}054{,}246 - [(1{,}405)(134{,}764)/8]}{247{,}703 - [(1{,}405)^2/8]}$$

$$= 406.694 = 406.7 \text{ (rounded to one decimal)}$$

$$\hat{\alpha} = -54{,}580.$$

Hence,

$$\widehat{E(Y|X)} = 16{,}845.5 + 406.7(X - 175.6),$$

or

$$\hat{Y} = 406.7X - 54{,}580.$$

It is more usual to simply write $\hat{Y}$ rather than $\widehat{E(Y|X)}$.

$$s_{Y|X}^2 = \frac{186{,}436{,}074 - 406.7\{24{,}056{,}246 - [(1{,}405)(134{,}764)/8]\}}{6}$$

$$= 4{,}886{,}723.3;$$

$$s_{Y|X} = 2{,}210.6.$$

(a) To test $H: \beta = 0$ versus $A: \beta \neq 0$, use the statistic

$$t = \frac{(\hat{\beta} - \beta)}{s_{Y|X}} \sqrt{\sum (X_i - \bar{X})^2} \qquad \text{with 6 d.f.}$$

or

$$t = \frac{(406.694 - 0)\sqrt{949.88}}{2{,}210.6} = 5.7.$$

H is rejected at the 5 percent level; i.e., the regression is significant at the 5 percent level.

(b) The second question may be answered in two ways that are equivalent. First, a 95 percent confidence interval may be found for the egg count of an individual herring 182 mm in length. Here $m = 1$, $X_0 = 182$. The required confidence interval is

$$\hat{Y}_0 \pm s_{Y|X}t_{0.05}\left[1 + \frac{1}{n} + \frac{(X_0 - \bar{X})^2}{\sum_{i=1}^{n}(X_i - \bar{X})^2}\right]^{1/2}.$$

Since t has 6 d.f., $t_{0.05} = 2.45$. $\hat{Y}_0 = 19,448$. Therefore, the required confidence interval is

$$19,448 \pm (2,210.6)(2.45)\left[1 + \frac{1}{8} + \frac{(6.4)^2}{949.88}\right]^{1/2};$$

i.e., $19,448 \pm 5,854$ or $(13,594; 25,302)$. Since with 95 percent confidence, it may be asserted that a 182-mm herring should have an egg count of between 13,594 and 25,302, the observed value, viz., 33,859, seems unlikely. It may be from a different population, or a measurement error may have been made.

The second approach is to form the t statistic

$$t = \frac{\bar{Y}_0 - \hat{Y}_0}{s_{Y|X}\left[\dfrac{1}{m} + \dfrac{1}{n} + \dfrac{(X_0 - \bar{X})^2}{\sum_{i=1}^{n}(X_i - \bar{X})^2}\right]^{1/2}}.$$

Here $m = 1$ and $\bar{Y}_0$ is $Y_0 = 33,859$.

$$t = \frac{33,859 - 19,448}{2,210.6\sqrt{1 + \dfrac{1}{8} + \dfrac{(6.4)^2}{949.88}}} = 6.03.$$

Since the 5 percent point of t with 6 d.f. is 2.45, the hypothesis that the observation $(X_0 = 182, Y_0 = 33,859)$ comes from the same population as the first set of observations is rejected. That the second approach is equivalent follows from the fact that the alternative here is two-sided.

Summary of Test Rules for Regression

1. $H : \alpha = \alpha_0$; the test statistic is

$$t = \frac{(\hat{\alpha} - \alpha_0)\sqrt{n\sum(X_i - \bar{X})^2}}{s_{Y|X}\sqrt{\sum X_i^2}} \qquad \text{with } n - 2 \text{ d.f.}$$

2. $H : \beta = \beta_0$; the test statistic is

$$t = \frac{(\hat{\beta} - \beta_0)}{s_{Y|X}}\sqrt{\sum(X_i - \bar{X})^2} \qquad \text{with } n - 2 \text{ d.f.}$$

3. $H : E(Y|X_0) = E_0$; the test statistic is

$$t = \frac{(\hat{Y}_0 - E_0)}{s_{Y|X}} \sqrt{\frac{1}{n} + \frac{(X_0 - \bar{X})^2}{\sum (X_i - \bar{X})^2}} \qquad \text{with } n - 2 \text{ d.f.}$$

4. $H : (\bar{X}_0, \bar{Y}_0)$ belongs to the specified population where $\bar{X}_0$ and $\bar{Y}_0$ are the averages of a new sample of size m; the test statistic is

$$t = \frac{(\hat{Y}_0 - \bar{Y}_0)}{s_{Y|X}} \sqrt{\frac{1}{m} + \frac{1}{n} + \frac{(\bar{X}_0 - \bar{X})^2}{\sum (X_i - \bar{X})^2}} \qquad \text{with } n - 2 \text{ d.f.}$$

In each case, if the alternative is one-sided, the hypothesis is rejected when t is outside the specified critical level in the proper tail. If the alternative is two-sided, the hypothesis is rejected when $|t|$ is outside the specified critical level.

Correlation

In the first half of this chapter we studied the relationship between the expected value of a dependent random variable Y and an independent variable X, which might have been random or not. The emphasis was on prediction of Y, and the values of X were only used to aid in this prediction. In this half of the chapter both X and Y are random variables, and we wish to study the *joint* relationship between them. For the moment, we drop Assumptions 1, 2, and 3, which we needed in the first half of the chapter.

In particular we wish to estimate the population correlation coefficient. Recall that for finite sample spaces Cov (X, Y) was defined as

$$\text{Cov } (X, Y) = \sum_x \sum_y (x - EX)(y - EY)p(x, y),$$

where the summation is over all points (x, y) in the joint sample space of (X, Y). The correlation coefficient ρ_{XY} is defined as

$$\rho_{XY} = \frac{\text{Cov } (X, Y)}{\sigma_X \sigma_Y}.$$

The *sample covariance*, which is denoted by s_{XY} and used to estimate Cov (X, Y), is defined as

$$s_{XY} = \frac{1}{n - 1} \sum_{i=1}^{n} (X_i - \bar{X})(Y_i - \bar{Y})$$

$$= \frac{1}{n - 1} \left[\sum_{i=1}^{n} X_i Y_i - \frac{1}{n} \left(\sum_{i=1}^{n} X_i \right) \left(\sum_{i=1}^{n} Y_i \right) \right] \qquad \text{(computing formula)}$$

for ungrouped data and

$$S_{XY} = \frac{1}{n-1} \sum_{i=1}^{k_1} \sum_{j=1}^{k_2} f_{ij}(X_i - \bar{X})(Y_j - \bar{Y})$$

$$= \frac{1}{n-1} \left[\sum_{i=1}^{k_1} \sum_{j=1}^{k_2} f_{ij} X_i Y_j - \frac{1}{n} \left(\sum_{i=1}^{k_1} f_{i \cdot} X_i \right) \left(\sum_{j=1}^{k_2} f_{\cdot j} Y_j \right) \right]$$

(computing formula)

for grouped data, where

$$k_1 = \text{number of groups of } X;$$

$$k_2 = \text{number of groups of } Y;$$

$$f_{ij} = \text{frequency of the } i\text{th class of } X\text{'s and the } j\text{th class of } Y\text{'s};$$

$$f_{i \cdot} = \sum_{j=1}^{k_2} f_{ij} = \text{frequency of the } i\text{th class of } X\text{'s};$$

$$f_{\cdot j} = \sum_{i=1}^{k_1} f_{ij} = \text{frequency of the } j\text{th class of } Y\text{'s};$$

$$n = \sum_{i=1}^{k_1} f_{i \cdot} = \sum_{j=1}^{k_2} f_{\cdot j} = \sum_{i=1}^{k_1} \sum_{j=1}^{k_2} f_{ij} = \text{total number of observations};$$

$$X_i = \text{midpoint of the } i\text{th class of } X\text{'s};$$

$$Y_j = \text{midpoint of the } j\text{th class of } Y\text{'s}.$$

Finally, the *sample correlation coefficient*, denoted by r, is defined to be

$$r = \frac{S_{XY}}{S_X S_Y}.$$

As with the population correlation coefficient it can be shown that $-1 \le r \le 1$ or $r^2 \le 1$.

Example 10.8 Heights and weights of men

The following are the heights (in inches) and weights (in pounds) of ten male statistics students. Find the sample covariance and sample correlation coefficient.

X	72	74	70	69	70	71	70	67	68	72
Y	155	166	170	155	148	160	150	160	160	166

Solution:

$$\sum X_i = 703 \qquad \sum Y_i = 1{,}590$$

$$\sum X_i^2 = 49{,}439 \qquad \sum Y_i^2 = 253{,}266$$

$$\sum X_i Y_i = 111{,}811$$

$$s_{XY} = \tfrac{1}{9}[111{,}811 - \tfrac{1}{10}(703)(1{,}590)] = 3.78,$$

$$s_X^2 = \tfrac{1}{9}[49{,}439 - \tfrac{1}{10}(703)^2] = 2.01,$$

$$s_Y^2 = \tfrac{1}{9}[253{,}266 - \tfrac{1}{10}(1{,}590)^2] = 50.67,$$

$$r = \frac{3.78}{\sqrt{(2.01)(50.67)}} = \frac{3.78}{10.09} = 0.37.$$

The sample covariance is 3.78 and the sample correlation coefficient is 0.37.

The sample correlation coefficient r is an estimator of ρ, a population parameter which measures a degree of relationship between X and Y. In particular, *if X and Y are jointly normal, $\rho = 0$ implies that X and Y are independent.* Thus, small values of r tend to suggest little relationship between X and Y.

This suggests the importance of testing $H : \rho = 0$ versus $A : \rho \neq 0$, when X and Y are jointly normal. For rejection of H implies that X and Y are dependent, while nonrejection of H is compatible with the belief that X and Y are independent. Table A2.7 shows the value of r_ϵ such that

$$P(|r| \geq r_\epsilon | \rho = 0) = \epsilon \qquad \text{for } \epsilon = 0.01,\ 0.05.$$

In other words, $H : \rho = 0$ is rejected in favor of $A : \rho \neq 0$ at the significance level 100ϵ percent if $|r| \geq r_\epsilon$. If, in Example 10.8, we assume that heights and weights are jointly normally distributed, then we may apply this test. We have $r = 0.37$ and $n = 10$. From Table A2.8, $r_{0.05} = 0.63$. Since $|0.37| = 0.37 < 0.63$, H cannot be rejected. That is, the evidence is not sufficient to give up the hypothesis of independence of heights and weights. The reader may find this strange at first since, intuitively, heights and weights should be dependent. The fact that we have not rejected H in this example is probably a result of sampling error associated with the small sample size. Even if $\rho = 0.7$ (which would imply that about 50 percent of the variation in weights is associated with height) there is about a 10 percent probability that r would be as small as 0.37. In short if the sample size is small, the Type II error may be large.

The concepts of regression introduced in this chapter provide additional insight into the correlation coefficient ρ and its estimator r, provided the assumptions for linear regression are satisfied. Suppose X and Y are both random. In some problems, only one variable needs to be predicted and in such problems this variable is always designated by Y. For example, if the two random variables are high school G.P.A. and freshman G.P.A., we automatically let Y represent the freshman G.P.A.'s since we would rarely, if ever, wish to predict high school G.P.A.'s from freshman G.P.A.'s. In other problems, either variable may need to be predicted from the other. For example, if the random variables are heights and weights, there is no reason to assume that one prediction is necessarily more important than the other. In this case we let either random variable be Y and make the following assumptions:

1. $E(Y|X) = \alpha + \beta X$,

   $E(X|Y) = \alpha' + \beta' Y$.

2. $V(Y|X) = \sigma_1^2$,

   $V(X|Y) = \sigma_2^2$.

In particular, when (X, Y) are jointly normal, Assumptions 1 and 2 are satisfied (see Chapter 9) and further, $\rho^2 = \beta\beta'$.

Now, a random sample $(X_1, Y_1), (X_2, Y_2), \ldots, (X_n, Y_n)$ on (X, Y) yields two sample regression lines, namely,

$$\hat{Y} = \widehat{E(Y|X)} = \hat{\alpha} + \hat{\beta}X,$$

$$\hat{X} = \widehat{E(X|Y)} = \hat{\alpha}' + \hat{\beta}'Y,$$

where

$$\hat{\beta} = \frac{s_{XY}}{s_X^2},$$

$$\hat{\beta}' = \frac{s_{XY}}{s_Y^2},$$

$$\hat{\alpha} = \bar{Y} - \hat{\beta}\bar{X},$$

$$\hat{\alpha}' = \bar{X} - \hat{\beta}'\bar{Y}.$$

EXERCISE

Show that $\hat{\beta}$ defined above is the same as $\hat{\beta}$ originally defined.

There are two sample regression lines because of the method we use to obtain a sample regression line. The sample regression line of Y on X minimizes the sum of the squared deviations of the observed Y's from their estimates; i.e., the vertical deviations of the observed points from the sample line are minimized. The sample regression line of X on Y minimizes the sum of the squared deviations of the observed X's from their estimates; i.e., the horizontal deviations of the observed points from the sample line are minimized.

If both sample regression lines are plotted on a scatter diagram, the reader should observe several things. First, both lines pass through the point $(\bar{X}, \bar{Y})$. Second, the regression of Y on X has slope $\hat{\beta}$. However, the regression of X on Y has slope $1/\hat{\beta}'$. By referring to their definitions, we see that the signs of $\hat{\beta}$ and $\hat{\beta}'$ (hence $1/\hat{\beta}'$) depend on the sign of s_{XY}. Thus, both lines have positive slopes or both have negative slopes unless $s_{XY} = 0$. In this case, the sample regression lines reduce to lines parallel to the X and Y axes. Third, since the two lines pass through a common point, they will reduce to a single line if and only if they have the same slope, i.e., if and only if $\hat{\beta} = 1/\hat{\beta}'$ or $\hat{\beta}\hat{\beta}' = 1$.

It is easily seen that, in general,

$$\hat{\beta}\hat{\beta}' = \frac{s_{XY}^2}{s_X^2 s_Y^2} = r^2,$$

so that the two sample regression lines reduce to one if and only if $r^2 = 1$, or $r = +1$ or -1. Since it is intuitively obvious that there can be one line if and only if all the sample points lie on a straight line, we see that $r = \pm 1$ if and only if all the sample points lie on a straight line.

The conditional variances σ_1^2 and σ_2^2 are estimated, respectively, by

$$s_{Y|X}^2 = \frac{1}{n-2} \sum_{i=1}^{n} (Y_i - \hat{\alpha} - \hat{\beta}X_i)^2$$

and

$$s_{X|Y}^2 = \frac{1}{n-2} \sum_{i=1}^{n} (X_i - \hat{\alpha}' - \hat{\beta}'Y_i)^2.$$

Using the definitions of r, $\hat{\beta}$, $\hat{\beta}'$, s_{XY}, s_X^2, and s_Y^2 allows these two equations to be algebraically manipulated to obtain

$$s_{Y|X}^2 = \frac{n-1}{n-2} s_Y^2 (1 - r^2)$$

and

$$s_{Y|X}^2 = \frac{n-1}{n-2} s_X^2 (1 - r^2).$$

Example 10.9   Heights and weights of men (continued)

Assuming that heights (X) and weights (Y) satisfy Assumptions 1 and 2, find the two sample regression lines and plot them on a scatter diagram.

Solution:

$$\beta = \frac{3.78}{2.01} = 1.88,$$

$$\beta' = \frac{3.78}{50.67} = 0.075,$$

$$\bar{X} = 70.3 \quad \text{and} \quad \bar{Y} = 159.0,$$

$$\hat{\alpha} = 159.0 - (1.88)(70.3) = 26.8,$$

$$\hat{\alpha}' = 70.3 - (0.075)(159.0) = 58.4.$$

The two sample regression lines are

$$\hat{Y} = 26.8 + 1.88X,$$
$$\hat{X} = 58.4 + 0.075Y.$$

A scatter diagram, along with the two regression lines, is shown in

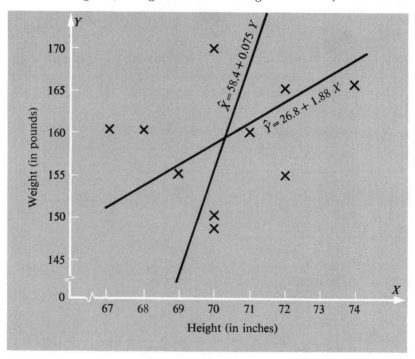

FIGURE 10.4   *The sample regression lines of height on weight and weight on height.*

Observe from the figure that the predicted weight of a male whose height is 70 in. is 158.4 lb while the predicted height of a male whose weight is 158.4 lb is 70.3 in. (not 70 in.). This is because the two lines do not coincide.

Still another interpretation of r, or more specifically r^2, is possible that, in fact, is often the more useful. To derive this, observe that

$$\sum_{i=1}^{n} (Y_i - \hat{Y}_i)^2 = \sum_{i=1}^{n} [(Y_i - \bar{Y}) - \hat{\beta}(X_i - \bar{X})]^2$$

$$= \sum_{i=1}^{n} (Y_i - \bar{Y})^2 - 2\hat{\beta} \sum_{i=1}^{n} (Y_i - \bar{Y})(X_i - \bar{X})$$

$$+ \hat{\beta}^2 \sum_{i=1}^{n} (X_i - \bar{X})^2$$

$$= \sum_{i=1}^{n} (Y_i - \bar{Y})^2 - \frac{\{\sum_{i=1}^{n} [(Y_i - \bar{Y})(X_i - \bar{X})]\}^2}{\sum_{i=1}^{n} (X_i - \bar{X})^2}.$$

The last line is obtained by replacing $\hat{\beta}$ by

$$\frac{\sum_{i=1}^{n} (X_i - \bar{X})(Y_i - \bar{Y})}{\sum_{i=1}^{n} (X_i - \bar{X})^2}$$

and collecting terms.

Divide both sides by $\sum (Y_i - \bar{Y})^2$ to get

$$\frac{\sum_{i=1}^{n} (Y_i - \hat{Y})^2}{\sum_{i=1}^{n} (Y_i - \bar{Y})^2} = 1 - \frac{[\sum_{i=1}^{n} (Y_i - \bar{Y})(X_i - \bar{X})]^2}{\sum_{i=1}^{n} (X_i - \bar{X})^2 \sum_{i=1}^{n} (Y_i - \bar{Y})^2}.$$

The last term on the right-hand side is r^2, so we have shown that

$$\frac{\text{Residual sum of squares about the sample regression line}}{\text{Sum of squares about the mean of the } Y\text{'s}} = 1 - r^2,$$

where we interpret $\sum_{i=1}^{n} (Y_i - \hat{Y})^2$ as the residual sum of squares about the regression line. Thus, by an argument similar to that in Chapter 9 for ρ^2, it follows that r^2 may be interpreted as an estimator of the variation in Y attributable to the variation in X (at least within our linear model with constant variance). The interpretation does *not* depend on the Y's being normally distributed. A similar argument shows that r^2 is an estimator of the proportion of the variance of X attributable to Y (provided that X is also a random variable).

In Example 10.8, where $r = 0.37$ so that $r^2 = 0.14$, only 14 percent of the variation in weight is attributable to variation in height (at least for these ten individuals) since r^2 is an estimator of the proportion of the variance in weights attributable to variation in heights. Since height is also a random variable, the interpretation that 14 percent of the variance in heights is attributable to variations in weight is also correct (for these ten individuals).

If the variable X is not random, it is not appropriate to calculate the regression

$$\widehat{E(X|Y)} = \hat{\alpha}' + \hat{\beta}'Y,$$

but it is proper to calculate r and r^2 by the formulas given above, and the latter interpretation of r^2 is useful.

Example 10.10   Egg counts of herring (continued)

In this example,

$$r^2 = \frac{[24{,}054{,}246 - \frac{1}{8}(1{,}405)(134{,}764)]^2}{[247{,}703 - \frac{1}{8}(1{,}405)^2][2{,}456{,}603{,}036 - \frac{1}{8}(134{,}764)^2]}$$

$$= 0.85.$$

Thus, 85 percent of the variation in egg count can be said to be associated with or attributed to variations in length, at least as estimated from this small sample. This is a very satisfactory value of r^2, and regression would be quite useful in studies on egg counts.

EXERCISE

In Example 10.9,

(a) predict Y when $X = 66$, 69, and 72 in.;
(b) predict X when $Y = 150$, 160, and 170 lb;
(c) check that $r = \sqrt{\hat{\beta}\hat{\beta}'}$.

Recall that it is customary to choose as Y the value to be estimated or predicted; as X the usable controllable variable from which the prediction will be made. In Example 10.1, the choice of calorie intake as X is indicated since this is the controllable variable. In Example 10.7, length is the variable that is easy to measure and it will be used to estimate egg count. Thus, length is chosen as the X variable though both are random variables. In this way, most regression models are reduced to the one considered in the first part of this chapter.

As remarked earlier in the chapter, a linear relationship between X and Y need not imply a cause-and-effect relationship. Aside from sample fluctuations, a high sample correlation coefficient may be due to

(a) A real cause-and-effect relationship.
(b) A "common part."
(c) "Selection."
(d) Their mutual relationship to a third random variable.
(e) The effect of trend in time.
(f) Related third variables used in the denominator of a rate or index.

Brief examples to illustrate this may be useful:

(a) A real cause-and-effect relationship is illustrated by heights of father (X) and sons (Y), where there is presumably a genetic effect.
(b) A "common part" is illustrated by freshman and university G.P.A.'s, since freshman grades are part of the total university G.P.A.'s.
(c) "Selection" is illustrated when attempts to make better prediction studies are made, where many possible prediction variables are examined and only those with the highest correlation selected. Such selected correlations or regressions are no longer random.
(d) Mutual relationship to a third random variable is illustrated by the heights of brothers and sisters (either may be X or Y). Both are affected by a third variable, their common inheritance, but neither is a cause for the other.
(e) The effect of common trends in time is illustrated by studies that have shown a positive correlation between minister's salaries and consumption of alcohol. One increases over time due to inflation and the other due to population increases.
(f) Use of related third variables in the denominator of a rate or index is illustrated by examples that have been given showing correlation between birth rates and the number of storks— because birth rates are higher in rural areas than urban ones and, of course, storks are more abundant in rural areas than urban areas.

■ Experiments

10.1   (a) Collect from each male in your class his barefoot height, Y (to the nearest inch), and the height of his father, X (to the nearest inch).

(b) Construct a scatter diagram of these data and plot on it the sample regression line of Y on X.

(c) Test $H : \beta = 0$ versus $A : \beta \neq 0$ at the 5 percent level.

(d) Find 95 percent confidence intervals for

   (i) The average height of all sons with fathers of height $X = 72$ in.

   (ii) The height of an individual son whose father's height is $X = 72$ in.

(e) If heights of succeeding generations are increasing, what does this imply about α? Test this hypothesis at the 5 percent level.

10.2   (a) Collect from each student in your class, the following information (where possible):

   X: average grade during last year at high school.
   U: scholastic aptitude test (S.A.T.) score.
   Y: average grade during first year at university.

(b) Make scatter diagrams for your data of (X, Y) and (U, Y).

(c) Find the sample regression lines of Y on X and of Y on U and plot them on the scatter diagrams.

(d) Test whether their slopes are significantly different from 0 (at the 5 percent level).

(e) If a student has a high school average of 70 percent and an S.A.T. score of 690, give two estimates of his first-year average at university.

(f) Compute r for both sets of data and decide which estimate in (e) is more likely to be close to the true average; i.e., which is the more useful predictor of freshman university grades?

   Note: This problem is better handled by multilinear regression where only one equation is found and both the value of U and X contribute to the one estimate of Y.

10.3   (a) Collect the barefoot heights X (to the nearest inch) and clothed weights Y (to the nearest pound) of each student in your class. Plot them on a scatter diagram.

(b) Omitting your own height and weight, use the rest of the data to construct sample regression lines of Y on X and X on Y.

(c) Find 95 percent confidence intervals for α and β. Can you reject $H : \beta = 0$ versus $A : \beta \neq 0$ at the 5 percent level?

(d) Repeat (c) for α' and β'.

(e) Test the hypothesis that your height and weight come from the same population as the rest of the class. (Use 5 percent as the significance level.)

10.4   (a) Use the observations X and Y collected in Experiment 9.3 to test the hypothesis that $\rho = 0$ at the 5 percent level.

*(b) If a copy of *Tables for Statisticians and Biometricians*† is available, find a 95 percent confidence interval for ρ and sketch it on a blackboard along with the others from your class. The theoretical value of ρ_{XY} that may have been determined in Experiment 9.3 is $\frac{1}{2}$. What fraction of the confidence intervals cover this value? What fraction do you expect to do so?

10.5   (a) Throw a dart at a dart board 30 times, aiming as closely to the center as possible. Measure and record the horizontal and vertical deviations of each throw from the center. Label these X and Y respectively.

(b) Find r, the sample correlation coefficient for your data.

(c) Assuming X and Y to be jointly normally distributed, test $H : \rho = 0$ at the 5 percent level.

(d) Give an intuitive reason for believing that H should be accepted. Since X and Y are normally distributed, what further can be said of them if you accept H?

■ Problems

10.1   The following data give the net profit Y in thousands of dollars for a small business over the last twelve years, X.

Year	1957	1958	1959	1960	1961	1962	1963	1964	1965	1966	1967	1968
Net profit (in thousands of dollars)	10.1	10.8	10.7	11.2	11.0	12.0	12.9	12.8	13.0	13.1	13.2	14.1

Plot a scatter diagram of the data. (Let 1957 be Year 1.) Find the sample regression line of Y on X and plot it on the scatter diagram. Estimate the profit for 1969 and 1970. Would you use this line to estimate the net profit ten years hence? Explain.

10.2   The following data give the length of time Y, in hours, for a headache to disappear after being given different dosages X, in grains, of aspirin.

Dosage	1	2	3	4	5	6
Time	1.5	1.3	1.8	1.0	0.9	0.9

† Edited by H. O. Hartley and E. S. Pearson (Cambridge, England: Cambridge University Press).

Plot a scatter diagram; find the sample regression line of Y on X and plot it on the scatter diagram. Estimate the time for a headache to vanish for a dosage of 1.5 grains. Comment on the assumption of linearity as the dosage increases.

10.3 The following data compare the number of days, Y, of absenteeism per year with the number of packs of cigarettes, X, smoked per day for employees sampled from a large factory.

Packs	0	0	0	0	1	1	1	1	2	2	2	3	3
Days	4	3	6	20	8	10	6	14	12	10	11	30	12

Plot a scatter diagram; find the sample regression line of Y on X and plot it on the scatter diagram. Estimate the number of days of absenteeism of an employee who smokes one pack per day.

10.4 The following data present a random sample from a population of adult males giving their schooling in years, X, and annual income in thousands of dollars, Y.

Schooling	9	9	9	10	10	11	12	12	12	16	16	19
Salary	3.0	4.5	10.0	6.0	6.5	8.0	6.0	10.0	15.0	8.0	16.0	20.0

Plot a scatter diagram; compute both sample regression lines and plot them on the scatter diagram. Which line presumably is of more value for predictive purposes? Predict the income of an individual who has ten years of schooling.

10.5 The following data present a random sample from the population of high school graduates giving their I.Q., X, and Grade 12 averages, Y.

I.Q.	95	95	100	100	100	100	100	105	105	105
Average	62	70	63	65	75	71	68	69	71	75
I.Q.	105	110	110	110	115	115	115	120	120	140
Average	76	85	60	75	75	80	70	60	85	95

Plot a scatter diagram; compute both sample regression lines and plot them on the scatter diagram. Which line is presumably of more predictive value? Estimate the average grade of all high school graduates whose I.Q. is 100.

10.6 The following data present a random sample from a population of adult males giving height in inches X and weight in pounds Y.

Height	72	69	74	70	70	67	69	73	70	72	71
Weight	155	149	166	150	170	150	155	195	148	165	160

Height	71	70	70	67	69	68	66	72	71	65
Weight	220	150	170	146	155	160	170	166	173	135

Plot a scatter diagram; compute both sample regression lines and plot them on the scatter diagram. Estimate the weight of a male whose height is 69 in. Estimate the height of a male whose weight is 150 lb. What fraction of the variation of weights do you estimate is accounted for by variation in heights?

10.7 Give three examples of pairs of random variables that are positively correlated. Give two examples in which the variables are negatively correlated. (If you have a major subject, try to obtain pairs that arise in your field.)

10.8 Find r, the sample correlation coefficient, for Problem 10.5.

10.9 Find r, the sample correlation coefficient, for Problem 10.6.

10.10 A dart is thrown at a circular dart board so as to hit as closely to the center as possible. The horizontal distance X and vertical distance Y (in feet) from the center are recorded for each throw giving the following results.

X	−0.8	0.2	0.2	0.0	−0.2	0.1	0.7	−0.2
Y	−0.7	0.0	0.5	0.6	0.3	−0.5	−0.7	−0.2
X	0.0	0.1	−0.5	0.5	0.6	0.5	−0.1	0.0
Y	−0.6	0.1	0.5	−0.3	−0.2	−0.6	−0.1	0.2
X	−0.2	0.5	0.0	−0.3	0.5	0.3	−0.1	0.6
Y	0.4	1.2	0.1	0.2	−0.2	0.5	−0.2	−1.1
X	−0.5	0.4	−0.3	−0.4	0.6	0.0		
Y	0.1	0.2	0.0	0.5	−0.5	−0.1		

Compute r, the sample correlation coefficient.

10.11 (a) Find 95 percent confidence intervals in Example 10.3 for the average G.P.A. and individual G.P.A. of students whose high school G.P.A. is $X = 2.4, 2.7, 3.0, 3.3,$ and 3.6. On graph paper, plot the sample regression line and the ends of the confidence intervals. Join these into smooth curves. Where are the confidence intervals smallest and hence most accurate? What can be said about the confidence intervals far away from the means?

(b) Find a 95 percent confidence interval for the current year's profit in Problem 10.1. What assumptions must be made about Y?

10.12 Test the hypothesis $H : \beta = 0$ versus $A : \beta \neq 0$ in Problem 10.2 ($\alpha = 0.05$). If you accept H, what does this imply about the worth of using X to aid in predicting Y?

10.13 Using Problem 10.3, find a 95 percent confidence interval for the average number of days lost by employees who smoke one pack a day. Find a 95 percent confidence interval for an individual who smokes one pack a day.

10.14 At a later time, another observation is taken as in Problem 10.4 and it is observed that $X = 12$, $Y = 25.0$. Does this come from the same population as the others? Use $\alpha = 0.05$.

10.15 Using the data of Problem 10.5, test the hypothesis that $\beta = 0$ and the hypothesis that $\rho = 0$. Use $\alpha = 0.05$. Why do you obtain the same answer to both parts?

10.16 Using Problem 10.6, find a 95 percent confidence interval for the weight of an individual whose height is 70 in. Does the observation $X = 70$, $Y = 300$ come from the same population ($\alpha = 0.05$)?

10.17 Test the hypothesis that $\rho = 0$ for Problems 10.8, 10.9, and 10.10 ($\alpha = 0.05$).

10.18 Explain intuitively why you believe $\rho > 0$ in Problems 10.8 and 10.9 and $\rho = 0$ in Problem 10.10.

10.19 A group of students is given an algebra placement test in May and again in September. The scores for ten students are as follows:

| May test | 19 | 21 | 16 | 16 | 12 | 13 | 18 | 13 | 18 | 20 |
| September test | 15 | 20 | 11 | 14 | 10 | 15 | 18 | 10 | 15 | 18 |

(a) Find the sample regression line for these scores.
(b) If you were told that another student got a May score of 15, what would you predict his September score to be?
(c) What is a 95 percent confidence interval for the Y predicted in (b)?
(d) If a university had some students entering with May scores and others with September scores, how would you use the results of

this problem? Would you be worried about the small number of observations? Why or why not?

10.20   A meteorologist is considering the usefulness of using the data on rainfall for June in predicting rainfall for July. Here is a sample of his data:

June rainfall (in inches)	3	5	2	1	2	6	8	7	2	10
July rainfall (in inches)	5	2	1	2	6	8	7	2	10	7

(a) Determine the regression equation that he would obtain from this data.
(b) Test $H : \beta = 0$ versus $A : \beta \neq 0$. What do you conclude from this?
(c) What is the predicted value of Y when X is 7?
(d) What is the standard error of such a prediction?

10.21   The following data show the heights in inches of a group of adult male first cousins.

	Height	COUSIN 1						
		60–62	63–65	66–68	69–71	72–74	75–77	Total
	60–62	2	0	3	2	4	1	12
	63–65	1	2	5	2	3	0	13
COUSIN	66–68	3	4	7	3	2	1	20
2	69–71	1	3	4	6	3	2	19
	72–74	2	2	2	3	5	1	15
	75–77	1	1	0	1	2	2	7
	Total	10	12	21	17	19	7	86

(a) Calculate r; state what assumptions are involved in testing $H : \rho = 0$ versus $A : \rho \neq 0$. Define ρ. What is the test result (5 percent significance level)?
(b) Find the two sample regression lines that can be calculated from these data.

10.22   Parents are often interested in predicting the eventual adult heights of their children. Physiologists have made studies on heights of children as related to their height at maturity. Here are some data from such a study.

X: height at age two (in inches)	29	30	32	34	35	36	36	37	38	39
Y: adult height (in inches)	61	63	63	67	68	68	70	72	70	71

(a) What is the linear equation by which you could predict adult height from height at age two?

(b) What is the predicted height for a 33-in. two-year-old?

(c) What is a 90 percent confidence interval for this prediction?

10.23   In a magazine article, a report is given of another study of height at age two and adult height. In this article, it is suggested that adult height (Y) can be obtained by the equation

$$Y = 2X - 1,$$

where X is two-year-old height.

(a) What additional information do you need to determine a confidence interval for such predictions?

(b) Suppose that the 95 percent confidence interval for the predicted adult height of a two-year-old whose height is 35 in. is 65–73 in. Does this mean that his adult height cannot exceed 73 in.? If not, what does it mean?

10.24   An anthropologist has the following data on skeletal measurements of prehistoric humans from fossil remains:

Arm length	28	32	34	35	37
Total height	59	61	65	66	69

(a) What is the linear equation he would calculate from these data to estimate the total height from a fossil with only the arm preserved?

(b) Suppose that he has another complete skeleton of height 68 in. There is some possibility that the arm bones have become mixed and do not belong to this skeleton. The arm in question is 38 in. long. Test this at the 10 percent level. What conclusion do you draw? What kind of error may you be making?

10.25   A car owner has the following data on gasoline consumption and miles driven.

Miles driven	84	168	53	95	123	80	138	178	201	155
Gasoline used (in gallons)	5.8	11.0	3.6	6.5	8.0	5.3	8.9	11.8	13.1	10.0

(a) Assume that $E(Y|X) = \alpha + \beta X$, $\sigma^2_{Y|X} = \sigma^2_1$ and estimate α, β, σ^2_1.

(b) A statistician suggests that obviously the regression line must pass through the origin. Test that $E(Y|X) = 0$ when $X = 0$ (5 percent level).

(c) If the hypothesis in (b) is rejected, does this mean that the linear relationship is completely unsatisfactory?

10.26 A sociologist has made a study of the relationship between time spent watching television (average number of hours per week) and high school grade point average. From a sample of 48 students, he obtained a correlation coefficient of -0.43.

(a) Test the hypothesis that in the population from which these students were sampled, there is no relationship between the variables indicated. Note the assumptions necessary to draw valid conclusions.

(b) What fraction of the variability of grade point averages may we estimate as being attributed to hours spent watching television?

10.27 In many cloud-seeding experiments, experimenters proceed as follows. Two similar areas are selected and the relationship between the rainfalls in the two areas is determined from past climatological records. Then in the experimental period, one area is seeded, one left unseeded as a control. Part of the climatological records are shown here, the rest being omitted to reduce the arithmetic.

Year	Area 1	Area 2
1946	9.8	8.8
1947	0.9	2.7
1948	6.8	7.3
1949	3.3	3.7
1950	2.5	2.9
1951	4.9	5.3
1952	1.7	1.9
1953	8.2	7.6
1954	7.1	7.0
1955	5.4	5.7
1956	4.4	4.0
1957	9.5	10.1
1958	5.0	5.3
1959	4.2	4.3
1960	6.5	6.9

(a) What is the regression of rainfall in Area 2 on Area 1?

(b) In 1961, cloud seeding was conducted in Area 2 and in this year the respective rainfalls were 4.7 in., 5.8 in. Test at the 5 percent level the hypothesis that cloud seeding has no effect against the alternative that it increases rainfall.

(c) How much would the rainfall have had to be in the seeded area (Area 2), when the rainfall was 4.7 in. in the unseeded area in order just to show a significant increase (5 percent level)?

*10.28 The following data show for various temperatures the average heights of grain seedlings 30 days after planting in an experimental plot.

Temperature (°C)	10	12	14	16
Height (cm)	3.4	4.6	5.6	6.9

(a) Estimate the regression of height on temperature.
(b) Estimate the expected height of the grain if kept at 5°C. Why may this estimate be criticized?
(c) The analysis in (a) assumes that there were the same number of plants in each plot. Suppose in fact there were 8, 12, 15, and 21 respectively. What is the estimated regression now?
(d) The different numbers might be due to the planting of seeds or to differential survival. Suppose that in all plots 25 seeds were planted and that the numbers given in (c) represent the survivors. Find the estimated relationship between percent survival and temperature. Would you extrapolate this to 20°C?

*10.29 The following data were obtained by a physiologist relating alcohol consumption X and reaction time Y of 12 subjects who were divided into groups of three and tested after consuming different amounts of alcohol.

Consumption (oz)	0	1	2	3
Reaction time (sec)	2.1	3.7	3.9	6.2
	1.4	3.1	4.7	6.8
	1.8	2.7	5.2	5.3

(a) Calculate the sample standard deviation for each of the four groups. Label these s_0, s_1, s_2, and s_3 (respectively) and plot against consumption (X). Estimate a linear relationship between s_X and X. Is it significant at the 5 percent level?
(b) Do you believe that as a result of (a) it is appropriate to use the linear regression model of this chapter to find a relationship between alcohol consumption and reaction time? Why or why not?

10.30   An old folk-saying is that a hot summer is usually followed by a cold winter. Indicate how you could use climatological data to test this. Be precise in defining the variable, the hypothesis, and the procedure.

*10.31   In a study of maximum-temperature forecasts, the following results were obtained:

Forecast maximum	75	50	59	48	47	71	69	83	71	63
Actual maximum	71	53	60	54	40	74	55	80	70	60

Test whether the linear relationship between forecast maximum and actual maximum has slope one (5 percent significance level). If the hypothesis is not rejected, does this prove that the forecasts are satisfactory? Discuss how else you might study the value of the forecast temperature.

*10.32   (a) A sociologist makes a study of education and "marital adjustment." For 83 couples, he finds a correlation of 0.48. He asserts this is significant at the 1 percent level. What does he mean? How much of the variability in marital adjustment is associated with educational factors?

(b) He has also correlated marital adjustment with several other variables, e.g., income ($r = 0.38$), age ($r = 0.56$), length of marriage ($r = 0.71$), age at marriage of husband ($r = -0.23$), age at marriage of wife ($r = -0.45$), "social compatibility of partners" ($r = 0.60$), age difference of couple ($r = -0.88$). The largest of these (numerically) is the last, which is significant of the 1 percent level. How is this probability statement obtained? Discuss its meaning and validity.

*10.33   The following are two time series:

	0	1	2	3	4	5	6
Index cost of living	100	108	111	124	125	130	139
Number of new cars purchased (in millions)	2.8	3.4	3.5	4.6	4.4	5.0	5.3

(a) Find the correlation coefficient between the two variables and test whether r is significantly different from zero.

(b) Criticize the analysis of (a).

(c) For each of the time series, fit a regression line and calculate the deviations $Y - \hat{Y}$ for each series. Denote these by d_1, d_2.

(d) Find the correlation between d_1, d_2.

(e) Do you think the ordinary test for significance of a correlation coefficient can be applied to the one found in (d)? Why or why not?

*10.34   A study is made to relate age of trees and diameter. Some data from the study are shown below:

Age (years)	1	2	3	4	5
Diameter (inches)	2	3	5	7	10

(a) Estimate the regression of diameter on age.
(b) Estimate the diameter of a five-year-old tree.
(c) Find the standard error of the estimate in (b).
(d) Another five-year-old tree is found to have a diameter of 5 in. Is this "unusual"? Discuss statistically.
(e) Let $e_i = Y_i - \alpha - \beta X_i$. Estimate e_1, e_2, e_3, e_4, e_5. Check these estimates by calculating $\sum_{i=1}^{5} e_i^2$, which should equal $3s_{Y|X}^2$. Why?

CHAPTER ELEVEN

Chi-Square Tests

Introduction

In Chapter 4 the theory of testing hypotheses was studied for the binomial parameter p. This problem arises where the random variable is the count of the number of successes in n independent trials. However the tests used there depended on the availability of binomial probability tables. Approximations for binomial probabilities were introduced in Chapter 6. In this chapter another approximation procedure equivalent to the use of a Central Limit Theorem is introduced.

Additionally, there are situations where a trial may not simply result in success or failure but may lead to one of several outcomes; these give rise to multinomial random variables, discussed in Chapter 9.

Examples of such random variables were given there. Many such situations lead to hypothesis-testing problems. In Example 9.4 (gene inheritance), experiments with three outcomes were studied, and it is often of interest to test whether sample data are in conformity with the hypotheses underlying the probability distribution, i.e., with Mendelian theory. Experiments also occur involving two or more series of binomial or multinomial trials and the interest is in the comparison of the results. Examples 1.6 and 1.8 illustrate such experiments.

All of these problems as well as the original binomial tests can be handled by a general family of procedures known as *chi-square* (or χ^2) *tests*, if the number of trials is not too small. Chi-square tests apply to count data, which are the outcomes of a series of independent experiments. The hypotheses tested usually specify something about the probabilities of these outcomes. We are led to calculate the expected value of the random variables and reject the hypothesis if the deviation between observation and expectation is "large." However, to avoid difficulties with combining deviations, some of which are plus, some minus, all are squared. As in the binomial and normal cases, the deviations are expressed in standard units.

Example 11.1 Sex ratios in chickens

A sample of 40 chicks yields 32 males and 8 females. Is this sample consistent (at the 1 percent significance level) with the hypothesis that the sex ratio in the population is 1:1?

Solution: The problem is to test $H : p = \frac{1}{2}$ versus $A : p \neq \frac{1}{2}$, where p = proportion of males in the population, and T = number of male chicks in the sample, and it is assumed that T is binomially distributed with $n = 40$. If H is true, $E(T) = 40(\frac{1}{2}) = 20$. Hence the number of males differs from the expected value by 12; there is also a corresponding difference in females from the expected value. These deviations are expressed in standard terms by squaring, dividing by the expected value, and summing. The resulting statistic has been given the symbol X^2. Here,

$$X^2 = \frac{(32 - 20)^2}{20} + \frac{(8 - 20)^2}{20} = 14.44.$$

Before commenting on the significance of this statistic it is useful to compare the procedure using the normal approximation based on the Central Limit Theorem. Using the normal approximation, we compute

$$|Z| = \frac{|T - np|}{\sqrt{np(1 - p)}} = \frac{|32 - 20|}{\sqrt{40 \cdot \frac{1}{2} \cdot \frac{1}{2}}} = 3.80,$$

and since $3.80 > 2.58$, $H : p = \frac{1}{2}$ is rejected at the 1 percent level in favor of $A : p \neq \frac{1}{2}$.

Now it is easy to check that $|Z|^2 = (3.80)^2 = 14.44$, so that the X^2 statistic calculated in this example is the square of the usual standardized normal random variable. This, in fact, can be shown algebraically, for

$$
\begin{aligned}
X^2 &= \frac{(T - np)^2}{np} + \frac{[n - T - n(1 - p)]^2}{n(1 - p)} \\
&= \frac{(T - np)^2}{np} + \frac{(T - np)^2}{n(1 - p)} \\
&= \frac{(T - np)^2}{n} \left(\frac{1}{p} + \frac{1}{1 - p} \right) \\
&= \frac{(T - np)^2}{np(1 - p)} \\
&= |Z|^2.
\end{aligned}
$$

Thus, to evaluate the approximate significance of the X^2 statistic, we need a table giving the probability distribution of the square of a normal variable. The top line of Table A2.8 shows such a distribution. It is easily checked that the 1 percent value, 6.64, is $(2.58)^2$, the square of the 1 percent value for the standard normal variable.

If H is true, the observed X^2 random variable is expected to be close to its expectation, so that X^2 is small; if H is false and the alternative A is true, then T will differ from np and X^2 should be large. Thus, if X^2 is large, H is rejected; small values of X^2 are consistent with H.

The Greek symbol χ^2 rather than its Roman equivalent X^2 is often used for this statistic. It is becoming more common to reserve the Greek symbol χ^2 for the family of tests (or the family of distributions) and to use X^2 for the statistics of this type. The use of the same symbol χ^2 for all three concepts is frequently confusing.

A χ^2 *distribution* is formally defined as the probability distribution of a random variable which is the sum of a finite number of squares of independent, standard normal random variables. The χ^2 distribution has one parameter, n, the number of independent squares that are

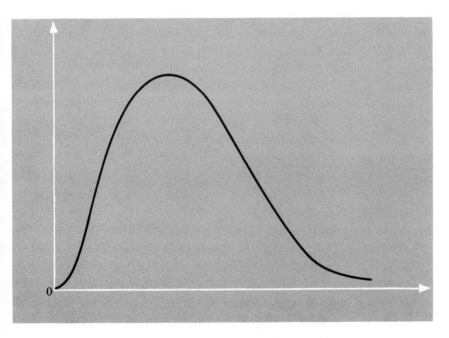

FIGURE 11.1 *A typical chi-square probability distribution.*

summed. A χ^2 distribution with parameter n is also called a χ^2 distribution with n degrees of freedom (d.f.). A typical example of a χ^2 distribution is shown in Figure 11.1.

The general procedure for χ^2 tests with a single set of binomial or multinomial random variables is now formulated.

Simple Chi-Square Tests

A sequence of n independent trials is observed; each trial may result in one of several outcomes, which we denote by $E_1, E_2, \ldots, E_k$. Let T_i = number of occurrences of E_i in the n trials, $(i = 1, 2, \ldots, k)$; the T_i are multinomial random variables, as defined in Chapter 9.

Let p_i be the probability that E_i occurs on any trial. Consider the hypothesis $H : p_i = p_i^0$ $(i = 1, 2, \ldots, k)$ against $A : p_i \neq p_i^0$ for at least one i $(i = 1, 2, \ldots, k)$, where $p_1^0, p_2^0, \ldots, p_k^0$ are k fixed nonnegative numbers, such that $\sum_{i=1}^{k} p_i^0 = 1$; recall also from Chapter 9 that for such multinomial random variables, $E(T_i) = np_i^0$ $(i = 1, 2, \ldots, k)$, under H. The statistic used to test H is

$$X^2 = \sum_{i=1}^{k} \frac{(T_i - np_i^0)^2}{np_i^0}.$$

In words, X^2 is the sum of squares of deviations of each observed value from its expectation divided by its expectation (often expressed as $\sum (O - E)^2/E$, using rather obvious symbols). If H is true, X^2 has a probability distribution that is approximately that of a χ^2 distribution with $k - 1$ degrees of freedom. The χ^2 approximation to the distribution of X^2 depends only on the number of terms entering into the sum. But like s^2, not all of these terms are "free," for

$$\sum_{i=1}^{k} T_i = n = \sum_{i=1}^{k} np_i^0,$$

so that

$$\sum_{i=1}^{k} (T_i - np_i^0) = 0.$$

There are only $k - 1$ essentially "free" terms and so X^2 is said to have $k - 1$ degrees of freedom. If X^2 is too large, H is rejected. The tabulated critical levels of the χ^2 probability distribution are tabulated for different values of the degrees of freedom in Table A2.8.

Example 11.2   Finding a defective machine

A statistics class performed Experiment 2.2 and got the following results:

x	Frequency
1	36
2	34
3	33
4	30
4	42
Total	175

Do these results conform with the hypothesis that $P(X = 1) = P(X = 2) = P(X = 3) = P(X = 4) = P(X = 5) = \frac{1}{5}$? Or, in the general notation, test $H : p_1 = p_2 = p_3 = p_4 = p_5 = \frac{1}{5}$. Here $n = 175$, and, if H is true, the expected value in each class is $E(T_i) = np_i = 175(\frac{1}{5}) = 35$.

$$X^2 = \frac{(36 - 35)^2}{35} + \frac{(34 - 35)^2}{35} + \frac{(33 - 35)^2}{35}$$
$$+ \frac{(30 - 35)^2}{35} + \frac{(42 - 35)^2}{35}$$

$$= 2.28.$$

From Table A2.8 looking along the line for which the degrees of freedom equal 4, we see that 2.28 is less than 7.79, the 10 percent critical level. The hypothesis $p_1 = p_2 = p_3 = p_4 = p_5 = \frac{1}{5}$ is not rejected at any usual significance level. Alternatively, it can be said that the significance probability of the observations given is approximately 0.69, as the student may ascertain from more complete tables. Nearly 70 percent of the time, a deviation as large as the one observed would occur due to chance fluctuations, if H were true.

Chi-Square Tests of Composite Hypotheses

If the hypothesis does not completely specify the expected values but leaves certain parameters unknown, these will have to be estimated from the observed data. Such a hypothesis is called *composite*. The estimation of each parameter is approximately equivalent to one more restriction. Alternatively, it may be said that the number of "free" terms entering into the calculations of X^2 is reduced by one. Consequently the degrees of freedom are reduced by one for *each* parameter estimated. A general setup that allows for this aspect and covers repeated series of trials is included in the following result.

Consider an experiment that consists of performing r independent multinomial subexperiments. In the jth subexperiment ($j = 1, 2, \ldots, r$), n_j multinomial trials are performed, during each of which one of the events $E_1, E_2, \ldots, E_k$ is observed. The events remain fixed from one subexperiment to another but their probabilities of occurrence may vary. It is assumed that during each of the n_j trials in the jth subexperiment, the probability that the event E_i is observed is p_{ij} ($i = 1, 2, \ldots, k$), where $p_{ij} \geq 0$ and $\sum_{i=1}^{k} p_{ij} = 1$. Let $n = \sum_{j=1}^{r} n_j$ be the total number of trials. A hypothesis is a prior belief in the p_{ij}'s ($i = 1, 2, \ldots, k; j = 1, 2, \ldots, r$). It may completely specify each p_{ij} as a number or only specify them partially, e.g., $p_{ij} = p_i$ independently of j, subject only to the restrictions that $p_{ij} \geq 0$ and $\sum_{i=1}^{k} p_{ij} = 1$ for $j = 1, 2, \ldots, r$. Let $\hat{p}_{ij}$ be the estimator of p_{ij} under the hypothesis and let $n\hat{p}_{ij}$ be the estimated expected number of occurrences of E_i in the jth subexperiment under the hypothesis. (For simplicity, write $n_j\hat{p}_{ij} = e_{ij}$.) The observed number T_{ij} of occurrences of E_i in the jth subexperiment is, of course, a random variable. The test statistic is

$$X^2 = \sum_{i=1}^{k} \sum_{j=1}^{r} \frac{(T_{ij} - e_{ij})^2}{e_{ij}}.$$

If H is true, X^2 is approximately distributed according to the χ^2 distribution with degrees of freedom equal to $r(k-1)$ minus the number of parameters estimated from the data.

Example 11.3   Cancer and smoking

In recent studies of cancer, samples of various populations have been selected and classified as "smokers" or "nonsmokers." Thereafter both groups are followed for a number of years, and for each group the number of deaths (for example) is recorded. A study of this type might lead to the data shown in the table at the top of page 273.

Such an experiment represents two series of trials: 200 in the first, 100 in the second; each trial may result in the event E_1 (death of the

	Deaths during study period	Alive at end of study period	Total
Smokers	26	174	200
Nonsmokers	4	96	100
Total	30	270	300

individual during study period) or in the event E_2 (individual is alive at end of study period). Let

p_{11} = the probability of death of a smoker in study period,

p_{12} = the probability of survival of a smoker in study period,

p_{21} = the probability of death of a nonsmoker in study period,

p_{22} = the probability of survival of a nonsmoker in study period.

The hypothesis of interest is $H : p_{11} = p_{21}, p_{12} = p_{22}$ versus $A : p_{11} \neq p_{21}, p_{12} \neq p_{22}$. If the hypothesis is true, then we have 300 binomial trials with a common probability of death p, and using the results of the section on estimation of p in Chapter 4, we have

$$\hat{p} = \tfrac{30}{300} = 0.10;$$

hence

$$1 - \hat{p} = 0.90.$$

The expected values computed on the basis of this estimate are conveniently set out in a 2×2 table.

	EXPECTED VALUES		
	Deaths	Survivors	Total
Smokers	$(0.10)(200) = 20$	$(0.90)(200) = 180$	200
Nonsmokers	$(0.10)(100) = 10$	$(0.90)(100) = 90$	100
Total	30	270	300

Once this is done, X^2 is easily written down and computed as

$$X^2 = \frac{(26 - 20)^2}{20} + \frac{(174 - 180)^2}{180} + \frac{(4 - 10)^2}{10} + \frac{(96 - 90)^2}{90}$$

$$= 1.80 + 0.20 + 3.60 + 0.40 = 6.00.$$

X^2 has an approximate χ^2 distribution with 1 degree of freedom. Why 1? We have $k = 2$, $r = 2$, and one parameter estimated from the data, namely $\hat{p}$. Therefore, the degrees of freedom $= 2(2 - 1) - 1 = 1$. It is seen that H is rejected at the 5 percent level; the significance probability of these observations is about 0.015.

Results of this type are typical of recent studies of cancer. While smokers are shown to have higher mortality rates from cancer of the lung and other diseases, this alone does not prove that smoking causes such increased death rates. Establishment of such a cause-and-effect relationship requires more sophisticated experiments, both medically and statistically, which we are not prepared to discuss here.

In Chapter 4 we emphasized the importance of keeping in mind the family of alternatives to the hypothesis tested. There are one-sided and two-sided families of alternatives; it is necessary to know which of these is appropriate before the correct test rule or significance probability can be computed. In many χ^2 tests the alternatives are necessarily two-sided, but in tests appropriate to a single binomial situation or in 2×2 tests when the number of degrees of freedom is one the alternatives may be one-sided. We illustrate this possibility by considering the data of Example 1.6.

Example 11.4 Cold inoculations

Recall the data of Example 1.6.

	Cold	No cold	Total
Inoculated group	14	16	30
Dummy shot group	24	6	30

This experiment also can be thought of as two series of trials, each trial being the experience of one of the soldiers. A trial results in the event E_1 (cold) or in the event E_2 (no cold). The evaluation of the results is a test of a hypothesis at, say, the 5 percent significance level. We formulate that hypothesis as follows: Let p_{11} be the probability that an inoculated soldier has a cold during the experimental period. Let p_{12} be the probability that a soldier who received a dummy shot has a cold. The hypothesis is $p_{11} = p_{12}$; here the alternative of interest is $p_{11} < p_{12}$ (the one-sided case—presumably the inoculation either makes no difference or has a beneficial effect). If this hypothesis is true, then the two groups of 30 might as well be considered one group of 60 in which 38 got colds. Hence, under the null hypothesis, the best estimate of the probability of a cold (during the specified time) is $\frac{38}{60}$, i.e., 0.633. Denote this estimate by $\hat{p}$. Then $1 - \hat{p} = 0.367$. Now it is possible to write down the table of expected values using this $\hat{p}$.

	EXPECTED VALUES		
	Cold	No cold	Total
Inoculated group	$(30)(0.633) = 19$	$(30)(0.367) = 11$	30
Dummy shot group	$(30)(0.633) = 19$	$(30)(0.367) = 11$	30
Total	38	22	60

As in Example 11.3, X^2 has 1 d.f. and has approximately a χ^2 distribution. The value of X^2 is easily computed from the tables of observed and expected values:

$$X^2 = \frac{(14 - 19)^2}{19} + \frac{(24 - 19)^2}{19} + \frac{(16 - 11)^2}{11} + \frac{(6 - 11)^2}{11} = 7.17.$$

Up to this point there is no difference between Examples 11.3 and 11.4. To obtain a one-sided test two steps are necessary.

First, compare the signs of $T_{11} - e_{11}$ and $p_{11} - p_{12}$ under A. If these are opposite, H is not rejected. If they are the same, we define $Z = \sqrt{X^2}$ and recall that Z has a probability distribution which is approximately that of a standard normal variable. H is rejected if Z exceeds the upper critical level, $z_{2\alpha}$ ($z_{2\alpha}$ is appropriate since this is a one-tailed test).

In this example, $T_{11} - e_{11} = -5$ and $p_{11} - p_{12} < 0$ under A so that we proceed to the second step; that is, we calculate $Z = \sqrt{X^2} = \sqrt{7.17} = 2.68$. For a significance level of 1 percent, $z_{2\alpha} = 2.33$ so H is rejected at the 1 percent level. (The significance probability of the observed random variable is 0.004.) Therefore, the conclusion is made that the inoculation does reduce the possibility of a cold. It is possible that we have committed an error in this decision. What error? With what probability?

[*Note:* The above procedure works for χ^2 tests with 1 degree of freedom; for certain models involving one-sided alternatives and more degrees of freedom more sophisticated techniques are necessary.]

Limits on the Use of the Chi-Square Approximation; *Continuity Correction

In the introduction to this chapter, it was noted that the χ^2 test is equivalent to the use of the Central Limit Theorem and hence becomes exact only as the number of trials becomes infinitely large. For any finite sample size the χ^2 test holds approximately; this means that the actual error probabilities differ somewhat from those specified. Numerous rules for use with χ^2 tests have been given, so that the error level actually realized is close to the desired error level.†

A simple rule which will be given here is: Do *not* use χ^2 tests if any expected number falls below 1. In some case, it may be possible to regroup categories if this happens. In other cases, exact tests or tables are available.

[*Note*: A further modification is sometimes suggested for handling χ^2 tests of the binomial problem (Example 11.1) or comparisons of two series of binomials (Examples 11.3 and 11.4). This is known as "Yates continuity correction" and consists of the following modification of the definition of χ^2 in these two cases:

$$\text{(Simple binomial)} \qquad X^2 = \sum_{i=1}^{2} \frac{(|T_i - np_i^0| - \frac{1}{2})^2}{np_i^0},$$

$$\text{(Binomial comparison)} \qquad X^2 = \sum_{i=1}^{2} \sum_{j=1}^{2} \frac{(|T_{ij} - e_{ij}| - \frac{1}{2})^2}{e_{ij}}.$$

This is, of course, related to the correction of one-half noted in the use of the normal approximation to binomial probabilities in Chapter 6. With this modification the actual error probability by the χ^2 test is well below the prescribed error probability. Recent research suggests that the refinement is usually too conservative, i.e., yields an actual error probability which is too far below the prescribed error probability, and hence is undesirable.]

Chi-Square Tests with an *r* × *c* Array

Example 11.5   Marriage in college and grades

The following data represent a statistically more defensible approach to the problem raised in Example 1.7. It is assumed that at the end of the sophomore year, 200 unmarried students are selected at random

---

† For a complete discussion of these rules, the student should refer to a paper by W. Cochran in the *Annals of Mathematical Statistics*, *33* (1952), pp. 315–345, particularly pp. 328–331.

from a college population. Three years later the following results are observed: Of these 200, 61 have married and 139 have not. The upper division G.P.A.'s of those who have graduated and the numbers who have not graduated are as follows:

	G.P.A.			Not	
	2.00–2.49	2.50–2.99	3.00–4.00	graduated	Total
Unmarried $j = 1$	65	24	18	32	139
Married $j = 2$	14	10	17	20	61
Total	79	34	35	52	200

It is interesting to ask whether the differences are due to chance. In terms of a statistical model, we write

p_{1j} = probability that a student in Group j graduates with G.P.A. between 2.00 and 2.49,

p_{2j} = probability that a student in Group j graduates with G.P.A. between 2.50 and 2.99,

p_{3j} = probability that a student in Group j graduates with G.P.A. 3.00 or better,

p_{4j} = probability that a student in Group j does not graduate in the time period noted.

The hypothesis is $H : p_{11} = p_{12}; \ p_{21} = p_{22}; \ p_{31} = p_{32}; \ p_{41} = p_{42}$. Under this hypothesis, the classification into married and unmarried is irrelevant and the second subscript can be dropped.

From the records of all 200 students, the probabilities *under the hypothesis* are estimated as

$$\hat{p}_1 = \tfrac{79}{200}; \qquad \hat{p}_2 = \tfrac{34}{200}; \qquad \hat{p}_3 = \tfrac{35}{200}; \qquad \hat{p}_4 = \tfrac{52}{200}.$$

Note that since these four $\hat{p}_i$'s are the only possibilities considered, they must sum to 1; hence the data is not used to estimate $\hat{p}_4$. It can be estimated by the relationship $\hat{p}_4 = 1 - \hat{p}_1 - \hat{p}_2 - \hat{p}_3$. Now a table of expected values is computed corresponding to the observed table above. If the null hypothesis is true, then the expected number of unmarried students graduating with G.P.A.'s between 2.00 and 2.49 is $(139)(\tfrac{79}{200})$, i.e., 54.9. Each of the other entries in the following table is calculated in a similar way.

Expected Table of Frequencies under Null Hypothesis

	G.P.A.			Not graduated	Total
	2.00–2.49	2.50–2.99	3.00–4.00		
Unmarried	54.9	23.6	24.3	36.1	138.9
Married	24.1	10.4	10.7	15.9	61.1
Total	79	34	35	52	200

(The right-hand totals should be 139 and 61 respectively but they differ because of rounding errors in the arithmetic.) Now X^2 is easily computed as follows:

$$X^2 = \frac{(65 - 54.9)^2}{54.9} + \frac{(24 - 23.6)^2}{23.6} + \frac{(18 - 24.3)^2}{24.3}$$

$$+ \frac{(32 - 36.1)^2}{36.1} + \frac{(14 - 24.1)^2}{24.1} + \frac{(10 - 10.4)^2}{10.4}$$

$$+ \frac{(17 - 10.7)^2}{10.7} + \frac{(20 - 15.9)^2}{15.9}$$

$$= 13.65.$$

How many degrees of freedom does X^2 have? This information is needed to enter the appropriate line of Table A2.8. By the general rule, d.f. = 8 − 2 (totals) − 3 (parameters estimated) = 3. Alternatively, since $r = 2$, $k = 4$, d.f. = $2(4 − 1) − 3 = 3$. Note that while there were four parameters, as pointed out, only three needed to be estimated from the data. Referring to line 3 of Table A2.8, it is seen that H is rejected at the 5 percent level.

This experiment indicates a difference in the college experience of students who marry after their sophomore year. It is to be pointed out that in this, like many similar experiments, it is difficult to distinguish between cause and effect.

Many experiments lead to results expressible in the form of the table in this example or, more generally, a table with r rows and c columns, showing the number of trials that ended in a particular result. *Such a table is called an $r \times c$ array.* It is usually asked whether the probabilities are the same for each row. The analysis proceeds exactly as in the example—a set of estimated probabilities are calculated by combining the results of all experiments. These are then used to compute expected values for each cell. Finally, it is easy to compute X^2, which has degrees of freedom as follows:

$$rc - r - (c - 1) = rc - r - c + 1$$
$$= (r - 1)(c - 1),$$

where rc is the number of cells, r is the number of totals, and $(c - 1)$ is the number of parameters estimated.

Chi-square tests are very simple and very useful omnibus tests; because of their simplicity and generality some investigators use them in situations where they are not appropriate. It is important to recall that χ^2 tests are valid where applied to random variables that arise from binomial or multinomial type experiments, that is, counts of outcomes in series of independent trials. The most serious errors in using χ^2 tests are:

1. Using them for random variables that are not counts. (Often they are applied to percentages, which is quite erroneous.)
2. Using them for data that arise in trials that are not independent. This occurs particularly in biological data but also in other fields. Such data, even though they are counts, must be analyzed by other methods.

■ Experiments

11.1   Choose at random 100 digits from telephone numbers in your local telephone book and test the hypothesis that each digit from 0 to 9 is equally likely. Test at the 5 percent level.

11.2   *Class experiment.* Have each member of the class write down the digits from 0 to 9 in some random order. In advance, a prescribed order is written down. Each student then counts the number of agreements with the prescribed order. For example, the prescribed order might be 7 5 3 4 2 6 1 8 0 9, while one student's order might be 6 4 2 7 3 9 1 0 8 5. It is seen that there is one agreement; viz., in place 7 the student has 1 in conformity with the prescribed order. The probabilities of having 0, 1, 2, ..., 9 agreements in an experiment like this, assuming that the sequences are written down at random, are as follows:†

$$P \text{ (no agreements)} = 0.37$$
$$P \text{ (exactly one agreement)} = 0.37$$
$$P \text{ (exactly two agreements)} = 0.18$$
$$P \text{ (exactly three agreements)} = 0.06$$
$$P \text{ (four or more agreements)} = 0.02.$$

† See W. Feller, *An Introduction to Probability Theory and its Applications*, vol. 1 (2nd ed.) (New York: John Wiley, 1957), p. 98.

Test the total class results to determine whether they are consistent with these probabilities. It may be mentioned that the Canadian Broadcasting Corporation conducted such an experiment on a nation-wide scale some time ago.

11.3   If the results of the experiments of Chapter 2 are available for all class members, it is useful to perform χ^2 tests to check whether the results are in agreement with the theoretical probabilities.

■ Problems

11.1   Use the χ^2 test to test $H : p = 0.75$ versus $A : p \neq 0.75$ in Problem 4.5. Test $H : p = 0.5$ versus $A : p < 0.5$ by means of the χ^2 test, using the data of Problem 4.9.

11.2   A traffic study divides the hours from 6:00 A.M. to midnight into six three-hour periods. From records it is found that the weekday automobile fatalities over a year in a city are classified as follows:

6 A.M. to 9 A.M.	8
9 A.M. to 12 noon	12
12 noon to 3 P.M.	3
3 P.M. to 6 P.M.	15
6 P.M. to 9 P.M.	16
9 P.M. to 12 P.M.	14

(a) Test the hypothesis that a fatality is equally likely to occur in any of these six periods.

It is more reasonable to ask whether fatalities occur in proportion to the traffic volume, regardless of the hour. The study has determined the relative traffic volumes as follows (the average being taken as 100):

6 A.M. to 9 A.M.	130
9 A.M. to 12 noon	60
12 noon to 3 P.M.	70
3 P.M. to 6 P.M.	170
6 P.M. to 9 P.M.	100
9 P.M. to 12 P.M.	70

(b) Test the hypothesis that the probability of a fatality is proportional to traffic volume.

11.3   In a cross of japonica with fine-striped maize, the offspring may be green, japonica, fine-striped, or a combination. Mendelian theory suggests that these will occur in proportions 9:3:3:1. In an experiment, E. W. Lindstrom obtained 135 seedlings and found, in the four categories, 82, 12, 33, and 8. Is the theory substantiated? (Test at the 5 percent level.)

11.4   In a cloud-seeding experiment, 80 clouds were selected for experimentation. Forty clouds were "seeded" and 40 untreated. The results of the experiment were as follows:

	Evidence of precipitation	No evidence of precipitation
Clouds seeded	12	28
Clouds unseeded	8	32

(a) Set out the hypothesis to be tested and the family of alternatives of interest. Define any symbols used.
(b) Perform the test of the hypothesis (at the 5 percent level) and state the conclusion.

11.5   A check is made on the number of sports fishermen who send in returns in a mail survey, by counting the number of fishermen for a one-week period early in the season, and one late in the season. Here are the results:

	Reporting in mail survey	Not reporting in mail survey	Total
Early-season count	91	145	236
Late-season count	31	93	124
Total	122	238	360

Is the proportion of returns the same early in the season as later on? (Test at the 1 percent level.)

11.6   The data of Example 1.8 are given again below. Test the hypothesis that the probability of the various grades in the statistics course is the same for all algebra grade classes (5 percent significance level). Also determine the significance probability of the observations by referring to more complete tables.

	Grade	STATISTICS CLASS A or B	C	D or E	Totals
ALGEBRA CLASS	A	5	2	2	9
	B	8	8	2	18
	C	6	10	5	21
	D	3	5	3	11
Total		22	25	12	59

11.7 A study is made at an eastern university of withdrawals during the freshman year. Here are some of the data collected:

High school grade point average for entering students	Number dropped out	Number remaining	Total
Less than 2.2	10	10	20
2.2 to 2.8	20	100	120
Above 2.8	10	50	60
Total	40	160	200

Test the hypothesis that the proportion dropping out is the same for each group. (Test at the 5 percent level.)

11.8 The following data have been compiled by a university counseling service on a group of male students entering university directly from high school.

	Degree obtained in five years	Degree not obtained in five years	Number
Married on entrance	5	5	10
Married before attaining junior standing	5	15	20
Married after attaining junior standing	50	20	70
Not married	240	160	400

Is there a significant difference among the four groups in regard to the probability of obtaining a degree in five years? Test at the 1 percent significance level. State carefully the hypothesis being tested.

*11.9 In a study of the fur seal on the Pribilof Islands, a sample of 20 seals was taken in each of five areas. They are classified as follows:

Age	AREA 1	2	3	4	5	Total
3	10	14	15	11	20	70
4	10	6	5	9	0	30
Total	20	20	20	20	20	100

To answer the question, "Is the age distribution the same for all areas?" the biologist must test a hypothesis.

(a) Set up a hypothesis H defining any parameters needed.
(b) Perform the test and state the conclusion.
(c) State in the words of this example the Type II error.

11.10 A record was kept of results of horse races according to starting position. The results for one month, those only for races with exactly eight horses, are as follows:

Starting post	1	2	3	4	5	6	7	8
Number of winners	29	19	18	25	17	10	15	11

Test at the 5 percent level the hypothesis that horses starting at each post are equally likely to win. (Note that Post No. 1 is at the inside of the track while No. 8 is at the outside. The X^2 test takes no account of the trend from 1 to 8—it measures only deviations. Alternative tests or additional procedures have been suggested to remedy this defect in situations when the order has some importance.)

11.11 A die-manufacturing company tests samples of its dice with a machine that throws them each 60 times. The results for one such die are:

Number	1	2	3	4	5	6
Frequency	8	9	11	11	14	7

What conclusions can be made as to whether the probability of each face's turning up is $\frac{1}{6}$, which it should be for a fair die? Test at the 5 percent level. What are the considerations in the choice of significance level?

*11.12   A sample of 100 families with three children from *Who's Who* reveals the following distribution:

Number of boys	3	2	1	0
Frequency	11	30	45	14

Are these data consistent with the hypothesis that the number of boys in families with three children is binomially distributed with $p = \frac{1}{2}$? (Set $\alpha = 0.05$.)

*11.13   In an experimental farm, cotton seeds were planted four to a hill. The results on 100 hills are shown below according to the number of seeds surviving after two weeks.

Number of survivors	0	1	2	3	4
Number of hills	30	8	31	10	21

Test the hypothesis that the number of survivors in each hill is binomially distributed with $n = 4$, p unspecified. Use $\alpha = 0.05$. [Since p is unspecified, it is necessary to estimate it from the data. Of 400 plants, $(1)(8) + (2)(31) + (3)(10) + (4)(21)$, or 184, survived. Hence the estimated probability of survival is $\frac{184}{400}$, i.e., 0.46.] Suggest a biological reason why the hypothesis is rejected.

11.14   A preliminary trial of a vaccine on 60 subjects (half received the inoculant, half a dummy shot) shows the following results:

	Inoculated	Not inoculated
Attacked	8	14
Not attacked	22	16
Total	30	30

Does the inoculant seem to have promise for this disease?

11.15   An instructor gives a fairly hard matching test involving ten questions to a class and notes the following results:

Classification	Frequency
None right	12
One right	8
Two right	6
Three or more right	4
Total	30

Can we conclude that these results might have been achieved by random guessing? (Recall the probabilities given in Experiment 11.2.)

11.16   Analyze the following data obtained in a sociological survey on the number of children according to the educational level of the father:

	NUMBER OF CHILDREN				
Educational level	0	1	2	More than 2	Total
Grade school	36	24	29	111	200
High school	20	26	19	35	100
University	10	18	27	45	100

State assumptions, hypotheses, and conclusions.

11.17   During a survey made on a college campus, a sample is taken by telephone contacts. The experimenter is not sure that a sample obtained by telephone contacts is properly random so he makes a number of cross checks. In particular, he checks the class structure of the sample. The distribution by years on the campus is as follows:

Freshmen	35 percent
Sophomores	27 percent
Juniors	20 percent
Seniors	18 percent

In the sample, the numbers from each of the four classes are 29, 21,

20, 24. Could this be a random sample from the known population? (Test at the 5 percent level.)

11.18   The following data show the results of a study that compared the way husbands and wives rated their marriage:

	HUSBANDS' RATING			
Wives' rating	Unhappy	Happy	Very happy	Total
Unhappy	37	24	6	67
Happy	12	38	12	62
Very happy	4	7	112	123
Total	53	69	130	252

Test the hypothesis that the probability a husband rates his marriage in these classes is the same for all classes of wives' rating. Another way of expressing this is that the classifications are independent. Note that the test would be the same if it were expressed as the probability a wife rates her marriage is the same for all classes of husband's rating. (Use a 1 percent significance level.)

*11.19   The following shows the classification of 127 college girls according to appearance and grade point average.

	APPEARANCE				
G.P.A.	Homely	Plain	Good-looking	Beautiful	Totals
Below 2.40	12	16	6	2	36
2.40–3.19	8	26	18	10	62
3.20 or above	4	10	12	3	29
Total	24	52	36	15	127

Analyze the data, state any assumptions, hypotheses, and conclusions. To what population do the conclusions apply? [*Note:* As in Problem 11.18, the data can be looked at in several ways. We can consider the probabilities of various classes of appearance for the given groups as defined by G.P.A., or the probabilities of the G.P.A. classes for the given groups defined by appearance. Because both classifications are not fixed in advance—that is, the marginal total for both rows and columns are random—it is more usual to test for independence of the two classifications. In symbols, we are testing the hypothesis that $p_{11} = p_1^{(A)} p_1^{(G)} \cdots$. Here

$p_1^{(A)}$ = probability a college girl is homely in appearance,

$p_1^{(G)}$ = probability a college girl has G.P.A. below 2.40.

The statistic X^2 is the same regardless of these different ways of considering the data. However its O.C. curve, which is beyond the scope of this course, will be different from one in the situation where some of the marginal totals are fixed by the experimenter.]

11.20 In a poll taken at the preview of a new movie, 54 of 100 men interviewed said they liked it and 36 of 100 women also reacted favorably. Test the hypothesis that there is no difference between the reactions of the men and women. State the hypothesis, defining any symbols used. Let the error probability equal 0.05.

*11.21 Decide on the basis of the sample data given in the following table whether students' interest in statistics is independent of their ability in mathematics. Use $\alpha = 0.10$. State the hypothesis and conclusion.

		ABILITY IN MATHEMATICS		
		Low	Average	High
INTEREST	Low	10	7	3
IN	Average	10	9	11
STATISTICS	High	15	14	21

11.22 (a) A doctor notices that he seems to have a large number of patients whose hearing in their left ear is better than in their right. He checks his files and finds that in 64 cases in which there is a difference, the left is superior 40 times. Discuss what he may validly conclude.

(b) He then classifies the results as to sex of a patient. How could he determine whether "left-earedness" differs between men and women? State in words or symbols what hypothesis he is testing.

11.23 Samples are taken of a planktonic organism in May and July and the following observations noted:

	May	July
Number sampled	48	64
Number mature	12	32

Is the change in the proportion of mature individuals significant at the 5 percent level? If so, estimate the change.

11.24 A game department survey is made to compare hunter success by various categories. One such comparison is the following:

	Number successful	Number unsuccessful	Total
Urban hunters	20	40	60
Rural hunters	30	30	60

Is the difference in success rates of urban and rural hunters significant (5 percent level)?

11.25 Various studies have been made on the season of birth by countries, climate regimes, etc. Here is a sample of such data on 265 British intellectuals classified by birth month.

Month	Number of births	Month	Number of births
January	24	July	18
February	25	August	20
March	23	September	23
April	21	October	25
May	19	November	27
June	16	December	24

(a) Test the hypothesis that the births are equally distributed among the 12 months.

For the British population as a whole the proportions of births by months are as follows:

Month	Proportion of births	Month	Proportion of births
January	0.080	July	0.082
February	0.086	August	0.078
March	0.092	September	0.078
April	0.095	October	0.080
May	0.091	November	0.077
June	0.086	December	0.075

(b) Does the distribution of birth months of the sample of intellectuals differ significantly from that of the general population?

11.26 Does sex ratio differ according to birth order? A number of studies have been made of this. Here is some data taken from *Who's Who in America.*

Birth rank	Male	Female	Total
1	146	132	278
2	109	104	213
3	65	64	129
4	37	33	70
5	12	10	22
6	10	7	17

(a) Test the hypothesis that $p = \frac{1}{2}$ for each birth rank (here p is the probability of a male birth).
(b) Test the hypothesis that p is the same for all birth ranks. [Use a 5 percent level in both (a) and (b).]

*11.27 A consanguineous marriage is one between relatives. In a study in Chicago the offspring of 109 consanguineous marriages were compared with the children of a group of unrelated parents. In particular, children were classified as to the presence or absence of major abnormality. The following results were found:

	MAJOR ABNORMALITY		
	Present	Absent	Total
Children of consanguineous marriages	8	184	192
Children of unrelated parents	0	163	163
Total	8	347	355

(a) Test at the 5 percent level the hypothesis H that the probability of a major abnormality is the same for the two groups.
(b) An assumption required for the valid application of a χ^2 test in (a) is almost certainly violated. What is the assumption?
(c) Suggest a way that the data might have been presented that would have avoided the problem noted in (b).

11.28   The following data show the sex composition of two university classes.

	ENGLISH 101		LATIN 101	
	Number	Percentage	Number	Percentage
Men	240	60	24	60
Women	160	40	16	40
Total	400	100	40	100

(a) Test the hypothesis $p = \frac{1}{2}$ for the English class (5 percent significance level); do the same for the Latin class.
(b) If the percentages were used in the χ^2 test, what would the results be? Observe that the use of percentages may be completely misleading because the variance depends on sample size information and sample size information may be lost when percentages are used.

11.29   In a test of color preference in babies (see Example 4.8), a psychologist offers a baby a choice between red and green balls; this is repeated 20 times. The same experiment is performed on five babies with the following results:

Ball chosen	1	2	3	4	5	Total
			BABY			
Red	18	14	10	3	15	60
Green	2	6	10	17	5	40

(a) Test the hypothesis that p, the probability that the red ball is chosen, is the same for all babies (5 percent level).

(b) On the basis of your conclusion in (a), would you regard a χ^2 test of $H : p = \frac{1}{2}$ as applied to the total as being appropriate?

11.30 Recall Problem 4.15; in that problem five subjects were tested on a polarized-light viewer. Their responses were either right or wrong. The results given are as follows:

Subject	Right	Wrong
1	12	0
2	4	8
3	7	5
4	7	5
5	8	4
Total	38	22

Test the hypothesis that p = probability of a correct response is the same for all subjects (5 percent level). [Recall Problems 4.15(a) and (b).]

11.31 Example 6.1 (catching a bus) suggested that in some circumstances the waiting times for a bus might be uniformly distributed. Suppose you set up an experiment to take observations on such waiting times. Observations on 56 people who are waiting for a bus yield the following data.

Time waited	0–10 minutes	10–20 minutes	Total
Number	20	36	56

(a) Analyze this information to determine if the hypothesis of uniformity is supported.

The analysis in (a) is dependent on a number of assumptions, e.g., that the observations recorded are independent. Suppose you found that the persons waiting for the bus had not arrived independently but happened to consist of 14 families each of size 4 so that the classification of independent units would be

Time waited	0–10 minutes	10–20 minutes	Total
Number	5	9	14

(b) Would your conclusion be altered? Recall the warning that a χ^2 test is validly applied to data obtained from independent trials.

11.32 A U.C.L.A. study on cancer of the lung reports on survival of patients classified by the diameter of the cancer lesion on discovery. The data presented are as follows:

Lesion diameter	Survived five years or more	Did not survive five years	Total
Less than 2.5 cm	45	40	85
2.5 to 4 cm	72	106	178

Is the difference significant at the 5 percent level? Do you think a one-sided or two-sided test is appropriate?

*11.33 In an experiment to determine whether a mosquito repellent is effective, two individuals (denoted A and B) are placed in a room with a single mosquito until it bites one of them. This is repeated 20 times. Then A applies the repellent and the experiment is repeated another 20 times. The results are as follows:

	A Bitten	B Bitten	Total
Preliminary test	12	8	20
Test with repellent	8	12	20

(a) Why is the preliminary test performed?
(b) What do you conclude about the value of the repellent to A?
(c) Can anything be concluded about the repellent to B?
(d) Suggest another way that the experiment might have been designed to test the value of the repellent to both A and B.

CHAPTER TWELVE

Nonparametric Tests

Introduction

In previous chapters, we studied tests of hypotheses concerning various random variables. In almost every case, we had to assume that the underlying random variable had a probability distribution of a certain form, usually binomial or normal. Then, specifying a hypothesis concerning the random variable was reduced to specifying a hypothesis concerning one or more of its parameters. This made our tests easy to construct, but we had to remember that each test was only completely valid *if the assumption was true*. Because there are random variables that are neither normal nor binomial, and to avoid having to make the assumption of normality in ignorance, statisticians have tried to find tests that do not depend on such assumptions. Further, it is occasionally necessary to make other assumptions that may be difficult to check—for example, the assumption of constant variance in regression analysis.

Usually, when random variables are not (even approximately) normal or binomial, it is hard to assume a given distribution for them. Thus, the tests proposed should be satisfactory no matter what distribution the random variable has (or should at least be satisfactory for a large class of distributions). Tests that satisfy such a condition are called *nonparametric tests* (or sometimes *distribution-free tests*), and the corresponding statistics are called *nonparametric statistics*. Much work has been done in recent years on nonparametric tests and the area is still growing rapidly. In this chapter, we try only to give a sample (not necessarily random) of this large area.

Sign Test for Paired Comparisons

The sign test for paired comparisons was one of the first nonparametric tests to be introduced, and it is still used in many statistical problems, both because of its simplicity and because of its good properties. Paired comparisons arise when one wishes to test the properties of a new treatment against an old treatment, no treatment, or a dummy treatment. (Treatment is used here to mean almost anything that can be investigated in an experiment.) For example, a treatment could be the giving of a sedative, the waxing of a car, the addition of an additive to a gasoline, increasing the dosage of a drug, the use of electric shock as a response for training purposes, etc. To make the conditions of the experiment as alike as possible, test subjects are chosen in pairs for their similarity, i.e., identical twins, sisters, brothers, cars that are of the same make and year, etc. In some experiments the subject can be used twice if the treatment does not seriously affect the subject. One of each pair, chosen at random, is given the new treatment and the other the old treatment (which may be no treatment or a dummy treatment). The hypothesis is, as usual, that the new treatment has the same effect as the old treatment. The alternative of interest is that the new treatment gives a better result than the old. To test this hypothesis, we observe n pairs and count the numbers of such pairs in which the new treatment gives a better result (ties are omitted). Under the hypothesis (and remembering that the pairs were chosen to be as similar as possible), the likelihood or probability of the new treatment's giving a better result is $\frac{1}{2}$; i.e., T, the number of pairs for which the new treatment gives a better result, is a binomial random variable with given n and $p = \frac{1}{2}$. If the alternative is true, then $p > \frac{1}{2}$. Our problem has been reduced to studying the random variable T with $H : p = \frac{1}{2}$ versus $A : p > \frac{1}{2}$. We have seen how to solve such problems in Chapter 4.

Example 12.1   A submarine test of car waxes

A car-wax producer claims its new car wax withstands water better than any standard treatment. To test this claim 15 cars are chosen, one side (chosen at random) is given a coat of the new wax, and the other side is given a coat of the standard wax. The method of application, etc., is the same for both sides. The cars are attached to a submarine and submerged for a fixed period of time. Upon surfacing, an impartial expert decides which side is waxier (if either). The results are as follows: the new wax gives a better result ten times, the standard wax two times, and neither three times. Can we accept the company's claim (at the 5 percent level)? (*Note:* This example is based upon procedures advertised in a television commercial.)

Solution: Let $T =$ number of pairs for which the new wax is judged better. We assume T is a binomial random variable with $n = 12$ and $H : p = \frac{1}{2}$ versus $A : p > \frac{1}{2}$.

From Table A2.1, the significance probability of the observation 10 is $P(T \geq 10 | p = \frac{1}{2}) = 0.019$. Since this is less than 0.05, we reject H at the 5 percent level and accept the company's claim.

Note that in the above example no numerical waxiness values were assigned to each side. Using nonparametric methods, we were able to arrive at an answer to our problem by means of simple comparisons. We might have tried to make up a waxiness scale and assign values to each side of each car. One merit of the nonparametric sign test is that it is not necessary to have a numerical scale since all that is needed are judgments of superiority. Such judgments and such a test are commonly used in taste or esthetic comparisons where it is difficult to assign numerical values but where it is possible to obtain evaluations of better or worse.

In any problem where one can decide which of a pair has yielded a better result, the sign test can be used. Sometimes the alternative may be $p < \frac{1}{2}$ or $p \neq \frac{1}{2}$, but the methods of Chapter 4 still apply. The sign test can be used when numerical values for each pair are available but we do not believe these values are normally distributed. It is often used even when it is believed that the underlying variables are normal because of its simplicity. Such usage has already been made, e.g., Problems 4.13 and 7.22, where comparisons were made between times of first and second calculations.

EXERCISE

In Example 12.1, what would you conclude if $n = 20$, the new wax is judged better 12 times, the old six times, and neither two times? Comment further on your answer.

Two-Sample Tests

In many experiments, it is not possible to find pairs which are identical in all respects for testing a new treatment against an old treatment (or against a control group). In such a situation, it is customary to use the new treatment on a random sample of size n and to use the old treatment (or no treatment) on an independent random sample of size m (m is not necessarily the same as n) and obtain $N = n + m$ random observations. In other problems, the statistician has samples from two populations and he is interested in knowing whether the population probability distributions may be assumed to be the same or must be taken to be different.

Two-Sample t Test†

If it can be assumed that the values in each experiment or sample are normally distributed with *the same variance*, the methods of Chapter 7 apply.

Formally, in this case we have observations $X_1, X_2, \ldots, X_n$, which are normally and independently distributed with mean μ_X and variance σ^2; we have observations $Y_1, \ldots, Y_m$, which are normally distributed with mean μ_Y and variance σ^2. Observe that the variances are *assumed* equal. We further assume that the two sets of observations are independent. The hypothesis to be tested is $H : \mu_X = \mu_Y$. The family of alternatives may be one-sided or two-sided. The test statistic is

$$t = \frac{\bar{X} - \bar{Y}}{s_p[(1/n) + (1/m)]^{1/2}},$$

where s_p^2 is the pooled sample estimator of σ^2 determined from the formula

$$s_p^2 = \frac{\sum_{i=1}^n X_i^2 - (1/n)(\sum_{i=1}^n X_i)^2 + \sum_{i=1}^m Y_i^2 - (1/m)(\sum_{i=1}^m Y_i)^2}{n + m - 2}.$$

The pooled variance s_p^2 has $n + m - 2$ degrees of freedom and hence t does also.

H is rejected at the 100α percent level if $|t| > t_\alpha$ when the family of alternatives is $A : \mu_X \neq \mu_Y$, and if $t > t_{2\alpha}$ when the family of alternatives is $A : \mu_X > \mu_Y$.

Example 12.2   Cigarette smoke and mice

The following data show weight gains of mice (in grams) in an experiment of the type discussed in Example 1.9.

---

† The two-sample t test is not a nonparametric test since the form of the probability distribution is assumed known. Thus, this test rightly belongs in Chapter 7, but is discussed here so as to compare it with the corresponding nonparametric test.

"Smokers"	13	14	12	18	15	11	13	17	12	13
"Nonsmokers"	21	16	21	18	18	19	19	17	22	23

Here, let X_i denote the weight gain of the ith "smoking" mouse and Y_i the weight gain of the ith "nonsmoking" mouse. (Note that X_i and Y_i have no relationship to each other—the mice in the experiment were not paired.) Calculate that

$$\sum_{i=1}^{n} X_i = 138, \quad \sum_{i=1}^{m} = 194, \quad \bar{X} = 13.8, \quad \bar{Y} = 19.4.$$

$$\sum_{i=1}^{n} X_i^2 = 1,950, \quad \sum_{i=1}^{m} Y_i^2 = 3,810.$$

$$s_p^2 = \frac{1}{18}\left[1,950 - \frac{(138)^2}{10} + 3,810 - \frac{(194)^2}{10}\right] = \frac{92.0}{18} = 5.11.$$

The hypothesis to be tested is $H : \mu_X = \mu_Y$ versus $A : \mu_X \neq \mu_Y$. The alternative is two-sided because we are really in ignorance as to the effect of smoking on growth in mice even though we may have the suspicion that smoking inhibits growth. The test statistic is

$$|t| = \frac{|-5.6|}{5.11(\frac{1}{10} + \frac{1}{10})} = 5.54.$$

Since the 1 percent critical level for t with 18 d.f. is 2.88, H is rejected at the 1 percent significance level.

In making this test we have assumed not only normality of the random observations but also that they are distributed with a common variance; the reader should check that the two *sample* variances are 9.07 and 9.16 respectively, which seem to be in accord with the assumption of equal population variances. Tests can be made for this assumption; such tests are more sensitive to the assumption of normality than the t tests of Chapter 7 are, and are not recommended for standard use.

Two-Sample Rank Test

We discuss now an alternative procedure that uses, instead of the actual random observations, their ranks, which are also random. Ranks are integers from 1 to $m + n$. Under the hypothesis, the rank corresponding to an observation has the same distribution as that of any other rank and hence has the same variance; thus, we avoid the problem of the assumption of the common variance needed in the two-sample t test.

The procedure is as follows:

1. Write the $N = m + n$ observations in order from smallest to largest, underlining those which correspond to the new treatment.
2. Under each observation write its rank in the combined sample. In case of ties, average the ranks of such ties and assign this average to each tied value.
3. Let W be the sum of the ranks of the new treatment values.

W is called the Wilcoxon–Mann–Whitney, or two-sample rank, statistic and we use it to test the hypothesis that the new and old treatments are identical. If this is the case then the ranks of the new treatment are likely to be scattered through the N ranks. Now the sum of the first N integers is easily computed to be $N(N + 1)/2$, and since n/N of the observations are those of the new treatment, we have the result that if the treatments are in fact identical,

$$E(W) = \frac{n}{N} \cdot \frac{N(N + 1)}{2} = \frac{n(N + 1)}{2}.$$

On the other hand, if, under the new treatment, the random variable being studied tends to take on larger values, then W tends to be large; if, under the new treatment, the random variable being studied tends to take on smaller values, then W is reduced, on the average. Thus, the hypothesis of no-treatment effect will be rejected if W differs significantly from its expected value, $n(N + 1)/2$.

The discussion above has been phrased in terms of treatment and control or new treatment and old treatment, but it applies equally well to comparisons of samples from two populations. In this case the treatment group is replaced by one of the samples, say, the observations on X. The same steps are followed through; since the test is symmetrical with respect to the groups it does not matter which is labeled the X group. Of course, in comparing a treatment and control group, the family of alternatives will often be one-sided, and hence the W test one-tailed, while in comparing two populations it is usual for the family of alternatives to be two-sided and thus the W test is two-tailed.

The exact distribution of W, under H, has been computed for small values of n and m.[†] Fortunately, for all but very small sample sizes (one or both less than 8), W is approximately normally distributed

---

[†] A table can be found in Donald B. Owen, *Handbook of Statistical Tables* (Reading, Mass.: Addison-Wesley, 1962).

with $n(N + 1)/2$ as expected value and $nm(N^3 - N - \tau)/12N(N - 1)$ as variance. Thus, we can set up a test or find a significance probability, as in Chapter 7.

The factor τ depends on the number of tied observations; if there are no ties, $\tau = 0$ and $V(W)$ reduces to $nm(N + 1)/12$. The factor τ is a sum; the number of summands corresponds to the number of ties; each summand is $(s + 1)(s)(s - 1)$ if there are s observations in the tied set.

Example 12.3 Effect of kindergarten on reading

The 31 students of a Grade 1 class are divided into groups depending on whether or not they have been to a kindergarten class. Both groups of children are taught to read, using the same material in the same way. At the end of the year a reading test is given to each class, and the following are the scores of each child, out of a possible test score of 30.

Group with kindergarten training	10	14	18	19	20	20	20	20
	21	21	22	23	26	26	29	30
Group without kindergarten training	9	10	11	13	14	19	19	19
	20	21	22	23	24	25	27	

Can we assume (at the 5 percent level) that kindergarten training affects learning to read as measured by this score?

Solution: Arranging the 31 observations in order and underlining those from the first group, we have

Score	9	10	10	11	13	14	14	18
Rank	1	2.5	2.5	4	5	6.5	6.5	8
Score	19	19	19	19	20	20	20	20
Rank	10.5	10.5	10.5	10.5	15	15	15	15
Score	20	21	21	21	22	22	23	23
Rank	15	19	19	19	21.5	21.5	23.5	23.5
Score	24	25	26	26	27	29	30	
Rank	25	26	27.5	27.5	29	30	31	

Therefore, $W = 2.5 + 6.5 + 8 + 10.5 + 15 + 15 + 15 + 15 + 19 + 19 + 21.5 + 23.5 + 27.5 + 27.5 + 30 + 31 = 277.5$.

Here, $n = 16$, $m = 15$, and $N = 31$, so that $E(W) = 16(31 + 1)/2 = 256$. We first compute τ before computing $V(W)$. There are 8 tied sets: 10, 10 ($s = 2$); 14, 14 ($s = 2$); 19, 19, 19, 19 ($s = 4$); 20, 20, 20, 20, 20 ($s = 5$); 21, 21, 21 ($s = 3$); 22, 22 ($s = 2$); 23, 23 ($s = 2$); and 26, 26 ($s = 2$). Hence $\tau = (3)(2)(1) + 3(2)(1) + (5)(4)(3) + (6)(5)(4) + (4)(3)(2) + (3)(2)(1) + (3)(2)(1) + (3)(2)(1) = 194$.

Finally,

$$V(W) = \frac{(16)(15)(31^3 - 31 - 194)}{(12)(31)(30)} = 635.83,$$

$$\sigma_W = 25.22,$$

$$Z = \frac{277.5 - 256}{25.22} = \frac{21.5}{25.22} = 0.85.$$

The significance probability of the observations is approximately $P(|Z| > 0.85) = 0.40$.

The significance probability is computed for a two-sided alternative. This is appropriate because of our initial ignorance as to the effect, if any, of kindergarten training on reading. It is concluded that the two groups do not differ significantly in regard to their reading scores.

Unless the sample sizes are small or there are many tied values, τ is usually negligible; even in this example with eight groups of ties in 31 observations, the computation of τ makes no difference to the final Z statistic, at least to two-decimal accuracy.

EXERCISE

Criticize the above example. Does it really test what we want to test?

Rank Correlation

The analysis of the relationship between two random variables (Chapter 10) is based on the assumptions of normality and on the assumptions that $E(Y|X)$ is linear in X while $V(Y|X)$ is independent of X. Again, these assumptions can be avoided and partial results obtained by replacing the random observations by their ranks. In other problems, only rankings are possible and an analysis based on ranks alone is therefore necessary. For example, if an employer is asked to rate ten employees for efficiency and pleasantness he would be hard pressed to assign numerical values but he might be able to rank the ten in order from first to tenth. The relationship of such ranked data is still measured by the sample correlation coefficient;

however when ranks are used, the formula for the correlation coefficient can be considerably simplified. This rank correlation coefficient was given first by Spearman and will be labeled here r_s to distinguish it from the usual correlation coefficient r, calculated from numerical data.

Let d_i be the difference of the ranks of the ith pair of observations. (It should be emphasized that the X's are ranked among themselves and also the Y's; there is not a joint ranking as in the two-sample problem discussed earlier in this chapter.) Then

$$r_s = 1 - \frac{6 \sum_{i=1}^{n} d_i^2}{n^3 - n},$$

where n is the number of pairs.

If the original data consist of numerical values, then it is possible to calculate r in the usual way from the actual data and from the ranks. These two different sample correlation coefficients are usually close. However, the rank correlation certainly does not come from jointly normally distributed random variables, and the tests of Chapter 10 are not applicable. In spite of this, the rank correlation can be used to test for independence of the two rankings. Tables for testing the hypothesis that there is independence are available for small sample sizes.

For our purposes, a normal approximation is again adequate for most hypothesis-testing purposes. If the two rankings are independent, then

$$E(r_s) = 0, \qquad V(r_s) = \frac{1}{n - 1},$$

so that an approximate test statistic is

$$Z = \sqrt{n - 1}\, r_s.$$

Example 12.4 Employee efficiency and pleasantness

An employer ranks ten employees as to efficiency and pleasantness and the following table results.

Employee No.	1	2	3	4	5	6	7	8	9	10
Efficiency ranking	1	2	3	4	5	6	7	8	9	10
Pleasantness ranking	3	1	8	2	4	6	5	9	7	10
$|d_i|$	2	1	5	2	1	0	2	1	2	0

$$r_s = 1 - \frac{6(44)}{10^3 - 10} = 0.73$$

Since $Z = \sqrt{9}\ (0.73) = 2.19$, it is immediately checked from Table A2.3 that $P(|Z| > 2.19) = 0.028$. Thus the significance probability of the observed ranks under the hypothesis of independent rankings is approximately 0.028, and it is inferred that there is in fact a relationship between the two rankings. (From tables, the exact significance probability of the observed ranks is 0.020, only slightly different from that found by using the normal approximation.)

Runs

Runs have been introduced in Examples 2.13 and 9.1. They can be used to test a number of hypotheses; in particular, runs are used to test some aspects of randomness. We will outline the procedure and then comment on its use in this section.

To test a sample for randomness by use of a run test, the sample median is found; *the sample median* is any number such that at least half the observed values are greater than or equal to that number and at least half are less than or equal to that number. (See Appendix 1, The Median; Percentiles.)

If N is odd, there is one median value, namely, the middle observation of the ranked observations. If N is even, then any value between the middle two ordered observations is a median. (The median can be defined uniquely as the average of these two observations.)

Each observation is replaced by the letter a if the observation is above the median, dropped if it is equal to the median, and replaced by the letter b if it is below the median. The total number of runs of a's and b's (after dropping all median values) is denoted by R. The hypothesis of randomness is rejected if R is too large or too small (small values of R being caused by clustering and large values by alternation).

As in the case of the r_s and W statistics, the distribution of R has been calculated for small sample sizes, but again a simple normal approximation is useful for moderate or large sizes. To use the normal approximation we need the expectation and variance of R, computed when the hypothesis is true. Let k be the number of a's and b's, i.e., the sample size minus the number of observations equal to the sample median.

Then

$$E(R) = \frac{k}{2} + 1,$$

$$V(R) = \frac{k}{4} \cdot \frac{(k-2)}{(k-1)}.$$

The test statistic is therefore

$$Z = \frac{R - [(k/2) + 1]}{\sqrt{(k/4)[(k-2)/(k-1)]}} = \frac{2(R-1) - k}{\sqrt{k(k-2)/(k-1)}}.$$

The hypothesis of randomness is rejected if $|Z| > z_\alpha$, at significance level α.

Example 12.5 Examination grades and order of completion of the examination

A professor keeps a record of the order of completion of one of his examinations. The scores, according to order of completion, are 99, 84, 58, 69, 89, 81, 81, 72, 52, 39, 66, 46, 51, 56, 73, 74, 97, 77, 57, 54. The ten lowest scores are those below or equal to 69; the ten highest scores are those above or equal to 72. Hence we relabel the observations; the runs are underlined:

<u>aa</u> <u>bb</u> <u>aaaa</u> <u>bbbbbb</u> <u>aaaa</u> <u>bb</u>

It is seen that $R = 6$; since the median is between 69 and 72, no observations are dropped and $k = 20$. Thus

$$E(R) = 11 \qquad \text{and} \qquad V(R) = \tfrac{20}{4}(\tfrac{18}{19}) = 4.74.$$

The test statistic is $Z = (6 - 11)/\sqrt{4.74} = -2.19$; the approximate significance probability of such a value of R, or of the corresponding Z, is 0.03. The implication of this result is that examination scores are not random with regard to order of completion of the examination, at least of the 5 percent significance level.

It should be emphasized that nonrandomness has many facets, some of which can be tested internally on the basis of sample observations. For example, if the sample is being drawn from a changing population, or if there is correlation between successive observations, then we say that there is nonrandomness, and it may be possible to determine this from the sample. On the other hand, if households are sampled and the interviewer only interviews from 9 A.M. to 5 P.M., he may get no information from households in which all adults, in particular the housewifes, are employed outside the home. Do you think such a sample would give proper information about the random variable: number of children per family?

Such nonrandomness might not be detected in the sample by any test. The problems associated with obtaining samples or designing experiments that are in conformity with probability models are many and complex and involve both statistical and nonstatistical aspects. It cannot be reemphasized too strongly that if the data collection is improper, so that the assumptions of the probability models are incorrect, then any analysis, no matter how sophisticated, may give incorrect or meaningless answers. In a shorter phrase: "Garbage in, garbage out."

Some students may well be puzzled by one part of these nonparametric tests; they are claimed to be distribution-free and yet we keep returning to the use of the normal distribution and finish the (approximate) test by forming a Z statistic. What has happened is that we have replaced the observations, about which we may be prepared to assume little, by ranks. Ranks are uniform random variables that are well-behaved and in particular have under the hypothesis tested a known mean and variance; moreover sums or means of even quite small samples of such uniform variables are close to being normally distributed. So the gain is in going over from an unknown distribution, which may possibly have bad properties, to one we know is well-behaved. Of course, if the original distribution was in fact well-behaved (in particular, normal, etc.) then we have sacrificed some information in going from original observations to ranks, though usually the loss is quite small.

Throughout this chapter and in the experiments and problems, it is seen that there is more than one way, in many situations, to test any proposed hypothesis. The statistician should, in any real problem, choose one procedure and stick with it. He should not use all the available tests and then choose the answer which best suits his convenience. Doing so alters the error probabilities in unknown ways.

■ Experiments

12.1   Draw two samples of random normal variables from Table A2.5, each of size 10: test $H : \mu_X = \mu_Y$ versus $A : \mu_X \neq \mu_Y$, using the two-sample t test and assuming that the variances are unknown. Use the two-sample rank statistic to test the same hypothesis. Do both at the 10 percent significance level. This experiment should be repeated 100 times (by the class in total) and a record kept of the number of rejections of $H : \mu_X = \mu_Y$ by both tests. (Since the observations are drawn from a table of random normal deviates, H is true, and in 100 trials we expect ten rejections on the average by either method.)

*12.2   Draw two samples of random variables from Table A2.5, each of size 10. Label these X's and Y's. To each of the Y's add 1.

Again test $H : \mu_X = \mu_Y$ versus $A : \mu_X = \mu_Y$, assuming that the variances are unknown and using a two-sample t test.

Use the two-sample rank statistic to test the same hypothesis. Do both at the 10 percent significance level. This experiment should be repeated 100 times (by the class in total) and a record kept of the number of rejections of $H : \mu_X = \mu_Y$ by both tests. [Since H is now not true ($\mu_Y = \mu_X + 1$), H should be rejected. However, the random observations are normally distributed and so the more efficient two-sample t test should give a few more rejections than the two-sample rank test. The true difference is not great and may be obscured by sampling errors.]

12.3 Take a sample of 10 random normal variables from Table A2.5; take a second sample from the same table, multiply each observation in the second sample by 2, and add 1 to the result. Denote the first set by X's, the second by Y's. Again test $H : \mu_X = \mu_Y$ versus $A : \mu_X \neq \mu_Y$ at the 10 percent level. Repeat the experiment 100 times (by the class in total) and record the number of rejections of H by the two-sample t test and the two-sample rank test. [In this case H is not true but the assumptions for the t test are not fulfilled (why not?), and the two-sample rank test should give more rejections than the two-sample t test.]

■ **Problems**

12.1 A company claims that its new gasoline additive gives better gasoline mileage. To test this claim 20 cars are chosen. One gallon of ordinary gasoline is placed in each car and it is run until the gasoline is used up; the mileage is recorded to the nearest tenth of a mile. The same experiment is repeated with the additive, and the random mileage is again recorded.

(a) Test the hypothesis that the additive is of no value ($\alpha = 0.05$) using the sign test, if the following data result:

With additive	15.6	20.9	25.1	18.6	12.8	16.0	19.9	20.6	18.1	22.8
Without additive	14.3	18.1	25.0	18.8	11.6	16.0	17.3	18.4	16.1	20.6
With additive	20.9	23.1	17.9	21.2	18.6	17.3	23.6	21.4	25.0	14.1
Without additive	21.1	23.0	16.9	21.2	16.7	18.1	20.9	19.3	22.3	14.3

(b) Since the observations are paired (both are obtained from the same car), the appropriate procedure to analyze the numerical values is to calculate the differences and test the hypothesis that the true mean difference is zero. This assumes normality of such differences. Perform the test and compare your result with that of (a).

12.2 The packaging department of a large food company claims to have designed a more eye-catching package for one of its products. To test this claim, 100 people are asked to choose between the old and the new package with the following results:

New package	55
Old package	35
No preference	10

Use the sign test to see if these results are significant at the 5 percent level.

12.3 A research chemist claims to have discovered a new drug which increases a person's I.Q. To test this claim, two I.Q. tests (which have been standardized so as to have the same mean and variance) are administered to each of ten persons. One test, chosen at random, is administered before the drug and the other after the drug.

(a) Use the sign test to see if the results significantly (5 percent level) favor the drug.

Before drug	110	115	100	95	95	130	110	120	100	125
After drug	115	105	115	110	90	135	105	125	120	115

(b) Could any other test be applied to try to validate the chemist's claim? If so, how would it be performed and what assumptions would be involved?

12.4 A psychologist believes, on the basis of past experience, that green-tinted walls in hospitals aid the recovery of patients. To test his belief, 20 pairs of patients (each pair of patients matched as closely as possible) are chosen. One of each pair, chosen at random, is put in the usual white-walled room; the other in a green-walled room. The results are as follows:

Faster recovery in green room	11
Faster recovery in white room	7
Recovery time same in both rooms	2

(a) Use the sign test to see if we can accept the psychologist's belief at the 5 percent level.

(b) Because of physical limitations the hospital might not be able to choose pairs of exactly matched patients. Instead it might simply have a sample of patients who are assigned randomly to the two types of rooms. If this were the case and recovery time were available for each patient, how would we test the psychologist's belief?

12.5   A diet supplement claims to increase weight gains in young pigs. In a test of this claim, 15 pairs of pigs are chosen. Each pair is chosen from the same litter and matched as closely as possible. One of each pair, chosen at random, is given the usual diet for one week and the other is given the usual diet plus the diet supplement. The weight gains (to the nearest tenth of a pound) are recorded and the results are as follows:

Regular diet	5.6	4.7	4.6	4.3	5.8	6.0	6.0	6.3
Diet plus supplement	6.7	4.7	5.2	5.1	6.3	5.8	7.1	6.4
Regular diet	6.2	5.1	5.3	5.8	6.2	6.0	5.4	
Diet plus supplement	5.7	6.8	5.9	5.8	6.5	7.1	5.4	

Use the sign test to see if the diet supplement significantly increases weight gains. Use a 5 percent significance level. If normality of the observations were assumed, what would be the appropriate test procedure? [*Hint:* Recall Problem 12.1(b).]

12.6   Two Grade 1 classes, chosen to be as alike as possible, are taught to read by two different methods. One class with 20 students uses the regular method. The other with 21 students uses a new experimental method. At year end, a reading test is given to each class. The individual scores are as follows:

Old method	20	19	19	18	18	18	17	17	17	17	17
	17	16	16	16	15	14	12	11	7		
New method	20	20	20	19	19	19	19	18	18	18	17
	17	17	17	17	17	16	16	16	16	10	

Use the two-sample rank test to see if the new method is significantly better at the 5 percent level. Compare the results obtained by using the two-sample *t* test. Can you use the sign test here?

12.7   In a test of the claim that marriage lowers university grades, twelve students are chosen at random from the population of all the students who are married at the end of their second year and ten students are chosen at random from the population of all students who are unmarried at the end of the second year. Their third-year G.P.A.'s are listed below.

Married students' G.P.A.'s	3.5	3.3	3.2	3.0	2.8	2.6
	2.6	2.6	2.5	2.5	2.3	2.0
Unmarried students' G.P.A.'s	3.7	3.4	3.4	3.3	3.1	3.0
	2.9	2.9	2.6	2.6		

(a) Use the two-sample rank test to see if unmarried students have a higher G.P.A. Use a 5 percent significance level.

(b) Use the two-sample t test on this data.

12.8   Ten I.Q.'s are sampled from Grade 10 students at one high school and 15 are sampled at another high school with the following results:

School 1	100	103	104	110	115	118	120	125	128	132
School 2	90	94	96	98	101	102	105	106	108	109
	111	112	113	114	131					

Use the two-sample rank test to see if the samples come from a common population ($\alpha = 0.05$).

12.9   The heights (in tenths of inches) of ten adult males are chosen at random from among all adult American males and from among all adult Canadian males, with the following results:

American males	68.1	69.3	70.9	70.9	71.1
	71.3	71.6	72.5	73.6	74.8
Canadian males	67.0	68.0	69.1	69.7	70.1
	70.8	71.4	72.3	72.4	75.1

Use the two-sample rank test to see if heights of American and Canadian males come from the same population.

12.10   Use the run test ($\alpha = 0.05$) to see if the following sample of 25 sugar sack weights (to the nearest hundredth of a pound), taken in order from the production line, can be regarded as a random sample.

1.08	1.08	1.09	1.11	1.11	1.11	1.12
1.09	1.10	1.10	1.09	1.12	1.13	1.11
1.11	1.12	1.07	1.11	1.08	1.07	1.08
1.10	1.12	1.13	1.10			

If you reject the hypothesis of randomness, inspect the data and try to find a plausible reason for your rejection.

12.11 A series of 20 rockets is fired at a target one mile away: the distance traveled by the rocket (measured to the nearest hundredth of a mile) is measured and recorded in order of shooting. Test these results for randomness, using the run test and $\alpha = 0.05$.

1.12	0.98	1.10	0.96	0.99	1.04	1.01
0.95	0.99	1.06	1.03	1.01	0.96	0.98
1.03	1.02	1.01	0.97	0.98	0.99	

If you reject the hypothesis of randomness, try to suggest a reason for doing so.

12.12 Two judges are asked to rank 12 sculptures in order from 1 to 12 with the following results:

Judge A	1	2	3	4	5	6	7	8	9	10	11	12
Judge B	4	7	1	2	5	3	10	8	6	11	9	12

Find the rank correlation coefficient and test ($\alpha = 0.05$) the hypothesis of no correlation against the one-sided alternative of positive correlation.

12.13 Ten different makes and models of cars varying within $300 in actual price are shown to two men, who are asked to rank them from 1 to 10. The following results give their rankings:

A	1	2	3	4	5	6	7	8	9	10
B	1	3	4	2	7	5	6	8	10	9

Find the rank correlation coefficient and test the hypothesis of no correlation versus the one-sided alternative of positive correlation.

12.14 (a) Convert the data of Problem 10.5 into ranks (averaging ties) and find the rank correlation coefficient. (b) Compare r_s with the value of r obtained in Problem 10.8. (c) Test the hypothesis of no correlation versus the one-sided alternative of positive correlation. (d) Compare the result of the test in (c) with the result of Problem 10.17.

12.15 (a) Convert the data of Problem 10.6 into ranks (averaging ties) and find the rank correlation coefficient. Compare r_s with the value of r found in Problem 10.9. (b) Test the hypothesis of no correlation versus the one-sided alternative of positive correlation. Compare this with the result of Problem 10.17.

12.16 A state parole board consists of five members; each member grades each potential parolee from 0 to 10. Prisoners may thus obtain a total score (adding the five separate scores) of 0 to 50. Prisoners with a score of 35 or higher are paroled. A statistician assigned to the board makes a study of the scores of those parolees who violate their parole and those who do not. He finds in his study of 74 parolees that 48 violated their parole while 26 did not. The 48 parole violators had a mean score of 41.4 (standard deviation 3.5) while the 26 nonviolators had at release a mean score of 41.8 (standard deviation 4.2). He analyzes this and asserts that the difference is not significant and that therefore the parole score is of no value in deciding whether or not to parole prisoners.

(a) Set this up as a test of a hypothesis, state the assumptions necessary, and perform the test which is presumably the basis of the statistician's statement of nonsignificance.

(b) Comment on the further conclusion made by the statistician. Is it valid?

(c) Set up an experiment which the parole board might undertake to see if their score procedure is of value in predicting parole violators.

12.17 In a growth study a number of pairs of twins are used as subjects. Of each pair, one twin receives antibiotic treatment for all minor illnesses (treatment); the other receives the treatment only for emergencies (control). The investigator measures their weight gain over a three-year period. Here are some of his results (weight gains in pounds):

Pair	1	2	3	4	5	6	7	8	9	10
Twin 1 (treatment)	28	23	27	30	18	26	30	19	17	22
Twin 2 (control)	25	26	26	25	24	30	32	21	24	28

Analyze the data and draw any conclusions that seem appropriate.

12.18 Here are the scores of twelve students on two successive tests in a statistics course.

Test 1	25	13	20	9	18	14	14	19	11	26	21	17
Test 2	30	21	21	11	22	29	14	17	23	15	14	17

(a) Calculate r and r_s; test both for significance at the 5 percent level. What hypotheses are being tested and what assumptions are involved?

(b) A student asked to analyze these data performs a two-sample t test. Is this appropriate? If so, in what circumstances? What is the hypothesis he is testing?

(c) What other test statistic might be used in place of the one used in (b)?

12.19 In an experiment, two groups of 100 experimental fish are placed in aquaria. One aquarium is twice as large as the other; both groups receive the same amount of food, however. The aim of the experiment is to determine whether crowding has a significant effect on growth rate.

(a) State what should be measured and what statistic might be calculated to answer this question.

(b) If the significance probability of the statistic computed in (a) is 0.51, would you state that the experiment has proved that crowding has no effect on growth rate?

12.20 The rank correlation test might also have been applied to Example 12.5 (grades and times on examinations). Compare the results of this test with that obtained in the example.

12.21 Recall the data of Problem 5.17 (grade point averages). Use the run test to test for randomness ($\alpha = 0.05$). Suppose the data were obtained by sampling students in the university library; do you think the sample obtained would be a random sample from the university? Would your test tell you anything about this?

12.22 Use the rank correlation test on the data of Problem 5.20 to determine if there is a time sequence in the observations of the diameters of Saturn's rings ($\alpha = 0.10$).

12.23 Recall the data of Problem 5.23; suppose you found that the first 24 observations had been made by one doctor and that he then had turned the experiment over to his assistant, who made the last 26 observations. Can you test whether there is a significant difference between the two? How? Under what assumptions? Perform the test.

*12.24 Use the two-sample t test to test at the 5 percent level the hypothesis $H : \mu_X = \mu_Y$ versus $A : \mu_X \neq \mu_Y$, where μ_X = mean of male salmon population and μ_Y = mean of female salmon population (referred to in Problem 5.16). This test requires the assumption that the variance of the two populations is the same. When the assumption is made, it is easy to proceed from the test statistic to a confidence interval estimate for $\mu_X - \mu_Y$. Find this confidence interval (with confidence coefficient 0.95).

Summarization of Data

Introduction

In most statistical problems a large quantity of data is usually obtained from which the statistician wishes to extract all pertinent information, if possible. Of course, one can simply keep all the data in a raw (unprocessed) form, and this is now possible when one can store vast quantities of data in a computer. However, without such help, even moderately large amounts of data are unwieldy. We wish to find ways of summarizing the body of data that will make it more manageable without losing any essential information contained in the data, and also ways of presenting the data in understable form. The first step in summarizing data is grouping, i.e., putting each observation into a class.

Classifying Data

If the data are categorical, each category is automatically a class, and there is no problem in assigning each observation to its category. If the data are numerical, one must decide first how to choose the classes. There are no hard and fast rules but only a few general guidelines.

1. Classes should be chosen so that every observation falls into one and only one class.
2. The number of classes should be neither too small (e.g., 1 or 2) nor too large (e.g., 100 or 200). Generally, some number of classes between 5 and 15 will do.
3. If possible, classes should be of equal width so as to simplify later work.

Numerical data (observations) normally come in decimal form (rounded off to some number of significant places, e.g., hundredths, tenths, whole numbers, nearest 10, nearest 1,000, etc.). Find the smallest and the largest observation, take their difference, divide the difference by 5 and by 15, and choose some convenient number between as the class width. The class width should be calculated to the same accuracy as the data. Choose next some number just below the smallest observation as the lowest class boundary. A convenient choice is a number that has one more decimal accuracy than the data and terminates in 5. For example, if the lowest observation is 0.073, the lowest class boundary could be 0.0725, though 0.0715 or 0.0705 would also do but might lead to empty classes. The remaining class boundaries are found by successive addition of the class width to the lowest class boundary. All observations may now be assigned to one class and since the class boundaries cannot coincide with any of the observations, no ambiguities in assignment can arise.

The upper limit to any class is referred to as the *upper class boundary*. Note that the upper class boundary for one class will coincide with the *lower class boundary* for the next class. The *class midpoint* is defined to be that number which is halfway between the upper and lower class boundaries. It is, then, the average of the two. The *class width* is the difference between the upper and lower class boundaries. (From now on, UCB and LCB will be used as abbreviations for upper and lower class boundary.)

Having chosen the classes, one then makes a tally of the number of observations falling into each class, this number being called the *frequency* of the class. A complete *frequency distribution* should include the class boundaries, class midpoints, and frequencies. For certain purposes only some of these columns are required. For other purposes, some new columns are required. Two such are the "*greater than*" *cumulative frequency* and the "*less than*" *cumulative frequency*. To obtain the "less than" cumulative frequency for any UCB, it is necessary to add up the total number of observations whose values are less than this UCB. Thus, the largest UCB will have as cumulative frequency the total number of observations, since every observation will be smaller than this largest UCB. It is convenient to add one more class at the beginning of the table. This class will have frequency zero and the cumulative frequency corresponding to its UCB will be zero.

To obtain the "greater than" cumulative frequency corresponding to each LCB, add up the total number of observations whose value is greater than this LCB. The smallest LCB will have cumulative frequency equal to the total number of observations, since every observation is larger than the smallest LCB. For convenience, one adds one more class at the end of the table. This class will have frequency zero and its LCB will have cumulative frequency zero.

Each frequency or cumulative frequency can be changed to a *relative frequency* or *relative cumulative frequency* by dividing the corresponding frequencies by the total number of observations, and to a *percentage frequency* or *percentage cumulative frequency* by multiplying the relative frequency or cumulative relative frequency by 100.

Note: If the data are regarded as a random sample from some population, these relative frequencies are estimates of the corresponding probabilities for the population.

The following example will be used to illustrate the various definitions. The data are taken from Problem 5.20 (Saturn's rings).

38.91	38.93	39.17	39.57	39.30
39.35	39.14	39.29	39.40	39.28
39.41	39.36	39.42	39.41	39.43
39.02	38.86	39.21	39.60	39.45
39.32	39.31	39.04	39.46	39.03
39.25	39.47	39.32	39.33	39.62
39.40	39.20	39.30	39.43	39.36
39.01	39.51	39.17	39.54	39.72

The smallest observation is 38.86; the largest observation is 39.72; their difference is 0.86. Dividing this by 5 and by 15 yields 0.172 and 0.057. A convenient class width is 0.10. The smallest lower class

TABLE A1.1

Class midpoint	Frequency	UCB	"Less-than" cumulative frequency	LCB	"Greater-than" cumulative frequency
38.795	0	38.845	0		
38.895	3	38.945	3	38.845	40
38.995	4	39.045	7	38.945	37
39.095	1	39.145	8	39.045	33
39.195	4	39.245	12	39.145	32
39.295	9	39.345	21	39.245	28
39.395	10	39.445	31	39.345	19
39.495	5	39.545	36	39.445	9
39.595	3	39.645	39	39.545	4
39.695	1	39.745	40	39.645	1
39.795	0			39.745	0
	$n = 40$				

boundary can be chosen as 38.845; the class boundaries are therefore 38.845; 38.945; 39.045; 39.145; 39.245; 39.345; 39.445; 39.545; 39.645 and 39.745. The first class midpoint is half way between 38.845 and 38.945, i.e., 38.895; other class midpoints can be obtained by adding 0.10 successively to 38.895.

The data of Problem 5.20 (Saturn's rings) are presented in Table A1.1.

Graphing Data

The Histogram

Assume first that all the classes have the same width. Plot the class boundaries on the horizontal axis of a graph and erect a bar for each class with the interval between the UCB and LCB as base, the height of the bar being proportional to the frequency. Such a graph is called a *histogram*. A histogram for the data of Table A1.1 is presented in Figure A1.1.

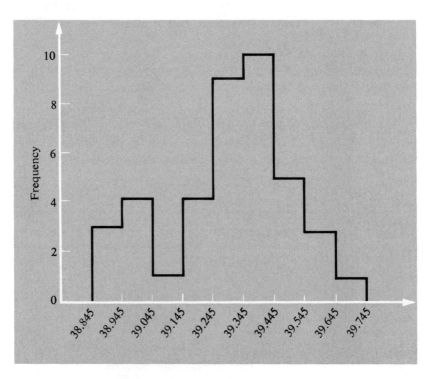

FIGURE A1.1   *A histogram for the data of Problem 5.20.*

If the class widths are not equal, then the bar height must be modified. If one class has a width twice the others, its height should be halved. If one is three times as wide, its height should be cut to one-third, etc. This is equivalent to saying that in general the *area* of each bar should be proportional to the frequency in the corresponding class.

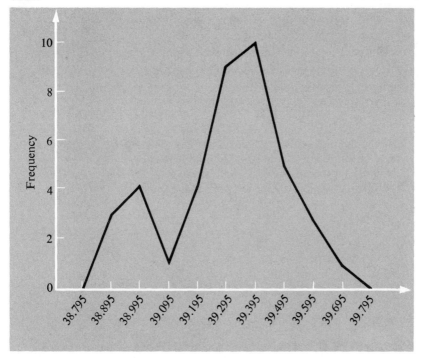

FIGURE A1.2   *A frequency polygon for the data of Problem 5.20.*

The Frequency Polygon

Assuming first that all classes are of equal width, the class midpoints are plotted on the horizontal axis of a graph and points are plotted above these points, the height of the points being proportional to the frequencies. These points are joined by straight lines and the resulting graph is called a *frequency polygon*. For convenience, extra midpoints are added at either end with frequency zero so that the frequency polygon starts and ends at zero. If the class widths are unequal, then the heights are modified exactly as in the case of a histogram. A frequency polygon for the data of Table A1.1 is presented in Figure A1.2.

Cumulative Frequency Polygons

To draw a "greater than" cumulative frequency polygon, plot the LCB's on the horizontal axis of a graph, and above each LCB plot a point corresponding to the total frequency that is greater than this LCB. For convenience, add one extra LCB at the upper end whose cumulative frequency is zero, so that the "greater than" cumulative frequency polygon ends at zero. The "less than" cumulative frequency polygon is constructed similarly, by using the UCB and cumulative frequencies less than each such boundary. An extra UCB is added at the lower end, so that the graph starts at zero. Cumulative frequency polygons are presented in Figures A1.3 and A1.4 for the data of Table A1.1.

Note: Any polygon or cumulative polygon can be changed to the corresponding relative or percentage polygon simply by changing the scale on the vertical axis, i.e., by dividing each number on the scale by the total number of observations in the case of the relative frequency and multiplying this by 100 for the percentage frequency.

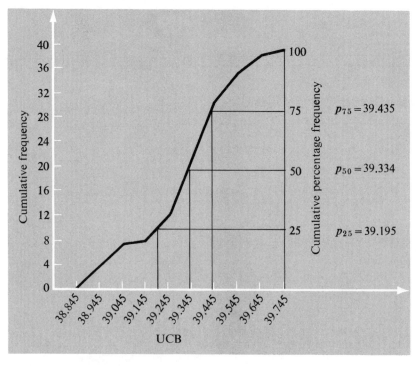

FIGURE A1.3 *A cumulative "less than" frequency polygon.*

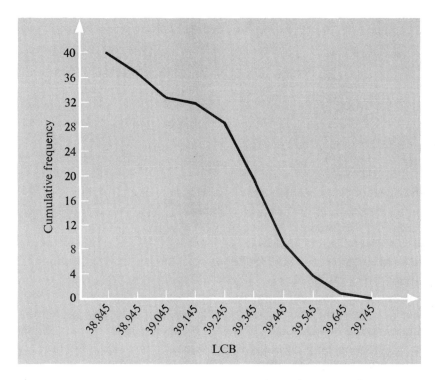

FIGURE A1.4 *A cumulative "greater than" frequency polygon.*

The Median; Percentiles

The arithmetic mean of the observations ($\bar{X}$, as defined in Chapter 5) is an unbiased estimator of the population mean μ, but if the population is not symmetrical neither μ nor its estimator $\bar{X}$ may be an appropriate summarizing statistic. For example, consider the six observations, 2, 2, 2, 2, 1004, 2, which have mean 169. It may well be felt that 169 does not represent this set of observations. An alternative summarizing statistic is the median, which very roughly is the middle value. (For this set of observations, the median is 2.) More specifically, the sample *median* is any number that has the property that half the observations lie at or below it, half the observations lie at or above it. If there is an odd number of observations, say, $2k + 1$, the median is uniquely defined as the $(k + 1)$st ordered observation, ordering from smallest to largest. If there is an even number of observations, say $2k$, the median is any number between the kth and $(k + 1)$st ordered observations, though it is customary to choose, in this situation, the number which is midway between the kth and the $(k + 1)$st observation.

The median of 2, 2, 2, 2, 2, 1004 is 2, since there are six numbers and 2 is half way between the third and fourth numbers. Note that 2 is much nearer the bulk of the data than 196. The median of 2, 3, 4, 8, 9 is 4, the third number. The median of 8, 16, 32, 40, 41, 42, 40, 98, 1004, 1070 is 41.5, since the fifth and sixth numbers are 41 and 42, the midpoint of which is 41.5.

The median is not the only descriptive statistic of interest that divides the observations into two classes. There is a family of such statistics called *percentiles*. For example, the 90th percentile is the number that separates the lower 90 percent of the observations from the upper 10 percent. More generally, we define the xth percentile, denoted as p_x, to be that number such that exactly x percent of the ordered observations lie at or below it. Thus, the median is, in fact, the 50th percentile, or p_{50}. The data may not uniquely define the xth percentile and some practical modifications then are necessary, particularly with grouped data. For grouped data any percentile, including the median, will fall within some class interval. To obtain an exact value we proceed by linear interpolation. To write down a formula for p_x, we define l_x and u_x to be the UCB's of the two adjacent classes such that less than or exactly x percent of the observations fall below l_x while more than x percent of the observations fall below u_x. Finally, let the cumulative percentage frequency corresponding to l_x be p_1 and corresponding to u_x be p_2. Note that $p_1 \le x < p_2$ by definition. Then,

$$p_x = l_x + (u_x - l_x) \frac{x - p_1}{p_2 - p_1}.$$

Use of this formula and of the linear interpolation involved is illustrated with the data taken from Problem 5.20 (Saturn's rings). To calculate the median, we observe in Table A1.1 that 12 of 40 observations lie below the UCB, 39.245, and 21 of the 40 observations lie below the UCB, 39.395. Thus, in the notation above $l_x = 39.245$, $u_x = 39.345$, $p_1 = \frac{12}{40} = 0.30$, $p_2 = \frac{21}{40} = 0.525$, and hence

$$\text{Median} = p_{50} = 39.245 + (0.100)\left(\frac{0.50 - 0.30}{0.525 - 0.30}\right)$$

$$= 39.334.$$

(The student should note that if the median were to be calculated from the raw data, the value obtained would be 39.325; the discrepancy is due to the grouping process. Like the slight discrepancies grouping causes when we calculate $\bar{X}$ and S^2, it is unimportant.) Verify that $p_{75} = 39.435$.

Any percentile can be determined very easily from a cumulative percentage polygon by graphical interpolation as is seen by referring to Figure A1.3, where the percentiles p_{25}, p_{50}, and p_{75} are shown.

Tables

TABLE A2.1   *Binomial Probabilities:* $P(T=t) = \dfrac{n!}{t!\,(n-t)!}\,p^t(1-p)^{n-t}$

$$n = 10$$

t \ p	0.05	0.1	0.2	0.3	$\frac{1}{3}$	0.4	0.5	0.6	0.7	0.8	0.9	0.95
0	0.599	0.349	0.107	0.028	0.017	0.006	0.001					
1	0.315	0.387	0.268	0.121	0.087	0.040	0.010	0.002				
2	0.075	0.194	0.302	0.234	0.195	0.121	0.044	0.011	0.001			
3	0.010	0.057	0.201	0.267	0.260	0.215	0.117	0.042	0.009	0.001		
4	0.001	0.011	0.088	0.200	0.228	0.251	0.205	0.111	0.037	0.006		
5		0.002	0.026	0.103	0.137	0.201	0.246	0.201	0.103	0.026	0.002	
6			0.006	0.037	0.057	0.111	0.205	0.251	0.200	0.088	0.011	0.001
7			0.001	0.009	0.016	0.042	0.117	0.215	0.267	0.201	0.057	0.010
8				0.001	0.003	0.011	0.044	0.121	0.234	0.302	0.194	0.075
9						0.002	0.010	0.040	0.121	0.268	0.387	0.315
10							0.001	0.006	0.028	0.107	0.349	0.599

TABLE A2.1   (*Continued*)

$n = 12,$ $p = 0.5$

t	$P(T = t)$
0	
1	0.003
2	0.016
3	0.054
4	0.121
5	0.193
6	0.226
7	0.193
8	0.121
9	0.054
10	0.016
11	0.003
12	

TABLE A2.1   (*Continued*)

$n = 16$

t \ p	0.5	0.6	0.7	0.8	0.9
1					
2	0.002				
3	0.009	0.001			
4	0.028	0.004			
5	0.067	0.014	0.001		
6	0.122	0.039	0.006		
7	0.175	0.084	0.019	0.002	
8	0.196	0.142	0.049	0.006	
9	0.175	0.189	0.101	0.020	
10	0.122	0.198	0.165	0.055	0.003
11	0.067	0.162	0.210	0.120	0.014
12	0.028	0.101	0.204	0.200	0.051
13	0.009	0.047	0.146	0.246	0.142
14	0.002	0.015	0.073	0.211	0.275
15		0.003	0.023	0.113	0.329
16			0.003	0.028	0.185

TABLE A2.1   (*Continued*)

$n = 18$

t \ p	0.5	0.7	0.9
1			
2	0.001		
3	0.003		
4	0.012		
5	0.033		
6	0.071	0.001	
7	0.121	0.005	
8	0.167	0.015	
9	0.185	0.039	
10	0.167	0.081	
11	0.121	0.138	0.001
12	0.071	0.187	0.005
13	0.033	0.202	0.022
14	0.012	0.168	0.070
15	0.003	0.105	0.168
16	0.001	0.046	0.284
17		0.013	0.300
18		0.022	0.150

TABLE A2.1 *(Continued)*

$n = 20$

t \ p	0.05	0.1	0.2	0.3	0.4	0.5
0	0.358	0.122	0.012	0.001		
1	0.377	0.270	0.058	0.007		
2	0.189	0.285	0.137	0.028	0.003	
3	0.060	0.190	0.205	0.072	0.012	0.001
4	0.013	0.090	0.218	0.130	0.035	0.005
5	0.003	0.032	0.175	0.179	0.075	0.015
6		0.009	0.109	0.192	0.124	0.037
7		0.002	0.054	0.164	0.166	0.074
8			0.022	0.114	0.180	0.120
9			0.007	0.065	0.160	0.160
10			0.002	0.031	0.117	0.176
11			0.001	0.012	0.071	0.160
12				0.004	0.036	0.120
13				0.001	0.015	0.074
14					0.005	0.037
15					0.001	0.015
16						0.005
17						0.001
18						
19						
20						

TABLE A2.1   *(Continued)*

$n = 20$

t \ p	0.6	0.7	0.8	0.9	0.95
0					
1					
2					
3					
4					
5	0.001				
6	0.005				
7	0.015	0.001			
8	0.036	0.004			
9	0.071	0.012	0.001		
10	0.117	0.031	0.002		
11	0.180	0.065	0.007		
12	0.150	0.114	0.022		
13	0.166	0.164	0.054	0.002	
14	0.124	0.192	0.109	0.009	
15	0.075	0.179	0.175	0.032	0.003
16	0.035	0.130	0.218	0.090	0.013
17	0.012	0.072	0.205	0.190	0.060
18	0.003	0.028	0.137	0.285	0.189
19		0.007	0.058	0.270	0.377
20		0.001	0.012	0.122	0.358

TABLE A2.1 (*Continued*)

$n = 25$

t \ p	0.5	0.6	0.8	0.9
0				
1				
2				
3				
4				
5	0.002			
6	0.005			
7	0.014	0.001		
8	0.032	0.003		
9	0.061	0.009		
10	0.097	0.021		
11	0.133	0.043		
12	0.155	0.076		
13	0.155	0.114	0.001	
14	0.133	0.147	0.004	
15	0.097	0.161	0.012	
16	0.061	0.151	0.029	
17	0.032	0.120	0.062	0.002
18	0.014	0.080	0.111	0.007
19	0.005	0.044	0.163	0.024
20	0.002	0.020	0.196	0.065
21		0.007	0.187	0.138
22		0.002	0.136	0.226
23			0.071	0.266
24			0.024	0.199
25			0.004	0.072

TABLE A2.1 *(Continued)*

$n = 30$

t \ p	0.2	0.5
0	.001	
1	.009	
2	.037	
3	.078	
4	.133	
5	.172	
6	.179	
7	.154	.002
8	.111	.005
9	.068	.013
10	.035	.028
11	.016	.051
12	.006	.081
13	.002	.112
14	.001	.135
15		.164
16		.135
17		.112
18		.081
19		.051
20		.028
21		.013
22		.005
23		.002

TABLE A2.2 *Random Numbers*

67493	86321	44356	57479	62650	28346	91557	33121	23439	28441
86369	92202	72986	29227	64539	85780	08630	52970	02167	47606
58955	24640	18811	42015	37771	77973	72019	71199	59051	19776
31692	07549	81795	59460	25727	98344	59784	46433	16013	69551
95947	83746	93201	62696	32370	25230	03070	42785	00211	09455
79309	95649	89044	42908	21952	70242	09978	89120	18564	97125
55103	07499	32223	33817	13079	51109	49526	81008	79291	77796
61824	68198	84436	76734	43396	95948	85106	40229	66975	72752
05617	67055	51837	70929	90932	97662	83046	98814	24755	32744
14515	84512	51719	54315	26809	49675	28615	58294	70181	49775
68255	41529	55685	84680	17886	27257	11700	95277	20046	65704
25058	32544	51951	83557	05345	13124	06772	11935	28450	94832
97547	69411	86855	73838	74389	78997	86118	43048	61308	56682
19594	17937	75916	32913	17760	72391	39977	17337	81166	35726
00654	48222	88807	07759	90123	04726	84385	26094	59749	11880
12385	74414	45166	59615	79287	73206	47710	80636	10486	91979
73701	37762	22542	39911	52750	51843	76972	79729	11471	68019
76070	85960	87114	30841	63521	07104	40701	34920	05968	14852
49820	72106	57069	55703	01785	18704	36055	30859	81586	52184
69304	81074	44731	28928	68024	14799	66305	08933	52680	06073
12548	35991	67295	89768	60426	18959	88665	67384	78285	80614
82501	59454	18973	03065	38147	89436	31277	95590	30198	27157
04540	99464	68841	22252	52079	12965	48762	23175	67108	04452
11268	67442	35323	05511	62332	12761	47098	74549	78938	27703
71403	61252	01359	47250	25483	54386	96967	94952	97855	74403
53825	41490	17050	97314	38878	33582	80270	48135	02611	88287
28791	32772	77936	35126	10663	93352	12620	07243	77925	23694
67960	48440	04310	71462	19711	81090	60217	75712	31498	15171
33878	73591	28993	32215	25723	34755	42981	94384	35092	77019
92286	55758	57053	39567	11418	26204	69019	98807	18631	63323
15713	71811	65332	44906	02709	53339	59334	00205	03820	85897
85139	73374	13913	88421	25522	24207	89556	50540	85217	50148
93132	94206	58555	28258	03679	97485	08294	19915	36383	55997
45951	37674	34947	32665	71469	93680	37463	26700	59725	87680
26720	80067	47362	35922	98726	91863	36774	43169	80809	81918
37797	57281	65920	27012	69225	81624	90232	20228	46723	03167
02670	46418	00765	58193	69759	38548	01421	09001	20776	89797
31399	17260	05191	44821	18578	89345	41238	67444	37466	29109
11338	36430	02675	51351	89119	47652	23322	12799	84538	77601
16984	31317	35353	34927	12776	02670	46938	15795	53440	59149
61377	24809	86664	84206	48751	16797	46293	76575	86752	71796
13107	89135	33001	04793	50705	50373	20012	32500	08473	97106
49101	60006	66886	84259	01253	32431	39571	15135	99265	71911
42576	93753	10082	91537	13189	64648	66361	64190	12470	58109
70999	60095	54641	49783	35487	86116	41577	03198	69820	91881

TABLE A2.2 *(Continued)*

67630	22312	11545	41425	52307	54200	12606	92974	37314	78514
36777	46008	94589	38563	16590	08023	51371	09247	64012	36794
41106	36471	43006	19585	09317	63753	79484	68950	29543	77391
33186	88262	68415	99707	10269	95255	98586	99178	86083	08743
76795	04192	54767	74962	88238	64583	02433	11548	44926	22429
44833	30254	82604	61033	83751	27854	03627	95102	46359	42522
97953	71599	54991	96295	29091	39836	77563	65486	97103	29594
29839	71065	25869	36505	77002	27985	33856	52000	32909	13260
09907	18729	60739	92888	52355	41080	10923	24879	56078	74073
83966	10798	01110	00064	64125	07225	60127	86437	59160	28142
48647	09598	12497	84972	08100	89571	65242	55477	77901	00814
27165	20700	13991	65270	82905	07445	78253	48981	40806	38860
59687	50051	00992	83288	38752	10517	23290	80397	73835	70622
03627	95066	11054	55386	87642	87337	51904	36980	48056	23566
53293	14073	46818	97240	65200	54212	24813	89834	26112	77292
13954	29240	77552	54931	37301	97155	81247	16586	37338	02797
65307	19608	31625	40947	79001	72049	01093	83458	07524	56382
90679	63308	38413	68098	85609	75053	78265	61501	47636	07464
38572	24995	70497	62739	75143	97600	22138	39130	78106	03139
66751	50455	00925	16789	38626	11315	13173	54533	42884	98117
78526	19921	42104	25129	02963	34263	55108	12432	20486	01967
36986	53268	89145	43600	08132	50149	98616	28995	34896	82324
59751	13553	31026	47557	29710	83661	08871	91197	76526	38233
43007	20053	72670	16692	42187	89384	80414	90876	58977	46902
07666	97786	05977	23700	86753	79925	06227	71385	43019	32532
72961	05281	34446	36785	54471	39302	48907	66992	89114	12617
81282	50948	90176	64839	56003	03771	37254	18777	08461	85650
99613	17464	07079	15292	54674	79717	99845	47058	34639	27777
82638	94589	38433	87855	64954	27044	01408	95645	84282	23487
70245	13447	26544	05742	00445	75703	22048	50506	51499	36274
41449	76674	84720	58159	36127	48228	94359	10382	88831	32324
02586	63435	64677	95316	59146	33798	94671	19308	34415	06004
13999	73671	08043	71184	43516	50551	96892	20637	51646	81226
25156	30020	50173	22298	97869	95646	85477	08441	65459	70493
88512	16052	08458	82229	89534	58998	67124	20384	00720	13817

TABLE A2.3 *Standard Normal Probabilities* $P(0 < Z < z)$

z	.00	.01	.02	.03	.04	.05	.06	.07	.08	.09
0.0	.0000	.0040	.0080	.0120	.0160	.0199	.0239	.0279	.0319	.0359
0.1	.0398	.0438	.0478	.0517	.0557	.0596	.0636	.0675	.0714	.0753
0.2	.0793	.0832	.0871	.0910	.0948	.0987	.1026	.1064	.1103	.1141
0.3	.1179	.1217	.1255	.1293	.1331	.1368	.1406	.1443	.1480	.1517
0.4	.1554	.1591	.1628	.1664	.1700	.1736	.1772	.1808	.1844	.1879
0.5	.1915	.1950	.1985	.2019	.2054	.2088	.2123	.2157	.2190	.2224
0.6	.2257	.2291	.2324	.2357	.2389	.2422	.2454	.2486	.2517	.2549
0.7	.2580	.2611	.2642	.2673	.2703	.2734	.2764	.2794	.2823	.2852
0.8	.2881	.2910	.2939	.2967	.2995	.3023	.3051	.3078	.3106	.3133
0.9	.3159	.3186	.3212	.3238	.3264	.3289	.3315	.3340	.3365	.3389
1.0	.3413	.3438	.3461	.3485	.3508	.3531	.3554	.3577	.3599	.3621
1.1	.3643	.3665	.3686	.3708	.3729	.3749	.3770	.3790	.3810	.3830
1.2	.3849	.3869	.3888	.3907	.3925	.3944	.3962	.3980	.3997	.4015
1.3	.4032	.4049	.4066	.4082	.4099	.4115	.4131	.4147	.4162	.4177
1.4	.4192	.4207	.4222	.4236	.4251	.4265	.4279	.4292	.4306	.4319
1.5	.4332	.4345	.4357	.4370	.4382	.4394	.4406	.4418	.4429	.4441
1.6	.4452	.4463	.4474	.4484	.4495	.4505	.4515	.4525	.4535	.4545
1.7	.4554	.4564	.4573	.4582	.4591	.4599	.4608	.4616	.4625	.4633
1.8	.4641	.4649	.4656	.4664	.4671	.4678	.4686	.4693	.4699	.4706
1.9	.4713	.4719	.4726	.4732	.4738	.4744	.4750	.4756	.4761	.4767
2.0	.4772	.4778	.4783	.4788	.4793	.4798	.4803	.4808	.4812	.4817
2.1	.4821	.4826	.4830	.4834	.4838	.4842	.4846	.4850	.4854	.4857
2.2	.4861	.4864	.4868	.4871	.4875	.4878	.4881	.4884	.4887	.4890
2.3	.4893	.4896	.4898	.4901	.4904	.4906	.4909	.4911	.4913	.4916
2.4	.4918	.4920	.4922	.4925	.4927	.4929	.4931	.4932	.4934	.4936
2.5	.4938	.4940	.4941	.4943	.4945	.4946	.4948	.4949	.4951	.4952
2.6	.4953	.4955	.4956	.4957	.4959	.4960	.4961	.4962	.4963	.4964
2.7	.4965	.4966	.4967	.4968	.4969	.4970	.4971	.4972	.4973	.4974
2.8	.4974	.4975	.4976	.4977	.4977	.4978	.4979	.4979	.4980	.4981
2.9	.4981	.4982	.4982	.4983	.4984	.4984	.4985	.4985	.4986	.4986
3.0	.4987	.4987	.4987	.4988	.4988	.4989	.4989	.4989	.4990	.4990
3.1	.49903	.49906	.49910	.49913	.49916	.49918	.49921	.49924	.49926	.49929
3.2	.49931	.49934	.49936	.49938	.49940	.49942	.49944	.49946	.49948	.49950
3.3	.49952	.49953	.49955	.49957	.49958	.49960	.49961	.49962	.49964	.49965
3.4	.49966	.49968	.49969	.49970	.49971	.49972	.49973	.49974	.49975	.49976
3.5	.49977	.49978	.49978	.49979	.49980	.49981	.49981	.49982	.49983	.49983
3.6	.49984	.49985	.49985	.49986	.49986	.49987	.49987	.49988	.49988	.49989
3.7	.499892	.499896	.499900	.499904	.499908	.499912	.499915	.499918	.499922	.499925
3.8	.499928	.499931	.499933	.499936	.499938	.499941	.499943	.499946	.499948	.499950
3.9	.499952	.499954	.499956	.499958	.499959	.499961	.499963	.499964	.499966	.499967
4.0	.499968									

SOURCE: A. Hald, *Statistical Tables and Formulas* (New York: John Wiley, 1952), Table 2. Reprinted by permission of the author and the publisher.

TABLE A2.4   *Poisson Probabilities*

t \ μ	0.5	1	2	3	4	5
0	0.607	0.368	0.135	0.050	0.018	0.007
1	0.303	0.368	0.271	0.149	0.073	0.034
2	0.076	0.184	0.271	0.224	0.147	0.084
3	0.013	0.061	0.180	0.224	0.195	0.140
4	0.002	0.015	0.090	0.168	0.195	0.175
5		0.003	0.036	0.101	0.156	0.175
6		0.001	0.012	0.050	0.104	0.146
7			0.003	0.022	0.059	0.104
8			0.001	0.008	0.030	0.065
9				0.003	0.013	0.036
10				0.001	0.005	0.018
11					0.002	0.008
12					0.001	0.003
13						0.001

SOURCE: E. S. Pearson, *Biometrika Tables for Statisticians* (Cambridge, Eng.: Cambridge University Press, 1954), Table 39. Reprinted with permission of the author.

TABLE A2.5   *Normal Random Variates*

0.013	1.201	0.625	0.458	1.055	0.134	−0.784	−2.991	1.138	1.189
1.390	1.186	1.191	0.355	1.125	0.596	0.868	−0.861	0.391	0.114
2.113	−1.477	−1.507	0.583	0.657	0.103	0.333	−1.443	0.699	0.129
0.316	1.353	0.961	1.196	−0.525	0.161	1.666	0.425	−0.009	−0.285
0.626	0.116	0.467	1.009	1.733	0.899	0.365	−0.510	−0.276	−0.404
−0.552	1.728	0.221	−0.015	0.812	1.006	−0.322	−0.718	0.343	−0.138
1.577	2.991	−0.118	0.271	−0.054	−1.216	1.218	0.568	0.508	−0.091
0.588	−1.749	0.507	0.856	−1.938	−0.570	0.484	0.347	0.323	1.298
−0.324	−0.672	1.325	−1.650	0.074	−0.106	0.449	1.783	0.505	−0.959
0.200	−2.044	−0.826	1.572	−0.270	−0.306	1.844	−1.832	−0.950	0.304
−0.171	−0.437	0.130	0.351	1.150	−1.070	−0.460	0.706	0.766	−0.266
−0.270	0.328	−0.088	0.747	−0.604	−0.751	0.238	0.048	−0.207	−1.232
1.100	0.473	−0.737	1.003	0.647	0.099	−1.606	−1.415	−0.524	−0.764
0.061	−0.509	−0.387	−0.908	1.075	0.503	1.365	−0.014	−1.542	−0.976
−1.051	1.818	1.040	0.755	−0.277	0.160	−0.842	−0.116	−0.094	0.438
−0.106	−0.806	0.240	−1.219	0.681	1.979	1.227	0.630	1.296	−0.357
−0.553	−0.192	−0.675	−0.816	−0.952	0.399	−0.787	1.215	−0.714	0.159
1.308	−1.018	−0.586	−0.438	−0.202	0.979	0.177	−0.147	−1.680	−0.428
1.491	0.503	−1.240	1.113	−0.474	−1.606	0.637	−0.905	2.018	2.693
0.162	−0.497	−0.638	−0.266	0.953	−2.019	0.824	0.270	−0.145	0.123
−0.746	0.259	0.562	−1.011	−0.439	−0.080	0.145	0.101	−0.238	0.549
−0.087	0.274	0.649	−0.456	−0.227	0.561	0.145	0.725	−0.177	0.528
0.183	0.880	−0.947	−0.823	0.074	−0.979	0.383	1.427	−0.768	0.268
−1.414	0.570	−0.162	0.578	1.445	0.248	−0.119	1.373	0.807	−0.397
−0.335	−0.295	0.342	−0.374	−1.523	−1.457	−2.278	0.471	−1.314	0.262
−0.064	−0.631	0.294	−1.198	−1.393	0.201	−2.419	−1.091	−2.488	−1.528
−0.679	−1.693	0.400	0.028	0.618	−0.941	0.267	−0.197	1.436	0.097
0.790	0.357	0.849	1.235	0.355	−0.431	0.079	0.019	1.305	−0.237
0.823	0.607	−1.022	2.609	0.584	−0.108	−1.124	0.155	1.523	−1.443
−1.161	−1.220	−1.173	0.428	0.235	0.018	1.477	1.355	0.149	−2.152
2.011	−0.018	0.569	1.410	−0.486	−0.110	−0.199	1.528	−1.193	0.642
0.924	−1.499	2.218	−0.208	−0.228	1.153	−0.654	1.387	−0.112	2.618
−0.725	−0.477	0.568	−0.944	−0.938	−0.163	0.107	0.162	0.992	−2.827
0.596	−1.163	0.678	0.450	0.724	−0.090	−0.676	0.661	0.320	1.039
0.359	−0.907	0.790	−1.790	−0.494	1.429	−0.221	0.668	0.032	0.263
−0.245	0.718	0.895	0.432	1.718	−1.119	1.154	−0.311	−0.674	−0.620
0.932	0.448	1.827	0.030	0.214	0.066	1.288	0.607	−0.074	0.379
0.238	−0.072	0.538	0.391	−0.599	−0.119	−2.146	−0.520	−1.811	−0.787
0.403	−1.427	−1.919	−0.922	−0.272	0.901	0.739	0.710	0.508	0.525
0.981	−1.020	−1.523	−0.227	0.031	−0.452	0.647	−0.220	−0.468	−0.366
0.291	0.096	1.128	0.122	2.178	−0.113	−0.471	−0.801	0.987	0.552
0.702	0.926	0.005	−0.014	0.743	−1.094	−1.084	−0.082	1.926	1.840
−1.319	2.055	−1.005	−0.025	−0.655	0.878	−0.235	−1.461	1.531	−1.680
−0.189	−0.628	−0.439	−0.171	−0.756	0.792	1.050	0.144	−0.005	1.725
−1.883	−0.579	1.459	−0.224	0.066	−0.352	0.038	−0.432	0.099	−0.384

TABLE A2.5   (*Continued*)

0.471	−0.360	0.862	1.159	−0.907	0.763	−1.899	−0.899	−0.334	−0.215
−0.144	−0.965	1.079	−0.213	−0.438	−0.476	−1.176	1.715	0.843	0.719
1.309	1.616	−1.208	−1.003	−0.001	−0.099	−2.351	0.118	0.268	−0.613
0.549	0.662	−0.565	0.154	−0.697	−0.013	0.985	−0.963	0.768	2.022
0.170	0.485	0.697	−0.087	−0.211	−2.147	−0.652	−0.513	−0.356	−0.228
0.353	1.894	−0.902	−1.903	−0.496	0.588	−0.448	0.589	−0.327	0.099
−0.358	−0.161	−1.429	0.500	0.789	0.986	−2.440	0.012	−0.169	−0.374
0.161	0.114	−0.366	1.182	1.507	0.381	0.386	−0.504	0.233	0.406
0.687	−1.654	0.437	−0.264	−1.336	−0.145	0.122	0.914	1.060	0.738
−0.302	−0.033	0.852	−0.871	0.553	0.335	0.371	−0.420	0.214	0.339
0.684	2.714	−0.358	0.324	0.183	1.095	−0.050	−1.754	1.125	0.540
2.467	0.051	0.106	−0.937	−0.303	0.880	−0.525	−0.095	0.186	−1.344
−0.765	−0.875	−0.059	0.165	−0.433	0.883	−1.342	1.564	−0.243	−0.431
2.102	1.378	−0.261	−0.686	−1.413	1.504	0.284	0.587	1.137	1.372
−1.376	0.179	−1.039	0.173	−1.621	−1.748	0.456	0.370	−0.319	0.320
0.492	0.821	−1.424	−0.725	0.099	−0.343	−0.743	−0.882	−0.733	1.853
0.702	1.852	0.309	1.363	0.635	−0.044	0.280	−0.411	0.772	0.169
1.878	−1.005	0.121	0.986	−0.240	−0.084	0.460	−0.773	0.470	−0.774
1.878	0.659	1.168	−1.564	0.549	−1.793	0.454	−1.628	0.637	0.100
−0.342	−3.148	0.696	1.553	−0.029	−0.157	0.377	1.953	0.596	1.031
−0.567	−0.211	−1.725	−0.510	0.489	0.517	−0.183	−1.280	0.661	−0.668
−0.451	−1.270	−1.082	1.484	0.652	0.701	−1.400	−1.222	−0.378	−1.343
−0.127	0.897	−0.791	0.960	0.014	0.924	1.205	1.034	−0.014	−1.302
1.684	−0.419	1.133	−1.376	1.514	−2.581	1.493	−1.632	1.067	−1.689
−0.453	0.372	−1.192	−0.835	−1.637	−0.005	0.320	−1.064	−0.203	0.628
−1.751	−1.037	1.387	−0.543	0.740	0.571	−0.046	−0.226	−0.694	0.270
−0.852	0.727	−0.046	−0.304	0.587	0.609	1.175	2.410	0.842	1.357
0.077	−0.079	−1.918	1.308	−0.802	0.037	2.411	0.684	1.097	1.096
0.395	−1.902	0.215	−0.490	0.473	0.602	−0.203	−0.153	0.905	0.941
−0.742	0.666	−0.392	−0.502	−0.014	0.633	−0.351	−0.701	−1.009	−0.234
−0.709	−1.237	−0.594	−0.684	1.183	−1.586	−0.678	−0.685	−0.427	0.320
0.582	−0.656	0.026	1.395	0.346	−0.451	0.260	1.299	0.791	1.215
0.236	−2.029	−2.507	−0.624	−1.024	2.815	1.170	−1.088	0.161	−0.739
0.910	0.425	2.357	1.804	−0.724	0.254	0.838	−0.426	0.496	−1.779
1.543	0.918	1.637	−0.582	1.201	0.843	−0.812	1.509	−1.484	−1.947

TABLE A2.6   *Critical Levels for the t Distribution*

Significance level α	10% 0.10	5% 0.05	2% 0.02	1% 0.01
Degrees of freedom				
1	6.314	12.706	31.821	63.657
2	2.920	4.303	6.965	9.925
3	2.353	3.182	4.541	5.841
4	2.132	2.776	3.747	4.604
5	2.015	2.571	3.365	4.032
6	1.943	2.447	3.143	3.707
7	1.895	2.365	2.998	3.499
8	1.860	2.306	2.896	3.355
9	1.833	2.262	2.821	3.250
10	1.812	2.228	2.764	3.169
11	1.796	2.201	2.718	3.106
12	1.782	2.179	2.681	3.055
13	1.771	2.160	2.650	3.012
14	1.761	2.145	2.624	2.977
15	1.753	2.131	2.602	2.947
16	1.746	2.120	2.583	2.921
17	1.740	2.110	2.507	2.898
18	1.734	2.101	2.552	2.878
19	1.729	2.093	2.539	2.861
20	1.725	2.086	2.528	2.845
21	1.721	2.080	2.518	2.831
22	1.719	2.074	2.508	2.819
23	1.714	2.069	2.500	2.807
24	1.711	2.064	2.492	2.797
25	1.708	2.060	2.485	2.797
26	1.706	2.056	2.479	2.779
27	1.703	2.052	2.473	2.771
28	1.701	2.048	2.467	2.763
29	1.699	2.045	2.462	2.756
30	1.697	2.042	2.457	2.750
40	1.684	2.021	2.423	2.704
60	1.671	2.000	2.390	2.660
120	1.658	1.980	2.358	2.617
∞	1.645	1.960	2.326	2.576

Note: The value tabled is t_α, where $P(|t| > t_\alpha) = \alpha$. The value tabled on the line labeled ∞ is z_α where $P(|Z| > z_\alpha) = \alpha$.

SOURCE: E. S. Pearson, *Biometrika Tables for Statisticians* (Cambridge, Eng.: Cambridge University Press, 1954), Table 12. Reprinted with permission of the author.

TABLE A2.7 *Critical Levels for the Distribution of the Sample Correlation Coefficient r*

Significance level	5%	1%
ϵ	0.05	0.01
Sample size n		
4	0.950	0.990
5	0.878	0.959
6	0.811	0.917
7	0.754	0.874
8	0.707	0.834
9	0.666	0.798
10	0.632	0.765
11	0.602	0.735
12	0.576	0.708
13	0.553	0.684
14	0.532	0.661
15	0.514	0.641
16	0.497	0.623
17	0.482	0.606
18	0.468	0.590
19	0.456	0.575
20	0.444	0.561
21	0.433	0.549
22	0.423	0.537
27	0.381	0.487
32	0.349	0.449
42	0.304	0.393
52	0.273	0.354
62	0.250	0.325
102	0.195	0.254

Note: The value tabled is r_ϵ, where $P(|r| > r_\epsilon) = \epsilon$, based on samples from a bivariate normal distribution with $\rho = 0$.
SOURCE: Table A2.7 is taken from Table 6 of Fisher & Yates, *Statistical Tables for Biological, Agricultural and Medical Research*, published by Oliver & Boyd, Ltd., Edinburgh, by permission of the authors and the publishers.

TABLE A2.8 *Critical Levels for the Chi-Square Distribution*

Significance level α	10% 0.10	5% 0.05	2% 0.02	1% 0.01
Degrees of freedom				
1	2.706	3.841	5.412	6.635
2	4.605	5.991	7.824	9.210
3	6.251	7.815	9.837	11.345
4	7.779	9.488	11.668	13.277
5	9.236	11.070	13.388	15.086
6	10.645	12.592	15.033	16.812
7	12.017	14.067	16.622	18.475
8	13.362	15.507	18.168	20.090
9	14.684	16.919	19.679	21.666
10	15.987	18.307	21.161	23.209
11	17.275	19.675	22.618	24.725
12	18.549	21.026	24.054	26.217
13	19.812	22.362	25.472	27.688
14	21.064	23.685	26.873	29.141
15	22.307	24.996	28.259	30.578
16	23.542	26.296	29.633	32.000
17	24.769	27.587	30.995	33.409
18	25.989	28.869	32.346	34.805
19	27.204	30.144	33.687	36.191
20	28.412	31.410	35.020	37.566
21	29.615	32.671	36.343	38.932
22	30.813	33.924	37.659	40.289
23	32.007	35.172	38.968	41.638
24	33.196	36.415	40.270	42.980
25	34.382	37.652	41.566	44.314
26	35.563	38.885	42.856	45.642
27	36.741	40.113	44.140	46.963
28	37.916	41.337	45.419	48.278
29	39.087	42.557	46.693	49.588
30	40.256	43.773	47.962	50.892

Note: The value tabled is χ_α^2, where $P(X^2 > \chi_\alpha^2) = \alpha$. For larger degrees of freedom, the fact that $\sqrt{2X^2} - \sqrt{2\nu - 1}$, where ν is the number of degrees of freedom, is approximately a standard normal random variable may be used to derive critical levels.
SOURCE: Table A2.8 is taken from Table 4 of Fisher & Yates, *Statistical Tables for Biological, Agricultural and Medical Research*, published by Oliver & Boyd, Ltd., Edinburgh, by permission of the authors and the publishers.

References

With the ever increasing availability of texts, monographs, and papers in all areas of probability and statistics, the student should be able, with the advice of his instructor or librarian, to find material on almost any topic he may wish to investigate more deeply. The following books and articles are of general interest in various areas and do not necessarily treat any at a deeper level.

BERNSTEIN, L. A. *Statistics for Decisions*. Grosset and Dunlap, New York, 1965.

HOGBEN, L. *Mathematics for the Million*. Revised edition, Norton, New York, 1968.

HOGBEN, L. *Statistical Theory*. Revised edition. Norton, New York, 1968.

HUFF, D., AND I. GEIS. *How to Lie with Statistics*. Norton, New York, 1954.

MORONEY, M. J. *Facts from Figures*. Penguin, Baltimore, 1957.

REICHMANN, W. J. *Use and Abuse of Statistics*. Oxford, New York, 1962.

ROBERTS, H. V., and W. A. WALLIS. *Statistics: A New Approach*. Free Press, New York, 1956.

SLONIM, M. J. *Sampling in a Nutshell*. Simon & Schuster, New York, 1960.

TIPPETT, L. H. *Statistics*. Third Edition. Oxford, New York, 1968.

ZEISEL, H. *Say It with Figures*. Harper & Row, New York, 1968.

In addition to these general books, there are a large number of statistical articles in the *International Encyclopedia of the Social Sciences* (Crowell, Collier and Macmillan, New York, 1968). These articles in general will be accessible to students who have only a basic background in statistics and will amplify some of the topics in this course or provide information on topics only alluded to in problems. Ten particularly appropriate articles are listed below:

Counted Data	Goodness of Fit
Decision Theory	Hypothesis Testing
Errors	Quality Control
Estimation	Quantal Response
Fallacies, Statistical	Sample Surveys

339

Answers to Selected Problems

Chapter 2

2.1 0.72

2.2 $\frac{15}{16}; \frac{1}{4}$

2.3 $\frac{1}{6}; \frac{1}{6}$; yes; no; no

2.4 (a) $\frac{1}{2}$
     (b) $\frac{3}{8}$
     (d) yes; yes

2.5 0.368

2.6 (a) 0.970
     (b) 0.9997

2.7 (a) $2p_1(1 - p_1)$;
         $p_1^2 + (1 - p_1)^2$
     (b) $6p_1p_2p_3$; $p_1^3 + p_2^3 + p_3^3$;
         $\frac{2}{9}; \frac{1}{9}$; 0.108; 0.244

2.8 $\frac{2}{3}$

2.9 0.9999; 0.9999897;
     independence

2.13 $\frac{1}{3}; \frac{2}{9}$

2.14

x	p(x)
0	$\frac{3}{10}$
1	$\frac{6}{10}$
2	$\frac{1}{10}$

$E(X) = \frac{8}{10}; V(X) = \frac{9}{25}$;
For sample of size 3,
$\quad E(X) = \frac{12}{10}; V(X) = \frac{9}{25}$

2.15

x	p(x)
2	$\frac{1}{2}$
3	$\frac{1}{2}$

$E(X) = \frac{5}{2}; V(X) = \frac{1}{4}$

2.16 $P(X = i) = \frac{1}{4}$ for
      $i = 1, 2, 3, 4$;
      $E(X) = \frac{5}{2}; V(X) = \frac{5}{4}$

2.17 (a) 0, 1, 2, 3, 4
      (b) $P(Y = i) = \frac{1}{5}$;
          $i = 0, 1, 2, 3, 4$
      (c) $E(Y) = 2; V(Y) = 2$
      (d) $Y = X - 1$
      (e) $E(T) = 20; V(T) = 20$

2.18

x	p(x)
3	$\frac{1}{6}$
4	$\frac{1}{6}$
5	$\frac{2}{6}$
6	$\frac{1}{6}$
7	$\frac{1}{6}$

$E(X) = 5; V(X) = \frac{5}{3}$

2.19

x	p(x)
0	$\frac{1}{3}$
1	$\frac{4}{9}$
2	$\frac{2}{9}$

$E(X) = \frac{8}{9}; V(X) = \frac{44}{81}$

2.20 (b)

x	p(x)
0	$\frac{1}{3}$
1	$\frac{1}{2}$
3	$\frac{1}{6}$

(c) $E(X) = 1$; S.D.$(X) = 1$

2.21 $E(X) = 3; V(X) = \frac{62}{15}$

2.22 0; 20

2.23
x	p(x)
2	$\frac{2}{10}$
3	$\frac{3}{10}$
4	$\frac{4}{10}$
5	$\frac{1}{10}$

$E(X) = 3.4; V(X) = 0.84$

2.24
x	p(x)
0	$\frac{9}{24}$
1	$\frac{8}{24}$
2	$\frac{6}{24}$
4	$\frac{1}{24}$

$E(X) = 1; \text{S.D.}(X) = 1$

2.25
x	p(x)
0	0.6588
1	0.2995
2	0.0399
3	0.0017
4	0.00002

2.26
x	p(x)
2	$\frac{1}{10}$
3	$\frac{2}{10}$
4	$\frac{3}{10}$
5	$\frac{4}{10}$

$E(X) = 4; V(X) = 1$

2.27
x	p(x)
-4	$\frac{1}{16}$
-2	$\frac{4}{16}$
0	$\frac{6}{16}$
2	$\frac{4}{16}$
4	$\frac{1}{16}$

$E(X) = 0; V(X) = 4$

2.28 (a) $E(X) = 6; V(X) = 4$
(b) $E(X) = 5.5;$
$V(X) = 3\frac{1}{4}$

2.29 $E(Y) = 3; V(Y) = 2$

2.30 $E(X) = 1/m;$
$V(X) = (m - 1)/m^2$

2.31 $E(Y) = 10/m;$
$V(Y) = 10(m - 1)/m^2;$
$2, \frac{8}{5}; 5, \frac{5}{2}$

2.32 $\frac{1}{12}; (k! \, n - k!)/(n - 1)!;$
$\frac{1}{12}; \frac{2}{5}$

2.33 $\frac{1}{5}; \frac{1}{15}$

2.35 (a)
z^*	$p(z^*)$
$-2/\sqrt{2}$	$\frac{1}{5}$
$-1/\sqrt{2}$	$\frac{1}{5}$
0	$\frac{1}{5}$
$1/\sqrt{2}$	$\frac{1}{5}$
$2/\sqrt{2}$	$\frac{1}{5}$

(b) 0; 1

2.37 0.10

2.38 0.78

2.39 $\frac{25}{32}$

2.40 $\frac{1}{70}$

Chapter 3

3.1 $(\frac{1}{2})^{20}$

3.2 0.215; 4; 2.4

3.3 (a) $E(T) = 4; V(T) = 2$

3.4 (a) 0.054; 0.968
(b) 0.074; 0.132

3.5 (a) $\frac{63}{64}; \frac{6}{64}$

3.6 (a) (i) 0.137; (ii) 0.213
(b) (i) 0.026; (ii) 0.993

3.7 (a) Integers 0 to 16
(b) 8
(c) Independence

3.8 $\frac{1}{256}; 1; \frac{3}{4}$

3.9 0.058

3.10 0.033

3.11 (a) 0.036
(b) 0.641

3.12 0.058

3.13 (b) 0.048

3.14 0.982

3.15 (a) 0.078
(b) 0.328

3.16 (a) 0.175; 0.132
      (b) 0.805; 0.989
      (c) 0.012; 0.122

3.17 (a)

t	$p(t)$
0	0.6561
1	0.2916
2	0.0486
3	0.0036
4	0.0001

      (b) $E(T) = 0.40$;
          $V(T) = 0.36$

3.18 $E(T) = 1$; $V(T) = 0.9$

3.19 (b) 0.590
          0.328
          0.168
          0.078
          0.031

3.20 (a) 0.729
      (b) $\frac{1}{10}$
      (c) 0.344

3.21 2; 0.033

3.22 (a) 0.005; (b) 0.006
      (c) 0.010; 0.012

3.23 Binomial $n = 5, p = 0.9$;
      0.00001; 0.00031

3.24 (a) 0.349
      (b) 0.006
      (c) 0.056
      (d) 0.600
      (e) 0.917
      (f) $\frac{3}{10}$; 0.033
      (g) $\frac{2}{10}$; 0.0235

3.25

p	$P(T > 15\vert p)$
0.5	0.006
0.6	0.050
0.7	0.238
0.8	0.630
0.9	0.997
1.0	1.000

3.26

Z^*	$p(z^*)$
-2	$\frac{1}{16}$
-1	$\frac{4}{16}$
0	$\frac{6}{16}$
1	$\frac{4}{16}$
2	$\frac{1}{16}$

3.27 Bound $< \frac{1}{4}$; exact $= 0.039$

3.28 (a)

p	$P(T \geq 2)$
0	0
0.05	0.086
0.1	0.264
0.2	0.625
0.3	0.851
0.4	0.954
0.5	0.989
0.6	0.998

      (b)

0	0
0.05	0.226
0.1	0.410
0.2	0.672
0.3	0.832
0.4	0.922
0.5	0.969
0.6	0.990
0.7	0.998

3.29 0.9999; 0.0005

3.30 0.989; 0.999; 0.918

3.31 (a)

p	$(1 - p)^{10}$
0.001	0.99
0.01	0.904
0.05	0.600
0.10	0.349

      For $p = 0.001$,
      (b)

x	$p(x)$
1	0.99
11	0.01

      $E(X) = 1.10$
      $V(X) = 0.99$
      For $p = 0.01$,
      $E(X) = 1.96$
      $V(X) = 8.68$
      For $p = 0.05$,
      $E(X) = 5.00$
      $V(X) = 24.00$

For $p = 0.10$,
$$E(X) = 7.51$$
$$V(X) = 22.72$$

Chapter 4

4.1   0.132; no
4.2   Reject H if $T \geq 16$
4.3 $H: p = \frac{1}{2}$; $A: p > \frac{1}{2}$;
      0.05; yes
4.4   Reject H if $T \leq 3$ or $T \geq 13$
4.5   Significance probability is
      0.058
4.6 $p \neq \frac{1}{2}$; 0.116; yes
4.7   Reject H if $T \geq 18$
4.8   Reject H if $T \geq 11$
4.9 $H: p = \frac{1}{2}$; $A: p < \frac{1}{2}$;
      0.000; yes
4.10 $H: p = \frac{1}{2}$; $A: p \neq \frac{1}{2}$;
      H is rejected if $T \leq 3$ or
      $T \geq 13$; 0.212
4.12 $A: p > \frac{1}{2}$; 0.049
4.13 Significance probability is
      0.146
4.14 H is rejected (significance
      probability is 0.022)
4.15 (c) H is rejected if $T \leq 1$
      or $T \geq 11$
4.16 Significance probability is
      0.078
4.17 0.588; no
4.18 $H: p = \frac{1}{2}$; $A: p \neq \frac{1}{2}$; 0.11
4.19 $H: p \leq 0.80$; $A: p > 0.80$;
      reject H if $T = 20$;
      if $p = 0.90$, $P(H$ is rejected$)$
      $= 0.122$
4.20 0.0001
4.21 $V(T/n) = 0.009$ if $n = 10$
             $= 0.0009$ if $n = 100$
4.22 0.033
4.23 H is rejected (significance
      probability is 0.012)
4.24 H is rejected
4.25 H is rejected

4.26

$P(H$ is accepted$)$
5 percent level

p	$n = 10$	$n = 20$
0.6	0.954	0.875
0.7	0.851	0.583
0.8	0.625	0.193
0.9	0.264	0.011
1.0	0	0

1 percent level

p	$n = 10$	$n = 20$
0.6	0.994	0.950
0.7	0.972	0.762
0.8	0.842	0.348
0.9	0.651	0.043
1.0	0	0

4.27

$P(H$ is accepted$)$

p	5 percent level	1 percent level
0.0	0	0
0.1	0.011	0.133
0.2	0.195	0.588
0.3	0.583	0.892
0.4	0.874	0.985
0.5	0.958	0.998
0.6	0.874	0.985
0.7	0.583	0.892
0.8	0.195	0.588
0.9	0.011	0.133
1.0	0	0

4.28

p	$P(H$ is accepted$)$
0.6	0.741
0.7	0.391
0.8	0.084
0.9	0.002
1.0	0

4.29

p	$P(\text{accept } H)$
0	0
0.1	0.068
0.2	0.403
0.3	0.755
0.4	0.933

0.5	0.980
0.6	0.933
0.7	0.755
0.8	0.403
0.9	0.068
1.0	0

4.30 Significance level is 0.006

4.31 0.598

4.32 (a) $H: p = 0.1$;
 $A: p > 0.1$; 0.043
 (b) 0.994

Chapter 5

5.1 718 in.; 0.447 in.

5.2 7; 5.35; 5.35

5.3 70; 20

5.4 17; 7.1

5.5 12,000 lb; 800 lb²

5.6 $\left[\dfrac{M(1-M)}{16}\right.$

$\left. \times \left(\dfrac{1}{n_1} + \dfrac{1}{n_2} + \dfrac{1}{n_3} + \dfrac{1}{n_4}\right)\right]^{1/2}$

5.7 $\left(\dfrac{1}{\sigma_1^2} + \dfrac{1}{\sigma_2^2}\right)^{-1}$

5.8 $E(\text{total}) = 10$ hours
 S.D.(total) = 0.79 hours
 Bound 0.0064

5.9 (a) Mean = 2.78
 S.D. = 0.48
 (b) 0.398

5.10 (a)

h	$p(h)$
45	$\frac{1}{15}$
50	$\frac{2}{15}$
60	$\frac{3}{15}$
65	$\frac{4}{15}$
70	$\frac{5}{15}$

 (b) 62.33; 62.89

5.11

$\bar{x}$	$p(\bar{x})$
1.75	$\frac{1}{15}$
2.00	$\frac{1}{15}$
2.25	$\frac{2}{15}$
2.50	$\frac{2}{15}$
2.75	$\frac{3}{15}$
3.00	$\frac{2}{15}$
3.25	$\frac{2}{15}$
3.50	$\frac{1}{15}$
3.75	$\frac{1}{15}$

For $n = 2$, $E(\bar{X}) = 2.75$;
 $V(\bar{X}) = 0.2917$
For $n = 3$, $E(\bar{X}) = 2.75$;
 $V(\bar{X}) = 0.1458$

5.12

x_2	$p(x_2)$
1	$\frac{1}{4}$
2	$\frac{1}{4}$
3	$\frac{1}{4}$
4	$\frac{1}{4}$

$x_1 + x_2$	$p(x_1 + x_2)$
2	$\frac{1}{20}$
3	$\frac{2}{20}$
4	$\frac{3}{20}$
5	$\frac{4}{20}$
6	$\frac{4}{20}$
7	$\frac{3}{20}$
8	$\frac{2}{20}$
9	$\frac{1}{20}$

5.13

x	$p(x)$
2	$\frac{1}{9}$
$2\frac{1}{2}$	$\frac{2}{9}$
3	$\frac{3}{9}$
$3\frac{1}{2}$	$\frac{2}{9}$
4	$\frac{1}{9}$

5.14 $E(Y) = n$; $V(Y) = n/3$
 For $n = 2$,
 $E(Y) = 2$; $V(Y) = \frac{2}{3}$

5.15 37.5; 5.5

5.16 (a) 24.49; 1.03
 (b) 23.83; 1.13

5.17 (b) $\bar{X} = 2.475$
 (c) $s^2 = 0.6125$

5.18 16.5; 5.9

5.19 98.60; 0.049

5.20 39.3075; 0.0407

5.21 4.45; 4.79

5.22 52.92; 477.43

5.23 120.0; 113.26

5.27 $V(X_1 + X_2) = \frac{1}{3}$;
$V(X_1) + V(X_2) = \frac{1}{2}$

5.28 $V\left(\dfrac{X_1 + X_2}{2}\right) = V(\bar{X}) =$

$\dfrac{\sigma^2}{2}\left(\dfrac{4-2}{4-1}\right); \sigma^2 = \dfrac{1}{4}$

$V(X_1 + X_2) = 2^2 \cdot \frac{1}{4} \cdot \frac{1}{2} \cdot \frac{2}{3}$
$= \frac{1}{3}$

5.29 $E(T) = 40p$;
$V(T) = 40p(1 - p)$

Chapter 6

6.1 980; 13,100

6.2 0.9876; -0.3050; 0.9370

6.3 -0.0606

6.6 67.8

6.7 (a) August 31; (b) 0.4920
(c) Noon August 7 to noon
August 23

6.8 0.00021

6.9 0.1458

6.10 122.2

6.11 No; probability increases
from 0.0227 to 0.0367

6.12 (a) 33,000; 212.1 lb
(b) 29,400; 196.3 lb

6.13 0.141; 0.00020

6.14 S.D. = 0.51; 0.6730

6.15 0.0094

6.16 $E(W) = 10$;
(a) $V(W) = \frac{40}{12}$
(b) $V(W) = \frac{100}{12}$

6.17 (a) 0.50
(b) 10.8 to 16.2

6.18 (a) 0.25
(b) 0.0088

6.19 8.14 days

6.20 51.99 seconds

6.21 0.2061

6.22 0.0478

6.23 0.0570

6.24 (a) 0.0571
(b) 0.0571

6.25 0.1056; 0.3372;
0.6628; 0.8944

6.26 0.3174; 0.022

6.27 0.0228; yes

6.28 0.3954

6.29

p	$P(H$ is accepted$)$
0.1	0
0.2	0.00074
0.3	0.1093
0.4	0.6134
0.5	0.9090
0.6	0.6134
0.7	0.1093
0.8	0.00074
0.9	0

6.30 0.440; 0.988

6.31 $H : p = 0.05$; $A : p < 0.05$;
0.125; no

6.33

p	$P(H$ is accepted$)$
0.01	0.264
0.02	0.594
0.03	0.801
0.04	0.909

For $p = 0.025$,
$P(H$ is accepted$)$
$\simeq 0.098$

6.34 Significance probability of T
= 24 is 0;
$H : p = \frac{1}{20}$; $A : p \neq \frac{1}{20}$
Yes, number of accidents is
significantly greater than
would be expected by
chance.

6.35 Expected proportions:

Length	Male	Female
$20\frac{1}{2}$	0.00014	0.0032
21	0.00068	0.0081
$21\frac{1}{2}$	0.00308	0.0216
22	0.0111	0.0479

$22\frac{1}{2}$	0.0305	0.0877
23	0.0696	0.1365
$23\frac{1}{2}$	0.1207	0.1671
24	0.1732	0.1722
$24\frac{1}{2}$	0.1897	0.1467
25	0.1716	0.1052
$25\frac{1}{2}$	0.1185	0.0592
26	0.0676	0.0284
$26\frac{1}{2}$	0.0293	0.0113
27	0.0106	0.0049
$27\frac{1}{2}$	0.00294	—
28	0.00063	—

6.36

Class	Proportion
< 99.5	0.0268
99.5–104.5	0.0453
104.5–109.5	0.0890
109.5–114.5	0.1404
114.5–119.5	0.1786
119.5–124.5	0.1827
124.5–129.5	0.1605
129.5–134.5	0.0898
134.5–139.5	0.0533
139.5–144.5	0.0229
144.5–149.5	0.0087
> 149.5	0.0020

6.37 With probability 0.75 G lies between $-\$71.56$ and $+\$61.04$

6.38 0.0622

6.39 0.368

6.40 0.0062

6.41 (a) 64.68
     (b) 0.0548
     (c) 64.68 lb; 0.00069

Chapter 7

7.1 Machine is stopped if $\bar{X} < 1.0673$ or $\bar{X} > 1.1327$

7.2 0.2380

7.3 Machine is stopped if $\bar{X} < 1.0752$ or $\bar{X} > 1.1248$

7.4 Machine is stopped if $\bar{X} < 1.0018$ or $\bar{X} > 1.0182$

7.5 0.1587

7.6 Yes; yes; no (significance probability is 0.00158)

7.7 0.0146

7.8 H is rejected if $T \le 18$ or $T \ge 32$

7.9 Significance probability is 0.00096

7.10 H is not rejected

7.11 $t = -1.43$; H is not rejected

7.12 $t = 2.39$; H is rejected at the 5 percent significance level

7.13 If this is a test of $H : p = 0.24$ against $p \ne 0.24$, the significance probability of the observation is 0.1030.

7.14 $t = 1.23$; seeding is of no effect if H is not rejected

7.15 H is rejected if $\bar{X} < -0.985$, $t = -0.516$; by either method H is not rejected

7.16 $t = -2.41$; H is rejected at the 5 percent significance level

7.17 H is rejected if $\bar{X} < 2.254$ or $\bar{X} > 2.646$; H is not rejected since $\bar{X} = 2.35$ (5 percent significance level)

7.18 H is rejected if $\bar{X} < 2.352$ or $\bar{X} > 2.548$

7.19 0.0074; H is rejected; no

7.20 $t = 1.33$; H is not rejected

7.21 Significance probability is 0.0348

7.22 (a) H is rejected if $\bar{X} < -11.01$ or $\bar{X} > 11.01$
     (b) 0.15

7.23 $t = 0$; H is not rejected

7.24 $t = 2.07$; H is not rejected at the 5 percent significance level

7.25 $t = -0.65$; difference is not significant (5 percent)

7.27 (a) $t = 0$
(b) Type II error made
(c) Take more observations

7.28 $t = -1.58$; difference is not significant

7.29 H is rejected if $T \geq 62$.

7.30 (i)   Significance level
(ii) Alternative of interest
(iii) Type II Error level
(iv) Variance or an estimate of it

7.32 (b) $H:p = 0.3; A:p < 0.3$
(d) H is not rejected at the 1 percent level

7.33 (a) $Z = 3.08$; H is rejected at the 5 percent significance level
(b) 0.0020
(c) Yes, since P (H is rejected) $= 0.9987 > 0.80$

7.34

μ	$P(H$ is accepted$)$
1.05	0.853
1.06	0.2810
1.07	0.5832
1.08	0.8413
1.12	0.8413
1.13	0.5832
1.14	0.2810
1.15	0.0853

7.35

μ	$P(H$ is accepted$)$
1.05	0.0233
1.06	0.1191
1.07	0.3409
1.08	0.6480
1.12	0.6480
1.13	0.3409
1.14	0.1191
1.15	0.0233

7.36 0.8413

7.37

μ	$P(H$ is accepted$)$
1.07	0.00028
1.08	0.0301
1.09	0.3821
1.10	0.8997
1.11	0.9979

7.38 0.0207

7.39 (a) Same as answer to Problem 7.30
(b) 0.9793

7.40 (a) Reject H if $\bar{X} < 0.49934$ or $\bar{X} > 0.50066$
(b) 0.99960

7.41 If out of 40 samples 21 or less are sterile, then the water is declared safe.

7.42 H is rejected if $T \leq 22$ or $T \geq 38$

p	$P(H$ is accepted$)$
0.2	0.00019
0.3	0.0793
0.4	0.6023
0.6	0.6023
0.7	0.0793
0.8	0.00019

7.43 (a) H is rejected if $\bar{X} > 523.5$
(b) 0.7896
(c) $n = 70$

7.44 (a) 0.00079
(b) 0.3557

Chapter 8

8.1 (1.974, 2.976)

8.2 (a) (98.53, 98.67)
(b) (98.47, 98.73)

8.3 (0.14, 0.48)

8.4 (0.49, 0.95)

8.5 (a) 4.38, 3.10, 2.20
(b) 0.48, 0.32, 0.22

8.6 (a) (0.16, 0.32)
     (b) (0.12, 0.36)
8.7 (12.0, 35.0)
8.8 (1100.9, 1135.1)
8.9 (a) Yes
8.10 (a) σ or s
     (c) (58.4, 102.6) lb
8.11 (a) Interval is 0.20 ± 0.08
         which has length 0.16
         < 0.2
8.13 (a) (5.59, 8.11)
     (c) No
8.14 (a) (1.82, 3.78)
     (b) (2.715, 2.745)
8.15 Point estimate is at center of
     confidence interval
8.16 (a) Second if σ is known
     (b) 0.10
     (c) Larger sample or
         smaller confidence
         coefficient
     (d) No
8.17 (a) (48.23, 49.77)
     (b) Use larger confidence
         coefficient; get longer
         interval
8.18 Tends to zero; tends to
     $z_\alpha \times \sigma / \sqrt{n}$
8.19 (24.40, 24.58)
     (23.73, 23.93)
8.20 39.3075 ± 0.0040
     39.3075 ± 0.0102
     39.3075 ± 0.0215
     39.3075 ± 0.0408
     39.3075 ± 0.0525
     39.3075 ± 0.0625
     39.3075 ± 0.0823
8.21 0.796
8.22 (a) (2.15, 2.55);
         H is not rejected
     (b) $\bar{X} \pm t_{0.05}(s/\sqrt{n})$
8.23 $(-0.87, 0.47)$;
     H is not rejected
8.24 (98.15, 98.75)

8.25 (0.92, 18.92);
     H is rejected; significance
     probability of 9.92 lies
     between 0.05 and 0.10
8.26 (a) (0.508, 0.758)
     (b) H is rejected
8.27 (a) Sample size
     (b) $n = 2$ (6025.7, 6081.7)
         $n = \infty$ (6049.4, 6058.0)
8.28 (a) 98.4
     (b) Confidence interval
         with 95 percent confi-
         dence is 98.4 ± 11.5
8.29 $\hat{\mu} = 4.39$; $\hat{\sigma} = 1.71$
8.30 (a) (0.563, 0.655)
     (b) (0.455, 0.549)
     (c) (0.512, 0.612)
8.31 No; he wants to test
     $H : p \le \frac{1}{2}$ against $A : p > \frac{1}{2}$;
     H is rejected at the 5
     percent significance level
8.32 (a) (619.9, 670.1) acres
     (b) (61490, 67510) acres
8.33 375.5 to 500
8.34 No; it will require
     approximately 298
     observations to meet the
     specified requirement
8.35 (a) Sample mean
     (b) Confidence interval
     (d) $n = 664$
8.36 (20.5, 30.9) minutes

Chapter 9

9.1

x \ y	1	2	3	4
0	$\frac{16}{81}$			
1		$\frac{16}{81}$	$\frac{16}{81}$	
2		$\frac{8}{81}$	$\frac{8}{81}$	$\frac{8}{81}$
3			$\frac{4}{81}$	$\frac{4}{81}$
4	$\frac{1}{81}$			

$E(X) = \frac{4}{3}$; $V(X) = \frac{8}{9}$;
$E(Y) = \frac{7}{3}$; $V(Y) = \frac{68}{81}$;
$\rho = 0.51$

9.2 $E(Y/X = x) = 3 - 0.5x$;
no

9.3

x＼z	2	3	4	5
1	$\frac{1}{10}$	$\frac{1}{10}$	$\frac{1}{10}$	$\frac{1}{10}$
2		$\frac{1}{10}$	$\frac{1}{10}$	$\frac{1}{10}$
3			$\frac{1}{10}$	$\frac{1}{10}$
4				$\frac{1}{10}$

$E(Z|X)$ is linear in X

9.4 (a) $5, 10, 5, \frac{15}{4}, 5, \frac{15}{4}$,
$-2.5, -\frac{1}{3}, -\frac{1}{3}$
(b) 0.00017; zero

9.5 0.059; $\frac{5}{4}$

9.6 $\hat{p} = 0.44$; confidence
interval: $(0.34, 0.54)$

9.7 -10; 64

9.8 $-np(1 - p)$; -1

9.9 155; 84.75

9.10 1000; 37,800; $x_0 = 619.0$;
$x_1 = 1381.0$; no

9.11 Estimated cost is $4,500;
estimate of $V(E)$ is
14,343,750

9.12 (a) 940
   (b) (i) $V(\text{Enrollment}) = 248$
   (ii) $V(\text{Enrollment}) = 371.9$
   (iii) $V(\text{Enrollment}) = 124.1$

9.13 (a) $f(t_1, t_2, t_3, t_4) =$
$$\frac{5!}{t_1!\, t_2!\, t_3!\, t_4!} \times$$
$$\left(\frac{1}{4}\right)^{t_1} \left(\frac{1}{4}\right)^{t_2} \left(\frac{1}{4}\right)^{t_3} \left(\frac{1}{4}\right)^{t_4}$$
   (b) $E(T_1) = \frac{5}{4}$;
   $P(T_1 = 0/T_4 = 4) = \frac{2}{3}$;
   $P(T_1 = 1/T_4 = 4) = \frac{1}{3}$

9.14 215, 150, 635;
130.75, 127.50, 197.75

9.15 (a) $P(X = 0/Y = 0) = \frac{1}{3}$;
   $P(X = 1/Y = 0) = \frac{1}{3}$;
   $P(X = 2/Y = 0) = \frac{1}{3}$;

$P(X = 0/Y = 1) = \frac{1}{2}$;
$P(X = 1/Y = 1) = \frac{1}{2}$;
$P(X = 2/Y = 2) = 1$
   (b) $\rho = \frac{1}{2}$

9.16 (a) 4; 12; 4
   $\frac{16}{5}$; $\frac{8}{5}$; $\frac{16}{5}$
   (b) 20; $\frac{56}{5}$
   (c) $(X, Y), (Y, Z)$ are
   independent

9.17

x＼y	0	1	2
0	$\frac{1}{8}$	$\frac{1}{8}$	
1	$\frac{1}{8}$	$\frac{2}{8}$	$\frac{1}{8}$
2	0	$\frac{1}{8}$	$\frac{1}{8}$

$P(X = 0) = \frac{1}{4}$;
$P(X = 1) = \frac{1}{2}$;
$P(X = 2) = \frac{1}{4}$;
$P(X = 0/Y = 0) =$
   $P(X = 1/Y = 0) = \frac{1}{2}$;
$P(X = 0/Y = 1) =$
   $P(X = 2/Y = 1) = \frac{1}{4}$;
$P(X = 1/Y = 1) = \frac{1}{2}$;
X and Y are dependent

9.18 $P(X_0 = 2, X_1 = 0, X_2 = 0,$
   $X_3 = 1) = \frac{3}{27}$;
   $P(X_0 = 1, X_1 = 1, X_2 = 1,$
   $X_3 = 0) = \frac{18}{27}$;
   $P(X_0 = 0, X_1 = 3, X_2 = 0,$
   $X_3 = 0) = \frac{6}{27}$;
   not independent

9.19

x＼y	0	1	2
0	$\frac{1}{10}$		
1	$\frac{2}{10}$	$\frac{4}{10}$	
2		$\frac{2}{10}$	$\frac{1}{10}$

not independent

9.20 (X, Y, Z) are multinomial
with parameters $n, \frac{1}{4}, \frac{1}{2}, \frac{1}{4}$;
marginally X, Y, Z are
binomial $(n, \frac{1}{4}), (n, \frac{1}{2}), (n, \frac{1}{4})$;
Y/X is binomial $(n - X, \frac{2}{3})$;
$Z(Y$ is binomial $(n - Y, \frac{1}{3})$;
not independent

9.21

x \ y	0	1	2	3
0	$\frac{1}{10}$	$\frac{1}{10}$	$\frac{1}{10}$	$\frac{1}{10}$
1	$\frac{1}{10}$	$\frac{1}{10}$	$\frac{1}{10}$	
2	$\frac{1}{10}$	$\frac{1}{10}$		
3	$\frac{1}{10}$			

$P(X = i/Y = 0) = \frac{1}{4}$
$(i = 1, 2, 3, 4)$;
$P(X = i/Y = 1) = \frac{1}{3}$
$(i = 1, 2, 3)$;
$P(X = i/Y = 2) = \frac{1}{2}$
$(i = 1, 2)$;
$P(X = 1/Y = 3) = 1$;
conditional distribution of
Y, given X, is similar

Chapter 10

10.1 $\hat{\alpha} = 9.85$, $\hat{\beta} = 0.34$;
1969: $\hat{Y} = 14.27$;
1970: $\hat{Y} = 14.61$

10.2 $\hat{\alpha} = 1.73$, $\hat{\beta} = -0.14$;
$X_0 = 1.5$, $\hat{Y} = 1.53$

10.3 $\hat{Y} = 6.90 + 3.52X$;
for $X_0 = 1$, $\hat{Y}_0 = 10.42$

10.4 $\hat{Y} = -5.16 + 1.21X$;
$X_0 = 10$, $\hat{Y} = 6.94$;
$\hat{X} = 7.48 + 0.49Y$

10.5 $\hat{Y} = 17.09 + 0.51X$;
$\hat{X} = 55.80 + 0.72Y$;
$X_0 = 100$, $\hat{Y} = 68.09$

10.6 $\hat{Y} = -103.81 + 3.81X$;
$\hat{X} = 60.15 + 0.0595Y$;
$X_0 = 69$, $\hat{Y}_0 = 159.08$;
$Y_0 = 150$, $\hat{X}_0 = 69.07$;
22.7 per cent ($r^2 = 0.227$)

10.8 $r = 0.6085$

10.9 $r = 0.476$

10.10 $r = -0.2291$

10.11 (a)

X_0	Average
2.4	1.585, 2.447
2.7	1.835, 2.565
3.0	1.954, 2.816
3.3	1.982, 3.156
3.6	1.973, 3.535

X_0	Individual
2.4	0.785, 3.247
2.7	0.991, 3.409
3.0	1.154, 3.616
3.3	1.275, 3.863
3.6	1.362, 4.146

(b) (13.70, 15.52)

10.12 $t = -2.126$; H is not
rejected

10.13 (6.43, 14.41) days;
(0, 25.05) days

10.14 $t = 4.37$; no, it does not

10.15 $t = 3.25 > 2.10$;
$r = 0.6085 > 0.444$;
H is rejected in both cases

10.16 $t = 0.08$; the observation
does not belong to the
population from which the
sample of 10.6 drawn

10.17 $H : \rho = 0$; rejected in first
two problems, but not in
the third

10.19 (a) $\hat{Y} = -0.50 + 0.91X$
(b) $X_0 = 15$, $\hat{Y}_0 = 13.15$
(c) (8.00, 18.30)

10.20 (a) $\hat{Y} = 3.96 + 0.22X$
(b) $t = 0.63$; H is not
rejected
(c) $X_0 = 7$, $\hat{Y}_0 = 5.50$
(d) 3.35

10.21 (a) $r = 0.102$; $H : \rho = 0$ is
not rejected
(b) $\hat{Y} = 61.69 + 0.10X$;
$\hat{X} = 61.15 + 0.10Y$

10.22 (a) $\hat{Y} = 30.01 + 1.08X$
(b) 65.65 in.
(c) (63.35, 67.95) in.

10.23 (a) Sample size n;
$s_{Y/X}^2$, $\sum (X_i - \bar{X})^2$, $\bar{X}$
(b) No

10.24 (a) $\hat{Y} = 26.40 + 1.13X$
(b) $t = -0.89$; H is not rejected at 10 percent significance level

10.25 (a) 0.2749, 0.0637, 0.0207
(b) $t = -2.05$; H is not rejected
(c) No

10.26 (a) $H: \rho = 0$ is rejected at 1 percent level
(b) 18 percent

10.27 (a) $\hat{Y} = 0.94 + 0.87X$
(b) $X_0 = 4.7$, $\hat{Y}_0 = 5.03$; $t = -1.39 < 1.77$ (one-sided test); H is not rejected
(c) 6.01 in.

10.28 (a) $\hat{Y} = -2.35 + 0.58X$
(b) 0.55 cm
(c) $\hat{Y} = -2.40 + 0.58X$
(d) $\hat{Y} = -53.2 + 8.4X$; in (d) Y = percent survival; X = temperature

10.29 (a) $s_0 = 0.35$, $s_1 = 0.50$, $s_2 = 0.66$, $s_3 = 0.75$, $s_X = 0.361 + 0.136X$; $t = 12.36$
(b) No

10.31 $t = -0.54$

10.32 (a) Test of $H: \rho = 0$; 23 percent

10.33 (a) $r = 0.9912$; $H: \rho = 0$ is rejected
(c) $\hat{X} = 100.82 + 6.25t$; $\hat{Y} = 2.90 + 0.414t$ where X = cost of living index, Y = new cars purchased
(d) 0.87

10.34 (a) $\hat{Y} = 0.60 + 0.20X$
(b) $X_0 = 5$, $\hat{Y}_0 = 9.4$

(c) 0.80
(d) $t = -5.5$
(e) $\hat{e}_1 = 0.60$, $\hat{e}_2 = -0.40$, $\hat{e}_3 = -0.40$, $\hat{e}_4 = -0.40$, $\hat{e}_5 = 0.60$

Chapter 11

11.1 $X^2 = 10.01$ (1 d.f.), 12.80 (1 d.f.)

11.2 (a) $X^2 = 10.89$ (5 d.f.)
(b) $X^2 = 17.63$ (5 d.f.)

11.3 $X^2 = 9.83$ (3 d.f.)

11.4 (b) $X^2 = 1.07$ (1 d.f.)

11.5 $X^2 = 6.67$ (1 d.f.)

11.6 $X^2 = 3.97$ (6 d.f.)

11.7 $X^2 = 12.50$ (2 d.f.)

11.8 $X^2 = 14.43$ (3 d.f.)

11.9 $X^2 = 14.76$ (4 d.f.)

11.10 $X^2 = 16.33$ (7 d.f.)

11.11 $X^2 = 3.2$ (5 d.f.)

11.12 $X^2 = 3.36$ (3 d.f.)

11.13 $X^2 = 145.58$ (3 d.f.)

11.14 $Z = 1.61$ (one-sided test)

11.15 $X^2 = 2.68$ (3 d.f.)

11.16 $X^2 = 22.98$ (6 d.f.)

11.17 $X^2 = 4.12$ (3 d.f.)

11.18 $X^2 = 177.96$ (4 d.f.)

11.19 $X^2 = 11.67$ (6 d.f.)

11.20 $X^2 = 6.55$ (1 d.f.)

11.21 $X^2 = 4.91$ (4 d.f.)

11.22 (a) $X^2 = 4.00$ (1 d.f.)

11.23 $X^2 = 7.19$ (1 d.f.)

11.24 $X^2 = 3.43$ (1 d.f.)

11.25 (a) $X^2 = 5.38$ (11 d.f.)
(b) $X^2 = 9.04$ (11 d.f.)

11.26 (a) $X^2 = 0.71$ (1 d.f.)
= 0.12 (1 d.f.)
= 0.00 (1 d.f.)
= 0.23 (1 d.f.)
= 0.18 (1 d.f.)
= 0.53 (1 d.f.)
(b) $X^2 = 0.62$ (5 d.f.)

11.27 $X^2 = 6.95$ (1 d.f.)

11.28 (a) $X^2 = 16.00$ (1 d.f.)
      $X^2 = 1.60$ (1 d.f.)

11.29 (a) $X^2 = 27.92$ (4 d.f.)

11.30 $X^2 = 11.91$ (4 d.f.)

11.31 (a) $X^2 = 4.57$ (1 d.f.)
      (b) $X^2 = 1.14$ (1 d.f.)

Chapter 12

12.1 (a) $n = 18$, $T = 14$;
      significance probability
      is 0.016; H is rejected
      (b) $t = 3.15$; H is rejected

12.2 Difference is significant

12.3 (a) Significance probability
      of $T = 6$, $n = 10$ is
      0.377; H is not rejected
      (b) Paired t test; $t = 1.02$

12.4 (a) Significance probability
      of $T = 11$, $n = 18$ is
      0.241
      (b) Two-sample t test

12.5 Significance probability of
      $T = 10$, $n = 12$ is 0.019;
      H is rejected at the 5

percent significance level; t
test on paired differences

12.6 $W = 501$; $z = 160$;
      $t = -1.59$ (in this case H
      is rejected)

12.7 (a) $W = 144$; $z = 193$
      (b) $t = 2.02$

12.8 $W = 166$; $z = 2.00$

12.9 $W = 118$; $z = 0.98$

12.10 $R = 8$; $z = -1.50$

12.11 $R = 10$; $z = 0.46$

12.12 $r_s = 0.741$; $z = 2.46$

12.13 $r_s = 0.915$; $z = 2.74$

12.14 (a) $r_s = 0.432$
      (c) $z = 1.88$

12.15 (a) $r_s = 0.541$
      (b) $z = 2.42$

12.16 (a) $t = 0.44$ (72 d.f.)

12.17 $t = 1.65$ (9 d.f.)

12.18 (a) $r = 0.152$; $r_s = 0.075$

12.20 $r_s = -0.330$; $z = 1.44$

12.21 $R = 11$; $z = 0.46$

12.22 $r_s = 0.271$; $z = 1.69$

12.23 $t = 0.013$

12.24 $t = 9.65$; confidence
      interval is (0.53, 0.79)

Index